IRAN AT THE PARIS PEACE CONFERENCE

IRAN AT THE PARIS PEACE CONFERENCE

International Diplomacy and the Pursuit of Imperial Nationalism

Philip Grobien

I.B. TAURIS
LONDON · NEW YORK · OXFORD · NEW DELHI · SYDNEY

I.B. TAURIS
Bloomsbury Publishing Plc, 50 Bedford Square, London, WC1B 3DP, UK
Bloomsbury Publishing Inc, 1359 Broadway, 12th Floor, New York, NY 10018, USA
Bloomsbury Publishing Ireland, 29 Earlsfort Terrace, Dublin 2, D02 AY28, Ireland

BLOOMSBURY, I.B. TAURIS and the I.B. Tauris logo are
trademarks of Bloomsbury Publishing Plc

First published in Great Britain 2024
This paperback edition published 2026

Copyright © Philip Grobien, 2024, 2026

Philip Grobien has asserted his rights under the Copyright,
Designs and Patents Act, 1988, to be identified as Author of this work.

For legal purposes the Acknowledgements on p. xviii constitute
an extension of this copyright page.

Series design by Adriana Brioso
Cover image © Sueddeutsche Zeitung Photo/Alamy Stock Photo

All rights reserved. No part of this publication may be: i) reproduced or transmitted in any form, electronic or mechanical, including photocopying, recording or by means of any information storage or retrieval system without prior permission in writing from the publishers; or ii) used or reproduced in any way for the training, development or operation of artificial intelligence (AI) technologies, including generative AI technologies. The rights holders expressly reserve this publication from the text and data mining exception as per Article 4(3) of the Digital Single Market Directive (EU) 2019/790.

Bloomsbury Publishing Inc does not have any control over, or responsibility for, any third-party websites referred to or in this book. All internet addresses given in this book were correct at the time of going to press. The author and publisher regret any inconvenience caused if addresses have changed or sites have ceased to exist, but can accept no responsibility for any such changes.

A catalogue record for this book is available from the British Library.

Library of Congress Cataloging-in-Publication Data
Names: Grobien, Philip, author.
Title: Iran at the Paris Peace Conference: international diplomacy and the pursuit of imperial nationalism / Philip Grobien.
Other titles: International diplomacy and the pursuit of imperial nationalism
Description: London; New York : I.B. Tauris, 2024. |
Includes bibliographical references and index.
Identifiers: LCCN 2024005950 (print) | LCCN 2024005951 (ebook) |
ISBN 9780755651856 (hardback) | ISBN 9780755651894 (paperback) |
ISBN 9780755651870 (epub) | ISBN 9780755651863 (ebook)
Subjects: LCSH: Paris Peace Conference (1919–1920) | Iran–Foreign relations–Great Britain. | Great Britain–Foreign relations–Iran. | Reconstruction (1914–1939)–Middle East. | Iran–Politics and government–1911–1925. | Iran–History–Qajar dynasty, 1794–1925. | World War, 1914–1918–Territorial questions–Iran.
Classification: LCC D651.P4 G76 2024 (print) | LCC D651.P4 (ebook) |
DDC 940.3/141095505–dc23/eng/20240208
LC record available at https://lccn.loc.gov/2024005950
LC ebook record available at https://lccn.loc.gov/2024005951

ISBN: HB: 978-0-7556-5185-6
PB: 978-0-7556-5189-4
ePDF: 978-0-7556-5186-3
eBook: 978-0-7556-5187-0

Typeset by Integra Software Services Pvt. Ltd.

For product safety related questions contact productsafety@bloomsbury.com.

To find out more about our authors and books visit www.bloomsbury.com
and sign up for our newsletters.

*In memory of my grandparents,
Nectar and Jonathan Marzeki.*

CONTENTS

List of Figures	ix
List of Maps	x
Prologue: The Paris Peace Conference	xi
Acknowledgements	xviii
Transliteration and Dates	xix
List of Abbreviations	xx
INTRODUCTION: IRAN AT THE CROSSROADS	1
Conceptualizing Iran's outlook	4
Imperial nationalism	6
Paris: Policies and personalities	10
Historiography and sources	16
Chapter 1	
THE NINETEENTH CENTURY, THE GREAT GAME AND THE SQUEEZING OF IRAN	19
Encounters and the advent of Russian confrontation	19
Britain: A symbolic toe in the water	23
Economic hegemony and the Qajar playbook	27
The quad-lateral balancing act	31
Conclusion	32
Chapter 2	
AN ENLIGHTENMENT	35
Intellectual inheritance	36
Direct action	38
More contemporary foundations	39
Occupation and war	45
The question of international law	48
Conclusion	50
Chapter 3	
A NEW DAWN	51
Towards the dream of peace	52
Iran and the preparation for peace	54
The delegation	62
Foreign reaction to Iran's delegation and plans	66
The delegation goes to Paris	71
Conclusion	73

Chapter 4
SPRINGTIME IN PARIS — 75
- January and February — 75
- March and April — 83
- Controlling the narrative — 95
- Conclusion — 98

Chapter 5
THE CAUTERIZATION OF INDEPENDENCE — 99
- May — 99
- The British vision — 101
- The Triumvirate — 104
- The Anglo-Persian Agreement — 110
- June, July and August — 114
- Criticism of the agreement — 116
- Conclusion — 120

Chapter 6
THE PERSISTENCE OF NOSRAT AL-DOWLEH — 123
- Nosrat al-Dowleh — 123
- Countering the narrative — 131
- Squaring the circle — 132
- Round two — 137
- Russia and the endgame — 144
- Conclusion — 149

Conclusion: A reassessment — 151

Appendix — 161
Notes — 174
Selected Bibliography — 197
Index — 207

FIGURES

1	One of many pictures of the Big Four in Paris. From left to right, Woodrow Wilson, Georges Clemenceau, David Lloyd George, and Vittorio Orlando	11
2	Lord Curzon, Viceroy of India, in the full regalia (1899–1905)	13
3	A young and uncertain Ahmad Shah Qajar, photographed during the First World War	15
4	Portrait of Prime Minister Vosuq al-Dowleh, painted between 1900 and 1917	56
5	One of very few images of Moshaver al-Mamalek	64
6	From right to left: Mohammad Ali Foroughi and Mirza Hossein Khan Ala in Paris	65
7	One of few images of most of the Iranian delegates photographed in Istanbul. All sporting the Fez which was very popular in Iran at the time. Picture includes Adolf Perni, Mohammad Ali Foroughi, Ehtesham al-Saltaneh and Mirza Hossein Khan	72
8	A young Nosrat al-Dowleh	125
9	The Guildhall, London, 1919: Right to left, prominent British representatives: Lord Curzon, Prince Albert, Sir Horace Brookes Marshall (London Lord Mayor). Right to left, prominent Iranians representatives: Ahmad Shah, Nosrat al-Dowleh, Mohammad Ali Foroughi	135

MAPS

1	Territorial claims put forward by Iranian delegation 1919. A simplified version of the map developed by the delegates in Paris	xxi
2	Territory lost under treaties of Golestan and Turkmanchai. Showing the extent of Russian expansion	22
3	Transcaucasian Confederation. Showing the territorial divisions between the Armenians, Azerbaijan and Georgian Republics. Interpreted and based on available information	46
4	Territorial claim for Transcaspian. Expanded section of 1	88
5	Territorial claim for Caucasus. Expanded section of 1	89
6	Zohab. Expanded section of 1	109

All maps have been drawn by the author. ©2024. Maps are purely illustrative, locations and distances are approximate. Maps were compiled from numerous sources.

PROLOGUE: THE PARIS PEACE CONFERENCE

Within days of the hostilities beginning on the Western Front, Iran was drawn unwillingly into the First World War. One of the first duties of the young Ahmad Shah, fresh from his coronation, was to announce Iran's neutrality.[1] This hopeful, but not confident, announcement was ignored and Iran was invaded by the Ottomans in late 1914 which prompted a Russian and subsequent British military reaction. Consequently, northern Iran was to become the backdrop to numerous military engagements between Ottoman and Russian forces, which was to result in frequent exchanges of Iranian territory. Iran's territory had become a battleground for British, Russian and Ottoman forces as well as German intrigue.

Iran's ability to protect its borders and provide a functioning government, never a source of optimism, had crumbled further during the war years. Civilian populations had been displaced and Iran had suffered periodic famines and epidemics. Despite convening Iran's parliament, the *Majles*, parliamentarians were, much like the government, overwhelmed by the huge difficulties that Iran faced. Many parliamentarians, in a further reminder that Iran's neutrality meant little, disregarded the proclamation of neutrality which had warned 'let none of our officials, whether on sea or on land, take any action either for or against any of the belligerent States'.[2] Apathy and desperation had turned many nationalists towards Germany as a counterpoint to past Russian and British hegemony.

Yet despite Iran's deprivations, Iran had worked towards sending a delegation to the Paris Peace Conference. In fact, Iran had decided to do so months before the guns fell silent on 11 November 1918. The delegation arrived in Paris on 23 January 1919 and immediately set to work. In the next months, Iran went to meetings and sponsored events, discussing and negotiating with other nations and would-be nations, both big and small. The strategy was to give vent to Iran's suffering during the war and to give voice to its aspirations for the future. They were not to be alone in this endeavour. Many nations, some of them largely unaffected by the First World War, went to Paris and for nearly two years Paris evolved into the 'capital of the world'.[3] This fascinating, yet largely overlooked period in Iranian history will be examined in this book.

My account of Iranian foreign policy forms part of the wider story and consequences of the Peace Conference. Originally seen as 'a great constructive experiment',[4] the Peace Conference was soon regarded as a failure. Noble ideas and new global institutions had failed to bring about satisfaction and peace. However, narratives of the Peace Conference and its outcomes have changed since 1920. More recently, there has been a more balanced understanding of the momentous and ultimately overwhelming task of re-ordering the world.[5] The prevailing analysis of failure, which had helped to obscure the hopes and experiences of the people and politicians of the period, has been re-assessed. In fact, there is now a perception that the various treaties and decisions, whatever their faults, did not make the Second World War inevitable.[6]

The Peace Conference gave breath to many political ideologies which had been bubbling up in the previous century. Questions of sovereignty, independence, nationalism and international law were given greater impetus by the calamity of the First World War, and thereafter, the desire for change. While these questions remain an area for continued examination for European scholars, they have been seldom addressed to the lesser nations, particularly in the colonial and imperial setting of the Middle East. Despite developing a better understanding that some of these ideas have provided beacons for the smaller nations, determined to free themselves from colonial or imperial rule,[7] Iran, long buffeted by imperial pressure from Britain and Russia, has largely been ignored.

Nevertheless, both the war itself and the preparations for peace were to be defining moments in Iran's long history. Much like Belgium, Iran had not fought in the First World War but had provided a battlefield for the Allied and Central powers. Now, in 1919, Iran saw the possibilities of a more positive resurrection through the new world order which the peace talks in Paris appeared to provide. The pronouncements of President Woodrow Wilson were to be particularly enticing. In 1916, in President Wilson's Peace Note, two important points were made. He advocated to protect 'the rights and privileges of weak peoples and small states' from aggression and proposed to 'consider the formation of a league of nations to insure [sic] peace and justice throughout the world'.[8] By 1918 these thoughts and desires were to be consolidated in President Wilson's famous Fourteen Points,[9] that posed ideas which were to become labelled as self-determination such as 'political and economic independence', and 'autonomous development' within Europe. The Iranians were to take heart from these pronouncements as well as his more specific intentions towards the Ottoman Empire.

The Ottomans had fought as a Central power, and its dissolution as an empire was now one of the primary concerns of the Allied powers in Paris when it came to decisions outside the European sphere. President Wilson had suggested the separation of the Turkish portions from other ethnicities, which had been part of the Ottoman Empire. He also proposed 'a free, open-minded, and absolutely impartial adjustment of all colonial claims', taking into account the 'sovereignty the interests of the populations concerned' and the controlling power. Iran, like many other nations, and would-be nations in the Middle East, saw in these pronouncements an opportunity to unshackle themselves from a semi-colonial existence.

In fact, the First World War had had a transformative effect throughout the Middle East. The war had helped to develop and hasten inchoate ideas of ethnic independence and nationalism. In Arab lands, Britain had stoked nationalist ideas among the tribes to ensure military success against the Ottomans. Further east, dormant ethnic nationalisms in the region of Transcaucasia were also invigorated. Previously part of Iran's Empire and more recently part of Russia, Armenia, Azerbaijan and Georgia had provided the territories over which the Ottomans and

Russians had fought during the First World War. Now, since the end of the war, Russian forces had disintegrated and the defeated Ottomans had been repatriated. The end of the war had resulted in an administrative and political vacuum – a geographical and political space – which had allowed the Armenians, Azeris and Georgians to believe in the possibility of independence.

In truth, while President Wilson had become the flag-bearer for ideas such as self-determination and the creation of institutions of peace, his ideas were not new. Many of the ideas and shibboleths extolled and put forward at the Paris Peace Conference had in fact been bubbling up in the previous century. Ideas of 'self-determination' had been espoused by those on the left of world politics. The socialist revolutionary Rosa Luxemburg expressed the rights of nations within the context of internationalizing socialism.[10] Vladimir Lenin, critical of Rosa Luxemburg's interpretation of the nation as an abstract, took a different view and defined self-determination in terms of 'political self-determination'.

Ideas for creating world institutions were likewise not new but had previously surfaced as part of the pacifist agenda. The League to Enforce Peace (1915–23) had been formed in the United States and promoted the formation of a body to keep international peace after the war had ended. The British League of Nations Society (1915–18), pacific and anti-war, also predated President Wilson's League of Nations. It too looked towards internationalizing relations between countries to prevent war.

Nevertheless, the 'left' and its proponents were very much on the fringe of world politics in 1919, and it was President Wilson who had the stature to pursue and push through change. His ideas were to be looked upon favourably, and it was he who appeared as the prime motivator of ideas such as self-determination and the League of Nations. These ideas, at least at first, appeared to promote values that could also aid those in the Middle East who had developed nationalist impulses and who pursued independence. Soon, however, it would become obvious that there existed a disconnect between ideas of self-determination, the ideals and workings of the League of Nations attributed to President Wilson, and what the ethnicities and nations in the Middle East understood from them.

The problem was that the ideas of self-determination and the development of the League of Nations on which these peoples, semi-colonies and colonies depended had been developed for and were to be used by the Anglo-Saxon world predominantly in Europe. However, even when it came to applying these notions to Europe the interpretation and scale were unforeseen. Very soon after the Fourteen Points were publicized President Wilson seemed to feel hostage to the ideas he had put in motion. He had, in fact, never uttered the word 'self-determination' and had originally not seemed to understand the consequences of his nascent wishes. In 1919, he told Congress, 'When I gave utterance to those words, I said them without the knowledge that nationalities existed, which are coming to us day after day.'[11] The problem was that while in theory the idea of self-determination prompted nationalist programmes for people such as the Poles, it was never clear where the dividing line would be. Do you stop at ethnicity, language or religion?[12] In most cases it did not matter as those who had the ability were creating (or re-creating) their own political states. In fact, the Allied powers including President Wilson found that they were often merely rubber-stamping political unions which had already taken place.[13]

Whatever President Wilson may have understood about 'self-determination' and how it was to be applied to Europe, there is no doubt that he saw it applied to the colonial world in a more limited form.[14] That was where the League of Nations came into the picture. No doubt, the League of Nations had been intended to provide a forum in which countries, both big and small, could voice and resolve their differences short of going to war. However, membership of the League of Nations was subject to certain criteria. Member states had to have 'a stable government and settled frontiers' and be 'self-governing'.[15] This was a very tall order for some following the war. For those states or would-be states who could not achieve such a standard, Article 22 allowed for the League of Nations to institute a mandate system to assist aspiring nations and colonies in achieving membership.

So, both the issues of self-determination and the operation of the League of Nations raised problems of application for ethnicities and nascent states. On the one hand, the definition of what self-determination meant was so vague that it allowed it to be tailored to political requirements; self-determination would mean whatever the independence-seeking state wanted it to be. On the other hand, once used, it was a definition that was unlikely to mesh with the definition used by the League of Nations. Failure to meet the definition put forward by the League would necessitate the instituting of a mandate to bring the state up to par. The reality was that Article 22 in its Covenant gave the League of Nations a role within the continuity of colonialism. Peace did not augur the diminishing of colonial and imperial practices outside Europe; rather, they were simply to morph into something slightly more intellectually and politically palatable.

Article 22 was to rely on a 'standard of civilization', a definition that was articulated within European terms of reference. On a practical level, this included all the elements we might expect to have in a modern nation-state: '(a) Basic institutions of government and public bureaucracy, (b) the organizational capacity for self-defense, (c) a published legal code and adherence to the rule of law, and (d) recognition of international law and norms, including those on the conduct of war and diplomatic exchange.'[16] On another level, this might include the approval or dislike of religion, ethnicity or a myriad of 'scientific' theories such as Social-Darwinism and Aryanism.

Notions of what it meant to be civilized were vital in the development of international law. The nineteenth century had seen the rise of international law, its implementation beginning to provide a meaningful legal framework for states and people's rights. Now, states and would-be states were looking for a measure of protection and equality under international law. Yet, as the nineteenth century had shown, the development of international law had been anything but fair. In fact, international law had been part of the civilizing mission of many European countries. While the rights of states and people were now embodied in the Covenant of the League of Nations Charter, this did not necessarily mean, given the definitions at hand, that much would change post-war.

There was also another hurdle. The British and French did not consider ideas of self-determination appropriate to the Middle East as it directly affected their interests. A series of formal and informal arrangements with France during the war concerning the Middle East had made it clear that Iran would come under Britain's sphere of interest.[17] The most infamous agreement, the Sykes-Picot Agreement (1916), confirmed that Britain would be free to affect its strategic interests in a wide swathe towards India which included Iran. The British had, in fact, begun planning for peace in the Middle East remarkably early during the First World War. The various recommendations of the de Bunsen committee which reported on 30 June 1915[18] all pointed towards extensive British influence throughout a dissolved Ottoman Empire. The four solutions that the committee arrived at included the annexation of all Ottoman territory, dividing the territories into spheres of influence, leaving the Empire in place but rendering it submissive and finally splitting the Empire into separate administrative and semi-autonomous units.

More critically when it came to the question of a post-war Iran, the de Bunsen committee clarified one important issue. Britain had agreed to give Russia the 'possession of Constantinople, the European coast from the Black Sea to the end of the Dardanelles, the Asiatic shore of the Bosphorus [sic], the islands in the sea of Marmora, and Imbros and Tenedos' in exchange for a 'revision' of the Anglo-Russian Agreement of 1907,[19] which had split Iran into zones of British and Russian political and economic influence. By 1919 arrangements with the Russians in relation to Iran had become moot as the Russians had left the Iranian sphere as the Bolsheviks were busy consolidating the Russian revolution. The British had come out of the First World War as the predominant power in and around Iran.

The question of what to do with Mesopotamia, roughly modern-day Iraq, which had been part of the Ottoman Empire and which neighboured Iran to the west, was ever present in the de Bunsen committee's deliberations. Pledges had been made to the Sheik of Mohammerah, chieftain of the port of Mohammerah, a port in Iran on the Shatt al-Arab waterway, that Basra would never again be a commercial threat under Ottoman/Turkish authority. There were also other commercial and strategic considerations that would impact British decision-making. The facilitation of trade ensured by free river navigation, railway connections with India and not least the protection of the oil wells that dotted the Ottoman/Mesopotamia and Iranian border pointed towards a solution larger than the simple annexation of the Basra region. The protection of Basra necessitated the protection of Bagdad which meant control of Mosul. The British were already anticipating the control of what was to become Iraq as a prerequisite to prevent either France or Russia from imposing any type of control on the immediate region at any point in the future.

President Wilson's ideas about the nature and conduct of imperialism were also not straightforward. On the one hand, President Wilson preached ideas of self-determination and autonomy; on the other hand, the United States' own policies towards smaller states were themselves colonial and the Americans had an Empire, albeit smaller, of its own. He saw no double standard in his views. An admirer of the British Empire,[20] he saw American involvement as a civilizing and educational mission – a paternalist streak that was comparable with Lord Curzon's attitudes, someone who would go on to play a large part in Britain's policy towards Iran.

For now, the many attendees of the Paris Peace Conference were not burdened by the political realities that were to come. Paris was the magnet that attracted a mixed bag of bigger and lesser nations who were captivated by the possibilities of a new world order and what that might mean for their peoples. Some seeking nationhood, like Greece, saw the opportunities in the break-up of the Ottoman Empire. A delegation from Egypt, then still a British protectorate, went to Paris demanding independence.[21]

Closer to home, the Armenians, Azeris and Georgians had all seen the opportunity to organize politically and to establish states which encompassed nationalist ideas based on territorial sovereignty. They had bought into the ideas of self-determination and all had one common goal to be admitted to the conference and to have their independence recognized and protected within a territorial context. Yet there were some nuances.

The Georgian delegation, under Nikoloz Chkheidze and Irakli Tsereteli, who were both socialists, wanted a future that guaranteed their sovereignty while at the same time needing a protector or a mandate power, despite what this might mean in the development of a socialist state. Georgian demands were small when compared to the Armenians.[22]

The Armenians sent two delegations, a result of the sectarian nature of the region in which a multitude of political groups had been attempting to garner control and secure a nationalistic route to power. In this case, one delegation, the Armenian National Delegation, recognized by the Allies, was led by Boghos Nubar Pasha. The other, the Armenian Republic, was led by Avetis Aharonian. Boghos Nubar Pasha represented the Turkish Armenians and the diasporic Armenians and Avetis Aharonian was a member of the Dashnak Party, a far more socialist and revolutionary political entity. Both groups eventually came together to form a joint memorandum at the Peace Conference.[23] The joint memorandum had declared Armenia's independence as hard-won through war and the sacrifices of its people. Armenia claimed that far from being inactive it had fought throughout the war and deserved the status of a belligerent state. Armenia also attempted to secure the sympathy of the allies, quoting its losses fighting its Ottoman oppressors, and describing the massacres of its people perpetuated by the Ottomans. In addition to claiming territory and reparations they also asked for a mandate to be established under the United States.

The Azeris also sent a delegation, led by Ali Marden Bek Topchibashev, president of the first Azeri parliament, but were the last to arrive in Paris. They also claimed their independence, that 'Wilsonian principles' be applied, that they be admitted to the League of Nations, and for the United States to extend military aid and to establish diplomatic relations with them. Significantly, they expressed more forcefully than either Armenia or Georgia, the fear of the reconstitution of the Russian Empire.

The question of a resurgence of Russian dominance in the region overshadowed all questions of independence and territorial sovereignty. Whether it was to be the re-establishment of the Russian Empire or a new Bolshevik Empire, it would have meant the loss of recently won independence for many inchoate states in the Caucasus. The success of the Bolsheviks in the civil war in Russia also concerned the Allies as they gathered in Paris. Uncertainty and fear over Bolshevik success in Europe were somewhat mirrored in the Caucasus. It was a fear that the head of the Kurdish delegation was tuned into.

Sharif Pasha (1865–1951) represented the Kurds in Paris and represented what was a large ethnic group that had primarily existed as part of both the Iranian and Ottoman Empires. Sharif Pasha may have led Kurdish nationalist claims but it was not obvious what backing he had amongst the dissolute Kurdish tribes. Arguably, they were to be the least organized group in the region and suffered from not having an effective focal point for their nationalist impulses. They also asked for independence, but unlike the Armenians, Azeris and Georgians, they had not declared and secured it in any fashion. Nevertheless, in pandering to fears of Bolshevism, Sharif Pasha was to argue that a Kurdish state would help to stabilize tensions in the region and 'create a buffer zone against the threat of Bolshevik Russia'.[24]

Most extraordinarily of all perhaps, an Assyrian delegation also arrived in early 1919 and demanded Assyrian nationhood not seen for nearly 2000 years.[25] Yet, like the Armenians, Azeris, Georgians and Kurds, they were so taken by ideas of self-determination that they sent delegates to the Paris Peace Conference. Believing that there was a possibility of independence or self-government, they put forward proposals that established territorial sovereignty – territory, which was to be contested by all, given the patchwork nature of ethnic distribution in the region, including Iran.

An Iranian delegation also went to Paris but there was to be one significant difference; it, unlike the ethnicities in the immediate vicinity, was already an established nation. In Paris, the Iranian delegation sought to re-establish sovereignty independent of unwanted impositions from foreign powers and to re-establish its pre-1828 borders. Iran's Parisian diplomacy was the spearhead of a febrile period in which she sought to right the wrongs of the past and to take what she considered its rightful place amongst the important nations of the world.

Acknowledgements

I have always been interested in history: curious as how people and situations could be manifestly impacted by events completely out of one's control. This was something indelibly emphasized to me in 1979. I had not known, as I returned to go back to school in England at the beginning of January, that the changes Iran was undergoing were to be permanent. My interest in Iranian history and politics has at times been intense, all to affect a greater understanding of a magnificent, yet flawed, country – the country in which I had spent my formative years and the land of my mother.

In middle age, I went back to university and, after an MA in Global History and a doctorate in Iranian studies, I have sought to better understand the history of Iran. I grew an interest in both the development of Iranian nationalism and the delimitation of Iran's borders. It was my thesis supervisor, Professor Ali Ansari, who first mentioned that I should consider looking at Iran's participation at the Peace Conference in Paris in 1919. This book is the result of those endeavours.

I have written this book on an overlooked period in Iranian history which has frequently been reduced to a simplified trope that the Qajar dynasty was simply a period of failure. I feel that it is still the case that too often Iranian history, to those outside academia, has been condensed to simplified and negative ideas about Iran. This book, therefore, seeks in a small way to help to remedy some ingrained perceptions of Qajar history and Iranian history more generally. It is therefore my hope that non-Iranians and non-academics may find this monograph of interest.

It is customary to thank colleagues, friends and family members for their direct or indirect impact on this book. However, in truth, it is difficult to articulate the actual beginning of this book and the list is therefore overwhelming. I will therefore keep the list short. I would like to thank Professor Ali Ansari, my thesis supervisor, for his help and nurture without which I would also have ignored this period in Iranian history. Also, I would like to thank Dr Hurivash Ahmadi Dastgerdi who helped me re-engage with the Persian language and the intricacies of nineteenth-century Persian. Finally, I would like to thank my wife, Fiona, for her patience and editing skills.

TRANSLITERATION AND DATES

This book uses a simplified form of Persian transliteration. It is based on the *Iranian Studies* scheme but, excepting (') for *ayn*, diacritical marks are not used. The transliteration has been made as a Persian speaker might be expected to see it. This includes Persian rendering of Arabic names and words. Place names and names of individuals have been represented in their common format, but reference notes retain original Persian and English words. Idiosyncratic reference notes have been transliterated as was.

Reference will be made to 'Iran' and 'Iranians' throughout, though reference to 'Persia' in original material, treaties, etc., has been preserved. The ill-defined transition from Ottoman to Turkey-controlled Iraqi lands, *c.* 1911, requires an inexact change of reference from Ottoman to Turk.

As was the habit of the time, reference notes will show the use of two dating systems, the Islamic Lunar and the Solar calendar. All dates are provided as the Gregorian equivalent in the text.

ABBREVIATIONS

AI	Kaveh Bayat and Reza Azari Shahrzayee (eds), *Amal-e Iraniyan az konferans-e solh-e Paris ta qarardad-e 1919 Iran va Engelis* (Iran: Pardise Danesh, 1392)
DBFP	Documents on British Foreign Policy
FO	Foreign Office files, UK National Archives
FRUS	Papers relating to the Foreign Relations of the United States
IOR	India Office Records, British Library
MAF	Mohammad Afshin Vafaie and Pejman Firouzbakhsh (eds), *Yaddashtha-ye ruzaneh-ye Mohammad Ali Foroughi az safar-e konferans-e solh-e Paris (Desambr-e 1918–Ut-e 1920). Requested by Iraj Afshar, Chap-e panjom. (Tehran: Sokhan, 1394)*
Mss	Additional Manuscripts, India Office Records, British Library
WO	War Office files, UK National Archives

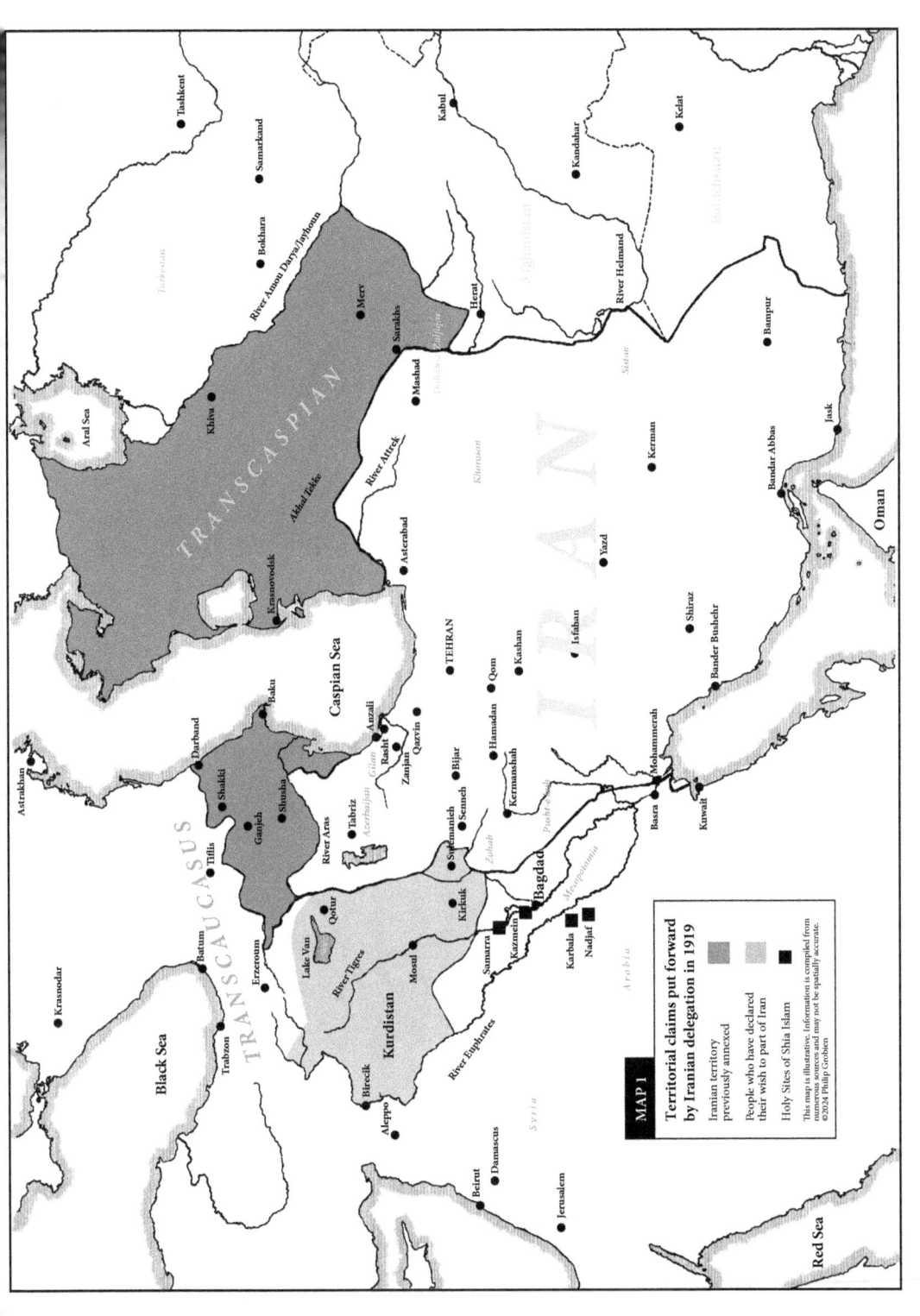

INTRODUCTION: IRAN AT THE CROSSROADS

Iran, at the end of the First World War, had been energized by notions of self-determination and the development of international institutions devoted to peaceful and lawful interaction. Internationalizing Iran's semi-colonial existence, and its loss of territory would, they hoped, bring their plight to a wider audience. At the upcoming Peace Conference in Paris, they expected that an Iranian delegation would be able to put forward plans which would throw off the hold of its 'stronger neighbours' who they believed were actively 'weakening her and suppressing her independence'.[1] This would lead to Iran re-establishing its sovereignty over its past imperial territory.

The war had been a defining period for Iran. It seemed, if nothing else, a fitting conclusion to a period of ever-increasing weakness which had permeated the previous and early twentieth century. Buffeted by the interests of the British and Russians and the tussle between them for supremacy, as well as Ottoman territorial incursions that Iran had countered with difficulty, Iran had become a semi-colonial state. Iran remained avowedly independent, a principle confirmed many times by the British and Russians, but, in reality, subject to their economic and political domination.

The inability of Iran to manage its own affairs and to defend its territory had become progressively more acute over the long nineteenth century up to the First World War. Yet in 1919, with its territory occupied by foreign forces and a government unable to manage either periodic epidemics or famines let alone insurgencies, Iran's diplomatic elite saw an opportunity for change. At a time when Iranian politicians and people considered that only the dissolution of Iran as an entity could be worse, Iran embarked on a diplomatic enterprise that was driven by nationalist impulses. Iran's diplomacy was to be innovative, consistent and persistent.

Much of the historiography of this period has not credited Iran's deliberate pursuit of a planned and coordinated policy. The immediate post-war period has more often been analysed through the prism of the Anglo-Persian Agreement pushed through by Britain and intended to implement a *de facto* protectorate over Iran. The Anglo-Persian Agreement symbolized then and, to this day, the abject and complete surrender of Iran to foreign imperialism. The agreement has also been seen as the nadir and end of a feeble Qajar dynasty – a period of confusion and decay in contrast to the more muscular government that epitomized the

Pahlavi dynasty. Yet, there was much more to this period than the Anglo-Persian Agreement and the narrative is far more complex and nuanced. Even the agreement itself requires a reassessment.

Despite the narrative of reforms under the Pahlavi dynasty, which had followed the Qajar dynasty and with which it has been unfavourably contrasted, Iran had still sought reform. Despite the government's tenuous control of the country, Iranian politicians continued to submit proposals to the British which included financial and military reforms. As Oliver Bast correctly suggested, more significant diplomatic and political progress was possible in the latter Qajar era than previously thought and that the narrative was not simply one of a *discourse of disintegration*.[2] The, for so long, accepted narratives of the Anglo-Persian Agreement have camouflaged a period that showed considerable intellectual development in Iran of ideas concerning reform and constitutional development.

These desires were to harden in the immediate post-war period. The year 1919 was to serve as a juncture in Iranian politics in which there was a decisive move to develop a state infrastructure and bureaucracy commensurate with a modern state – the development of state institutions for protection, education, finance, taxes, etc., within a specified territory. Or, to put it another way, the provision of a state structure afforded the mechanisms with which to govern. This would form part of the broader morphing of Iran from a dynastic to a national state – a pattern where nationalist sentiments and loyalty to the state, rather than to the Shah and Qajar dynasty, were increasingly permeating the Iranian bureaucracy.[3]

However, this precarious and turbulent period in Iranian politics, which had begun just before the war's end and tailed off in 1920, and which was to be spearheaded by the sending of a delegation to the Peace Conference in Paris, did not advocate a nation-state as we would normally understand it. Iran was to put forward a new and consolidated nationalism in Paris, based on the need for modern state structures but within the context of an imperial Iran. This *imperial nationalism* envisioned an independent and modern Iran, though one which encompassed, to a great extent, the territory of its eighteenth-century Empire.

The definition of this period as one of *imperial nationalism* may, at first glance, appear to be one of contradiction. Theories of nationalism have usually relied on the rights of people to be collectively independent, yet Empire implies the political control over a multitude of diverse peoples. *Imperial nationalism*, as defined here, is not antagonistic, but rather a description of Iran's diplomacy during this period. Iran set out a nationalist manifesto that included independence from foreign interference and territorial sovereignty within an imperial setting. In a nutshell, Iran wished to modernize and return to its imperial borders before their contraction which had taken place during the long nineteenth century. Iran's independence and sovereignty claims were therefore heavily dependent on an idea of Empire that was both cultural and territorial (see Map 1). Certainly, the nationalists who argued for Iran's rights in Paris were relying on an interpretation and idea of Iran grounded in history, myth, culture and territory.

This book examines the nature and implications of Iranian diplomacy after the First World War – a diplomacy that looked to the future, in securing an independent, modern state that was still anchored in Iran's imperial past. Iran's interaction with European Empires operating in the region, the loss of territory, independence and the subsequent evolution of an Iranian enlightenment, led to the building of the foundations for a national state rather than providing the dying embers of the Qajar dynasty. It proposed a path that suggested a distinctly Iranian modernity. Never before had Iran's politicians and statesmen articulated such a consolidated vision for their future. Above all, Iran's *imperial nationalism* shows that they had learned from the past and were now able to develop a proactive diplomacy.

For readers curious about Iran and the more general aspects of Iranian history, this book offers an insight into the attitudes and diplomacy of a minor nation, Iran, which sought to elevate itself within an international context at the Paris Peace Conference, attempting to stand up to European imperialism. For students of Iranian history, my research points to a number of themes, some of which are revisionist. The narrative points to an Iran, who, despite the many impediments, made good use of modern methods in establishing a foundation for Iran's diplomacy. Iran's mission was also forward-thinking and aspirational and everyone, without exception, agreed that Iran needed to be reformed. Yet, within these broad objectives, there existed different viewpoints as to how this could be achieved. Compelling in this narrative are clearer ideas of the roles of Iranian politicians, the Shah and the British.

Ahmad Shah (1898–1930) took a far more involved role in Iran's mission to Paris than previously thought. At the same time, Vosuq al-Dowleh (1868–1951), the prime minister, along with a small clique of cabinet ministers, showed little appetite in sending a delegation to Paris and was rather ambivalent to their hopes for success. Whilst paying lip service to the aims of the Paris mission, Vosuq al-Dowleh was to use the delegation to help develop his own ideas for reform. His ideas were to mesh with the British, who opposed Iran's delegation to Paris, not only because it did not fit into their own plans in Britain's imperial backyard, but also because they had plans of their own. Lord Curzon and Sir Percy Cox had developed ideas regarding the re-generation of Iran which were singular and at odds with some in their own government as well as in Iran. The result, the Anglo-Persian Agreement, was in fact a 're-vitalization' of Iran which went far beyond what other British politicians had intended. Not only does it present Lord Curzon's paternalistic impulses to Iran but it also promotes the role of Sir Percy Cox in a more nuanced light. The Iranian's *desiderata*, both in Paris and the secretive negotiations with the British for the Anglo-Persian Agreement, were remarkably consistent. Both included elements of reform and sovereignty and formed part of Iran's foreign policy during the period and cannot be separated in this analysis.

Too much of the narrative of this period has been seen from the British perspective and this book will hopefully explain the Iranian narrative more fully and reach a more balanced perspective. Ultimately, it is hoped that this overlooked period in Iran's history will be integrated more fully into the narrative of Iranian nationalism and that the examination of Iranian nationalism needs to incorporate the idea of Empire more fully.

Conceptualizing Iran's outlook

The development of *imperial nationalism* and the issues which were to drive Iranian diplomats in Paris were informed by several paradigms and events, all of which were interlinked, and which require further clarification and definition. These include the changes to Iran's geo-political outlook, Iran's reaction to British and Russian modernity, and Iran's adaption to both paradigms.

The first is the altered geo-political outlook in which Iran found herself at the beginning of the nineteenth century. Iran had never been isolated from the West, but its relationship with the West and particularly the Empires of Britain and Russia now undertook a radical turn. In 1799, The East India Company vanquished Tipu Sultan of Mysore and from that point onwards controlled all of India. British political designs now included the protection of India and the security of its trade routes. It was natural, therefore, that Iran, which both bordered India and had a geographical vantage point over the Persian Gulf, would come to form part of British security and trade strategies. Threat assessments to India during the very early part of the nineteenth century came from Napoleonic France. However, when this threat failed to materialize, the British turned their attention, albeit slowly, to the growing threat of Russia towards their Indian dominions.[4]

Russia, under Catherine the Great, had reignited an interest in the Transcaucasus and Transcaspian[5] first shown by Peter the Great. Between 1801 and 1828 Russian aggression grew and the expansion of its Empire pushed towards the Caucasus and what had been considered Iranian territory. Iran fought two wars against the Russians which led to two penal defeats. Under the Treaty of Golestan (1813) Iran lost many of its Caucasian provinces. The second war, resulting in the Treaty of Turkmanchai (1828), would not only lead to the disastrous loss of more of the Caucasus and Nakhchevan, but also a reassessment by the British of the Russian threat to Iran and therefore India.

Between 1828 and 1919 Iran became a pawn in what was to be called the *Great Game* and the political and diplomatic strategies in which the British and Russians vied for regional supremacy. It was during this period that a pre-modern Iran, largely agrarian and pre-industrial, was faced with Empires that had significant technological, military and organizational advantages. What followed was a period of dialectical change in which Iran was to appropriate, absorb and then apply Western achievements to its own paradigm. The course of this exchange was progressive but also slow and erratic. It also included the appropriation of a different language – a language that included the vocabulary of Western ideas such as sovereignty and independence. By 1919 Iran was to use these modern arguments, methods and language in their diplomacy of *imperial nationalism*.

There are two parts to this narrative of Iranian appropriation. The first part is to understand the rise of nationalism within the context of 'Western' ideas and philosophies and how they were applied. The second part is to understand the nature of reform and modernization in Iran not as the fountainhead of Iranian nationalism, but as a means to an end and the development from a dynastic to a national state.

In fact, the development of nationalism in Iran would nourish and be fed by an 'Iranian awakening' and 'enlightenment',[6] in which Iranian intellectuals were to grapple with the nature of the appropriation of Western ideas to Iran. There was a slow but determined change in Iranian society and the growth of an Iranian polity – a society which evolved ideas of *vatan* (homeland) and *mellat* (nation) and what it meant to be a *vatanparast* (patriot). Ideas that would be disseminated through newspapers, and discussed in the bazaars and coffee houses of Iran, thereby further aiding the rise of national consciousness. There were also notable signposts to this gradual, but by no means constant and consistent change. One can note the rise of nationalism in the Tobacco Rebellion (1890) and the *Enqelab-e Mashruteh* (Constitutional Revolution) between 1906 and 1911. The Constitutional Revolution served to bring together different public spheres of public criticism[7] and involve diverse and wide-ranging socio-political groups.

The second part is the facilitation of nationalism through modernization. Without an evident pathway towards achieving an independence unfettered by British and Russian hegemony, Iran's elite saw economic reform as a mechanism towards political change. In other words, a national revival might be secured through modernization. However, modernization was mainly sought through the negotiation of European concessions which, in effect, meant the importing of modern methods and technologies. The course of this strategy, if the haphazard awarding of concessions could be defined as such, was highly dubious. For example, the losses and penal treaties which followed both wars with Russia had shown the deficiencies of the organization of and inferiority of the Iranian Army. Yet the narrative of Iran's ability to modernize its army for future wars or protection was held back by the inability of Iran's rulers to grasp the nettle. While Fath Ali's heir, Abbas Mirza, did allocate time and expense to modernizing Iran's army, any real chance was forestalled by his death in 1833. From that point on, any modernization of the army and other arms of government was to be fitful or non-existent.

In fact, the only consistent thread was the ambivalence to modernization which coloured all the Qajar rulers from Fath Ali Shah (1772–1834) to Ahmad Shah, the last Qajar Shah. Much has been written about the revered Prime Minister of Iran Amir Kabir (1807–52) and his motivation to modernize Iran's governmental structures but his was to be a small interlude of light soon snuffed out by court jealousies and his eventual assassination. In many ways, the uncertainty shown by the Qajars towards modernism was highlighted by the longest-serving Shah, Naser al-Din, who ruled between 1848 and 1896 and who had ordered the assassination of Amir Kabir. He did not consider his long reign as an opportunity to modernize Iran's government infrastructure as he saw any changes as a threat to his patrimonial rule and dynasty. His intention was 'to stay in power and to amass wealth'.[8] He would do this by extending concessions to foreigners in greater and greater volume. He once told Jakob Eduard Polak, his personal physician and a doctor who performed an important role in bringing modern medicine to Iran, 'If only no European had ever set foot in my country, we would have been spared all these tortures. But since these aliens have penetrated, I intend to take as good and as much advantage of them as possible.'⁹ Clearly one of the advantages to be taken was the money from concessions which fuelled his lifestyle. Another advantage lay in the usefulness of modern methods. If a modern invention or method was useful in helping him have greater control of his reign, and he could benefit from it, then he was more motivated to employ it. In the words of Abbas Milani, Naser al-Din Shah 'had to domesticate modernity into a servile tool of his despotism'.¹⁰

By any yardstick of progress, the Qajar dynasty cannot be called successful or fruitful. However, even the short synopsis above shows that these assumptions are not absolute. The much-criticized actions of accepting ever-greater numbers of concessions for financial gain in fact also allowed for a modicum of modernization, while at the same time avoiding greater penitence towards either the British or the Russians. It was a method, however haphazard, of bringing in modern technologies and techniques while simultaneously towing a middle path.¹¹ Some concessions were vital and successful, the most evident being the introduction of the telegraph.

These concessions would, however, represent a double-edged sword. On the one hand, Iran could fitfully modernize, but on the other hand, each new concession furthered British and Russian commercial interests in the country which had the diplomatic backing of their respective governments. Some concessions at least had practical advantages and many brought hard currency into the country through either commission or premium payments. However, concessions known as capitulary rights offered to the Russians and subsequently British governments following the Treaty of Turkmanchai were to be a heavy burden on Iran's economy. For example, the treaty allowed Russian merchants and companies to pay only a 5 per cent tariff on exports to Iran and no tariffs on internal trade. These rights, which Iranian traders did not have, put Iranian commerce and any nascent industry at a disadvantage. In fact, when examined collectively with numerous other rights that were given to the British and Russians, such as the legal immunity to be tried by their own courts rather than the Iranian court system, one can begin to understand the frequent and emotive responses to foreign 'interference' in Iran, which still resonates today.

While scholarly consensus is that modernization has played a role in Iranian nationalism, defining its role is rather more problematic. Using analytical frameworks where modernization has been the precursor or foundation of nationalism is unhelpful in the analysis of Iranian nationalism.¹² The problem is one of timing; or as Afshin Marashi has articulated, there have been 'sequencing' issues of Iranian industrialization and nationalism. To put it another way, Ali Ansari has eloquently suggested, 'While in the West nationalism has increasingly been seen as the child of modernity, an unfortunate progeny, in Iran modernisation was the handmaiden of nationalism.'¹³

Imperial nationalism

Frequently used concepts and frameworks of nationalism are equally problematic when employed to describe and analyse the growth of nationalism in Iran. John Breuilly articulated nationalism as a form of a political movement, which must be seen in the 'context of the modern state and the modern state system'.[14] Of course, Iran did not have a modern state system. One analytical framework that has many adherents, if not as a guiding paradigm but as a method for getting into the debate about Iranian nationalism, is the work of Benedict Anderson. He argued that nationalism had not been invented and fabricated as Ernest Gellner had suggested,[15] but imagined through a binding political community.[16] There are some theoretical problems in how this binding can actually take place, or as one scholar suggested, 'If the condition for a community to be considered imagined is that the only way to perceive it as a whole is to refer to its image, then all social groups, even the smallest, are imagined communities.'[17] Moreover, Benedict Anderson, like others, has emphasized the use of modern technology and in particular print technology for the spread of the imagined national community[18] – the timing of which is difficult to articulate when it came to Iran.

This brief study of nationalism shows how difficult it is to use broad conclusions and European articulations about nationalism within the Iranian context.[19] As Afshin Marashi has suggested the development of nationalism in Iran has other defining features. Though societal transformation was critical to nationalistic impulses, the language of and pull of nationalism was guided by the Iranian elite and not public spheres from below. Moreover, the result of a public mobilization of nationalism was to lead, in the Constitutional Revolution, into a pluralist and diverse understanding of the nation.[20] There will always be idiosyncrasies when applying a European framework of analysis of the growth of nationalism in Iran. Not only are most ideas of nationalism borne out of a European context, but the language and modality are Western.

None, for example, even those who look at the Middle East,[21] give an account of the role of Empire and how Empire might influence more modern ideas of identity. Accounts of nationalism in the Austria-Hungary and Ottoman Empires fundamentally address the break-up of these empires into separate nation-states on ethnic lines. Separatist nationalist urges throughout the Austria-Hungary Empire were sufficiently advanced for the Empire to be dissolved soon after the First World War. The emergence of an ethnically purer Turkey from the Ottoman Empire was also the result of un-making rather than making of Empire. In Iran, no tribal, ethnic or provincial nationalism as a single political movement seriously troubled the integrity of Iran's Empire.[22]

Frontier Fictions by Firouzeh Kashani-Sabet[23] remains the only study of Iranian nationalism that attempts to locate ideas of Iranian nationalism within the context of land. She has suggested that there has been a continuous link between land and culture, which eventually took a more nationalistic path.[24] The idea of Iran had developed over time and side by side with the fluctuations and conflicts that affected Iran's land and frontiers. While the link between territory and nationalism is a vital element of *imperial nationalism*, it is the territorialization of this nationalism within a defined and delimited modern state which is crucial to this study. It is not a pre-modern cultural idea of ruling over peoples rather than territory.[25]

Now, for the first time, these delegates were establishing a defined territory of what the Iranian Empire meant in geographic terms. They were defining borders suitable for the modern age. If borders were now to be fixed, then they needed to be positioned adequately as befitted the Empire of Iran. Of course, in the event, forcible territorialization took place under the Pahlavi dynasty and on the basis of Iran's 1919 borders, but the definitions were being established by the delegates in 1919. They seemed to understand the importance of establishing a distinct *Persianate* connection between their idea of nationalism and territory.

On the one hand, they understood that the greatness of Empire had always been intrinsically linked to territory and that the loss of territories over the last 100 years which had damaged Iranian perceptions needed to be addressed. On the other hand, they had now learnt the necessity of a territorial state, with fixed borders as a necessary element in building a modern nation-state. Arguably, these delegates were very aware of this, as they had also learned the lesson that the delimitations that had already taken place, and the territory lost, had helped raise the consciousness of the nation.

The study of Iranian nationalism over the *long duree*, encompassing the Qajar and Pahlavi dynasties, the Iranian Revolution of 1979 and the Islamic Republic, has been contested and the source of much debate concerning the relative merits or demerits of many elements, not least the role of modernization, religion, race and ethnicity. The nationalism which the Iranian government and representatives put forward in Paris provides a nuanced interpretation of the discussion of Iranian nationalism. *Claims of Persia before the Conference of the Preliminaries of Peace of Paris* suggested that Iranian nationalism was rooted in an Iranian identity. It suggested an ethnic and *Persianate* foundation as the glue which was to define its territorial limits – ethnic, or as Anthony D Smith has described an 'ethnie', which incorporates facets such as a collective name, a common myth of descent, a shared history, a distinctive shared culture, a sense of solidarity and an association with a specific territory[26]; *Persianate*,[27] as articulated by Marshall Hodgson, in the extent of Iranian language, culture and literature, throughout the region. This allowed a nationalism that was both ethnic and cultural and therefore imperial, covering people of different descents. The programme put forward envisaged the resurgence of Empire and the reclaiming of parts of the Transcaucasus, Kurdish regions and the Transcaspian – all of which were now considered part of the Iranian 'imperial' identity.

The importance of Empire has more recently become of greater interest in the construction of national identity. The leaderships of China and Russia have all suggested that they be defined as Civilizational States. This self-identification serves political needs for exceptionalism and relies heavily on cultural uniqueness anchored in an imperial past. Together with a distinct racial ethnicity and language, a Civilizational State evinces a modern state structure within a long-term geographical location. Fundamental to a functioning Civilizational State is the acquiescence of the population to varying illiberal attitudes. Authoritarianism for the good of the many goes hand-in-hand with the promotion of 'group harmony' and the rejection of individualism.[28] The final point of difference between democracies in the West is the importance and rejection of, and insulation from, Western values.

Arguably, a representation of a Civilizational State was contemporaneous with the development of Iran's diplomacy. Japan was indeed proof that a non-Western state could modernize on its own terms, independent of Western imperialism.²⁹ Japan's Meiji Restoration in 1868 had sought to modernize in order to 'save its cultural heritage, not transform it'.³⁰ Though there was awareness in Iran of Japan's modernization, especially after it defeated the Russians in 1905, it is not clear what the Iranian elite took from Japan's obvious progress.

Modern Turkey has also been defined as a Civilizational State, building a modern and illiberal state on the foundations of its Ottoman and imperial past. Moreover, before and during the First World War, Ottoman Turkey had embarked on an irredentist programme of its own. In response to losing territory in the west and nascent nationalist urges from their Christian minorities, the Ottomans looked to the east where people of Turkic origin resided and who could be morphed into an ethnically Turkish Empire. This pan-Turkism³¹ was also to be influenced by sections of the Young Turk movement who drummed up support from Muslims of Turkic origins as far away as India.

Imperial nationalism differed from the concept of Civilizational State and pan-Turkism in two respects.³² Firstly, they did not reject individualism or envisage authoritarian rule, as they expressed Iran's reform under the umbrella of a continuing constitutional monarchy. Secondly, they expected a role for a modern state that differed from pan-Turkism and a Civilizational State. Clearly, with this understanding we must evaluate and define what manner of 'state' was envisaged.

Definitions of a modern state range widely. Normative ideas of the state as both a symbol of and means of authoritarian control and therefore a threat to liberty prevail, especially in the Middle East. In fact, it is sometimes difficult to differentiate between characterizations of the state and government. In Iran's case, we must look at the modern state in terms of the achievements of the Constitutional Revolution. The Constitutional Revolution had resulted in Iran having its first constitution, a constitution which set up a constitutional monarchy with a *Majles* (Iran's parliament) to conduct the business of government. It did not result in the development of the mechanisms of government and the ability of lawmakers to put laws into practice. Progress in this regard did not go far enough and in truth the constitutional changes were not completed. Soon the revolution, which had ushered in a new political and social landscape in Iran, was on the defensive during a period of greater turmoil in which the gains of the revolution had to be safeguarded.

Freedoms brought about by the constitution led to many social movements or revolutionary societies (known as an *anjoman*) and a proliferation of newspapers. The first *Majles* met in 1907 and signalled a new era in Iranian politics. Thereafter, progress was slow, and the revolution was buffeted by anti-constitutional forces and at times the bloody intervention of Russia. This period of immense change and political enthusiasm was also to be a period in which Iran was to be at its weakest. In 1907 the British and Russians chose to partition Iran into spheres of influence. This action reflected a spiritual and practical blow to the reality of Iran's independence and sovereignty, which the new constitution was meant to accompany. By 1911 Iran's progress towards constitutional monarchy appeared dead under the dictatorial leadership of Mohammad Ali Shah, Ahmad

Shah's father. Further developments were caught up in internal divisions, foreign intervention and ultimately the First World War.

Given that the nationalists in Paris defined sovereignty expressed in terms of Empire, ideas of nation-building do not serve as useful definitions as they do in the Pahlavi era. Nation-building implies the imposition of an element of homogeneity not reflected in Paris. The intention was purely one of state-building with attention largely given to affecting the mechanisms of government. The modern state that these nationalist and political elite foresaw was not only institutional but also spatial and visual. On a functional level it would include a civil service, police, a standing army, national taxation, national education and public health. On a political level it would include territorial sovereignty defined by fixed borders and extending state functions to the periphery of Iran and a policy devoted to developing adherence to the idea of a modern Iran and visual representations such as the flag.

Readers of Iranian history, or indeed imperial, colonial, and post-colonial history, would be aware of the challenges in pursuing independence. Iran, during the nineteenth and early twentieth centuries, has been characterized as a pre-modern nation unable to progress as it would like because of British and Russian interference. This argument remains one of the broadest elements argued in the *Claims of Persia before the Conference of the Preliminaries of Peace of Paris*. It is also a partial narrative. Iran could have, given will and ability, changed the path that successive Shahs had kept it on during the Qajar dynasty. By 1919 there can be no doubt that all of Iran's elite, politicians and diplomats believed that state-building was a vital prerequisite for survival. This sentiment was also echoed by the British – probably a unique period in which the British and Iranians were to agree. Most, if not all, of the political elite had been participants in the Constitutional Revolution, had become the backbone of successive Iranian governments and were now determined to finish the job by introducing reforms and a strong centralized government.

Paris: Policies and personalities

Iran's fortunes in Paris, and its programme more generally, came to rely on a small group of powerful politicians, political elite and intellectuals. The most powerful politicians were the so-called 'Big Four' who would be the ultimate decision-makers and arbiters of peace. They were British Prime Minister David Lloyd George, US President Woodrow Wilson, French Prime Minister Georges Clemenceau and Italian Prime Minister Vittorio Orlando. In reality, it was David Lloyd George, Georges Clemenceau and Woodrow Wilson who made the important decisions, including those which affected Iranian concerns. The narrative and analysis in this book rely heavily on these influential and powerful people, and a greater understanding of these individuals is needed to evaluate events and arguments developed in this book.

Figure 1 One of many pictures of the Big Four in Paris. From left to right, Woodrow Wilson, Georges Clemenceau, David Lloyd George, and Vittorio Orlando. ©Public Domain.

Formally and informally, the Americans were to provide a diplomatic outlet for Iranian views. As suggested in the prologue, President Wilson's ideas regarding the immediate peace and its aftermath would hang over Peace Conference more heavily than those of Georges Clemenceau and David Lloyd George. His impact on the proceedings was far greater than one would assume given America's late entry into the war in 1917 and its relatively small casualties. However, as detailed in the prologue, his utterances were never explained fully, and detail was at times lacking. He seemed either unable or unprepared to understand how his theoretical arguments could be put into practice in the real world – a world in which less high-minded attitudes and desires were to hold sway. It seemed that when faced with the question of what would happen with the dissolution of the Ottoman Empire, he was happy to bow to British imperial needs and strategies. A man of contradiction he was liked and disliked in equal measure. Despite an appreciation of the British Empire, President Woodrow Wilson and his entourage were to become increasingly suspicious of British actions towards Iran and their attitudes towards Iranian representation in Paris.

President Wilson was, therefore, to be a friend to Iranian aspirations in Paris. He, together with Robert Lansing (Secretary of State) and John Caldwell (Minister to Iran), was favourably inclined to give Iran a hearing. Robert Lansing (1864–1928) was an experienced international lawyer whose opinions President Wilson often ignored. John Caldwell (1875–1922) was cut from a different cloth. A non-career appointee, he was a humanitarian prone to help Iran and Iranians in addition to his political office.

The British were represented by David Lloyd George (1863–1945). He had seen the importance of fighting the war in the Middle East and now, equally, saw opportunities for the British in the dissolution of the Ottoman Empire. Much of this was driven by his visceral hatred for the Turks. He also saw no reason to share the spoils of war in the region with his Allies. After all, the British Army had, without them, beaten the Ottomans and at the end of the war were the pre-eminent power in the Middle East and David Lloyd George's approach was to keep it so. He claimed that Britain was now entitled to play the dominant role in the Middle East and would do what he could to enable that.[33] Where he could, he would avoid oversight from the other powers of British interests by excluding them from agendas and playing the American's 'anti-imperialist ire against the claims presented by Italy and France'.[34] Such actions sought to keep any conference oversight away from Mesopotamia and Iran. At times the British were very successful in their endeavour. In fact, the British had managed to secure recognition of the Egyptian Protectorate even though a delegation from Egypt was en route to the Peace Conference to further claims for independence.

David Lloyd George's strategy was successful despite his ignorance of the Middle East, its history and geography. It was successful because he was reliant on capable men such as Lord Balfour and in particular Lord Curzon. Lord Balfour (1848–1930), the foreign secretary, was in Paris with Lloyd George and had left Lord Curzon (1859–1925) in London as acting foreign minister. Though slightly older, Balfour was a contemporary of Curzon's, but had managed a far more successful political career and had been prime minister. Left to his own devices, Lord Curzon came to play a pivotal role in British diplomacy towards the Iranians between 1918 and 1920. He helped formulate and impose British policies towards Iran's attendance in Paris and negotiated the Anglo-Persian Agreement.

Lord Curzon's interest in the East and Iran had probably begun as early as his student days in Eton. It was an interest that would be furthered by his travels to Iran. When still a young man, his first trip to Iran lasted a mere three months but led to the creation of the double volume *Persia and the Persian Question*. This work would begin to establish him as an Iranian expert. His travels were also to imbue in Lord Curzon a deep belief in the civilizing nature of the British Empire, a notion which, given his knowledge of the eastern lands, revolved around the security of British India. Lord Curzon and President Woodrow Wilson shared several characteristics and opinions. They both cultivated dislike from their peers and were seen as arrogant, uncompromising and unduly set in their ways – particularly when situations changed. A deep sense of patrimonialism drove both him and President Wilson, which coloured President Wilson's outlook on the international stage and Lord Curzon's attitude towards the Iranians. Lord Curzon had always remained deeply sceptical of the 'Persian character' and Iran's ability to change and reform itself.

Figure 2 Lord Curzon, Viceroy of India, in the full regalia (1899–1905). ©Public Domain.

Sir Percy Cox (1864–1937) had become temporary Minister to Iran in September 1918. Notably of the same mindset as Lord Curzon with regard to Iran's inability to reform itself, he seemed at first to be a useful negotiator and conduit for British post-war strategy. His selection had been opposed by Iran who commonly opposed appointments from the Government of India as they felt that Indian officials brought many unwelcome attitudes and practices with them. There was, from the Iranian point of view, little to recommend him. Not only was he an Indian Army officer but he had been a Political Resident and responsible for British interests in the Persian Gulf and had, during the war, served as the chief political officer to the Indian Expeditionary Force and would eventually become Britain's Civil Administrator in Bagdad.[35] As the Iranians feared, his experiences in southern Iran and Mesopotamia would serve to inform his attitudes towards them. Despite his knowledge and experiences in Iran, his inability to understand the post-war environment and to drive forward ideas without sufficient reflection made him, eventually, more of a liability.

The British strategy would be primarily driven by Lord Curzon and Sir Percy Cox. It followed the general approach of excluding other Allied powers from what they considered their backyard and was motivated by arriving at a very British solution to the 'Persian Question' –how to develop a coherent policy towards Iran and how to bring Iran into a ring of compliant states which would provide a buffer to, and protection of, British India. Practical decisions had to be made regarding Iran's attendance in Paris and how to make Iran more compliant and reliant on Britain. For Iran, the problem was two-fold. Firstly, how to get Britain to buy in to their agenda and then at the same time stay on the right side of the most powerful commercial and military Empire in the region. Iran required British help in gaining access to the Peace Conference yet were arguing for the withdrawal of Britain from Iranian affairs. Iran's transformation into a truly independent state necessitated help from those involved in its domination and semi-colonial status.

In contrast with other literature on the subject, this book, using primary sources in the British archives, will help to see the actions of Lord Curzon and Sir Percy Cox in a more nuanced light. The role of Sir Percy Cox, which has been somewhat demoted to Lord Curzon's, will be assessed, as will different interpretations of Lord Curzon's attitude towards the 'revitalization' of Iran. In the same way, Iranian newspapers and archive material will be used to give a fuller understanding of the role of the Iranians during this remarkable period.

This material shows that Ahmad Shah Qajar had played a larger role than has been previously understood in Iran's post-war policies. Ahmad Shah Qajar was to be ousted in a coup by Reza Khan in 1925 who would go on to establish the Pahlavi dynasty. He came to the throne as a minor in 1909 when his father, Mohammad Ali Shah, was forced into exile. Between 1909 and 1914 and until Ahmad Shah gained his majority, he was supported by two regents. His legacy, as a weak monarch, too young and inexperienced to lead Iran, albeit in the capacity of a constitutional monarch, has endured. Indeed, his reign fits in well with the narrative of a dynasty on the ropes, unable or unwilling to counter the many threats that Iran faced.

Contemporary assessments of his suitability for the Iranian throne were also critical. Mohammad Ali Foroughi, who went to Paris as part of the delegation, considered the Shah out of his depth and 'not made for the monarchy'. Ahmad Shah was reported to have said about himself that 'it would be better to be a cabbage seller in Switzerland than Shah of such a country'.[36]

However, while Ahmad Shah may not have been the best Shah Iran could have hoped for, he was, towards the end of his reign, far more able. The first part of his reign, between 1914 and 1918 during the First World War, was symptomatic of a young man out of his depth. In the second period, between 1919 and 1920, he played a more significant role in Iran's new-found nationalist diplomacy. It was Ahmad Shah who set in motion the discussions and planning for Iran's strategy in Paris. It was he who picked the leader of Iran's delegation and who was to follow his instructions. During this period, he showed an ability that the British had not

Figure 3 A young and uncertain Ahmad Shah Qajar, photographed during the First World War. ©Public Domain.

foreseen – a role that remains largely unrecognized to this day. He managed to get like-minded intellectuals, diplomats and politicians to buy into the strategy.

Iran's political elite had grown up during a period of profound intellectual and political change in Iran. When not educated abroad they grew up open to European intellectual influences. Some were revolutionaries, some were very religious and some were not. It seems, however, that while their objectives towards Iranian political and social reform might have been divergent most of the diligent were imbued with the idea of Iranian reform. Without question all the delegates who went to Paris were nationalists who sought Iranian reform.

The delegates who were to go to Paris were pulled from this intellectual niveau, but while they had a good understanding of Iran's needs, they were venturing into the realm of international politics of which they had limited experience. As Mansoureh Ettehadieh has argued, this meant that they were at a disadvantage in understanding the sometimes nuanced relationship between the Allies, and the more parochial concerns of the British, French and Americans. This meant that the delegates were not able to mould their approach to the exigencies of the individual Allied countries. Another point which is sometimes missed but will become obvious as the narrative in this book unfolds was that the delegates who made up the delegation were not part of a single party or political group but were individuals who had their own ideas for Iran's reform.[37]

Historiography and sources

Research on the relation between nationalism and territory remains limited. *Frontier Fictions* is the only in-depth study of the synergy between the development of Iranian nationalism and Iranian territory. It develops the idea that the process of nation-building and nationalism had not just been umbilically linked to land, but that this process pre-dated and followed the establishment of the modern state.[38] A valuable tool for all researchers of this period, it does, however, cover a wider period and does not address the immediate post-war diplomacy in any detail.

Specific research that discussed the diplomatic issues of the time concentrates more on the development and ultimate failure of the Anglo-Persian Agreement. For example, Homa Katouzian discussed the period as a dialectical narrative of chaos and arbitrary rule, in which the Anglo-Persian Agreement played a significant part, and in which the chaos ultimately enabled the rise of Reza Khan and the Pahlavi dynasty.[39] In some respects, Houshang Sabahi's research on this period of Iranian and British diplomacy also pointed to the rise of Reza Khan as a solution to Britain's security needs.[40] Notably, Shaul Bakhash discussed the nature of the Anglo-Persian Agreement and how it formed part of a wider discourse of modernization.[41] William Olson's analysis examined the role the Anglo-Persian Agreement played in Britain's search to determine a cogent post-war policy towards Iran in order to secure its wider imperial interests.[42]

Most critically useful for this study has been the work of Oliver Bast. His research has established that Iran's role in the First World War was far from a failure and that its precarious neutrality in fact saved Iran's independence.[43] He has further established the essential elements of Iran's diplomacy during this period and given voice to the much-maligned Vosuq al-Dowleh, who, instead of a traitor, has rather been portrayed as a man devising and running 'a cleverly exercised diplomatic strategy'.[44] While the characterization of Vosuq al-Dowleh may require greater support to completely vindicate his actions, the man can to some extent be separated from the policy, which, given the state of the nation, had value. That is to say, despite his shortcomings he did what he felt was best for his country.

Oliver Bast's conclusions regarding Vosuq al-Dowleh remain at odds with Iranian narratives of his role in the Anglo-Persian Agreement where the agreement is frequently and derogatively referred to as 'Vosuq al-Dowleh's Agreement'. The narrative of the agreement has been often boiled down to accusations that Vosuq al-Dowleh sold Iran for 200,000 tomans.[45] Persian research has since developed to view the agreement, and Vosuq al-Dowleh's role in it, in a more considered manner. This includes research by Kaveh Bayat others.[46]

I have striven to provide a more balanced study of this febrile period in Iranian politics. British archives remain important, as do other English language and European newspapers of the period. This book, however, relies heavily on Iranian source material. One is the diary of Mohammad Ali Foroughi, the second most important delegate, who made copious diary entries and who recorded the ups and downs of the delegation. It is his diary of the period which gives a contemporary account of what the Iranians were trying to achieve and offers an insight into how they were determined to circumvent the obstacles in their path. In fact, his diary supplies the chronological structure of the book.

The other is the considerable Persian archive material which has been collated in the excellent archive of Iranian diplomatic communications assembled by Kaveh Bayat and Reza Azari Shahrzayee.[47] It is this, as far as I can see little-used archive, which has provided a vital source on which to build the framework for Iran's diplomacy. In the same way, Iranian newspapers have been used to give a fuller understanding of the role of the Iranians during this remarkable period.

Chapter 1

THE NINETEENTH CENTURY, THE GREAT GAME AND THE SQUEEZING OF IRAN

Many of the factors that informed Iran's diplomacy in 1919 were deep-rooted and can be traced back to the beginning of the nineteenth century. In 1789, the Qajars, a tribe of Turkmen descent, became the new ruling dynasty in Iran. The beginning of this dynasty was to coincide with changes in the geopolitics in the immediate region. Now, Iran was progressively to be part of a new paradigm – the ever-increasing weakness of the Qajar dynasty mirrored by the ever-increasing involvement of the British and Russians in Iran.

More specifically, between 1800 and 1828, the nature of the Qajar dynasty was to coincide with British and Russian interest in Iran which would set the patterns for the future – patterns which were to be detrimental to Iran's development and sovereignty and from which Iran was unable to escape. Iran was to become unable or unwilling to face the increasing diplomatic and military pressures exerted on it by the Russians and British as they were involved in a confrontation for domination of the region, which was to be, at times, also informed by European politics. Without a doubt, all Iran's *desiderata* put forward in Paris in 1919 can be traced back to this period in which Iran's imperial territory was not only substantially reduced but in which its own local power had come under threat.

Encounters and the advent of Russian confrontation

British involvement in Iran prior to 1800 had been primarily commercial. In the main it concerned the Persian Gulf, an area in which the East India Company, Britain's foremost trading and commercial powerhouse, had become dominant. Politically, Iran was not considered important enough to have a British mission and travel to Iran was generally deemed only befitting for explorers and archaeologists who were attracted to Iran given its imperial past. Most famously the Sherley Brothers[1] and Sir John Chardin[2] were to spend some time at Iranian courts. Russians also travelled to Iran to explore and to trade, though less in numbers than the British. Russian diplomatic missions had instilled in the Iranians a belief that Russians were nasty, uneducated and clownish, Uzbegs.[3] In general, therefore, from the European point of view, Iran was not politically important enough prior to 1800 for diplomatic communication and representation to be maintained. However, it was well integrated into local and global trade and not cut off from Western or more Eastern influences.[4]

Comparisons with Iran's glorious past, real or imagined, were to be inevitable. British travellers to Iran came with preconceptions of the past which were to be tested by the present. The unshakable notion was that Iran, an Empire and people with a rich cultural past, had fallen on hard times. Russians came to Iran, manifesting a moral and positional superiority of Christian Europeans and intent on a civilizing mission.[5] For the British, imperialist values, Victorian ideas and ethnic classifications all had a role to play. Certainly, envoys and officers from the East India Company and the Government of India came to Iran schooled in Asiatic diplomacy and possibly flawed assumptions that Iranians could be treated as Indians were.[6] Once in Iran, British attitudes towards a pre-modern Iran only hardened. However, the greatest criticism of Iran was reserved not for the people but for the Qajar Shahs and Iran's ruling elite. Sir John Malcolm (1769–1833), writing his history of Iran, referred to the ministers and chief officers who 'speak any language but that of flattery and deceit; and who are, in short, condemned, by their condition, to be venal, artful and false'.[7] A Persian speaker, Malcolm, was from boyhood an East India Company man.

These underlying attitudes, however, only coloured an increasing British diplomatic and political interest in Iran: an interest that had been supercharged by Tipu Sultan's defeat at the battle of Seringapatam in 1799 – a defeat which marked the end of resistance to the East India Company and the beginning of its control of India. The East India Company, a commercial venture, was now in complete control of a vast territory which had huge commercial implications for the British government. Now, not only did India have to be protected from both local and European powers but the trading and commercial routes to Britain and from India needed to be secured.

Another important development was Russian territorial expansion southwards. Under Peter the Great, in the eighteenth century, Russia had made sporadic forays into the Transcaucasus and Transcaspian before retreating until the reign of Catherine the Great who reignited an interest in expanding Russian interest in these territories. Towards the end of the eighteenth century, Georgia, which had previously been part of the Iranian Empire, had been taken over by Russia. In 1795, Agha Muhammad Khan, the first Qajar Shah, had recaptured Georgia only to see it once again be lost to the Russians. In 1795, Agha Muhammad Khan (1742–97), the first Qajar Shah, had recaptured Georgia only for his successor to see it once again be lost to the Russians in 1799. This annexation was seen by the Iranians as the opening salvo of a greater threat to Iran's lucrative provinces.[8] Iran's reaction to Russia's expansion into what had been part of the Iranian Empire and Russia's increasing diplomatic and military aggression was to lead to two wars, the results of which remained a constant source of irritation.

The touchpaper for the first war (1804–13) was lit by the invasion of Yerevan, in present-day Armenia, by the Russians under General Tsitsianov (1754–1806). He had only arrived in the Caucasus in 1803 but was quick to give vent to his desire to add territories to the Russian Empire. He was very much the 'model' Russian soldier. He has been described as 'arrogant, cruel, contemptuous of Muslims, and not nearly as great a commander as he believed himself to be'.[9] His self-publicity was to mask his limitations but he nevertheless came to epitomize the standard for Russian military officers who would push the boundaries of Russian expansion, sometimes even ignoring orders from St Petersburg to do so. Russia's expansion into the Transcaspian, later in the decade, was to be driven by men of similar nature and capacities.

Despite superiority in manpower, logistics and arms, Russia was quite ineffective in its first forays. Russia was also at war with France, the Ottomans and Sweden at the time. Despite limitations in manpower and arms, General Tsitsianov attacked and sought to bring other Khanates who were subject to Iran under Russian control. As Russia annexed further territory the Iranians began to see the Russians as not only a threat to their local hegemony but also a threat to the Qajar's legitimacy.[10] After all, the Qajars were still a new dynasty and needed to prove themselves worthy of the Iranian Empire. In the longer run despite superiority in manpower Iranian forces were no match for the better-equipped and better organized Russian forces and the war ended when Iran sued for peace in 1812. The Treaty of Golestan (1813), which followed the war, was to be very penal for Iran and under this treaty, Russia was the recipient of Georgia, Darband, Qobba, Baku, Shirvan, Shakki, Ganjeh, Moghan and parts of Talesh (see Map 2).

This was to be Iran's first lesson in the reality of Russian expansion and modern warfare. Iran's pre-modern army, which depended on the Shah's household army as a hardcore bolstered by tribal cavalries,[11] was no match for a modern army. Consequently, Abbas Mirza, Fath Ali Shah's heir, set out to create a modern army on European lines with the help of the British. This army's first task was to take on the Ottomans in 1820 when Fath Ali Shah decided to attack Ottoman Mesopotamia in an attempt to regain some of the territory lost during the preceding Safavid dynasty.[12] The Ottomans were eventually routed by the Persians, under Abbas Mirza himself, at Khuy in 1822. Unhappily for the Iranians, Abbas Mirza could not force a concrete resolution on the Ottomans as 'cholera then devastated his own troops, forcing him to seek peace from the pliant Sultan'.[13]

Iran's military success against the Ottomans seemed to bear out the promise of Iran's new-found approach, and the Iranian Army, bolstered by its efforts against the Ottomans, went to war again with the Russians. Research on the resumption of hostilities in 1826 has illuminated several causes. These have included the religious fervour created by the *Ulema* and the call for *Jihad* to redress the loss of Muslim territories and protect Muslims from further Russian aggression, and the pro-war stance of Abbas Mirza and, therefore, by definition, the weakness of Fath Ali Shah in preventing war. Overlooked has been, in my opinion, the structure of the Treaty of Golestan which offered Russia opportunities for further expansion. The Treaty had, purposely, left many territorial issues unresolved and allowed Russia to absorb disputed territories that had not been decided on. Indeed, it was an expansion into the contentious area of Gokchai which had pushed Fath Ali Shah into a corner from which he felt had no choice but to react. The territorial dispute of Gokchai provided the trigger for the second war between Russia and Iran (see Map 2).

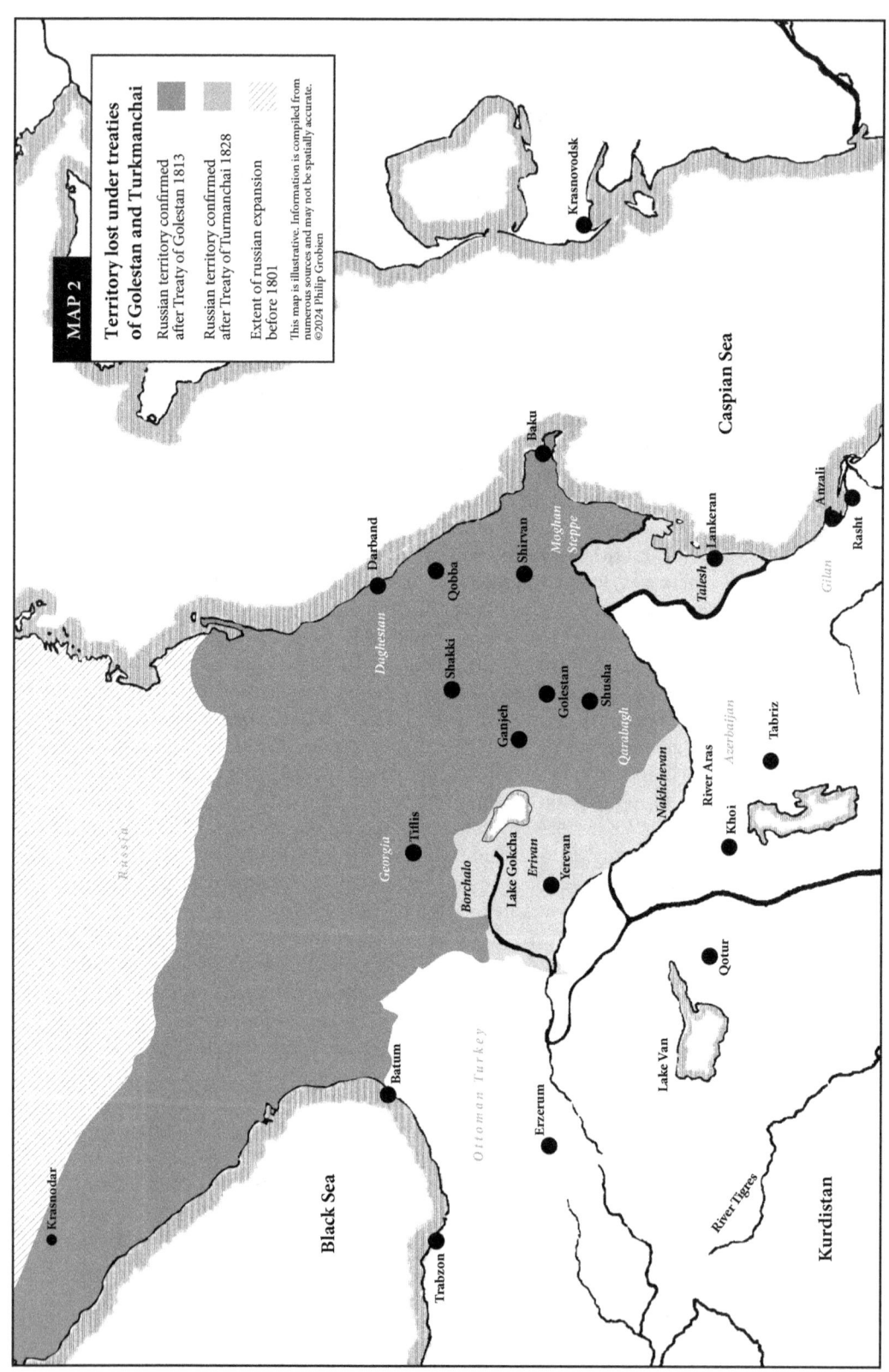

Again, the war began well for the Iranians. In less than a month, Iranian forces had reoccupied Shirvan, Shakki, Ganjeh and were at the gates of Tiflis (Tbilisi). However, the Russians reorganized and the *Persianate* uprising of people under Russian yolk never materialized as the Iranians had expected.[14] Soon the Russians turned the tide and after the loss of Tabriz, the Iranians sued for peace. The Treaty of Turkmanchai was catastrophic for the Iranians and Erivan and Nakhchevan became Russian territory (see Map 2). In addition, significant reparations were forced on Iran, Russia was given a say in Fath Ali's succession and Iranian ships lost the right to sail on the Caspian.

So, Russia had, between 1800 and 1828, annexed large swathes of territory that the Iranians had considered part of their Empire. Russian expansion had shown that Iran was no match for the Russians militarily and, significantly, that Russian regional hegemony was here to stay. It was also during this time frame that Britain and the East India Company opened a greater political dialogue with Iran. Whilst the Russian strategy was simple and direct, Britain's was not. Treaties were negotiated and diplomatic channels were opened but as we shall see when Britain's diplomacy is referenced and evaluated against the significant territorial Russian gains it was to come up short, for Iran's interest and indeed their own. The narrative of British diplomacy during this period was not only short-sighted and naïve but significantly showed a lack of strategy. British muddled thinking was in fact to set a pattern of involvement in Iran which was to be the hallmark of British diplomacy, at least up to 1919.

Britain: A symbolic toe in the water

British politicians, diplomats and military agreed that the trading routes to India had to be protected and that India's military security was paramount. However, Iran's place in that strategy was never to be truly defined. In 1800, Sir John Malcolm's mission to Iran had been initiated to procure a commercial and political treaty with Iran which intended to solve the problem of military engagements between the Iranians and the Afghans and to counter French interest and intrigues towards India.[15] The French threat to India had appeared in the shape of Napoleon's landing and subjugation of Egypt in 1798. From Egypt, the French were expected to work towards the Persian Gulf and India. It was a threat, however, that was never to materialize.

What had, of course, materialized was the Russian attack on the Iranian provinces in the Caucasus. Britain, now for the first time, found its actions circumscribed by European political exigencies. As they were now allied with Russia against Napoleon in Europe, Britain was unable to help Iran. The Treaty of 1801 had enlisted Iranian help against threats from the Afghans and French but had not mentioned Russian aggression. Nevertheless, the Iranians were to feel aggrieved and let down.

So, if Britain would not protect Iran, as Iran had agreed to protect British interests in the region, then the French might. In 1807 Iran entered into a treaty with the

French expected to guarantee Iranian territorial integrity. The Iranians had backed the wrong horse, however, as Napoleon's rather insubstantial foray into the Middle East had ground to a halt. Iran was to be again isolated diplomatically and was forced to turn to the British once again. The treaty of 1809, adjusted and ultimately finished as the Definitive Treaty of 1814 (*Mofasal*), voided and superseded other treaties with European nations. It necessitated Iran to protect India and allowed, if necessary, British soldiers on Iranian soil. In exchange for British political primacy in Iran and the possibility of having foreign troops in Iran, the Iranians received only one thing of substance in return: that was the certainty that the British would come to Iran's aid if invaded by a European country or, if that was not possible, to provide funds for Iran's defence.

The treaty had been concluded by Sir Gore Ouseley (1770–1844), ambassador extraordinary and plenipotentiary to Iran, who had also offered to 'help' Iran in concluding the aforementioned Treaty of Golestan. During that matter he had enthusiastically agreed to go to St Petersburg to advocate on behalf of, and negotiate for, the Iranians. Sir Gore Ouseley's correspondence with the Foreign Office makes it plain that he was anything but an honest broker. After all, a quick resolution to the war would keep the Russians onside, crucial given the war against Napoleon, and might kill off any further talk of Britain paying a subsidy to the Iranians under the terms of the 1801 treaty. All of which might also secure India from Russian threats.[16]

Sir Gore Ouseley's next move, the Definitive Treaty, however one-sided, had given Britain all that she wanted and had only obliged Britain to protect Iran from Russian aggression. Britain now spent the next fifteen years attempting to get out of this commitment in any form possible. In 1815 Sir Henry Willock (1790–1858) became chargé d'affaires to Iran and continued to play a careful balancing act between the Iranians and Russians. Nevertheless, this balancing act tended to appease the Russians more and he saw his role as primarily defensive and as far as the Russians were concerned, non-confrontational.

When Sir Henry Willock could not prevent another military confrontation between Russia and Iran, he began to wriggle out of British commitments to protect Iran; he was at pains to point out that the Iranians had caused the war,[17] though he had also agreed that Russia had been the aggressor.[18] In truth, though Iran's decision to go to war with the Russians was a military misjudgement, there is much evidence to suggest that the pressure on Iran was so great that it had no choice but to initiate military action. Still, Britain's diplomatic stance once again meant that Britain had to find a way out of its obligations to protect Iran from Russian aggression. The Definitive Treaty therefore was a significant milestone in what were early days of British and Iranian diplomacy. It showed that Iran was not to be treated as an equal and that agreements between the two countries could be reneged in spirit or in substance.

Britain had found out rather late in the day that the main threat to Iran and therefore India was to come from Russia rather than France. This may seem strange given the two wars and Russian expansion into new territories ever closer to Iran, not to mention Russian expansion towards the Black Sea at the expense of the Ottomans. This threat appeared clear as the Russians had been threatening the Ottoman Empire as they sought warm-water port facilities in the Bosphorus. Some, the knowledgeable ones, did raise alarm bells. Sir John Malcolm had believed the Russian threat to Iran and hence to India had always been clear. In a devastating critique of Russian aggression towards Iran, Sir John Malcolm claimed that there was no doubt that Russian policy was to establish direct influence over Iran and that Britain was abetting them in this process. Not only were British 'Hot and Cold proceedings' allowing the Russians to achieve their expansionist policies but there had to be a point at which the British could not let the Russians advance any further and Iranian independence was crucial to 'the continued tranquillity if not security of our possessions in India'.[19]

Despite this, and even accepting the political restrictions that European *realpolitik* had imposed during the Napoleonic wars, politicians either misread or were slow to react to the Russian threat. British inaction in this respect led to a realization as late as 1828 that Russia was now able to dominate Iran politically and was thus an even greater threat to India. British muddled thinking on Iran had begun at the highest levels in British politics. Richard Wellesley, who had been foreign secretary between 1909 and 1912, during the Napoleonic wars, had naturally not wanted to antagonize the Russians but also sought to turn Iran into a protectorate.[20] Robert Castlereagh, who had taken over from Richard Wellesley in 1812, feared that turning Iran into a protectorate would undoubtedly divert Russia from the Grand Alliance in Europe against Napoleon[21] and decided to withdraw the British military mission.[22] He also assumed that mediating between Iran and Russia meant asking the Iranians to do what the Russians were asking.[23] George Canning, who succeeded him in 1822, was more than happy to wash his hands of Iran and gave control of the Iranian Mission back to the East India Company.[24]

This reticence to get involved also raises another facet of British political engagement in Iran. Both Sir Gore Ouseley and Sir Henry Willock had been appointed by the Foreign Office (though Sir Henry Willock was to be chairman of the East India Company), and this gave them a European bias to the Iranian paradigm. In practice, this meant that European demands carried greater weight than possible and conceivably ephemeral threats to India. Sir John Malcolm and indeed Sir Harford Jones (1764–1847), who had negotiated the 1809 treaty which had been morphed into the Definitive Treaty, were East India Company men and more prone to view direct threats to India. This schism in approach was effectively permanent as East India Company officers, and officers of the subsequent India government,[25] were to hold views less impacted by European politics. It is notable that there were to be frequent splits in strategy towards Iran between the Foreign Office and the India government, and consequently towards Russia.

These differing backgrounds were to manifest themselves in diverse plans to protect India. As Edward Ingram has suggested, policies ranged from using Iran as an ally for India, a protectorate under British control, a strategic barrier or no-man's land or even a military desert, or a buffer state.[26] It was the idea of the buffer state that was to gain traction as the years wore on and which invited two differing approaches in protecting India from the Russians. Masterly activity 'wanted to promote relations with the border tribes, and to provide for the defence of India outside India – that is, to utilise Persia, Afghanistan, and Baluchistan as outworks in Indian defence'.[27]

Closely related to masterly activity was the idea of having a forward policy where the bulwark, or buffer to Russia, was as far from India as possible. Its antithesis, masterly inactivity, assumed a laissez-faire attitude best described as a 'stationary or defensive policy … and a "wait and see" policy towards Russia'.[28] These methodologies expressed much about the haphazard methods upon which India's security was to rely. Overall, the competing strategies did nothing more than lead to confusion in policy and compelled the British to be reactive to situations and events, rather than being proactive and setting the policy agenda.

Disjointed and confused policies were also to become obvious on the ground. Whether officials came from the Foreign Office in London or the India government fundamentally altered how policies were enacted. Towards the end of the nineteenth century, success in selecting 'their man' ensured that 'their' argument carried the day. As India government officials were often relied on, given their experience in India, and their ability to cope with harsh conditions, policies were carried out even if they had emanated from the Foreign Office. Adroit in numerous skills – explorers, engineers and diplomats – they would provide boots on the ground.

In fact, another example of increasing British interest in Iran was the duplication of envoys and posts which were to blossom in the nineteenth century. This had become such a problem that a gentlemen's agreement had to be reached in 1860 to prevent overlapping interference and duplication of efforts.[29] Despite the fact that consular and diplomatic posts were to be divided between the India government and the Foreign Office, differences were to continue.

Overall, Britain's involvement in Iran between 1800 and 1828 highlighted several elements and problems in its diplomatic approach. In the first place, political considerations with Iran were to be affected by European concerns to which Iran had no party to. Secondly, and connected to the first point, Russia as a large land-based power had a foot in European and Middle Eastern and consequently Iranian policymaking. Thirdly, that Britain, through its diplomatic vacillation, had shown a deep-rooted wish not to get entangled in Iran, and as Edward Ingram memorably pointed out, the British would have preferred 'to defend the Indian Empire to the last Persian'.[30]

So, by 1828 two paradigms were in place. One was that Russia was showing a single-minded attitude to territorial expansion. The other was that given India, European expediencies and differing outlooks within the wider British government, no one strategic response would be available to Russian aggression or indeed a coherent policy towards Iran. All policies towards Iran were only to be tangential and a by-product of India. Nevertheless, the *Great Game* was now afoot in Iran, and the Russians and British were to vie for diplomatic supremacy in Iran at least up to the First World War.

Contingent yet part of the diplomatic pressure which Britain and Russia were to assert in Iran was the development of ever-increasing economic and commercial engagement. It is in this narrative, and the discussion concerning the commercial attitudes of these two imperial powers, that we can discern patterns of Qajar diplomacy and attempts to counter their domination. One thing was clear by 1828, the Iranians were beginning to understand, primarily through the ineffective Definitive Treaty, that Britain could not be relied upon, and Russia was to be feared.

Economic hegemony and the Qajar playbook

Of great long-term significance in the future domination over Iran was the capitulation rights, commercial treaties and rights to place consular envoys in Iranian towns which Iran was forced to accept by the Treaty of Turkmanchai.

On the face of it the right to place consular envoys in Iranian towns, which was extended to the British in 1841, may not seem a large concession, but in a pre-modern country such as Qajar Iran it would help to develop Iran into a semi-colonial state. In effect, foreign nations were able to impose their own administrations. There seemed to be little that the Qajars could do to prevent this. Given the instability and administrative disintegration between 1722 and 1797 under the Safavid dynasty, Qajar bureaucracy had not inherited an organized and structurally stable bureaucracy. Whether a large and functioning bureaucracy would have made a difference is hard to know. Under the Qajar's, government bureaucracy remained small and informal. The administration of the Qajar government was the mirror image of Qajar tribal leadership and authority. It displayed many features of what can be 'Classical patrimonialism' and a kingdom that was 'an extension of the Shah's household and subject to his personal authority', with 'no distinction between property and office, and offices were often sold as a source of revenue and patronage by the shah and his officials'.[31] In this environment, without a robust state infrastructure that reached, or could reach the peripheries of the country, Iran was unable to prevent the osmosis of dual and *ersatz* foreign governments.[32]

This took place in two ways. Firstly, the British and Russians developed an almost permanent presence at court. Secondly, they created a modern bureaucracy which reached areas of Iran that were seemingly out of Iran's own government's reach. The British and Russians developed a system of Political Residents and Consul Generals in major towns. The flexible nature of Qajar state relations with tribes allowed the British to insinuate themselves into the governmental system and they communicated with tribal leaders and landholders directly to promote their own interests; thus, regional affiliations were a direct result of the administrative weakness of the Qajar state. This was particularly the case in southern Iran, a region of British commerce.[33]

Wide-ranging capitulatory rights had been first negotiated by Sir John Malcolm in 1801 for British merchants in Iran.[34] These privileges included the right to live wherever they wanted, build, sell, rent houses, recover debts owed to them and 'to suffer no obstruction' if wanting to leave Iran. However, it was the Treaty of Turkmanchai which had established a framework for foreign trade that put

Iranian merchants at a disadvantage. The privileges provided to the Russians under this treaty established a single 5 per cent *ad valorem* tax on imports and exports. This privilege was soon established for other nations, including Britain, despite protestations from Iranian merchants to protect their domestic industries and 'safeguard the balance of payments'.[35] In 1903 agreements signed with Britain and Russia replaced the *ad valorem* tax with taxes specific to the products in question based on weight.[36] Though this was an improvement, Iranian merchants had operated under an economic disadvantage for many years. They were still subjected to many taxes for which foreigners had been exempt. These privileges, and others, had ultimately played a large part in the demise of indigenous industries.

These rights had developed a two-tier economic system in which the Iranians were to be disadvantaged. Russian trade with Iran grew exponentially and accounted for 70 per cent of total trade and 50 per cent of all imports by 1914.[37] Though Britain's trade with its Empire was a remarkable 25 per cent of the nation's output,[38] trade with Iran, whilst increasing between 1800 and 1914, was very low. Relatively, however, the effect on Iran as a trading partner was enormous. It is probable that between the 1830s and 1860s, Britain accounted for 50 per cent of Iran's total trade.[39] Internal trade was also affected and disadvantaged by the fact that the British did not have to pay the duties that Iranian traders did.[40] The result was that Iran's trade with its immediate neighbours diminished considerably, further isolating Iranians from more local trading options.[41] Crucially, unable to shelter from these imports and special capitulary rights, Iran's small industries simply succumbed.

Whilst capitulatory rights had been given away, the issue of concessions allowed the Qajar Shah's to exercise a degree of control. Concessions given to foreign governments and foreign companies in Iran were to grow exponentially towards the First World War and the number of concessions given to foreigners in Iran was considerable, even by the standards of other middle eastern countries.[42] As touched on in the introduction, Naser al-Din Shah showed an ambivalence towards concessions. Yet, more concessions were given out during his rule than at any other Qajar Shah. One reason was simply the length of time he was in power but the increase in commercial competition between the British and Russians, as well as some other European countries, also coincided with his rule.

The *Great Game* and the competition between Russia and Britain for political and commercial supremacy were to play a large part in both the nature and frequency of concessions. Though concessions were risky propositions for foreigners, the commercial benefits for them were more obvious than those for Iran. The reasons, benefits and disadvantages, of concessions are so varied that it is difficult to establish a working thesis for all concessions. However, an analysis of concessions is vital in understanding their political and economic impacts, how they might have helped modernize or reform Iran and how they impacted Iran's *desiderata* in Paris.

One point that is sometimes missed is that before the Constitutional Revolution, financial renumeration for concessions went to the Shah. So, venality was certainly one reason. This was clearly the case during Naser al-Din Shah's reign as concessions were used to supplement his lifestyle. Still, concessions were also instrumental in attracting capital and much-needed hard currency to Iran. Each concession offered different levels of financial renumeration. As they were negotiated on their own merits and were contractually different, many of them demanded advance payments and/or rents. Some, such as those concessions which relied on unskilled labour, did involve local employment possibilities. These types of concessions predominantly revolved around the granting of rights for the exploration and exploitation of natural resources. Iran was rich in minerals and natural resources and the British were keen to exploit them. A detailed report had, in 1886, listed some of the most important ones. This included boxwood, rock salt, borax, saltpetre, alum, gypsum, naphtha, sulphur, coal, iron, manganese, cobalt, copper, lead, gold, silver, slate, quicksilver, zinc, tin, precious stones, marble and porphyry.[43]

Other concessions that were not reliant on the exploitation of resources were to offer a greater conundrum for Naser al-Din Shah and his attitude towards those that include modernization and reform remains complex. He both accepted the need for modernization and feared it at the same time. He was reported to be fascinated by the mechanics of modern inventions, and his trips to Europe and purported letters to Napoleon III regarding the introduction of modernity into Iran may be evidence of this. At the same time, his fascination with the modern tools of the Industrial Revolution was tempered by the filth and smog it created and therefore its appropriateness to Iran. Sir Henry Drummond Wolff (1830–1908), minister to Iran between 1887 and 1991, came closest to successfully describing Naser al-Din's outlook when he pointed out, 'The Shah fears the approach of civilization as being likely to curb his power, and to check his autocratic and arbitrary tendencies.'[44]

One concession that fits this profile of an acceptable concession was that of the telegraph. Under the unimpressively titled *The Engagement entered into by the Persian Minister for Foreign Affairs* in 1862, Britain and Iran agreed to construct the first line between Khanaqin (at the border with Ottoman/Mesopotamia) and Tehran, then Isfahan, Shiraz and Bushire. Though the British were very keen to establish quick communication with India following the Indian Mutiny in 1857, which necessitated a connection through Iran, in truth the mutiny had only hastened its implementation. Indeed, Iran had already embraced the telegraph. It is apparent that Naser al-Din Shah and the Iranians were already open to the possibilities of this new technology. Numerous small lines already existed in Tehran, connecting places frequented by the Shah and, by 1858, lines existed connecting the palaces of Golestan and Lalehzar and the Dar al-Fonun. The Shah had begun to appreciate the strategic necessity of the telegraph when he put in motion a plan to construct a line between Tehran and Mashad, to enable better security in the province of Khorasan.[45]

The connection of a telegraph line between Naser al-Din Shah's palaces and the Dar al-Fonun was not only an example of autocratic control but also showed his appreciation for new skills. The Dar al-Fonun polytechnic, established in 1851, had been imagined and constituted on European lines. The school was designed to develop the necessary modern skills for upcoming administrators and military personnel. It taught subjects such as medicine, mathematics, engineering and European languages. Credit for its introduction has become part of Amir Kabir's legacy. However, as Maryam Ekhtiar has suggested, while Amir Kabir may have been instrumental in establishing the Dar al-Fonun, credit for keeping it going needs to be given to Naser al-Din Shah.[46]

Other examples of concessions show a different side to Naser al-Din Shah but also illuminate how concessions had become a significant part of the *Great Game* and indeed how Iran's diplomacy in 1919 was to be informed. The notorious Reuters Concession, negotiated in 1872, exemplified the Iranian paradigm. It granted Julius Reuter 'an exclusive concession for a term of 70 years for the construction of railways, irrigation, and other works throughout the country'.[47] Or as Lord Curzon was to put it, the agreement was 'the most complete and extraordinary surrender of the entire industrial resources of a kingdom into foreign hands that has probably ever been dreamt of, much less accomplished, in history'.[48]

The Reuters Concession, despite being ratified by Naser al-Din Shah, was effectively paralysed by opposition from many quarters and soon cancelled. The Russians objected as it was an 'unprecedented privilege conferred not only upon the concessionaire, but on all England'.[49] The British, in the shape of Lord Glanville, were less than enthusiastic about Julius Reuters' approach. Julius Reuters had dangled the danger of Russian economic progress and Russian railway infrastructure in the Caspian region in asking for British backing if he ran into difficulties with the project.[50] Glanville's response, published in the *New York Times*, stated, 'We wish Baron de Reuter and his friends all success, both on their account and for the sake of Persia, but beyond this not one step would we go',[51] was kinder than the actualité,[52] where questions of competence and anti-Semitism were rife.

On the one hand, the Reuters Concession is an example of what can be seen as the purchasing of modernization on a wholesale basis.[53] On the other hand, it can be seen as the mortgaging of Iran's resources and possibly its future independence. What it did do was to spark an even greater and more sustained period of competition between Britain and Russia over the domination of Iran. In this case the fallout of this stillborn concession was not only domestic, but the episode enabled the British and Russians to press for other concessions. The genie was well and truly out of the bottle as both Russia and Britain sought other concessions as 'partial compensation for the cancelled Reuter concession'.[54] The Russians were able to secure the Falkenhagen concession in 1874 for the construction of a railway line and in 1889, Reuter, in lieu of the cancellation of the Reuters Concession was able to set up the state bank, the Imperial Bank of Persia. He was also able to begin the Persian Bank Mining Rights Corporation which, though went bankrupt, was instrumental in interesting William Knox D'Arcy in the search for oil.

One of the results of the *Great Game* was that, when a concession had strategic implications for both the Russians and British, some useful economic developments were prevented. The best example is the issue of railways. Neither Russia nor Britain was interested in giving the other the strategic advantage of developing a railway. As a result, Iran was not to benefit from the introduction of a railway system by the First World War. By then only two railways were built. One was a six-mile railway completed in 1888, which linked the shrine of Shah ʿAbdol Azim with Tehran, built by the Iranians. The other, and far larger railway, was completed by the Russians and linked a Russian terminus, Julfa with Tabriz, some ninety miles. The concession given to Russia to build the Julfa-Tabriz line was granted in anticipation of a concession being granted to a British syndicate to connect Mohammerah to Khorramabad.[55]

The quad-lateral balancing act

Naser al-Din Shah had become quite adept at negotiating a path between the economic and political desires of the British and Russians. In the case of concessions, the method of playing one imperial power off on another was not economically successful if the intention truly had been to modernize Iran. Politically, Abbas Amanat has argued that Naser al-Din should be given much credit for how he managed to navigate the competing imperial strategies and suggested that 'it is possible to argue that the idea of a buffer state was advanced by the European policy makers on both sides only when it became clear that they could neither advance their imperial ambition in Iran beyond a certain point nor disengage from Iran's political arena altogether'.[56]

In this way it has been suggested that playing one European power against the other had kept Iran politically servile and had held back reform and modernization but had more crucially preserved the existence of Iran. Politically, the British and Russians had not conceived the dissolution of Iran which would give either the upper hand. The problem was what happened when these Empires decided to work together to a common end. Here the results were mixed. In one example, these political and economic adversaries found common ground in the Anglo-Russian Convention of 1907.[57] This convention had divided Iran into three zones of influence: a Russian zone in the north, a British zone in the south and a neutral or buffer zone in the middle. The segregation of imperial interests in Iran formed part of a larger agreement, which took Tibet and Afghanistan into account, and from the British point of view aimed to lessen frictions between Russia and Britain and was intended to aid India's security. Despite a reassurance that Iranian sovereignty would be secured by this agreement, it was in reality a flagrant disregard of Iranian sovereignty and as we will see would form a large part of antagonism towards European imperialism in 1919. It is a mark of the intensity of Iranian feelings towards this agreement, and what it meant to Iranian territorial sovereignty that its abrogation was sought whenever possible.

One example of imperial cooperation was British and Russian mediation over the saga of the western border. Discussions and negotiations over the border, which stretched from Mount Ararat to the Shatt-al Arab in the Persian Gulf, would take some seventy years and would be largely finalized by the British and Russians in the face of Ottoman and Iranian disagreements over the delimitation of the border.

In fact, the arrival of the British and Russians into the Iranian diplomatic scene in the early part of the nineteenth century imposed a layer of complexity on the long-standing rivalry between the Iranian and the Ottoman Empires. An imperial rivalry that went back centuries had developed a greater cleavage with the development of differing views on Islam. The Sublime Porte had adopted the role of Caliph in 1517. From this point on, and until 1918, the Caliphate would remain with Ottomans, even though the bloodline to the Prophet Muhammad had been broken. Meanwhile in Iran in 1501, the newly crowned Shah Ismail announced that Shi'ism was to be the new official religion and thus Safavid Iran was to be clearly differentiated from the Sunni Ottoman Empire. Nevertheless, though this point of difference was politically useful, the Ottoman/Iranian relationship was to evince very little sectarianism. In fact, the relationship was to revolve more around questions of territorial supremacy.

Despite a victory over the Ottomans in 1823, the Ottomans were arguably still the dominant local imperial force at the beginning of the nineteenth century. Ottoman and Iranian antagonism was to become less relevant after 1830 though there was a resurgence between 1905 and 1919. Even so, the trading, and particularly the political relationship between Iran and the Ottoman Empire, was to be increasingly influenced by the British and Russians.[58] For one thing, the Russians had considerable interest in the warm water ports in the Black Sea and the Ottoman Empire was a significant impediment to their expansion in that region. Wars between the Russians and Ottomans had been numerous, beginning in the sixteenth century. By the nineteenth century Russian expansion into the Caucasus had not only brought the Russians a common border with Iran but Russia now shared a border with the Ottomans (see Map 5). So, some of Russia's political intentions in Iran, including their involvement in the negotiations on the western border, had a great deal to do with the Ottomans rather than the Iranians.

Britain, as noted above, always feared Russian expansion at the expense of the Ottoman Empire. This led, in the main, except for the issue of Greece, to keeping the Ottoman Empire intact. In much the same way as Britain's policy towards Russia had, as far as Iran was concerned, been reactive rather than proactive, its policy towards the Ottoman Empire was similarly that of a commitment to the status quo.

Conclusion

This brief survey of the diplomatic and political paradigm which had developed in nineteenth-century Iran demonstrates that pre-modern Iran had been forced to face modern British and Russian imperial practices and had been found wanting. Iran, with difficulty, had managed to skirt around the problem it faced by playing one imperial power off against the other, minimizing both the economic and political damage. In a very early, but perceptive analysis, Sir John Malcolm wrote in 1830:

> The power of Asiatic countries to resist invasion of a regular army depends less upon their riches than their poverty, the want of resources of their country, the unsettled habits of the inhabitants, and their being in fact intangible to the attack or regular force. **They yield like a reed to the storm, but are not broken.** [Emphasis added][59]

In addition, Iran's confrontation with Britain and Russia cannot be separated from European exigencies that had led to decisions which had little to do with Iran. As Iranians need to be reminded from time to time, for Britain and Russia, Iran was simply part of a larger picture and sometimes only a small cog. A pre-modern Iran was outmatched by two Empires who were intent on stamping their mark on the region. Iran was merely a footnote to wider strategies of political and economic dominance in the region.

In what has been set out we can see the inchoate beginnings of diplomatic engagement in Iran, which would ultimately see Iran develop into a semi-colonial country. Progress towards a penitent Iran, at the mercy of both Allied and Central Powers by the First World War, was gradual but persistent. Still, the Russians would be arguably more effective in getting their way in Iran. Their persistence led to considerable territorial acquisition at Iran's expense. Indeed, Russia's single-minded approach to exert political and economic control over Iran was faced with a wholly inadequate British response.

Established early on, British policies were reactive and, in choosing the line of least resistance, were inadequate, either to safeguard Iran or to prevent Russian aggression. Lord Curzon was right to believe that Britain had never developed a consistent plan or policy with regard to Iran that had come close to answering the 'Persian question'. There is much truth in the suggestion that Britain's lack of success in Iran was to revolve around the nature of British foreign policy, which was frequently reactive, memorably defined by Lord Salisbury as 'to float lazily down stream, occasionally putting out a diplomatic boat-hook to avoid collisions'.[60]

Nevertheless, Qajar policies and British and Russian political and economic hegemony were to give vent to dissatisfaction amongst the ruling elite, the *Ulema* and intellectuals who were to set their minds on the political, social and economic development of Iran. As we will see, what they had learnt from contact with British and Russians would lead to the growth of a national polity and nationalism – a nationalism which the Iranians would give vent to in Paris.

Chapter 2

AN ENLIGHTENMENT

It may seem a paradox, but despite the weakness of the Qajar state in the long nineteenth century and its semi-colonial existence, Iran went through its own intellectual and social enlightenment. This process was not only to lead to the Constitutional Revolution but was to provide the intellectual basis and backbone for Iran's diplomacy in 1919. Iran's aims at the Peace Conference were directly informed by an understanding of both Iran's political and economic difficulties and the inchoate solutions that had begun in the nineteenth century, but which also continued in the early twentieth century.

Increased connections with, in particular, the British would lead to the beginning of an interchange of information and European thought. As early as 1811, students, largely children of Iran's elite, were travelling to Europe and gaining knowledge of European thought and progress and bringing these ideas back to Iran.[1] Obviously, the Iranian elite also began to interact socially with the growing number of British and Russian officers, diplomats and in some cases academics who visited Iran. One was Edward Browne (1862–1926), an orientalist whose work articulated the progress towards a national renewal which could be held back, not by the Iranians themselves, but competing foreign powers.[2]

One route towards the exchange of information and ideas was through the growth of masonic lodges. Freemasonry, at times dogged by controversy today, was not only an important medium for the exchange of information but also for the importing of European ideas.[3] Iran's growing band of intellectuals (*roshanfekran*) became members and set up their own lodges in Iran. Another route was the development of newspapers in Persian, also set up by intellectuals. The Qajar period (1797–1925) saw the publication of over 100 newspapers,[4] many of which were published abroad and critical of Qajar rule and foreign meddling. Increasingly, books published in foreign languages were translated into Persian for pleasure[5] but also for education.[6]

The reach of newspapers, books and therefore the intellectual developments in Iran was not the province of the average, illiterate, Iranian. Unless read to, or part of political discussions in the various coffee houses in Iran, Iranians responded to what they saw. More obvious to them was the assimilation of foreigners into the fabric of Iranian life. The aforementioned osmosis of British and Russians into the governing infrastructure of Iran was obvious to people. Foreigners surveyed

Iran, ran the telegraph system and managed other visible representations of European modernism. It is important to note that Iranians seldom distinguished between foreigners and foreign officials. In fact, they were all tarred with the same brush. Iranian perceptions were not entirely flawed as both the India government and the Foreign Office were to form close bonds with British commercial ventures. The point was, often lost on the British, that the Iranians could not and sometimes would not distinguish between British officials and independent businessmen. The overall effect was the hardening of perceptions that foreigners, particularly the British and Russians, were either singularly responsible or partially responsible along with the Qajar dynasty for Iran's malaise.

Inchoate nationalistic ideas were, therefore, formed in response to a dynasty seemingly in collusion with foreigners. However, though foreign intervention was forcing Iranians to think hard about what they wanted, one aspect of foreign intervention has been hard to quantify: how the introduction and implementation of fixed borders and the shrinking of the Iranian Empire had affected questions of identity and ideas of nationalism in Iran – a process in which, either through military prowess or through participation in border negotiations, the British and Russians were participants. Increasingly, the introduction of physical barriers, requiring permissions to cross,[7] was developing mental barriers.[8]

Intellectual inheritance

Many leading intellectuals towards the end of the nineteenth century saw modernization as a method of reform and political progress. One of those was Mirza Malkam Khan (1833–1908). Malkam Khan, of Armenian extraction, was both a diplomat and would become the foremost critic of the Qajars during the reign of Naser al-Din Shah. He would come to promote concessions as a means of importing modernization and believed it was necessary to give concessions to foreign powers on whatever terms to attract capital and accelerate progress in Iran.[9] As we have seen, though, it is very difficult to present a beneficial economic case for the concessions made in the nineteenth century. Concessions that might have aided the economic infrastructure of Iran such as railways and roads all failed because of Anglo-Russian competition. Concessions that succeeded were ultimately foreign ventures whose profits and capital would eventually go back overseas. In addition, in contrast to the concessions contracted in Egypt and in the Ottoman Empire, the terms that Iran offered were inflated as many investors were put off by the risks of working in, and with, such an under-developed country and system of government.[10]

Concessions which were made to reform the bureaucratic or financial structure of Iran were to have similar difficulties. Increasingly, towards 1914, the bureaucracy of Iran was developed by employing citizens of 'neutral' or least inoffensive countries as the competition between the British and Russians made the employment of their citizens too difficult. In 1897 Joseph Naus, a clever Belgian who had a penchant for wearing Muslim clerical attire, was made director of

Customs. In 1911, more famously, Morgan Shuster, an American, was brought in to organize Iran's finances. Despite Shuster's neutrality he had to endure, but would ultimately fail, to operate in a country deadlocked by both imperial competition and petit rivalries amongst the Iranian bureaucracy. In the main, it remained the case that bureaucratic positions were bought and sold and/or given to members of the extended Qajar royal family with little regard to qualifications or ability. Some offices were even hereditary and corruption remained rife. Yet, as Shaul Bakhash has argued, some progress had been made under the brief premierships of Amir Kabir (Mirza Taqi Khan) and Moshir al-Dowleh, but these reforms were not to be permanent.[11]

If the idea had been for modernization to encourage the development of political reform, then it was becoming apparent that this would not happen. In fact, there was to be no correlation. Even in Egypt it had become obvious that the improvements in its economic infrastructure such as railways, ports, etc., had not resulted in political change. In truth any reforms were destined to operate within the straitjacket of Iran's bureaucracy. Qajar reforms were expected to work within well-established bureaucratic channels which were a product of a patrimonial system, and which survived at the behest of the Shah.[12] This is confirmed by the fact that neither Amir Kabir, Moshir al-Dowleh, nor particularly Mirza Malkam Khan, had articulated political change. There is no doubt that, frustratingly, when reading the many ideas that Mirza Malkam Khan put forward for reform and modernization, he never explained how they were to be implemented. He may have put forward a blueprint for modernism, but he left out the instructions. In many ways this appears to be the result of swallowing the benefits of modernity wholesale without an understanding of how it developed in Europe and therefore how it could develop in Iran.

Nevertheless, other intellectuals were busy articulating how Iran could come out of its current decrepitude, which seemed only to get worse. Mirza Fath Ali Akhundzadeh (1812–78) despite brought up and living in Russia identified with his Iranian heritage. Akhundzadeh, like the European philosophers he drew on, laid Iran's problems at the door of an outdated and ignorant religion, Islam, which was holding Iran back. Much like the work of Emmanuel Kant, who had compared Protestantism favourably with the backward nature of Catholicism, he too looked towards a more rational society in which Iranians were free of the shackles of a suffocating and esoteric religion. It would therefore come as no surprise that Akhundzadeh promoted education outside the religious schools and also lamented Iran's Arab inheritance. Mirza Aqa Khan Kermani (1854–97) was to be similarly driven to see Iran's malaise within the context of an Islamic Iran and anti-Arab sentiments which would ultimately drive his nationalism. Both Akhundzadeh and Kermani were to develop nationalist ideas based on an antithesis towards religion and Arabism and a re-centring of an Iranian identity with the past.

The promotion of the past glories of the Achaemenid and Sassanian Empires, under a more enlightened and liberating Zoroastrianism, is hard to counter. The past had to be greener, even more so since European orientalists were also comparing Iran's contemporary malaise with past glories. Iranian intellectuals, such as Akhundzadeh and Kermani, were supplementing their own ideas of Iran's past by re-learning its past from the European perspective. The method of absorbing or re-absorbing these ideas was to be found in assessments of Iran's rich poetic and historical literature. Much of this discourse would be developed from a single source, the *Shahnameh*, where the myths and legends of Iran's past were described by Ferdowsi.

The legends and myths of Iran's imperial past were useful in promoting Iranian uniqueness primarily by distinguishing the identity of Iranians from others. In the *Shahnameh*, a distinction was made between the lands of Iran and of *Turan* in the *Shahnameh* – *Turan* being Iran's mythical enemy. Much like the European Enlightenment, the development of an Iranian enlightenment also used the process of othering to promote the elements of Iranian or *Persianate* identity which were deemed worth keeping. An inchoate nationalism, using notions of the Iranian past and originality, combined with a cultural myths and legends, would provide the ground on which a nationalism based on Empire would ultimately be based at the Paris Peace Conference.

Yet, some intellectual discourse was not to provide a basis for Iran's *imperial nationalism*. The views of the now ostracized Mirza Malkam Khan, in the newspaper Qanun which he founded, did facilitate a channel for anti-Qajar views.[13] However, generally, intellectual criticism of the Qajar's and, in particular, Naser al-Din Shah was muted by the ruling elite. Intellectuals on the outside of Iran's diplomatic or bureaucratic circles would use newspapers, mainly printed outside Iran, to criticize the rule of Naser al-Din Shah. Akhundzadeh attacked the corruption and nature of Naser al-Din Shah's despotic rule and lamented missed opportunities for change. In fact, the growth of newspaper publications was to be an important element in criticism of the Qajar dynasty and served as a milieu for the exchange of information. Some would be more militant.

Direct action

Another intellectual Seyyed Jamal al-Din Asadabadi (1838/9–97), better known as al-Afghani, was to be far more militant. His anti-British sentiment and hatred for Naser al-Din Shah did not necessarily set him apart from other intellectuals; however, his belief in pan-Islamism,[14] and his participation in agitation, did. He was to be an interlocutor between the theoretical and the practical. Al-Afghani, motivated to get his hands dirty, would get involved in the Tobacco Rebellion of 1890, which foregrounded and forewarned future political change. From now on Iran's intellectual enlightenment was to be just one aspect of the more general criticism of Iran's malaise.

On one of the Shah's trips to Britain, Naser al-Din Shah agreed to a concession with a Major Talbot for the monopoly over the sale of tobacco throughout Iran. Thus, with one signature, he prevented the sale of tobacco by Iranian merchants and allowed a significant pleasure and pastime, second only to tea drinking, to be transferred to a foreigner. Not only had Naser al-Din Shah not learnt from the

Reuters Concession but he seemed oblivious to the groundswell of opinion which, not for the first time, would be organized against future Iranian Shah's.

The concession brought together the *Ulema*, the merchants, dissidents such as al-Afghani, and people together in mass dissent. It included a boycott, and eventually violent protests, before the concession was cancelled at great expense. As Shah, the only check on his power was the limit of his ability, in the main, to mediate between the interests of segments of Iran's society. Naser al-Din Shah had dangerously managed to ally the forces of the *Ulema*, merchants and many other parts of Iranian society against him.

At a time when Iran was suffering from an economic dislocation partially caused by Western dominance in Iran at the expense of the local economy and the fall in the international price of silver (on which Iran's economy was based), Iranians were becoming increasingly dissatisfied with the role and predominance of foreigners, particularly the British and Russians in the economic, social and political fabric of Iran. By the end of the nineteenth century, the various concessions and bureaucratic reforms had not helped Iran escape its pre-modern captivity but had increased it and had only engendered a backlash from a growing national polity.

More contemporary foundations

Many of the issues raised above, the development of an intellectual enlightenment and the growing national consciousness brought on by Iran's semi-colonial existence were to form part of the basis of Iran's diplomacy in Paris. In fact, all of Iran's delegates except for Moshaver al-Mamalek and Mohammad Ali Foroughi were born towards the end of Naser al-Din Shah's rule which was cut short by his assassination in 1897. Moshaver al-Mamalek was born in 1868 and had, by the end of the century, already started his career as a diplomat. Mohammad Ali Foroughi was twenty when Naser al-Din Shah was killed. Though recent history was to inform the new breed, they were all to be contemporaries of huge events in Iranian history which would also help form their ideas and opinions.

Mozaffar al-Din Shah (1853–1907) came to the throne in 1897. He was to prove to be no less an advocator of reform or partial to changes in Iran's concession practice than his father. He was to die a few months before Britain and Russians semi-colonial status was effectively rubber-stamped by the Anglo-Russian Convention of 1907. During his tenure, concessions were given out with ever-increasing regularity. The only stumbling block to the exponential growth of concessions was the competition between the Russians and British. None was to be more prominent than the question of oil which would come to be dominated, in the twentieth century, by the narrative of Iranian grievance in the face of British arrogance and greed.

The narrative of the search, drilling and growth of Iran's oil industry has been covered in depth elsewhere. It is a narrative that on the Iranian side epitomized British greed and fraud with little concern for the country that was being exploited.

On the British side it was a tale of reward for the undertaking of a risky venture that became a huge success story and the basis for what was to become British Petroleum. However, between 1911 and 1918, oil had become of such strategic importance to the security and protection of Britain and its Empire, it had now become a large factor in Britain's post-war aims in Iran.

The importance of securing oil supplies was the result of the considerable foresight of three men, Ernest Pretyman, Lord Fisher and Winston Churchill. It was a prescient Ernest Pretyman, working for the Admiralty, who attempted to dissuade William Knox D'Arcy from selling the concession when he was low on finance.[15] It was Lord Fisher, First Lord of the Admiralty, who had seen the need to convert the British Navy from coal to oil burning, and who asked Ernest Pretyman to form a committee to analyse how oil supplies could be appropriated and safeguarded.[16] Finally, it was Winston Churchill, who became First Lord of the Admiralty in 1911 on Lord Fisher's retirement, who was convinced in the efficacy and need both for an oil-fired navy and to secure adequate supplies.

Post-war, Britain's oil needs were hardly to diminish and securing Iranian oil supplies for British needs was never greater. It was, therefore, no surprise that the Eastern Committee had listed 'the enormous importance' of the oilfields in Iran.[17] The War Cabinet's Eastern Committee was set up in March 1918 and operated until January 1919 and chaired by Lord Curzon, replacing the Persia Committee. The Eastern Committee had no specific stated objectives and seemed only guided by its territorial limits, which included 'the entire western glacis of the Indian fortress'.[18] It would, however, be the axis of British policymaking in the Middle East going forward.

One cannot understate the importance of the Eastern Committee as both a vehicle for Lord Curzon to bully and control British policymaking in the Middle East and the preponderant and critical function it formed at the heart of the British government. Lord Curzon's private fiefdom was such that it was able to eat into the auspices and political territory of both the Foreign Office and India government. The committee, far from being organized to facilitate coordination, was to develop 'wide-ranging executive functions'.[19]

From the Iranian point of view, oil was a concession that needed to be modified. In the original agreement, Iran had agreed to receive 16 per cent of any profit. Over the following years, what became the Anglo-Persian Oil Company (APOC) took every advantage to reduce these royalty payments. These payments were completely withheld between 1916 and 1917 as a result of a dispute about wartime sabotage. Given the disingenuous methods by which the APOC had reduced and then stopped Iran's royalty payments, and how the APOC avoided arbitration, the issue of oil should have been placed at the top of the list of Iran's grievances. There are two reasons why it was not. For one, it was a large issue that would probably have taken away much of the Iranian focus on independence, sovereignty and territorial proposals. For another, more importantly, Iranian diplomats had decided not to antagonize the British as they had expected they would need their help in getting heard in Paris.

What has been seldom discussed is how this effective joint venture was to affect Iranian sensibilities. Naturally it did provide evidence to those who argued that the British government and British commercial interests were indistinguishable. Certainly this conflation was obvious when Indian Army soldiers were brought in to protect oilfields, a decision which it was thought would have a 'sobering effect' on the Bakhtiari tribes whose tribesmen had been paid for but had failed to protect the oilfields.[20] Not only was it clear why Iranians conflated the British government and the D'Arcy Oil Syndicate (pre-curser to the APOC) as one of the same, but it was also clear that territorial sovereignty was at risk if British soldiers could be drafted in by the British.

Paradoxically, Mozaffar al-Din Shah's rule would end with the signing of a new Constitution literally on his deathbed. The Tobacco Rebellion, it has been argued, had been a dress rehearsal for the Constitutional Revolution which began in 1905. Another economic crisis and rapid increases in food prices directed anger by merchants towards a government that seemed to be more intent on raising more customs revenue through the auspices of Joseph Naus, the director of Customs. Protests and violence again united the unholy trinity of the merchants, *Ulema* and intellectuals. This time, the protests would end in political and legal changes which defined a significant break with the past. A written constitution had established a *Majles* and the Supplementary Fundamental Law had established the Rule of Law and had decided on other layers to the constitution necessitated by a modern state.[21] The Constitutional Revolution had curbed the powers of the Shah, and Iran had therefore taken a major step in developing from a patrimonial system[22] of rule to one where the political system could transcend the death of the monarch.

In truth, the gains in revolution had been easier made than consecrated. The backlash came in the shape of Mozaffar al-Din Shah's son and successor, Mohammad Ali Shah (1872–1925), assisted by the Russians. The nature of this backlash was to be bloody and included another issue of territorial sovereignty when the Russians intervened in the revolution and occupied Tabriz in 1909. The issue of the removal of Russian forces from Tabriz, and more generally Azerbaijan in north-western Iran, was to be used as a political contest in which Iran could only lose. When the Iranian chargé d'affaires in St Petersburg asked when the Russian troops would be withdrawn from Iranian soil,[23] Russia replied that they would do so when Iran satisfied their conditions of providing an adequate environment for commerce and an ability to keep the peace. This was something that Russia's very presence in Azerbaijan proved that Iran could not do. Eventually, the Russians in 1911 linked the removal of their forces in exchange for the removal of the financial advisor Morgan Shuster. Morgan Shuster had to be sacked for Russian forces to be removed.[24]

Morgan Shuster, who had been in Iran for a matter of months, had not enamoured the Russians by either his appointment or his conduct in carrying out his duties. The British were likewise not happy, though they did not object to his appointment. Though a man of unquestioned abilities, he would step on many toes as he attempted to bring Iranian finances in line. This included his challenge to corrupt officials as well as the introduction of a special gendarmerie to collect taxes. Though his actions were at times high-handed, his respect for the *Majles* was total and his respect for the British and Russians lacking. He considered them generally 'manifestly hostile to Persia's welfare'.[25]

Morgan Shuster was to incite a backlash from the Russians who had failed to put the exiled Shah back on the throne and who had never hidden their backing for royalist and anti-constitutional forces. Russian forces had already intervened in Azerbaijan and had perpetuated a reign of terror and bloodshed in the city of Tabriz. Now, they used an incident in which Morgan Shuster had been authorized by the *Majles* to confiscate the property of Salar al-Dowleh and Sho'a' al-Saltaneh who had been involved in counter-revolutionary plotting. Using, as Morgan Shuster described, fictitious and dubious financial and political links to the Russians as a pretext, the Russians took the opportunity to issue several ultimata.

The first was the demand for an apology for insulting the Russian Consul against a threat of military action. This demand was indecently followed almost immediately by a second ultimatum which demanded three actions: the removal of Shuster and his assistant, to not engage any foreigners in the future without agreement from Russia and Britain, and finally a demand that Iran should pay an indemnity for the cost of Russian troops which had operated in Iran. As Abbas Amanat has pointed out, it was 'blatantly required that Iran reimburse the cost of the violation of its own sovereignty to an aggressor who, as it turned out, went on a rampage of massacres and maltreatment of defenceless Iranians'.[26]

Russia's actions in 1911 went much further than their previous involvement when the Cossack Brigade bombed the *Majles* in the furtherance of Mohammad Ali Shah's designs to defeat the Constitutional Revolution. The Cossack Brigade, which had been formed after a Russian mission to Iran, was a military force officered by Russians which turned out to be 'openly an instrument of Russian foreign policy and was completely beyond Iranian control'.[27] Morgan Shuster was eventually given his marching orders, though not by the *Majles* which stood by him, but by a concerned cabinet. Once again, much like the events of the Tobacco Rebellion, the events of 1911, and the ultimate, and the role of the Russians in it, had produced agitation and protest from a more politically astute polity. The members of the *Majles* were outraged but so were the *Ulema*, and protests by Iranian citizens, including women and children, punctuated yet another dismal chapter in Iran's history where its sovereignty seemed meaningless.

The events of 1911, and more generally those of the Constitutional Revolution, are so significant to future Iranian perceptions and diplomacy that they are worth specifying. Firstly, it showed that change was possible and that Iran could formulate a distinct path for itself. This was despite the emergence of disparate political groups and movements which had blossomed during the revolution. Secondly, it showed that progress would be slow, if not impossible, while the Russians were allowed to operate in Iran as they wished, not always supported, but never opposed by the British. The Russians had shown a capacity for violence and deceit.[28] British support for Russian actions, though sometimes tempering Russian brutality and overreach, had nevertheless continued.

It is easy to feel sorry for the British as they seemed captive to the 1907 Anglo-Russian Convention and therefore Russian actions. It seemed that the convention had allowed the Russians to give vent to whatever they wanted as long as it was within their designated sphere of influence. That would, however, miss the point. Sir Edward Grey (1862–1933), Britain's long-standing foreign minister (1862–1933), had happily and positively gone into the convention because he felt that the protection of Britain's financial interest in the south of Iran and the security of India could best be secured by it. More importantly, Sir Edward Grey saw an agreement with Russia as part of cementing the triple entente against Germany in the run-up to the First World War.

Once again, Iran's future was to be tied to European exigencies. But again, this explanation does not do justice to Sir Edward Grey's approach to Iran. He did not ignore Iran, as some commentators have suggested and as the volumes of his correspondence in the British Archives contradict. He was simply disinterested in Iran. Iran's well-being was of no interest to him and it is this which informed his decisions. While he found some support, those who had to deal with Iran were not of them. Sir Cecil Spring-Rice, British minister to Iran (1906–8), was caught completely off-guard by the 1907 Anglo-Russian Convention and said:

> They have thrown a stone into the windows here and left me to face the policeman. Neither Nicolson [Minister to St. Petersburg] or the F.O informed me that the agreement was signed till three days after it had been published here. This was, I suppose, a sign that the Persian public opinion was not to be considered.[29]

The India government was also against the convention. In a detailed reply to questions raised a few years earlier about plans to resist Russian intentions in Iran, any favourable policy towards the expansion of Russia's interests was to be resisted.[30] Lord Curzon was still viceroy of India at this point and he did not change his opinion when the convention was agreed. He considered the 1907 Anglo-Russian Convention as a betrayal to the Iranian people,[31] though it is likely that he was more bothered by the huge benefits that had just been given away to Russia on a whim.

Nevertheless, the attitude towards Sir Edward's role, in the Anglo-Russian Convention in view of Russian actions in 1911, was captured by an article in *The Economist* which painted a picture of a man whose abilities were stunted by his lack of knowledge of Iran. Indeed, his probity was also called into question:

> The discovery that Sir Edward Grey on his own avowal was actually supporting the Russian ultimatum to Persia – in open violation of the Anglo-Russian agreement as well as to the obvious detriment of British and Indian interest – gave an ugly shock to public opinion.[32]

It is hard not to compare the Russian 'playbook' and aggression, British appeasement and Iranian inadequacy in the early twentieth century, to the beginning of the nineteenth century. The only difference was that a more developed national consciousness was outraged and bitter that Britain, who had 'never missed a chance to point to England as a paragon of virtue', had 'participated in the rape of Persia'.[33]

With the wealth of archival material available today, the issues concerning the threat of Russia to Iran and, as the determinist logic went, to India can be assessed more fully. Without a doubt, Lord Curzon had been right in his criticism of the convention. Yes, the British had rewarded Russia who had undertaken a massive expansion southward in the 1880s and by now had taken considerable territory from Iran as well as being in a position to challenge the borders of Afghanistan. Also, the Russians would not 'abide by the self-denying ordinance' in the convention as their actions in 1911 showed.[34] However, was Russia still an existential threat to Iran? In truth, only the Iranians might have thought so.

Sir Edward Grey and Lord Curzon did not think so. Even the India government considered a Russian invasion of India through Iran as being both illogical and impractical. While political and economic subjugation was an aim, the elimination of Iran was not. Even if it was, one can argue that, despite Iranian misgivings at Paris that Iran had been violated by the 1907 Agreement, it was only the 1907 Agreement that had kept Iran intact. The agreement was the anchor that secured Russia from consolidating Iranian Azerbaijan under Russian rule during and following the Constitutional Revolution.

In addition, the British and Russians did in fact have an 'understanding' that Iran's territorial integrity should be, if not protected, at least acknowledged. In 1834, Britain and Russia arrived at 'a common understanding respecting the independence and integrity of the dominions of the Shah of Persia'.[35] This Understanding was re-affirmed in 1838 and in 1865. This Understanding has been largely ignored by researchers. After all, Russia's territorial gains in the Transcaspian in the latter half of the nineteenth century seemingly rendered the Understanding as irrelevant. However, a territorial nibble here or there did not mean that the essential sanctity of Iran would not be recognized. None of this was known to an Iran, which had become increasingly subordinate to Russian diplomacy, and frightened of its military might towards the end of the nineteenth century.

It was not until 1873, after Iran asked for its integrity to be recognized, that Britain finally told the Iranians that an Understanding with Russia existed which did just that.[36] It can be surmised that had Iran known, concerned as she was with Russia's expansion into what was considered Iranian territory, it might have acted differently. Peculiarly, the Iranians were told that the Understanding should not be made public as it could have implied distrust on the part of Britain towards Russia and raised doubts as to Russia respecting Iran's integrity.[37]

There is no doubt that the British could have used the Understanding to modify and restrict the actions of Russia. It is strange, but also unfortunately in keeping with British diplomacy towards Iran, that the British were happy to have an Understanding but not call on Russia when breached, thereby rendering it useless. In 1888, as Sir Henry Drummond Wolff was being briefed to take over as minister to Iran, it was notable that the British viewed the Understanding with some circumspection, calling it of a 'somewhat informal and indefinite nature'.[38]

Thirdly, and finally, it was becoming obvious that the Constitutional Revolution was only half won. The *Majles* was hampered without the means, or state infrastructure, to carry out policies. The period between 1905 and 1911 during the Constitutional Revolution had been a period of immense political turmoil and change, which furthered the British and Russian grip on Iranian politics and economics but which also came tantalizingly close to great political change.

Occupation and war

Battered by the imperial practices of Britain and Russia domestically and the disruption caused by the Constitutional Revolution, Iran was to face increased pressure on its borders and was to eventually, during the First World War, see its territory used as a battlefield. It has been the norm to see the actions of Russia and Britain, and especially the Ottomans between 1905 and 1911, and the First World War, as separate. Yet, given Russian and British attitudes in the run-up to the First World War, their military occupation of Iran was almost inevitable. Iran, unable to develop an internal and expansive police force, was also incapable of protecting its borders.

In fact, the major threat to Iran was to come from the Ottomans. From 1905 onwards the Ottomans, with ruthlessness, attempted the subjugation of northern Azerbaijan, encouraged by the weakness of the Iranian state and the turmoil of the Constitutional Revolution. The Ottomans were also to take advantage of Russian ill-timed lethargy. Russia's relative military decline, regional inattention and its military disaster against Japan and the 1905 revolution meant Russian minds and guns were, at least for the short term, elsewhere.

The Ottoman Empire had long-standing designs on Azerbaijan, the Caucasus and northern Iran in much the same way as the Russians. As a result of the 1877 Russo-Ottoman War the make-up of the Ottoman Empire had become less European and more Asiatic in ethnicity. This, combined with the promotion of Sultan Abdulhamid II, who, ascending the throne in 1876 as a champion of Sunni pan-Islamism, has led some to argue that Ottoman encroachment in Azerbaijan projected a largely religious component.[39] Religion was utilized to coalesce forces against Iran. However, though religion was to play a greater role in border politics than ever before, it was only part of the story. Over the longer period of Turkish territorial encroachment, Ottoman exploitation affirmed commercial railway interests, military pre-eminence and simple territorial seizure.

Between 1905 and 1911, the Ottomans, who were still in long-standing negotiations with the Iranians, British and Russians, within the context of the delimitation of the Ottoman/Iranian border, saw the benefits that territorial encroachment could bring. If greater gains could be made, and the Ottomans could galvanize inchoate nationalist tendencies along with Kurdish militancy to attempt

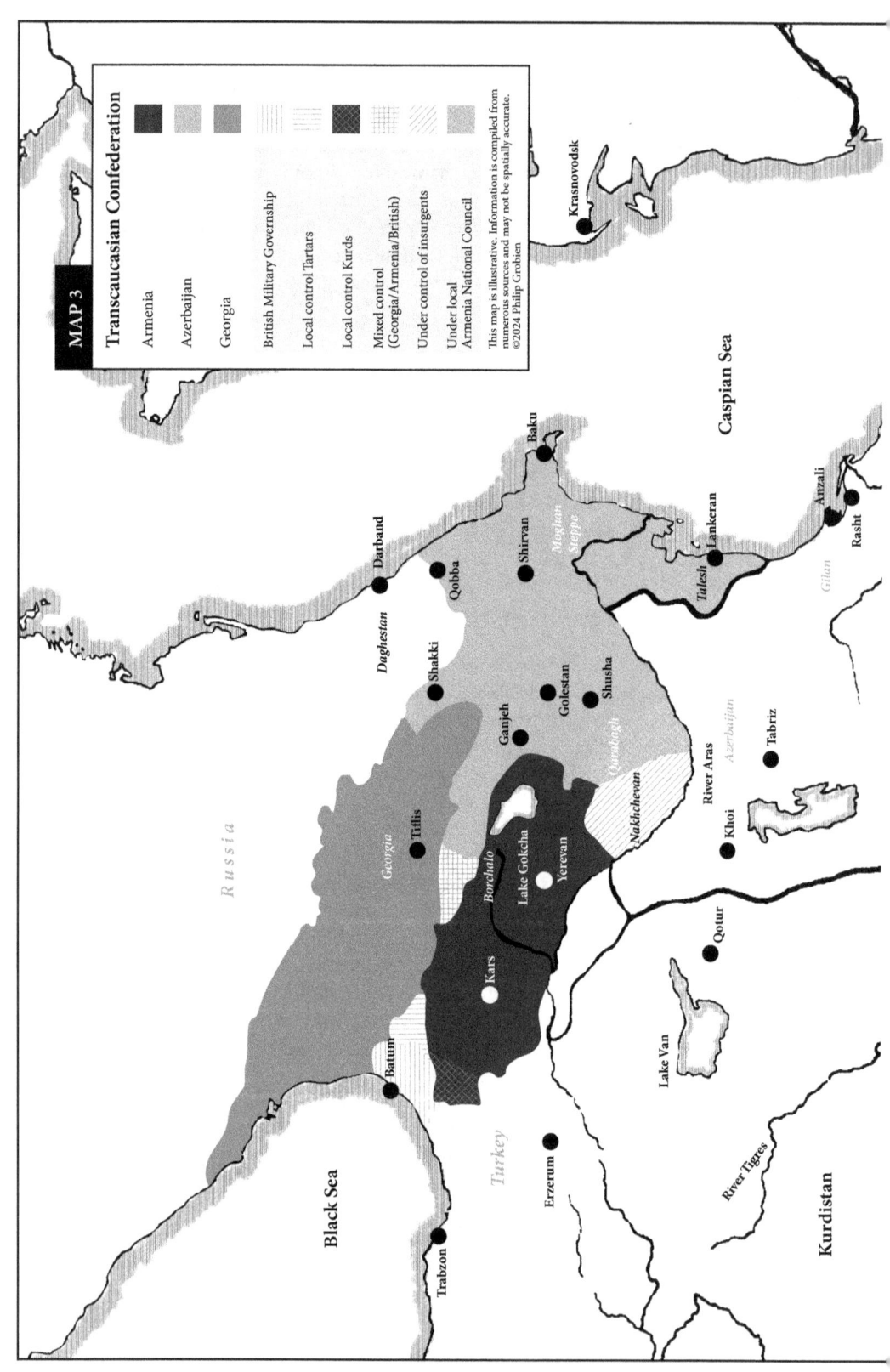

to push back borders towards Iran, then some of these territorial gains could be made permanent. By December 1911, the British and Russians were becoming concerned with the extent of Ottoman encroachments, and assembled a Mission of Investigation, to report its extent. The Joint Report was furnished together with a map showing the extent of Turkish encroachments overlaid on the *Carte Identique* which had been made and utilized to geographically pinpoint the territories in dispute. In the forthcoming August, the Russians submitted to Turkey a borderline that reflected the status quo of the 1905 border, which nullified Ottoman encroachments between 1905 and 1912.[40] This line, which had been established by the Mission of Investigation, was eventually accepted by the Turks in April 1913 and was to provide for a 'qualified acceptance of the Russian demands'.[41] Except for some small exceptions, it was the 1905 boundary line that was to be permanently delimited in the northern boundary section.

Without Russian and British intervention, Turkey would have been more successful in gaining, probably permanently, more disputed territory. Of course, the British and Russian had their own strategic interests in acting against the Ottomans in light of the Anglo-Russian Convention of 1907. In addition, Russia also had expansionist interests in the region and was more than happy to thwart Ottoman territorialization. But this was only to be a prelude to what was to come. Iran was invaded by the Ottomans in late 1914 which prompted a Russian and subsequent British military reaction.

Long discredited has been the idea that Ottoman military aggression during the First World War had been the result of German dominance and manipulation. Less discredited has been the idea that Ottoman war aims, particularly those in Azerbaijan and the Caucasus, were the result of a newfound 'Turkish' nationalism. While it is true that the Ottomans had undergone political changes of their own and had undergone their own constitutional revolution, it is not true that their territorial aims had changed. Even though they were now demonstrating a more forceful, and decidedly 'Turkish' nationalism, in practical terms Turkey's interest in northern Iran had only changed in language.

Enver Pasha, the minister of war, and a proponent of pan-Turkism, stood at the centre of this paradigm. His vision for a pan-Turkish or pan-Turanian state in the Caucasus would do much to drive military strategy. The strategy to develop a pan-Turkish state was pushed through despite military setbacks and was eventually achieved in summer of 1918. As a result of a final military push in April 1918, the Turks had occupied Azerbaijan and in September reached Baku. Also in summer, the Turks saw action against an Azeri and Armenian fugitive army around lake Urumieh and pushed into Iran as far south as Tabriz, Bijar and Zanjan.[42] Much of this progress was down to both the recent retreat and melting away of the Russian military, occupied with the recent Russian revolution. It was also down to the new paradigm the British found themselves and their own dithering strategies.

The Russians had provided the bulk of the manpower during the war and the British now faced dealing with the Turks on their own. With a small military force and low on ideas, the only strategy to repel an invasion by the Turks from the Caucasus was to occupy Hamadan and protect the road from the frontier to Tabriz.

Otherwise, the only other option offered was for the small British force in Iran to be simply deployed to protect the British Legation.

There is no doubt that the British in Tehran were concerned about the longer-term effects of the Turkish invasion of Azerbaijan. Iranian Azerbaijan could have formed part of a larger entity. If a pan-Turkish state could be formed, it could include the indigenous Turks around the Black Sea, Azerbaijan, Transcaucasia and the estimated two million Turks in Iran (at the time 20 per cent of the Iranian population). 'A Manual on the Turanians and Pan-Turanianism', published by British Naval Intelligence,[43] reflected the characteristics and nature of Turanism, but was evidently written to inform British officials regarding the threat and possibility of a union between some 50 million Turanians who were dispersed throughout Russia, the British dominions, Afghanistan and Iran.

Whilst Turkish designs for a new state ran out of time, coming to an end with the capitulation of the Central powers in late 1918, the reality was that it was already failing to be the cohesive entity they had hoped it would be. Turkish nationalist ideas did not find fertile ground. The Turks may have considered all of Azerbaijan as Turkish territory,[44] but these feelings were not mutual. Earlier in the war, the Azeris had not joined the pan-Turanian movement, and by the end of the war it was becoming clear that rather than joining a larger Turkish movement they were actively moving towards forming an independent republic.

New Azeri political parties had burst on the scene in 1917 and nationalism was to provide an increasing component of Azerbaijani identity.[45] The announcement of the Transcaucasian Federation on 22 April 1918 effectively showed that nationalism did not mean being attached to a Turkish Empire (see Map 3). In fact, as time wore on, needless Turkish aggression was having a negative effect. Ethnic cleansing, however mild, was never far away as the Turkish military occupied ethnically mixed areas. One Turkish officer, operating in Iranian Azerbaijan, specifically demanded a count of Armenians in the territory. He had previously stated that Khoi had been taken and 'that happily there were none [Armenians] left in Turkish territory'.[46] Indeed the British felt that the Turks had 'occasioned great dissatisfaction among the local population'.[47] This did nothing to help Turkish exertions in Iranian Azerbaijan in trying to establish a pan-Turkish state.

The Ottomans had never been able to interfere in Iran's internal politics as the British and Russians had done. Their role had been that of a regional military foe of long-standing. What Iran's relationship with the Ottomans illustrated was how incapable Iran had been of protecting its borders either during peace or during war. Iran could not protect itself against the Turanians at the door. The goal for Iran's elite was to reform Iran and re-make its territorial integrity to defy the Turks or others in the future.

The question of international law

In the nineteenth century, interactions between countries were balanced by an 'international society' or 'the notion that states and rulers of states are bound by rules and form a society or community with one another'.[48] Much of this, it has been argued, has developed from the Peace of Westphalia (1648).[49] The period between the Congress of Vienna in 1815 and the First World War represented the apogee of this political club and ideal. Despite the Crimean War, this outlet for international agreements had helped to keep the peace in Europe. Therein lay the problem as the 'international society' was not a club to which Iran belonged, as it was for the powerful European nations and empires only. Nevertheless, the practice of international law was to replace this long-standing practice of keeping the peace. Its implementation was beginning to provide a meaningful legal framework for states and people's rights.

The Constitutional Revolution had given voice to the idea of the Rule of Law. Yet, guaranteeing both individual rights and protecting society from arbitrary power[50] brought the question of international law into sharper relief. If Iran, as a minor and non-European power, had not prospered from the political intercourse of the international society, then it was hoped it may under international law. Iranian sovereignty could only be enabled and preserved under a system of international norms and values and a system of international law.

The problem was that there seemed little practical difference between an 'international society' and international law. Iran's elite could, during the long nineteenth century, only identify international law as enabling the hegemonic aspects of imperialism. For countries such as Iran, it was difficult to see how international law had in any way retarded the activities of European powers when it came to colonialism or imperialism. Even from the European perspective, it appeared that international law was not to be fully incorporated into the imperial project and European lawyers were not averse to have one rule in Europe and another for the 'orientals'.[51] They argued that Europeans 'were sufficiently similar for there to be an international law among them, and sufficiently different from non-European peoples so as to preclude the extension of such law to the latter'.[52] In this way the development of international law was beginning to be seen as part of the cultural process in Europe only. However, this did not stop the introduction of 'laws' that could be used to civilize the savage and to aid the conversion of non-Europeans into civilized behaviour.[53] In the final analysis, it would appear that 'Empire is never an advocate of an international law that can seem only an obstacle to its ambition'.[54] The Anglo-Russian Convention of 1907 was clearly an example of international law giving away to imperial imperatives.

As Iranians looked towards an equality in international law, they viewed favourably the emergence of an international community and international organizations such as the League of Nations which would help secure it. Iran's elite may even have been aware, at this point, of plans that the League of Nations would set up a permanent international court of justice. In this, they were not the only country that had been enticed by the notion of a new post-war order.[55] As we will see, Iran's delegation was to utilize their understanding of a future international legal framework on which to build their claim in Paris. Their arguments were not to be unsupported.

As early as 26 June 1918 a well-respected Indian Jurist and Muslim political leader, Ameer Ali, gave a speech at the Central Asian Society in which he outlined *The Rights of Persia*.[56] His argument for Iran to 'stand alongside the free nations of the West' was based on two parameters. Firstly, that Iran had great potential – a race rich in culture and a rich past, rich in natural resources and a people willing to work. Secondly, that in its struggle for liberty from oppression, Iran had shown 'progressive tendencies' despite opposition from Russia and home-grown absolutism. Ameer Ali, therefore, believed that Iran should be feted as a nation and have injustices such as lost territories repatriated. In fact, he asked, how could Britain not miss the great opportunity to help Iran in this regard? After all it was all that Iran deserved 'from her history, her economic potentiality, and from the vigour and self-restraint with which her people have won their liberty – far more than many of the Balkan nationalities'.[57]

This speech remains, to my knowledge, the only legal justification in the West for Iran's rights. Ameer Ali was an anglophile and sought to encourage a greater alliance between Muslims and, as he saw it, a benevolent Britain. That said, his speech, while encouraging the British to view Iran with greater goodwill, falls short of giving a more detailed legal argument regarding either Iran's place in international law or indeed how international law might be used to help Iran.

Conclusion

Iran had, over the long nineteenth century, been unable to shrug off the ever-increasing pressure of Britain and Russia over its independence. For Iran's political elite and those who would make up Iran's delegation in Paris, the First World War and Iran's role in it seemed to be the final sign, if one was needed, that Iran could not go on as it had in the past. If anything, Iran's control and administration of its own territory before the war were now more severely diminished.

Yet, as Iran's existence as a semi-colonial state and imperial football had become more pronounced, an intellectual enlightenment had merged with direct action and the Iranian populace was beginning to have a voice. Events such as the Tobacco Rebellion had shown a growing appetite for change – change which had been confirmed by the events of the Constitutional Revolution. The Constitutional Revolution had not only established a constitutional monarchy but had allowed an intellectual expression of the future of Iran. While the Constitutional Revolution remained the only tangible success amidst the ever-increasing attack on Iran's independence by Russia and Britain, it proved to be the educational grounding for Iran's political elite. Threats had provided new learning opportunities.

Chapter 3

A NEW DAWN

Battered by imperialism, a state existing in marginal sovereignty, Iran had come to a crossroads as the First World War was slowly coming to an end. Iran, more than ever, was now tapped into the range of international movements that the war had engendered. The ruling elite was beginning to see a solution to Iran's significant problems, not solely in relation to the British, Russians and Turks, but further afield. If Iran could take its case to the peace talks, then Iran may be able to escape the semi-colonial paradigm it had difficulty breaching. As the Iranian minister to The Hague was noted to have said, admittance to the peace talks represented the difference between Iran's survival as an independent state or a very different outcome, to perish in political slavery.[1] This would mean that Iran's ruling elite had to decide what they wanted from any peace process and how they wanted to proceed. In effect, Iran had to determine its place in a modern, more globalized world.

The failure of Iran to protect its neutrality during the First World War from the Turkish, Russian and British military had seemingly only underlined the systemic weakness of the Qajar state. This was despite the fact that Iran was also to fail to keep Russian and British forces out of Iran during the Second World War with an even more potent military force. Nevertheless, the end of the Qajar dynasty, and its paradigm of weakness, owes much to the positioning of the Pahlavi dynasty as a modernizing force in the country and as a counterweight to Qajar incompetence. Also pertinent was the prevailing narrative of the time, drawn largely from British sources, who portrayed Iran's efforts to regain its sovereignty as absurd given its problems.[2]

With some exceptions, such as Edward Browne, the British saw Iran's issues and problems as largely self-inflicted, ignoring their own part in them. Yet, this narrative neglects both the intellectual and political progress that Iran had made and the absolute necessity, as the Iranian elite saw it, to attempt to impose reform and change. Not only had the British not recognized the growing nationalism in the country but they had failed to understand the desperation that drove the Iranian elite to commit to change. In yet another paradox, the parlous nature of the country, rather than engendering a state of inertia, had instead fomented a drive towards change.

Towards the dream of peace

Iran's elite began thinking and planning for its post-war future a long time before the First World War had ended. In fact, planning began at a point when the Allied victory was by no means assured, or even envisaged by some Iranian politicians who were happier if the Germans had won. They held the view that the Germans might serve as a counterweight to British and Russian hegemony in Iran.

Not all of Iran's diplomatic moves appeared either well thought out or planned. In attempting to impose Iran's immediate sovereignty over a war-torn country, in January 1918, Ahmad Shah, rather impetuously, asked the British forces to leave Iran. Lord Balfour rightly felt that such a move would 'expose the country to further violations of neutrality on the part of their enemies'.[3] Balfour's entirely correct assessment of Iran's weakness merely highlighted the reality of Iran's circumstances and vulnerability. However, Ahmad Shah's request also underlined how Iran's wish to re-establish sovereignty eclipsed a realistic assessment of its inability to protect itself from incursions by other countries.

On 18 December 1916 President Wilson issued a 'Peace Note' which requested all belligerents to give voice to their terms on which peace could be restored. The secrecy behind the note was such that even other Allies, such as Britain, were caught flat-footed. The note, however, was well received by all neutral nations apart from Spain. President Wilson's Peace Note had been circulated in the press in Iran and a mere ten days later Ahmad Shah was petitioned by 300 Iranians to reply to it.[4] The Iranians were greatly appreciative of President Wilson's note, which had, as a preview to his fourteen points, highlighted the rights of weaker states and the formation of a League of Nations.[5]

By this point, Iranians had also become aware of Bolshevik ideas of self-determination as states, previously under Russian control, were recognized as independent.[6] The 'Declaration of the Rights of Peoples' gave heart to those Armenians, Azeris and Georgians who sought independence from the Russian Empire. For the moment this pronouncement had shown Lenin to be true to his principles. The hand of friendship was likewise extended to Iran. The newspaper *Iran* published an article quoting Pavel Nikolayevich Milyukov (1859–1943), the minister of Foreign Affairs, 'of the new and freedom-loving government of Russia'. The article tied in the Russian Revolution and the promise of Iran's future possibilities, untethered by Russian malevolence. Or, put another way, 'the antidote had replaced the poison'.[7]

Iran now entered a peculiar political relationship with the Bolsheviks. The Iranians had, not knowing where the wind would blow, tentatively recognized the Soviet Union in December 1917. Nevertheless, they remained wary of Bolshevik intentions towards Iran and, given that the Bolsheviks still had to win a civil war to rubber-stamp their assumption of power, it is fair to say that Iran's engagement with Soviet Russia was careful and targeted. Nevertheless, Iran did take steps to exploit this new-found friendship with Russia and the idea was circulated that an Iranian delegation should go to St Petersburg and see what could be achieved. However upbeat this proposal was, it would probably have been opposed by Britain who had just lost an ally in Tsarist Russia and whose relations with Bolshevik Russia seemed in abeyance. It is probable that the Iranians would have sought an agreement from Russia to either vacate the territories lost to Russia under the treaties of Golestan and Turkmanchai and/or ask for reparations. In the end no delegation was sent to St Petersburg.

It was also mooted that more should be done to officially involve Iranian intellectuals in Iran's cause. However, some Iranians had been acting unofficially for some time and pushing for change. Abroad, Iranian intellectuals were already pushing Iran's cause. In particular, the establishment of The National Committee (*Komiteh-ye Melliyun*) in Berlin during the First World War was to be a source of both information for and promotion of Iran's cause. It came about when the Germans invited Hasan Taqizadeh (1870–1970) to go to Berlin and set up an anti-imperialist and especially anti-Russian and British, political campaign. In time, it became more obvious that the Germans had also sought Hasan Taqizadeh out to agitate for German and Ottoman sympathy as well as to help Indian revolutionaries pass through Iran to get to India.

Hasan Taqizadeh was a prominent Iranian intellectual who had been an active participant in the Constitutional Revolution and was still a member of the *Majles* when the First World War broke out. At the time he was in exile in New York and looking for a channel for his views. His enthusiasm for the project was tempered by a streak of independence and he agreed to the German proposal as long as the movement remained independent.[8] It is notable that Hasan Taqizadeh had met with Mirza Ali Qoli Khan (1879–1966), the chargé d'affaires in the Iranian Embassy in Washington. Mirza Ali Qoli Khan was to serve on the Iranian delegation to the Peace of Paris.[9]

In Berlin, Hasan Taqizadeh became part of a loose group of influential members of Iran's intellectual and cultural elite which included Hasan Kazemzadeh (Iranshahr) (1883–1961), Mohammad Qazvini (1877–1949) and Mohammad Ali Jamalzadeh (1891–1997) amongst others.[10] Hasan Kazemzadeh had been furthering his education in Europe before he joined Hasan Taqizadeh. A nationalist writer, editor and multi-potentialist, he also spent some of the war years agitating in Iran. Mohammad Qazvini and Mohammad Ali Jamalzadeh were both distinguished literary scholars, also participated in writing for the group. The outlet for their ideas was to be the newspaper *Kaveh*, published from 1916 to 1922. *Kaveh*, at least until the defeat of Germany, supported Germany's strategic outlook and war aims. In addition, it sometimes supported pan-Islamic views but it always supported Iranian nationalism. The newspaper would find its way to Iran and was influential in the development of Iranian nationalism.

Hasan Taqizadeh wrote articles in *Kaveh* and was able to engage in discourses of sovereignty, self-determination and imperialism and apply them to the Iranian paradigm.[11] In this way Hasan Taqizadeh was to become an unofficial promoter of Iran's cause and *Kaveh* the organ for change. On 15 August 1917, tagged onto an article discussing the annual meeting of socialists in Stockholm, Hasan Taqizadeh outlined Iran's post-war *desiderata*:[12]

1. The Anglo-Russian Convention of 1325 [1907] regarding Iran should be abrogated and the political and economic independence of Iran should be restored.
2. Iran should be completely free to administer its finances and military and to have the right to hire advisors from foreign countries. Iran has the right to borrow from abroad.
3. Iran should have an independent customs and citizens should not be forced to pay capitalists in Moscow and London for necessities and the Iranian worker should not die of hunger.
4. Iran should have the right to sail on its seas and have the right to use its mines, to which the neighbouring states have exclusive rights.
5. Numerous concessions which have been taken by force hindering Iran's capabilities and violating its independence, and also all the obligatory restrictions and undertakings that have been taken by resorting to threat and ultimatum, should be abolished.
6. The complete restoration of Iran's independence so that the nation of Iran can freely provide for its own means of defence and development in its own land with peace and tranquillity.

This list of Iran's *desiderata*, though muddled, appears to be the first evocation of Iran's post-war demands. Yet, though it may seem the cornerstone of all other demands that Iran would turn out in the next few months, it was merely what other intellectuals and elite were already thinking. All of Iran's intellectual elite had similar ideas for Iran's salvation. At its heart, Iran's wishes were to be anchored by the ambition to be independent which necessitated the removal of unwanted foreign involvement in Iranian politics and finances.

One major difference between Hasan Taqizadeh's *desiderata* and the official and finalized one in Paris was that there was no demand for territorial restitution and reparations. Also, two further points should be noted: Firstly, Hasan Taqizadeh did not differentiate between Britain and Russia and was not restricted by the *realpolitik* of seeking British help to present their wishes at the Peace Conference in Paris as the official delegates would be. Secondly, the list is also an example of Hasan Taqizadeh's leftist leanings and as such did nothing to endear him to the British. This, allied to his close association with the German cause during the war, which he was eventually to see as a mistake, positioned him as a mere agent of German propaganda as far as the British were concerned. Nevertheless, Hasan Taqizadeh would carry on having an impact on the proceedings in Paris and to see him as a German lackey would ignore his importance, not only to Iranian nationalism, but also to Iran's immediate post-war diplomacy.

Iran and the preparation for peace

President Wilson's Peace Note had already prompted a response by the Iranian minister to the United States and he had articulated the hope that 'the Government of the United States will assist our oppressed nation to maintain its integrity and rights not only for the present but whenever a peace conference shall take place'.[13] The Iranian government now began planning for peace. In November 1917, Moshaver al-Mamalek, Iran's foreign minister, sent a memorandum to the Cabinet Office outlining a strategy to both harvest information and raise public opinion abroad for the Iranian cause.[14] More specifically, he called for 'special envoys' to be sent to both friendly and not-so-friendly countries.

In a peculiar intervention in early October 1918, nearly a full year later, Vosuq al-Dowleh in a memorandum to Iran's embassies in London and Paris had emphasized the importance of the American viewpoint and asked for their views on foreign consultants, the *Faqarat-e hashtganeh* (eight-point programme) and their negotiations with Britain to be relayed back to Tehran.[15] A seemingly perplexed Moshaver al-Mamalek who had already put much of this in motion in November 1917 replied with a memorandum of his own to the Iranian Cabinet in which he underlined the necessity of foreign relations but also the necessity for its work to be reflected by internal reforms. In a possible rebuke to Vosuq al-Dowleh he suggested how the international message needed to be mirrored at home.[16]

Though the November memorandum would form the basis of more tangible planning for Iran presenting its case at any possible peace conference what is more surprising is the date it was sent. The Russian threat to Iran had diminished for the time being as they were preoccupied with their revolution but otherwise the end of the war, either in Europe or in and around Iran, was by no means certain, as Moshaver al-Mamalek had stated. Still, the memorandum was effective in priming Iran's embassies in Europe and the United States to both articulate the elements that would go towards making up Iran's *desiderata* and to detail the nature of what a peace conference might look like and where it might take place.

Most of this information provided in this context would come from the embassies in Washington and Paris. It is questionable that the Minister in Washington, Mehdi Khan Qarazuglu, was chosen for his diplomatic skills. Little is known about him but he appeared to be related to Ahmad Shah's last mentor regent Abol-Qasim Khan Qarazuglu. An office which probably relied on nepotism, it is believed that when he returned to Iran he set up an agricultural college. However, Mirza Ali Qoli Khan, the chargé d'affaires, frustrated with the inaction of Mehdi Khan, the minister, proved to be a considerable fount of information and energy in promoting Iran's cause.[17]

His work and tenacity would earn him a place as one of the delegates to the Peace Conference. He was the right person in the right place at the right time. For one thing, Iran believed that persuading the United States in the shape of President Wilson to help Iran's cause would be imperative to Iran's policy of regaining its unfettered independence. And for another, it was at this time still a possibility that the Peace Conference might take place in the United States.

In Paris, Momtaz al-Saltaneh (1869-1954), Iran's minister, likewise began to court diplomats and promoted Iran's cause. He met with the king of England, the president and foreign secretary of France, the US ambassador and the king of Belgium.[18] The main aim was to prepare the ground and make these countries receptive to Iran's *desiderata* when it was presented.

Figure 4 Portrait of Prime Minister Vosuq al-Dowleh, painted between 1900 and 1917. ©Public Domain.

In contrast to Iran's hopes that the United States would support them, Iran's attitude towards France was more circumspect. While it was true that France had no territorial interests in and around Iran, their intentions as a British ally were unclear. The Sykes-Picot Agreement (1916) had left Iran out of any Franco-British bartering and within the British sphere of interest, but it was unclear if the Iranians knew anything about this secret agreement. In uncertainty, Iran was against any discussions regarding the furthering of European imperialism in and around Iran.

Moshaver al-Mamalek, in his November memorandum, had mentioned that some ministries were already collating and providing lists of damages caused by the war. In fact, in June 1917, the Iranian cabinet had ordered the setup of the *Komisiyun-e markazi-ye ta'yin-e khesarat* (Central commission for the specification of damages). The commission, under the auspices of the Ministry of Foreign Affairs, and with the assistance of both the Interior and Finance ministries, was tasked with the systematic determination of 'the amount of material and moral damage of crimes and all atrocities committed by foreign forces on the government and the people and subjects of Iran'.[19] Information provided by the provinces would be assessed in bi-weekly meetings held at the Ministry of Foreign Affairs.

It should be emphasized that this was a monumental undertaking given the parlous state of Iran. More impressively, given communication and transport difficulties, not to mention the territories under occupation, the Iranians went about their work with diligence. The task 'of assessing systematically the moral, financial and physical damage' was made more comprehensive by sub-commissions established to take reports for damages, on pre-prepared forms.[20] The commission's work was to prove useful for establishing the cost of the war and in providing the basis for Iran's argument for reparations.[21]

Much earlier in 1914, the Iranians had begun work on a *Ketab-e sabz* (Green Book)[22] to help establish Iran's neutrality during the war. The Green Book would give much-needed specific background to economic and political issues that had emerged because of the fighting. In this way the Green Book would also serve as part of the foundational basis for Iranian arguments put forward at the Peace Conference. When the delegates made it to Paris in anticipation of the Peace of Paris, Mohammad Ali Foroughi would carry on the process of detailing actions and progress in subsequent Green Books.

The Treaty of Brest-Litovsk (3 March 1918) between the Central Powers and Russia, which had followed Russian capitulation, was to provide a dry run for some of the *desiderata* taking shape for the main peace conference. The Iranians were intent on making their case at Brest-Litovsk. They sent two delegates to push for the realization of their neutrality and to get the Russian Army to leave Iranian soil. Moshaver al-Mamalek, one of the delegates, communicated directly with the German representative, Baron Richard von Kühlmann, who seemed open to Iranian sentiments. It is likely that von Kühlmann had also been influenced by the Iranian exiles in Berlin.[23] Iran's wish was crystalized when its sovereignty was re-asserted by article 7: 'In view of the fact that Persia and Afghanistan are free and independent States, the contracting parties obligate themselves to respect the political and economic independence and the territorial integrity of these States.'[24] In fact, Iran's case had been accorded a great deal of interest at the deliberations of Brest-Litovsk as both Russia and Germany seemed keen to give it what it wanted.[25] As if to further underline the changes in Iran's fortunes, a couple of months earlier, Leon Trotsky had declared that the Bolsheviks considered that the Anglo-Persian Convention of 1907 was no longer binding.[26]

Iran had seemingly succeeded at Brest-Litovsk and the Russians had unilaterally left the Anglo-Russian Convention. In fact, later in June, the Russians renounced all Iranian debts, all Russian concessions in Iran, and revoked consular oversight and jurisdiction of Russian subjects. All this seemed good news but it was the Iranians who, in October 1918, unilaterally decided to nullify all treaties made with Russia over the last 100 years.[27] Though not specifically indicated by the Iranian announcement, this would have included the Treaty of Turkmanchai and all treaties concerning the Transcaspian (see Map 4). Clearly the cancelling of many of the treaties with Russia, which had rubber-stamped the loss of significant territorial losses, signified the direction of Iran's diplomacy.

Russian bonhomie had not ended there and Karl Bravin, the newly minted Bolshevik Envoy to Iran, brought with him other notes that apologized for previous Russian misdeeds and envisaged and encouraged a more fruitful future relationship. Vosuq al-Dowleh had not been dazzled by these overtures as the Iranian government kept the new Soviet government at arms-length. Soon enough it was to become obvious that Russian actions, particularly in terms of military disengagement from Iranian territory, were not to progress as agreed.

Also, it is worth noting that even with the moderate success at Brest-Litovsk Iran's aims had been far greater. Moshaver al-Mamalek had outlined the following aims:[28] the revision of the Treaty of Turkmanchai and in particular the cancellation of capitulations and the ability for Iran to sail ships on the Caspian; recognition of Iran's rights concerning tariffs; freedom for Iran to grant privileges as it wanted; to hire advisors and officials from any country it wants; Iran's freedom to maintain military forces; removal of the right of Russian interference in Iran's internal affairs; restitution of rights that are based on written and oral contracts and the cancellation of specified concessions.

The Iranians felt great urgency in pursuing these measures and it is important to understand the precarious background which added impetus to these desires.[29] The Russian military had not completely abandoned their positions on Iranian soil and the Turks were still a threat, now even more so given the small British force operating in north western Iran. The overt political and military retrenchment of Russia from Iranian affairs had forced the British to reappraise their policy regarding the security of north-west Iran. Their decisions were to be underwhelming. Securing communications and repelling a possible invasion by the Turks were vital but somehow this was to be secured by no military occupation of the strategic areas vacated by the Russian forces or what the Foreign Office called unlimited concessions.

In April 1918, a month after the signing of the Treaty of Brest-Litovsk, the Turks took advantage of British dithering and re-invaded Azerbaijan and began a march to Baku. Sir Charles Marling (1862–1933), minister to Iran, was given an impossible brief and was asked to do what he could as long as Britain remained free of commitments. The quandary for Sir Charles Marling was to balance the possibility of making an alliance with Iran to stop a pan-Turanian state with the knowledge that there were no further British troops to help.[30] Iranian belief in Britain's ability to stave off the Turkish campaign for territorial acquisition was very low. So low, in fact, that in October they asked the British if the rumours, which were circulating regarding a separate Anglo-Turkish peace treaty that would give Iranian Azerbaijan to Turkey, were true. The Iranians were told that Britain was not in the habit of giving territory to its enemies and, if anything, the eventuality might be the other way around.[31]

Despite reservations regarding Iran's attendance at the Treaty of Brest-Litovsk, Marling wondered if his ability to protect northern Iran might be aided by a closer relationship with Iran. Given that Iran had asked the British for assistance in the event of a Bolshevik invasion,[32] an abandonment of Iran's neutrality seemed worthwhile.[33] On 30 September, the Eastern Committee even discussed the feasibility of an alliance with Iran.[34] However, Allenby's prospective victory in Palestine lessened the need for an alliance. It was pointed out that Iran's 'sole motives for coming in would be in order to appear at the Peace Conference as a belligerent with the hope of getting its independence guaranteed internationally and also of receiving a slice of Turkish territory in neighbourhood of frontier as compensation for injuries suffered'.[35] Nevertheless, it was against this background, in order to maintain an Iran friendly to Britain, that Sir Charles Marling thought that the 1907 Convention should be abrogated, the South Persia Rifles should be placed under neutral officers and that Iran should be admitted to the Paris Peace Conference.[36]

Nevertheless, planning and organizing for the peace settlement continued unabated. In November 1918, Ahmad Shah set about organizing a commission of former and current ministers in his palace to discuss the aim of Iran's foreign policy.[37] He did this seemingly to the exclusion of the cabinet and Prime Minister, Vosuq al-Dowleh. The result was the *Komisiyun-e ta'yin-e maqased va amal-e Iran* (Commission to determine the aims and intentions of Iran).[38] This would culminate in a two-pronged approach, to send a delegation to Paris and another one to the United States. The US approach was soon dropped as the League of Nations would not be convened in Washington as first believed.[39] Of course the high-ranking US diplomats and President Wilson were going to be in Paris anyway. It also made sense to put Iranian energies, which were already stretched, into sending a delegation to the Peace of Paris.

The commission began its work on 17 November 1918 and concluded on 11 December 1918. The first meeting was chaired by Moshaver al-Mamalek and attended by Mohammad Ali Foroughi, Mirza Hossein Khan Ala (1882–1964), Minister of Public Works and Entezam al-Molk (1882/1883–1929), working in the Foreign Office and head of the Passport Office. They would provide the ministerial core for the commission going forward. The commission used Iran's eight-point programme (see below) which had been developed so far as an agenda. The meetings concentrated, in the main, on topics that needed more work such as research into concessions and capitulations, tariffs, and territorial losses. At the first meeting, Moshaver al-Mamalek gave a summation of the background and outlined the reason for and duties of the meetings.

One issue, that of the probity of concessions, led to a report by Mo'azzam al-Molk, the head of the Office of Concessions.[40] Concessions were differentiated between those, particularly Russian concessions, which could simply be cancelled, and those which might be amended as they contained onerous contracts. Contracts that could be amended included, for example, those for the largely successful telegraph and postal concessions.[41] Concessions given to foreign nationals were also examined, seemingly one by one, and re-considered.[42] Capitulations were also reviewed in terms of Iran's 'territorial integrity and independence' and the question of Consul guards was raised to be included in any final document.[43] Furthermore, it was decided that a new customs tariff should be more in keeping with the economic interests of Iran as it would help the government increase its income.[44]

Another discussion led to a detailed synopsis behind the nature of territorial losses and the theoretical foundations for deciding what territories could and should be demanded. They would include territory that had been lost in military conflicts or that had military, geographical or tribal considerations. The emphasis was to be to unite those whose 'characteristics of people as a result of national and historical interests and shared religion, language, habits and customs' were alike.[45]

More specifically, Azerbaijan's economic and political importance to Iran and the possibility of reparations led the commission to discuss the need for more information from the region. They duly sent a fact-finding mission to Azerbaijan. The commission also deliberated the various communications by Mirza Reza Khan (Prince Arfa) about the region. Prince Arfa was a product of a bygone age and by this point a man of the *Ancien Regime* having been prominent in the reign of Naser al-din Shah. He had, amongst other postings, been minister to Russia and Turkey. By this point in semi-retirement, he put his considerable diplomatic and political knowledge towards Iran's claims in the Muslim Caucasus and the ferment caused by Turkish plans to constitute a Turanian state.[46]

Prince Arfa's work also helped to establish an ethnic and *Persianate* connection between Iran and the territories in the Caucasus lost to the Russians. It is particularly fascinating that Iran's interest in having parts of the Caucasus returned was discussed explicitly in terms of President Wilson's fourteen points and the question of self-determination.[47] It is also interesting to note that Prince Arfa passed on an exchange in which a Frenchman had declared that the issue of the Caucasus should be dealt with the sword and not the pen.[48]

Iran, of course, did not have an army capable of taking the Caucasus by force and would have to rely on the pen. As Iran was intent on establishing its *imperial nationalism*, territorial re-acquisition based on religion, ethnicity and *Persianate* elements were to apply. Much of the work of the commission, therefore, was taken up by the issue of territory. Early in the meetings it was decided that the delegates to the Peace Conference would be furnished with maximum, moderate and minimum territorial demands. This schema was to form the methodological basis for Iran's demands.[49]

In the Transcaucasus, on the border with Azerbaijan, the following borders were to be determined. The maximum would be to return Iran's borders to that of before the Treaty of Golestan. This would include the return of Georgia, Darband, Qobba, Baku, Shirvan, Shakki, Ganjeh, Moghan and parts of Talesh.[50] The moderate demands would be to return to the borders that existed prior to the Treaty of Turkmanchai which included more of Armenia, Nakhchevan and Talesh. The minimum demand was for the current border to follow the river Aras more completely, which would have repatriated Talesh and a small part of Armenia.

In the Transcaspian, rivers would dominate border limits. The maximum intention was to demand all the land up to the River Jayhoun (Amou Darya). The moderate target lay north-east to the river Murghab and the minimum requirement was to take the border up to the Tejen (Tejend) River (see Map 4).

The maximum and moderate demands included the appropriation of numerous railway lines developed by the Russians.

In the west, demands were more circumspect and it was acknowledged that the Turkish surrender of occupied territories would play a part in deliberations. Nevertheless, some further territorial seizure of parts of the River Tigris were noted.

Much like the decision not to ruffle British feathers by discussing its oil concession, it was further decided that issues concerning the eastern and southern borders would not be discussed at the Peace Conference. Britain had played a large part in the formation of the eastern border and consequently the defence of Afghanistan to the detriment of Iranian control. Iran had already had its fingers burnt. Naser al-Din Shah, early in his reign, in a vain attempt to re-establish control over Herat, had initiated a military action, which, despite securing Herat, also aroused the indignation of the British. British retribution was swift and following a declaration of war by Britain, the Iranians were forced to accept defeat. In the resulting Treaty of Paris in 1857, Iran was forced to relinquish all claims to Afghanistan.

Britain had no intention of relinquishing its semi-colonial hold on Afghanistan as it provided yet another buffer in protecting India. In the same vein, it was felt necessary to delimit the borders between India and Iran which is now the border between Pakistan and Iran. A fixed border, through the region of Baluchistan, established under the auspices of General Goldsmid, was also intended to do away with previous porous borderlands which the British deemed a security risk. British and Iranian archives suggest that there existed little appetite in raising the question of these borders, save for some small adjustments here or there. If anything, the Iranians would have been more intent on discussing the status of islands in the Persian Gulf, which had been occupied or tacitly controlled islands by the British.

In fact, only the question of the Persian Gulf islands was debated with any vigour. Other specific issues, which may have impacted Iran's relationship with the British, were also not further deliberated and finessed by the delegates in Paris. These specifically addressed the issue of Iran's non-existent railway and oil concessions both already discussed, as well as the reform of the Bank of Persia.[51] As we will see, the operation of the Bank of Persia as a foreign bank acting as both a commercial and state bank was surely a thorn in the side of Iran's much-vaunted need for independence.

The British remained suspicious of Iran's behaviour during the middle to latter part of 1918. They had been unhappy that Iran had sent a delegation to negotiate at the Treaty of Brest-Litovsk and unhappy with some of the noises concerning sovereignty in Iran. In addition to the aforementioned demand that British forces leave Iranian territory, the previous Iranian government of Samsam al-Saltaneh, in a similar vein to the Russians, had also declared the removal of consular oversight over all foreigners in Iran.

British were clearly troubled by the abrogation of the Foreign Office Tribunal and Kargozari Courts and the assumption that foreigners would now be dealt with by the Iranian court system. The Kargozar were a system of officials, part of the Ministry of Foreign Affairs, who acted as intermediaries between foreigners and Iranians. The Kargozari, therefore, reflected both the privileged position of foreigners in Iran and the tiered legal system in Iran.

Privately, the British thought that the Iranian cabinet had lost their minds, a thought reinforced by the knowledge that the Iranian cabinet had debated going further and nullifying all British concessions as well. Formally, the British replied that the announcement could not 'affect the existing status of foreigners in this country'[52] and determined that the action was 'null and void'.[53]

The delegation

In addition to discussing, determining and planning the nature of Iranian claims, the Iranian government set about picking the delegation which was to go to Paris. In much the same way that Vosuq al-Dowleh had been excluded from the commission whose responsibility had lain with Moshaver al-Mamalek and Iran's Foreign Office, he was also to be excluded from picking the delegates which Ahmad Shah undertook himself.[54] Ahmad Shah originally wanted his mentor and last regent Abol-Qasim Khan Qarazuglu, Naser al-Molk to lead the delegation.[55] When Naser al-Molk declined and Mostowfi al-Mamalek also turned him down, Moshaver al-Mamalek was chosen. The Shah's main concern was to send someone he trusted and someone who shared his views.

Ahmad Shah was very intent on not picking Vosuq al-Dowleh who was keen to go. Ahmad Shah disliked and distrusted Vosuq al-Dowleh whose premiership he felt had been forced onto him – not least because the British had lobbied heavily for him to become prime minister. The public line was, however, that Vosuq al-Dowleh was required to stay at home to deal with the considerable problems Iran faced,[56] but the British assumed correctly that the Shah did not trust him enough to let him go.[57] In fact, others in Iran's ruling elite also did not want Vosuq al-Dowleh to lead the delegation and representations were made to Ahmad Shah, asking him not to send Vosuq al-Dowleh to Paris.[58]

Moshaver al-Mamalek was third choice but he was also the polar opposite of Vosuq al-Dowleh. Born into a diplomatic family, his education included being exposed to foreign ideas at the Jesuit school in Trabzon. His reputation was mixed. On the one hand, he was characterized as a time server, sometime playboy and a man without diplomatic skills. His only advantage as a delegate seemingly was that he was fluent in French. On the other hand, he was considered a good, if mild, man, who conducted himself admirably in diplomacy and was a committed nationalist. He was also someone whom Ahmad Shah could trust.

The choice of Moshaver al-Mamalek, who was foreign minister, to lead the delegation was inconsiderate of British feelings. They had been keen for Vosuq al-Dowleh to go to Paris,[59] and when they did not get their way, they became even more unhappy with the choice of Moshaver al-Mamalek whom they considered a traitor.[60] The low opinion of Moshaver al-Mamalek, his abilities and political views were, if anything, to further harden after his role in securing help from the Germans at Brest-Litovsk.

To what extent the British felt that Moshaver al-Mamalek may have been a thorn in their political side, should he have remained in Tehran, is difficult to judge. However, if he were going to Paris then he might be isolated. This also aided Vosuq al-Dowleh, who may also have felt that it was useful to get the foreign minister as far away from Tehran as possible. Vosuq al-Dowleh mistrusted Moshaver al-Mamalek and it is probable that he feared his capabilities so much that he wanted to get him as far away as possible from Iran and prevent any obstruction by him.[61] In fact, Vosuq al-Dowleh may have considered the benefit of isolating the entire delegation which also included other non-desirables, such as Mohammad Ali Foroughi, in Paris.

Unfortunately, whatever the reasons, the choice of Moshaver al-Mamalek had two results. On the one hand, Ahmad Shah got to send someone he trusted and, on the other hand, Vosuq al-Dowleh was able to isolate Moshaver al-Mamalek in Paris, hamper Iranian progress at the Peace Conference and ensure that the delegation's work would suffer from the mutual distrust between these two men. As Moshaver al-Mamalek was not trusted by the British, it also meant that diplomacy between the Iranian delegation and the British in Paris would be strained from the outset.

In addition to Moshaver al-Mamalek, the core delegates were to be Mohammad Ali Foroughi, Mirza Hossein Khan Ala, Entezam al-Molk and Mirza Ali Qoli Khan who was to travel from Washington. In addition, Mohammad Ali Foroughi notes the following delegates also left for Paris: Rahim Khan, Ali Akbar Khan, Ashjeh al-Saltaneh. Added to these was ʹAbdol Hossein Khan (Moshaver al-Mamalek's son) and French advisor and jurist, Adolphe Perni.[62] Perni had come to Iran as a legal advisor in 1911 and would be largely responsible for the setting up of Iran's new legal system he would go on to form Iran's foremost law school. In all, some fifteen people left Iran as part of the delegation, though it is difficult to account for all of them.

Mohammad Ali Foroughi was a man of high intellect whose early career has been obscured by his more considerable role in the Pahlavi Dynasty. As an educator and prime minister under Reza Shah, his previous liberal leanings have been somewhat clouded by his extensive role in the Reza Shah government. His role in the Constitutional Revolution was characterized as an educator of the process of constitutionalism and an educator of members of the *Majles* rather than as a firebrand. In 1907, he published *Hoquq-e assasi (ya'ni) adab-e mashrutiat-e doval* (Fundamental laws or the rules of constitutionalism of states). This book described the notion of a constitutional monarchy. It went on to discuss the rights of the nation and the individual rights of the people – the freedom to live, have property, to have a home and a job, and to be equal in the eyes of the state and the law.[63] Though an elected member of the *Majles* for a number of years, Mohammad Ali Foroughi seemed more drawn towards the need to help establish the facets of a modern state and to educate people about it. At the *Majles*, he carried out administrative work and established the parliamentary library. By the beginning

Figure 5 One of very few images of Moshaver al-Mamalek. ©Public Domain.

of the First World War, he was minister of justice having also spent some time in the Ministry of Finance.

Mohammad Ali Foroughi was a committed nationalist. And, like many like-minded people, he had been part of the Constitutional Revolution which had ushered in a new political and social landscape in Iran. He had also seen the gains of the revolution buffeted by anti-constitutional forces and at times the bloody intervention of Russia. The First World War had seemed yet another hurdle to Iran's inability to institute change. Like others, Mohammad Ali Foroughi felt that the war had been a step backward in the construction of modern state structures and a strong centralized government. He felt that Iran had been unable to enforce its neutrality during the First World War because it did not have the structure and facilities at hand to do so.

Figure 6 From right to left: Mohammad Ali Foroughi and Mirza Hossein Khan Ala in Paris. ©Public Domain.

Mirza Hossein Ala, Mohammad Ali Foroughi's friend, inspired considerable animosity from the British. He had been educated in Britain when his father replaced Malkam Khan as minister. Returning to Iran after the Constitutional Revolution by the end of the First World War, Hossein Ala worked in the Iranian Foreign Office. After his work as part of the Iranian delegation in Paris, he became minister to Spain.[64]

As already noted, Mirza Ali Qoli Khan was chargé d'affaires at the Iranian Embassy in Washington. A nationalist, his political views had been nurtured by an affection for the role the United States might play in Iran. By this point, he had been in the United States since 1901. In 1915 he was appointed Consul General in

New York.[65] He married an American, Florence Breed, and remained in the United States for the rest of his life.

The nationalist credentials of Moshaver al-Mamalek and other delegates were also reflected in the hostility aimed towards them by the British. In addition to disliking Moshaver al-Mamalek, they regarded Mirza Hossein Khan Ala and Mohammad Ali Foroughi as patriots with 'visionary ideas as to Persia's ability to reform herself',[66] and likewise nationalist troublemakers. These delegates certainly exhibited common characteristics and ideals that bound them. Participants in the Constitutional Revolution, they were educated in the politics of the late nineteenth and early twentieth centuries and had developed views that encouraged sovereign independence. They were multilingual and able to translate European philosophy and modernity texts. They were active freemasons, which allowed them access to networks of European thought and reforms. Conversant with European philosophy, many had either travelled abroad or had been stationed abroad.

It is, at this point, worthwhile pointing out that though the delegates had been grounded in European philosophy and methods of modernization they were not innovators. They sought to adapt aspects of modernization to the Iranian paradigm. Mohammad Ali Foroughi was undoubtedly the leading Iranian intellectual in the delegation, but he was not a freethinker, nor able to elucidate an Iranian paradigm of change outside the European paradigm.

Vosuq al-Dowleh had been effectively sidelined from the planning process involved in sending a delegation to the Peace Conference. The choice of delegates and its leader had in fact caused a power struggle in Tehran, and though there had been different factions in government for some time it was obvious that this event caused a major cleavage in those who felt that Iranian progress was bound by sending a delegation to Paris and those who felt that another approach may be more likely to succeed. As we will see, this differing opinion was to hamper Iran's delegates in Paris. Vosuq al-Dowleh's only intervention in Iran's planning was to ask the delegation in Paris to direct its efforts to hiring foreign advisors and teachers to work in Iran. This included, as Mohammad Ali Foroughi recounted, French and American advisors and, if needed, even the re-hiring of Morgan Shuster.[67] The delegation was given extensive powers by Vosuq al-Dowleh to hire whomever they felt was necessary.

Foreign reaction to Iran's delegation and plans

The formation of Iran's delegation had come as a shock to the British, even more so when they discovered the makeup of the delegation. While they were not happy with the delegation, it seemed that they were caught off-guard by the firm and positive nature of Iran's intentions. Why this was the case is not easy to understand. After all, the British had some inkling during the war that Iran would, if possible, be at the Peace Conference. Immediately after the armistice with Turkey, Sir Percy Cox, minister to Iran, was informed of their decision to form a representative committee 'in regard to desiderata which Persia should seek from the Peace Conference'.[68] Barely three weeks later, Sir Percy Cox had an audience with Ahmad Shah, in which Iran's attendance had been raised. Ahmad Shah had told him that Iran's 'exceptional position in having been made a theatre of war by both sides' had made Iran's participation at any peace talks 'a burning question for Persians'.[69] On 20 November, in another meeting with a member of the Iranian government, Sir Percy Cox was given a preview of Iran's *desiderata*. These were listed in summation as:

1. Revision of treaties which had been forced on Persia.
2. Compensation for acts perpetrated on Persian soil.
3. Change of Customs Tariff and various other items.[70]

Sir Percy Cox, unable to confirm whether Iran would be able to go to the Peace Conference as a non-belligerent, equivocated. The British had so far held the line that Iran's acceptance at any Peace Conference would be a decision for the Peace Conference rather than themselves alone. Given this situation, it was now becoming obvious that Iran had to approach and get permission from all the Allied Powers.

On 21 November, Vosuq al-Dowleh submitted a formal memorandum listing Iran's demands to the French, British and US governments.[71] The memorandum was based entirely on the eight-point programme, the *Faqarat-e hashtganeh* and the work of the *Komisiyun-e ta'yin-e maqased va amal-e Iran* and would come to form the basis for all subsequent documents put forward to the Peace Conference in 1919. It listed Iran's *desiderata* as follows:

1. Persian government delegation to be admitted to the Peace Conference.
2. Annulling and cancellation of treaties, conventions and agreements which are in contravention to the territorial integrity and sovereignty of Iran. An undertaking and assurances to be provided towards safeguarding the future territorial integrity and sovereignty of Iran.
3. Iran to be indemnified for the losses inflicted during the war (reparations).
4. Economic independence of Iran.
5. Revision of treaties not cancelled and annulling of capitulations.
6. New commercial treaties and new customs tariff based on economic independence.
7. Revision of concessions not nullified.
8. The ratification of Persia's frontier lines and the restoration of Persian territory wrongfully taken.[72]

The version of the memorandum I have used was also sent to Iranian officials in Washington. Sent by Moshaver al-Mamalek to Ali Qoli Khan it also specified that, not only had been developed from the *Komisiyun-e ta'yin-e maqased va amal-e Iran*, but that its foundation was 'within the scope of the fourteen principles and conditions outlined by President Wilson'.

This memorandum also noted that the British had confirmed that an Iranian delegation would be received at the Peace Conference to 'furnish information whenever necessary, concerning matters relative to Persia'. Whilst not a ringing endorsement it certainly appeared that the British had acceded to Iranian demands to be accepted to the Peace Conference, though it seemed to depend on whether neutral states would be either admitted or called upon. Not put off, Ahmad Shah suggested that Iran be admitted along with Luxemburg as 'honorary members'.[73] The Iranians were certainly not in the mood to be put off.

In the meantime, the Americans asked for a more precise statement regarding the restoration of Iranian 'territory wrongfully taken' and received it on 7 January. Though Iran specified the restoration of territories in the Caucasus, they also mentioned that Iran was anxious to raise the recovery of certain islands in the Persian Gulf but stated that 'the Persian Government will probably not raise the question'.[74]

Despite the obvious wish not to antagonize the British, in view of not making a point about the islands under British control, the memorandum was not well received. The British moved to modify their position on Iran's attendance at the Peace Conference. Iran's attendance would now be subject to the agreement of other Allied governments.[75] Assuming that they would be unable to prevent Iran from going to the Peace Conference, the British began to assemble arguments to prevent them being heard.

On 17 December the British assembled a detailed internal memorandum outlining reasons why Iran should be prevented from attending the Peace Conference.[76] Access was to be denied on the basis that Iran had been non-belligerent during the First World War and that Britain wanted to be free to 'settle our post-war policy directly with the Persian Government'. The memorandum continued to describe the need for an Iranian policy, that reflected the security of India, and therefore any policy that promoted stability was ideal. If access to the Paris Conference could not be rebuffed, then various contingencies were also mooted, which included mandate powers – a mandate which, if politically acceptable, could be operated by the British but otherwise by a small 'neutral' power such as Belgium who might defer to Britain. All discussions regarding reparations for war damage and changes to Iran's borders were to be strenuously resisted and their status quo observed. Sir Percy Cox was to avoid any discussions regarding Iran's *desiderata*.

Less officially, the minutes of an Eastern Committee revealed Lord Curzon's antipathy towards an Iranian delegation going to Paris.[77] He confessed 'that Persia's claims with regard to the Peace Conference excite in me a good deal of irritation', and declared that Iran's claims were both feeble and untenable. He went on to declare that 'the ground she [Iran] alleges is that although she has not been a belligerent, her country has been the prey of warring armies, that she has been invaded from the West, and that she has suffered material damage' was not relevant as neutral countries would not get a hearing. Finally, he declared that most of Iran's proposed *desiderata* had nothing to do with the Peace Conference at all.

Lord Curzon's views on Iran's participation in Paris, more than any other, would do the most damage to Iran's participation at the Peace Conference. What is perhaps more striking is the nature of his argument. His opposition to Iran being heard was such that he had no issue describing the very war-like situation Iran had faced as a non-belligerent and in my opinion confirming the very reason why Iran might have been heard.

The minutes of this entire meeting which considered the future policy of Britain towards Iran, and which arrived at no firm conclusion, serve as a testament to British views concerning Iran and their relationship with Iran within the imperial context. The most important voices heard at the meeting on 19 December, in addition to Lord Curzon, were Lord Robert Cecil (assistant secretary of State for Foreign Affairs), Lancelot Oliphant, Sir Charles Marling (ex-British Minister to Iran), Edwin Montagu soon to be Lord Montagu (secretary of State for India) and Sir Hamilton Grant (foreign secretary to the Government of India).

British concerns for Iran were described as based on the inability of a weak, corrupt and incompetent ruling class unable to pull the country out of ever-increasing disorder and chaos. The consensus was that the British had tried to help the Iranians in any way they could, without cooperation or benefit. Where the British were forced to engage with the Russians as in the Anglo-Russian Convention or militarily within Iran's territory, they had done so because they had been forced to. Iran could not be left to its own devices: 'We cannot for two reasons leave Persia to slip into ruin; first, because it would be absolutely fatal to her own future and prosperity and, secondly, because it would be scarcely less dangerous to ourselves.'[78] So, in addition to Lord Curzon's paternalism toward resurrecting or at least preventing greater and further Iranian decline were political, security and imperial implications of keeping a foothold in Iran.

Some of these conditions mentioned in the meeting were immediate and concerned the disposition of the British military in Iran and cordons to protect Afghanistan and British trade interests in the Persian Gulf as well as other economic interests such as oilfields. Less immediately, given the British intention to secure a mandate in Mesopotamia, there was the more general question of Indian security. Britain now had 'a double Indian frontier touching Persian soil'.[79] That is to say that 'Persia … has the Indian frontier on one side of her and what is tantamount to a British frontier on the other'.[80] The security of British interests in and around India could never, therefore, be damaged or determined by a failing Iranian state.

What is clear from the Iranian perspective is not only the disdain observed on Iranian efforts to modernize their country, but the policy of dealing with Iranian politicians who would serve as British lackeys. Moshaver al-Mamalek was not 'a candidate whom we should have chosen' to lead the delegation to Paris but that Vosuq al-Dowleh was someone who the British could do business with. In fact, Lord Curzon remarked that Sir Charles Marling had brought Vosuq al-Dowleh to the premiership. Sir Charles Marling's conduct in doing so, not noted in this meeting, had in fact been quite extraordinary. At one point, in his plan to bring Vosuq al-Dowleh to power, he organized and paid for demonstrations to close the bazaars. When this failed, he went further and arranged for armed demonstrators to close the bazaars.[81] Notably, the British were now conducting their affairs much like the Russians and rather brazenly manipulating Iranian politics more and more to suit their interests. While they noted that Britain's standing was probably at its lowest ebb in Iran, they did not consider themselves in any way culpable.

Meanwhile, in Paris, Momtaz al-Saltaneh had worked to promote Iran's *desiderata* and had on 18 November invited some of the elite French foreign policymakers to a meeting. This would include the French Foreign Minister, Stephan Pichon, directors from the Quai d'Orsay (ministry of Foreign Affairs) and Charles Bonin, the new minister to Iran, who had not yet left for Tehran. Nevertheless, when Iran's eight-point programme had been made public, the French reaction was mixed.[82]

The French reaction to Iran's *desiderata* was on the surface supportive of the British position. Lord Curzon himself reported that he had received a note, which represented the views of Mr Pichon, that Iran had no right to be represented at the Peace Conference and should 'not be allowed to interfere in the discussions in any way'.[83] Raymond Lecomte, the soon-to-be-replaced French minister to Iran, ridiculed Iranian initiatives and recommended that Iran be denied entry to the Peace Conference. Raymond Lecomte had spent longer in Iran than most French ministers. More famous for his role in the 'Eulenburg Affair' and as one of Philippe, Prince of Eulenburg's lovers, his role during the First World War had been to support the Allied cause. His successor, Charles Bonin, who had gone to the meeting in Paris, also objected. He also viewed Iran's territorial claims as not credible, though he did seem to agree with some determination towards a guarantee for Iranian sovereignty and integrity.[84] France did not have any strategic interests in Iran until after the war when Charles Bonin was to embark on an ambitious project to increase French influence.[85]

There seemed to be some consensus towards Iran's entitlement, towards reparations and towards some of Iran's territorial claims, at least in so much that these claims might weaken the Ottoman Empire. However, in the final analysis, the Quai d'Orsay expressed the belief that though some commercial treaties might be renegotiated, the Iranians were to be discouraged from sending a delegation.[86] France's resolution to stand by Britain, its erstwhile ally, at least in public was appreciated by Britain, yet one gets the sense that the French might have prospered from Iran going to the Peace Conference. The Iranian delegation may have provided a nuisance factor, which may have worked in France's favour given their fear of being shut out of the Middle East.

As the memorandum sent by Moshaver al-Mamalek to Ali Qoli Khan had predicted, the United States was much more supportive of Iran's plans. In early November, John Caldwell, minister to Iran, had suggested that, given Iran's suffering during the war, it was only right to settle the Iranian question and that 'Persia's hope is in America'.[87] Also, on 20 November, at a banquet for the American Relief Commission held in the *Majles*, Prince Firuz Nosrat al-Dowleh (1889–1937), then at the Ministry of Justice, had remarked to Sir Percy Cox that the United States had already maintained that they would help Iran at the Peace Conference in 'very general terms'.[88]

The activities of the American Relief Commission in Iran require some explanation. Americans had been active in Iran as missionaries and had established a good reputation amongst Iranians. As the employment of Morgan Shuster had shown, the Americans were seen as a friendly and benevolent people and importantly, as they had no commercial or political interests in Iran, the antithesis of the British and Russians. In time, attitudes towards the United States would change but at the end of the war, America's image amongst the Iranians remained high.

The American Relief Commission had been set up in 1918 to raise funds and operate relief programmes to help Iranians through the devastation of the war. The American Relief Committee or Persian Relief Committee, set up in 1916, had been working to alleviate the hardships of Iranians during the war and after and had received funds from the American Relief Commission. The Persian Relief Committee was in fact run by John Caldwell, the US minister to Iran. His 'missionary' work in Iran had not only blurred the line between diplomacy and his humanitarian vocation but had also informed his political outlook. He believed that Iran's grievance was 'greater than and differs from the sufferings of other neutrals'.[89] The American Relief Commission had been set up by Dr Harry Pratt Judson (1849–1927), an educator who saw the need to finance relief in Iran. He, according to the British, reported back to President Wilson.[90] It is interesting to note that both John Caldwell and Dr Harry Pratt Judson were to meet with the Iranian delegation in Paris.

It is possible that American misgivings regarding the British attitude towards Iran's wish to be at the Peace Conference may have begun as a result of the interaction of John Caldwell and Dr Harry Pratt Judson. Certainly, the Americans had early reservations regarding the British attitude and believed that the vague British welcome for an Iranian delegation in Paris would at some point become a sticky diplomatic matter, or even be overturned. However, the Americans remained cautious and, though sympathetic to Iranian overtures to be represented, were not going to make a final decision on Iran's attendance until President Wilson reached Paris.[91]

Iran's newspapers were also keen to discuss the diplomatic issues facing the delegation and its mission to Paris. One article in the newspaper *Iran* discussed the severing of the Caucasus from Iran at the point of the Russian bayonet as doing little to negate the *Persianate* connections between the two. The length of time under Russian possession had in no way retarded these bonds. If the years that had passed had made the repossession of these territories a fantasy, then how come Poland or the Ukraine, who had been under the Russian cosh for longer, were also able to achieve independence?[92]

The delegation goes to Paris

With time running out, the delegation was asked to make its way to Paris for the Peace Conference. Despite the amount of research and preparation which had been completed, the *Komisiyun-e markazi-ye ta'yin-e khesarat* had not been completed, undone by the huge commitment of reporting damages under the strain of a nation dislocated by war.

It had become obvious to the British and French that nothing else could be done to prevent the delegation from attending the peace talks in Paris. The trip to Paris was also not without its dangers as the delegation would be travelling through regions affected by violence, local uprisings and the ever-changing political landscape affecting the post-Russian Transcaucasian territories. Nevertheless, the British and French, instead of making the trip as difficult as possible, helped in any way they could.[93] The optics of not helping the delegation reach Paris, and inviting disaster, was to be one step too far.

The delegation, apart from the members coming from the United States and those in France, left on 17 December in two cars. Despite car trouble, the entourage reached the port of Anzali, helped by drivers lent by the British, via Qazvin and Rasht. They boarded the *Avetik* to travel to Baku. After a few days in Baku, they took a train to Ganjeh. From there they went to the small town of Poylu, then on the Azerbaijan/Georgian border and eventually reached Tbilisi on 1 January; then by train to Batum, which the British had recently taken over from the Ottomans. They boarded the ship *Malioa* and arrived in Istanbul on 5 January.

In Istanbul, the delegates ran into a political spat between Ehtesham al-Saltaneh (1863–1936), Iran's minister to Turkey, and the remnants of Iran's provisional government called the *Mohajeran*. The *Mohajeran*, a motley crew of *Majles*

Figure 7 One of few images of most of the Iranian delegates photographed in Istanbul. All sporting the Fez which was very popular in Iran at the time. Picture includes Adolf Perni, Mohammad Ali Foroughi, Ehtesham al-Saltaneh and Mirza Hossein Khan. ©Public Domain.

deputies, newspaper editors and members of Iran Gendarmerie had all been supportive of the Germans during the war. They viewed the Germans as a hedge against the British and Russians and were keen to safeguard Iran's independence if the Central powers were to win the war. However, when Russian forces sped towards Tehran, they had left the capital to go to Qom and eventually made their way to Istanbul.

The delegates were enjoined to pleadings by Mirza Soleiman Khan, Adib al-Saltaneh and in particular Nezam al-Saltaneh, the head of the provisional government, that Ehtesham al-Saltaneh would not lift a finger to aid their repatriation to Iran. Mohammad Ali Foroughi was far from enamoured by Ehtesham al-Saltaneh's countenance and 'idiotic' arguments and was not impressed by al-Saltaneh's argument that the war had ended early because of his action – presumably in keeping the provisional government in Istanbul.[94] After a few days, the delegates left Istanbul on 15 January on a French naval dreadnought called the *Diderot* and reached France, docking at Toulon. Iran's delegation arrived in Paris on 23 January 1919 at 9.30 pm.

The journey from Tehran to Paris had at times been arduous, yet it would not have passed Mohammad Ali Foroughi's notice that their trip had been facilitated by British drivers and British help in securing hotel accommodations in Istanbul. The irony of using a Russian-built railway for part of the journey would likewise also not have escaped his notice. The trip had involved meeting Azeri, Armenian and Georgian bureaucrats and officials, which had given Foroughi cause to lament that they, rather than Iran, were better organized in the pursuit of their aims.[95]

Foroughi, who believed that the delegation should take any opportunity to speak to other interlocutors, was taken aback by Moshaver al-Mamalek's attitude. Moshaver al-Mamalek sought to avoid contact with others. In Istanbul, he instructed the delegates not to speak to the Azeri delegation to Paris who were also there. Moshaver al-Mamalek was reticent to involve the delegates in diplomatic discussions while out of touch with Tehran.[96] Mohammad Ali Foroughi, however, was starting to believe that al-Mamalek's passivity was at odds with the importance of their mission.

During the trip Adolphe Perni was to supply two sobering observations to Mohammad Ali Foroughi. The first was that the delegation's hope for success was limited by its leadership, Moshaver al-Mamalek, given that he was not liked by the British or the French.[97] While Moshaver al-Mamalek's reputation would play a part, it is inconceivable that the leadership would be given to anyone other than a nationalist. Perni's second point was to dissuade the delegates from putting forward political goals and to focus on economic issues.[98]

Conclusion

Iran's elite had determined, at one of the lowest points in Iranian history, that Iran's resurrection could be affected, or at least helped, by going to the Peace Conference in Paris. Iran had not only bought into and fully engaged with, the 'Wilsonian moment',[99] but, in Wilson's arguments for self-determination, had seen a route to escape what they reasoned was a lack of true independence and sovereignty.

The modern methods the Iranians had used to prepare and organize the delegation to the Peace Conference were nothing more than remarkable. Against the background of a war-torn country, they were able to develop the structure of a cogent nationalist plan which would be further refined in Paris. After many years of deference to Western attitudes and modernism, they were to use modern methods in pursuing their *desiderata*.

Iranian sources suggest that Ahmad Shah may have been far more involved in planning for Paris than previously appreciated. Vosuq al-Dowleh less so. A divergence in the strategy of the delegation and those of Vosuq al-Dowleh was beginning to be obvious as he was to have little to say in the planning undertaken by Moshaver al-Mamalek, and little to say in picking the delegation.

Iran's positive plan for the future had proceeded despite opposition from the British. However, it must be said that while generally hostile to Iran's proposals, British opposition had not really developed a head of steam. The memorandum which raised British opposition to Iran's *desiderata* in Paris was only sent the very day the delegates had left Tehran.[100] The meetings of the Eastern Committee had taken place as the delegation was en-route to Paris.

Official reactions by the French were in line with their ally, Britain, less than enthusiastic about Iran's *desiderata* and their mission in Paris. American sentiments were far more conciliatory and allowed Iran to hope that they might play a large part in the success of Iran's mission.

So far, the Iranian delegation had been given the necessary help and information with which to build the foundations for their diplomacy in Paris. Now the task was to both use and develop further the ideas and arguments into a more comprehensive and complete diplomatic strategy.

Chapter 4

SPRINGTIME IN PARIS

Contemporary British writers have not been kind to Iran's diplomatic efforts in Paris. One, in particular, painted an image of Iran's efforts as 'delegates [who] wandered about like souls in pain, waiting to be admitted through the portals of the Conference Paradise'.[1] As if researching amoeba under a microscope, travellers and diplomats were examined from far distant lands, who, seemingly, were only in Paris to add colour but otherwise get in the way of the real work of the Peace Conference, which was to bring a European peace.[2] It was certainly true that many of these countries, Iran included, had an inflated view of their own importance to their region and in fact to the wider world and that the British, French and others felt the most important work lay elsewhere. Yet, it was also true that it had been a 'world' war. If anything, it was the existence of European imperialism and colonial practices, both before and during the war, that had opened Pandora's box.

The Iranian delegation arrived in Paris and joined a whole host of non-belligerent but smaller 'nations' at the Peace Conference. These included Armenian, Assyrian, Azeri and Kurdish delegations, all of whom wanted to redefine their territories and borders. For most of these delegations, it could have meant independence and statehood. For all of them, including Iran, it would mean claiming contested territories.

January and February

The Iranian delegates were housed in numerous hotels around Paris. Mohammad Ali Foroughi was put up at the Hotel Mac Mahon near the Champs-Elysées. To his satisfaction, the delegates began work almost immediately. It was immediately decided that Mohammad Ali Foroughi would write Iran's request to be admitted to the Preliminary Peace Conference which was to be translated into French by Mirza Hossein Khan Ala.[3] Less satisfactory, to Mohammad Ali Foroughi, was that his opinion of Moshaver al-Mamalek had not improved. He criticized Moshaver al-Mamalek's passive nature, which he described as 'to sit and think and wait to see what cooked morsel will fall from the sky into his mouth'.

Nevertheless, Moshaver al-Mamalek seemed to have a clear strategy and methodology based around the eight points, the *Faqarat-e hashtganeh,* which could be enhanced by a diplomatic and public relations strategy. The first diplomatic contact was made when Moshaver al-Mamalek met with Jean Gout, the director of Eastern Affairs at the Quai d'Orsay. He gave Moshaver al-Mamalek a mixed interpretation of Iran's chances at the Peace of Paris. He suggested that though the Iranians would be listened to they would not be granted entry to the Peace Conference as neutrals, but would, however, be asked to join the League of Nations.[4]

On the same day, Vosuq al-Dowleh sent a telegram to Moshaver al-Mamalek asking him not to approach the conference to appeal for access. The Telegram declared:

> In the meantime, try to delay the recruitment of French teachers. Second, with regard to the negotiations that have taken place recently which in total could affect the whole plan, please do not start any negotiations that could impose any kind of undertaking on the government, until necessary instructions and information are sent to you soon. Third, please inform all the delegate members to follow this.[5]

Though not clear which negotiations Vosuq al-Dowleh was referring to, the work of the delegation, nevertheless, ground to a halt before it had really got going. Two days later Moshaver al-Mamalek responded to Vosuq al-Dowleh in a telegram eschewing the time delay and loss of impetus.[6] On 1 February another telegram was sent to Vosuq al-Dowleh which ended with the phrase 'waiting for instructions'.[7] Further telegrams on 3 and 6 February from Moshaver al-Mamalek to Vosuq al-Dowleh explained how the Iranian cause was losing impetus with Iran's suspension from negotiations and how others, in particular the Saudis and the Kurds, appeared to be making progress and their *desiderata* may be resolved without Iran being heard.[8] In one telegram the strain seemed palpable as Moshaver al-Mamalek declared that he saw no point in staying in Paris if he was not allowed to carry on.[9]

On 7 February, at an informal meeting that Moshaver al-Mamalek attended, Lord Balfour proclaimed how pleased he was that the Iranian government was in talks with the British government in Tehran.[10] A dumbstruck Moshaver al-Mamalek, who had heard nothing from Iran, did not let on that he hadn't a clue what Lord Balfour had been talking about and that he had been kept out of the loop.[11] In his diary, Mohammad Ali Foroughi recounted the unease that flowed through the delegation as this news had come on top of the telegram which had brought their work to a standstill. Mohammad Ali Foroughi, and presumably the other delegates, had seen Sir Percy Cox's fingerprints all over the telegram and believed he was behind it.[12] Moreover, the members of the delegates had always had their suspicions of Vosuq al-Dowleh and his predilection towards the British. They now feared the worst and felt that their work would be undermined and that the British would feel even less inclined to help the delegates.[13] In an unguarded moment even Moshaver al-Mamalek described Vosuq al-Dowleh to the rest of the delegates as a man of many faces.[14]

On 7 February a disconsolate Moshaver al-Mamalek wrote to Vosuq al-Dowleh and recounted the meeting with Lord Balfour.[15] This prompted an immediate reaction from Vosuq al-Dowleh who replied that discussions regarding the recruitment of advisors had taken place with the British and intimated that discussions regarding the eight-point programme should continue in Paris.[16] Further communications discussed the issues concerning the hiring of foreign advisors and the development the delegates had made in their arguments around the structure of the eight points. On 14 February Vosuq al-Dowleh wrote to Moshaver al-Mamalek, lifted the pause in negotiations, but also suggested that he did not call a halt to negotiations in Paris in the first place![17] The telegram from Vosuq al-Dowleh, lifting the brief hiatus, was followed by a series of telegrams by Moshaver al-Mamalek in which he deprecated the loss of time and initiative.[18]

This episode in which Vosuq al-Dowleh had, for the first time, intervened in the work of the delegation in Paris is critical when assessing the role of Vosuq al-Dowleh in both in Paris and his role in negotiating what was to become the Anglo-Persian Agreement. One interpretation has been that Vosuq al-Dowleh was in fact running a dual-track approach: negotiations in Paris and in Tehran directly with the British. This outcome is in line with recent research in which Oliver Bast rehabilitates Vosuq al-Dowleh's role in 1919.[19] Yet, if this was the case, then why would Vosuq al-Dowleh wait so long to confirm his instruction to Moshaver al-Mamalek?

The communication between Moshaver al-Mamalek and Vosuq al-Dowleh has been difficult to parse, given the more direct prose of Moshaver al-Mamalek and the elliptical responses of Vosuq al-Dowleh. It is certainly possible therefore that Vosuq al-Dowleh had not in fact called a halt to all negotiations but just those concerning the recruitment of advisors and that he had expected the delegates to carry on developing ideas and negotiating with foreign diplomats on Iran's eight-point agenda. But again, why wait so long to confirm it?

In truth, as his later telegrams to Moshaver al-Mamalek will show, he had little if any faith in the delegation's chances of success but did consider the delegation useful as a nuisance factor in his negotiations with the British. It is more probable, therefore, that Vosuq al-Dowleh had intervened in Moshaver al-Mamalek's brief in Paris to keep pressure on the British during deliberations in Tehran, negotiations which had only barely begun, rather than running a two-track approach.

An appraisal of the telegrams of this period points towards the interpretation that there were significant disagreements between Moshaver al-Mamalek and Vosuq al-Dowleh, and that Moshaver al-Mamalek had disregarded instructions from Vosuq al-Dowleh.[20] Given that Moshaver al-Mamalek was Ahmad Shah's choice it was more than likely that they were in communication with each other. If not, then Moshaver al-Mamalek was simply following Ahmad Shah's directions given to him before he left Iran.

The animosity between these two men also played a considerable role in the fractured communications between them. Though Vosuq al-Dowleh has been accused of not keeping Moshaver al-Mamalek sufficiently informed, Moshaver al-Mamalek was also guilty of not keeping the Iranian cabinet informed.

Communications between Vosuq al-Dowleh and Moshaver al-Mamalek were limited and terse, though we need to recognize that the process of affecting diplomacy via telegrams was, in those days, not easy. It is certainly true that communication did suffer from telegrams which may not have arrived at their intended target. In the final analysis, Moshaver al-Mamalek was Ahmad Shah's man,[21] and not Vosuq al-Dowleh's. Mistrust and a certain level of paranoia were not limited to Vosuq al-Dowleh and Moshaver al-Mamalek.

Also evident from Mohammad Ali Foroughi's diary was the level of mistrust between the delegates themselves and Mohammad Ali Foroughi vented his many opinions of his co-delegates as well-meaning but intellectually ill-suited to the endeavour. He liked Moshaver al-Mamalek as a person but questioned his diplomatic abilities and considered him too complacent to run the delegation. He thought Moshaver was guilty of keeping information to himself and not acting quickly or stridently enough when needed. He viewed Mirza Ali Qoli Khan, the minister to the United States, as too pro-American and working for closer ties with them. Altogether, he believed that many of the delegates had their own agendas.

Mohammad Ali Foroughi's greatest dislike was reserved for Momtaz al-Saltaneh, the minister to France, who also served as part of the delegation. It had seemed curious that Momtaz al-Saltaneh had reported nothing regarding the negotiations in Tehran even though he had a long meeting with Lord Balfour before Lord Balfour had met Moshaver al-Mamalek.[22] Momtaz al-Saltaneh had also reported that Stephen Pichon had no wish to see the delegation,[23] something that was made possible just a few days later. Labelled an egotist, Mohammad Ali Foroughi's dislike eventually led to hatred of the Iranian minister in Paris; Momtaz al-Saltaneh was considered a spy reporting directly to Vosuq al-Dowleh and therefore the British. There is some justification for this view as the British seemed to know what was going on in real time.

This conspiratorial atmosphere would have been considerably heightened if Mohammad Ali Foroughi, and other delegates, had known that Vosuq al-Dowleh was routinely showing their telegrams to Sir Percy Cox in Tehran.[24] The Iranian delegation had gone to some lengths to ensure secrecy by using a separate cypher for telegrams received in the Iranian Legation in Paris. However, the Iranian Legation in Paris was deciphering these telegrams and sharing them with the British.[25] The British also believed that there were leaks from their negotiations in Tehran.[26] From Mohammad Ali Foroughi's diary this would seem unlikely as the perceptions of the delegations towards the possibility of direct negotiations with the British in Tehran had been evident or at least feared for some time.

It is a matter of conjecture as to how much the interregnum between 28 January and 12 February had affected the work of the delegates. Mohammad Ali Foroughi had certainly carried on working and it is likely that he had finished Iran's request to be admitted to the preliminary Peace Conference during this period. This would come to be known as the *Requête adressée par le Gouvernement Persan à la Conférence des Préliminaires de Paix á Paris afin d'être admis à y participer*. During the interregnum there were frequent debates as to whether they should simply go ahead and present the request and inform Tehran as it was being done. Such was the fear that the delegation's work would be stopped in its tracks. Despite the delegation's assessment of Vosuq al-Dowleh's treachery they would not go that far. Moshaver al-Mamalek, the consummate diplomat, however disillusioned, would not countenance further action without a go-ahead from Vosuq al-Dowleh.[27]

In fact, though no official contact was made regarding Iran's entry to the Peace Conference, the diplomacy had continued. Moshaver al-Mamalek met with Stephen Pichon on two occasions. It was Stephen Pichon who urged him to put in Iran's *desiderata* as soon as possible.[28] He, along with Momtaz al-Saltaneh, also met with the French President Raymond Poincaré,[29] who promised to assist Iran. It may be that both Stephen Pichon and Poincaré were keen to meet with Moshaver al-Mamalek, less to help the Iranian delegation, than to gain intelligence regarding the Bolshevik threat to Iran.[30] After all, Stephen Pichon had originally shown scepticism towards Iran's *desiderata* or had at least taken the government line. There were, however, wider implications.

Both Pichon and Poincaré were members of the loosely knit *parti colonial* (colonial party). Less a party than a pressure group, it included politicians, members of the civil service and journalists. It was also a formidable force in French politics which did much to drive French policies abroad.[31] Stephen Pichon's career was an example as to how interwoven the activities of someone in high office was with extra-governmental colonial activities. Stephen Pichon had been foreign minister between 1906 and 1911 and resumed his work in the *parti colonial* by joining the *Comité de l'Orient* and *Asie Francaise* – two colonial pressure groups. He was also to become president of the newspaper *Le Petit Journal* and by doing so joined a whole host of newspapers owned and run by those affiliated to the *parti colonial*.[32] Sometimes the connections were more direct. Jean Gout, one of the first Frenchmen who had met with Moshaver al-Mamalek, was the director of Eastern Affairs at the Quai d'Orsay and a leading civil servant, and at the same time was also a member of *Asie Francaise*.

The French Prime Minister Georges Clemenceau who had become president of the Peace Conference was not a member of the *parti colonial*. Clemenceau's political priorities lay with Europe rather than anywhere else. Not only did Georges Clemenceau not have an interest in Empire but he had little interest in the middle eastern question. It is therefore of little surprise that the Iranian delegation would fail to see Clemenceau in February, but only got their chance when Clemenceau's relationship with the British was being affected by the issues of imperialism and colonialism in the Middle East. For the time being the delegation was restricted to meeting members of the *parti colonial*, who occupied key positions in the Quai d'Orsay and had colonial ambitions, and by their nature saw the British as an obstacle to French initiatives in Syria and possibly Mesopotamia.[33]

Nevertheless, at this point, while the Middle East was an integral part of the relationship between Britain and France, the contemplated break-up of the Ottoman Empire had not yet been discussed. Yet, as the delegation continued discussions with members of the French government and the *parti colonial*, it was becoming even clearer that the path to success for the Iranian delegation in Paris lay with the Americans and not so much the French. Following Moshaver al-Mamalek's meeting with Jean Gout in which Iran's ambitions had seemed reduced, Mirza Hossein Khan Ala met with John Caldwell, the American minister to Iran, who had made his way to Paris.[34] Moshaver al-Mamalek was keen to understand the American point of view.[35] John Caldwell, who had professed that Iran's wartime issues and sufferings had been so great that Iran was in a category of itself, supported Iran.[36] Still, the delegates had reservations. Not so much about American support but whether American ignorance of Iran might be utilized by the British to prevent their involvement in helping the Iranians achieve their goals.[37] Despite this underlying feeling the delegates had no choice but to work as best they could within the diplomatic limits that existed. They continued to seek greater intervention from the Americans.

The delegates met Sidney Edward Mezes, a member of the American delegation, at the Hotel Crillon. There, the delegates re-counted the negotiations in progress in Tehran and this prompted Dr Mezes to declare that he would see what he could do to help.[38] Subsequently, meetings with Edward Pratt, a previous envoy to Iran, and Edward House (1858–1938), President Wilson's trusted and influential advisor, paved the way to President Wilson. The meeting with Edward House, who understood the magnitude of the importance of the East, had been of particular importance as it had opened the diplomatic door to the president. Moshaver al-Mamalek was finally able to introduce himself, and other delegates, to President Wilson at an opera given in his honour. While the *Damnation of Faust* had helped to break the ice, Moshaver al-Mamalek had already met with the president's formidable wife, as had other members of the delegation.[39]

On 11 February, the telegram, in which Vosuq al-Dowleh had allowed the resumption of the delegates' activities and its approach to the Peace Conference, prompted invitations to be sent out for a formal reception at the Iranian Legation for a mixture of French ministers of parliament and officials, politicians, journalists and others who might be influential in Iran's cause. That same evening, Moshaver al-Mamalek met with President Wilson who encouraged him to press for access to the Peace Conference and promised that Secretary of State Lansing would do what he could to help.[40]

On 14 February the Iranian delegation officially applied for entry to the Peace Conference. Enclosed with a letter was a four-page document entitled *Requête adressée par le Gouvernement Persan à la Conférence des Préliminaires de Paix á Paris afin d'être admis à y participer.*[41] This document described Russian aggression towards Iran before the First World War, from the Treaty of Turkmanchai through to Iran's trials during the Constitutional Revolution. It then outlined the struggle Iran had faced at the beginning of the war to enforce its neutrality and how the Ottomans and subsequently the Russians had ignored it. Ultimately, Iran's neutrality ignored; Iran had become a theatre of war and suffered as a result. Finally, the document argued that given what had happened to Iran, it could not be compared with a neutral country, which had been pro-Allied, but which had not suffered at all. Some Allied powers had already indicated that Iran would be heard and Iran hoped that this promise would be kept and that Iran would be able, given the new era of justice, to find its own route towards reform and progress.

Mohammad Ali Foroughi had clearly not taken on board his conversation with Adolphe Perni in which it was suggested that the delegates should ignore political goals and concentrate on economic issues. The necessity to prove the devastation that had been wrought on Iran should have weighted more heavily than long past history which the Peace Conference was unlikely to want to repair. What is also apparent is the lack of data to support Iran's contentions. While it is true that the *Komisiyun-e markazi-ye ta'yin-e khesarat* had not been completed before the delegates had left Iran's shores, work had continued. Just two days after Iran's submission, Moshaver al-Mamalek received a telegram that itemized the material damage and deaths caused by Russia and the Ottomans.[42] In hindsight, had they known that this information was forthcoming, the delegates would have been advised to wait and incorporate the data.

The Iranian government in Tehran had, in an attempt to help the delegate's cause, published some of this data in the Iranian newspapers of the day. Even the outgoing French Minister to Iran, Raymond Lecomte, who had earlier ridiculed Iranian initiatives and recommended that Iran be denied entry to the Peace Conference, remarked that Iranian claims for reparation may be justified. He did, however, query the inaccuracies which may have existed in the list of damages.[43] So far, the Iranian government had accounted for a figure of 378,000,000 tomans, roughly equating to 126,000,000 pounds.[44] Much of this, 262,000,00 tomans, was accounted for in the region of Azerbaijan and made up purely of damages attributable to the Russians and Ottomans. At this stage, these figures included only material damages but even so it was not clear how these figures had been arrived at. Raymond Lecomte may have had a point. The telegram mentioned that the cost of casualties and deaths would follow in time, though these may have had even shakier methodological foundations. In June the Iranian Legation in Switzerland claimed that 30,000 Iranians had perished during the First World War.[45]

Moshaver al-Mamalek had met with the Italian Prime Minister, Vittorio Orlando, earlier in the month and it was with the help of Baron Sonnino, Italy's foreign minister, that Iranian participation at the Peace Conference was put on the agenda on 18 February. However, when the Council of Ten met, Lord Balfour declared that the question of Iranian participation did not arise as they had not been belligerents.[46] The question of belligerency and non-belligerency on which the British relied, at least when it came to public pronouncements, was, given the nature of the First World War, a strange method of deciding entry to the Peace Conference.

Other countries such as Belgium and Luxemburg had also been non-combatants but had been nevertheless the scene of much carnage. If Belgium could be allowed in, then why not Iran? If not Iran, then why Brazil who had joined the war in 1917 after several of their ships had been sunk by German U-boots. If neutral states such as Sweden were left out of the negotiations, what then when neutrality was violated by both sides? Equally, Iran, as a neutral country, had been afflicted far more than China which had gone to war but had suffered little.[47]

George Brandes, who had met Hasan Taqizadeh at the annual meeting of socialists in Stockholm on 15 August 1917, had also published *The World at War* in the same year. In a chapter devoted to Iran, he declared Iran the 'Asiatic Belgium', drawing comparisons between the fate of Belgium and Iran during the First World War. He disparagingly compared British promises to respect Belgium neutrality and how the British were unprepared to protect Iranian neutrality. He saw Iran forsaken for petroleum and the imperial needs of the British Empire.[48]

Despite some support from those on the left such as George Brandes, the delegates had to confine themselves to winning, the moral rather than the practical argument. The British had found a viable justification for preventing the Iranian delegation access to the Peace Conference. Yet, in truth, any argument that worked was enough to leave the question of what would happen to Iran post-war a British preserve. The fact is that not even the British believed in the argument which they had put forward. In a British government publication, a handbook for Iran, they concluded that Iran 'had suffered almost as much as Belgium'.[49]

Occupying some of the moral high ground was not going to be enough to achieve its objectives. It did, however, help to cement the distrust that the Americans felt towards the British and their machinations in keeping the Iranians a distance away from the Peace Conference. On the 19 February Moshaver al-Mamalek met with Robert Lansing again who offered American assistance and willingness to support Iran's request to be heard.[50]

The last two weeks of February were characterized by a delegation operating in the shadow of talks they believed were going on with the British in Tehran behind their backs. No telegram of note had been received from Vosuq al-Dowleh after his earlier and decisive intervention. Operating in these paranoic circumstances the delegation had nevertheless asked to be received at the Peace Conference and had made themselves known in political circles. Much of the time was taken up by further work on Iran's territorial claims and how they may be impacted by the claims from neighbouring ethnic nations.

The Iranian delegates, receiving news from the Transcaucasus through French newspapers, were forced to keep one eye on the various delegations that had made the trip to Paris. The delegates met with a representative of the Kurdish delegates, Sharif Pasha. Mohammad Ali Foroughi reported that Sharif Pasha had feared that his dream for an independent Kurdistan was becoming unstuck, caught as it was between the political and regional competition between Britain and France. Such were his fears that he was becoming more willing to accept the domination of Iran.[51]

This was certainly welcome news to the Iranian delegation but not as much as when they saw *The Armenian Question Before The Peace Conference*. The delegates had feared the political and diplomatic traction the Armenians had been receiving in the press and amongst the Americans. Massacres of Armenians during the First World War had resulted in considerable support in America and large sums had been raised for Armenian relief. A Christian ethnicity in the Caucasus naturally had support amongst the European nations. However, in the event, Armenian territorial claims largely excluded territory which Iran either held or claimed.[52] This 'gift' to Iran which included territory in which Armenian inhabitants were not insignificant was certainly a puzzle.[53] The Azerbaijani delegation, which Moshaver al-Mamalek had previously not wanted to meet with, was, at this point, still stuck in Istanbul waiting for visas.

It is tempting to see many of the *desiderata* that these nations were beginning to consolidate as being static but they were always evolving and were not only a factor in long-term desires but more immediate necessities. The Caucasus, which incorporated the aspirations of the Kurds, Armenians, Azeris and indeed the Georgians, were still in the process of constructing their borders and declaring their sovereignty. Despite separate nationalistic impulses, the early months of 1919 had resulted in improbable multi-ethnic associations. The hastily constructed Transcaucasian Federation, provided protection in view of the collapse of the Russian administration and military in the region in view of new-found Ottoman aggression, had brought together the unlikely federation of Georgia, Armenia and Azerbaijan (see Map 3). Nationalist urges had been put aside to fight off the Ottomans. The federation was not to survive the ethnic nationalist urges nor the political realities; the Azeris felt a kinship with the Muslim and Turkic speaking Ottomans, the Georgians preferred to go it alone and seek an alliance with Germany. That left the Armenians alone, depleted and weak, and therefore no match for the Ottomans.

Georgian independence was announced on 28 May, though it was as a protectorate of the German Empire. The announcement was long on the question of democracy, independence and neutrality, but was short on territoriality. In fact, Georgia's territory was not mentioned at all.[54] The Azeris and Armenians declared independence on the same day with declarations short on detail. In June, Georgia entered the region of Borchalo, which she claimed as its territory but which included Armenians and Azeris as well. This showed, in a nutshell, the issues that ethnic nationalism in the region faced, while ethnically separate the territorial living arrangements were not. In a real sense, the Georgians, Armenians and Azeris were all captive to the Iranian, Ottoman and Russian Empires, which had enabled these people to move around.

None of this would prevent the Georgians, Armenians and Azeris from claiming territory which was open to dispute. In Paris, Georgia's claim to Borchalo, a region just above lake Gokcha (Gokchai), was also claimed by Armenia; the Azeris would claim the corridor towards the Black Sea, which included Batum and which the Georgians considered theirs. Also, the Kurds in Paris would claim a homeland that the Iranians wanted to bring under their control. Such were the claims and counterclaims which coloured the national territorialization of the Caucasus.

March and April

On the first of March, Moshaver al-Mamalek wrote to Iran that he had not heard about the deliberations in Tehran and explained the necessity of knowing what was going on in Tehran so that the delegation made no diplomatic miss-steps in Paris.[55] There is certainly some logic to this. Vosuq al-Dowleh's attitude in not apprising Moshaver al-Mamalek again speaks to the fact that the diplomacy followed in Paris was never intended to be in concert with Vosuq al-Dowleh's own initiative in Tehran.

On 5 March, Mohammad Ali Foroughi briefly met with M. Pierre Crabites. He had written a lengthy document under the pseudonym Pier Patton entitled *Why The Peace Conference Should Requite Persia's Wrongs*.[56] The meeting was so fleeting that it is reasonable to suggest that though the delegation might have been happy with the production of this document, they had laid no claim to it. This polemical document set out how the 'primordial rights of the Persian people'[57] had been violated and appealed for help from the international community. M. Pierre Crabites was an interesting character. An American judge working in the Egyptian court system, he had developed considerable anti-British sympathies which he was happy to indulge in his writings.

The delegates continued to discuss and debate Iran's territorial *desiderata* in early March. These territorial claims were in fact still debated when they finally found a suitable cartographer to produce a map which was to be presented along with *Claims of Persia before the Conference of the Preliminaries of Peace of Paris*. In fact, the map was still being adjusted in content as the cartographer drew it. The basis for the territorial claims was the same as the maximum, moderate and minimum territorial demands worked out in Tehran. The choice of which to use had been left to the delegates who were the final arbiters of the political climate in Paris. Yet even so, the territorial claim up to the River Jayhoun and unspecified claims in the north-west were creating a rift in the Iranian delegation. Both Moshaver al-Mamalek and Mohammad Ali Foroughi thought these claims were excessive but Mirza Hossein Khan Ala won the argument.[58] In retrospect, Mohammad Ali Foroughi was to consider Iranian territorial claims as far too exaggerated. It was a position, he recalled, that Hasan Taqizadeh had also agreed with. Yet, even so, it was clear to him that some claims had to be made, and despite the grandiose nature of those claims, that they may yet bear fruit.[59]

On 8 March Ali Qoli Khan had invited the American ambassador and the entire American delegation to a dinner. The reception made the papers in the United States and at least one article reported the bonhomie between Iran and the United States. It was reported Robert Lansing had 'expressed the hope that Persia and America would join hands in building a new structure that will be eternal.'[60] An ecstatic Moshaver al-Mamalek reported back to Iran that in response to Ali Qoli Khan's speech in which he highlighted the friendship between the two countries, Robert Lansing was said to reply: 'No one in America, but in the world, wishes for the prosperity of Iran and its nation more than the President. He is and will be Iran's friend, and Iran can rely on this friendship in order to achieve its goals of peace and benevolence towards nations.'[61] Certainly, the warmness of the Americans seemed at variance to that of the British but as Ali Qoli Khan pushed the idea that Iran should look to the United States for advice and help, Mohammad Ali Foroughi remained concerned that a move towards the Americans would be both disapproved of, and opposed by, Britain, and even possibly France.

One reason why the question of a greater role for the Americans had such import was because Ahmad Shah had sent a direct message, outside the usual channels, asking the delegation to come to an agreement or accord with the Americans.[62] This stunning intervention can only be attributed to the Shah somehow getting wind of Vosuq al-Dowleh's negotiations with the British in Tehran. The delegates, as Ahmad Shah's agents in Paris, were happy to explore this. So far discussions with the Americans had been concerned with gaining access to the Peace Conference. In addition, one aim of the Iranian delegation was to foster closer ties with the French and Americans and specifically to sound them out regarding financial advisors.[63] But now, Moshaver al-Mamalek was to investigate establishing closer ties with the Americans on a much deeper and wider basis.

From the British archives one can see that the question of the United States playing a larger role in Iran had in fact also been raised separately by Moshaver al-Mamalek. At some point he must have asked Vosuq al-Dowleh for clearance to approach the Americans and see if they would be open to playing a greater role in Iran. This communication was received by Vosuq al-Dowleh who showed it to Sir Percy Cox and quickly shut down this approach.[64] Vosuq al-Dowleh's reply to Moshaver al-Mamalek explained that there was no point in substituting one enemy with another, Germany with America, and said that the whole cabinet and his majesty forbade it.[65] Of course, Ahmad Shah had specifically asked for the Americans to be approached. It would appear that there were notable exemptions to Vosuq al-Dowleh's blanket refusal.

Nevertheless, despite being warned off, it was the Americans, in the form of Edward House, who invited the delegation to a meeting discussing the impending formation of the League of Nations.[66] The delegates were now hopeful that they would secure a seat and it was decided that Mohammad Ali Foroughi would begin to write an address to the League of Nations in the event of membership being concluded. Debates on what this address might entail also included who might give it. In fact, no decision had been made as to who should go to the meeting. The letter had been received by the Iranian Legation but the idea of Momtaz al-Saltaneh representing Iran, rather than Moshaver al-Mamalek, was not that appealing given the suspicions some of the delegates had of him.

The delegate's exuberance regarding the invitation was tempered by a visit by Sharif Pasha who declared that the British had intimated that an independent Kurdistan might be possible after all.[67] In view of an earlier discussion with Moshaver al-Mamalek, in which it had been assumed that the Kurds would attach themselves to Iran, this came as a shock. Mohammad Ali Foroughi, rather than reasoning that this change might have been the result of a further evolution of British strategies, chose instead to blame Moshaver al-Mamalek for his naivety.[68] It was another sign of the shifting sands in which the Iranian delegation had to work in.

As the delegation was making some headway with the Americans and to a lesser extent the French, they were getting nowhere with the British government. Not only had the delegation been an unwanted distraction for the British but they had made no effort to meet with the delegates. It was obvious that the delegates were to be hampered by this attitude and Moshaver al-Mamalek had reasoned on several occasions that a trip to London might be worthwhile. Lord Curzon reasoned that there was no point in seeing the head of the delegation when negotiations were going on in Tehran.⁶⁹

British irritation towards the Iranian delegation was to become more intense in March as they sought to rebuff greater American involvement. Whilst Vosuq al-Dowleh had shut down the approach towards the Americans, he had, however, sanctioned the delegation to hire teachers from France. The hiring of French teachers had been stopped by the same telegram in which Vosuq al-Dowleh had told the delegation to stop its diplomatic activities a few days after they arrived in Paris. The hiring of French academics to teach in Iran had been normal practice as the Iranian educational system had been broadly set up on French lines. Again, the timing presupposes that Vosuq al-Dowleh's telegram had more to do with putting some pressure on the British in his negotiations with them.

In any event, no British opposition existed towards Iran becoming a member of the League of Nations. In a meeting over 20 and 21 March, designated for 'Neutral Powers', Iran became a founding member of the League of Nations. Moshaver al-Mamalek, in a telegram to the Iranian Foreign Ministry, reported Iran's diplomatic success in this regard and disclosed his wish for Iran to be one of four countries, which together with five supreme governments were intended to form the executive committee.⁷⁰

Iran's rather automatic membership of the League of Nations stood at odds with the limited credence its independence and sovereignty had generated in Paris amongst the Allies. Iran's status not great enough to have its *desiderata* presented to the Peace Conference but significant enough to be a certainty at the League of Nations. The Arabs, led by Britain's pick, Sheikh Feisal, who ostensibly represented innumerable tribes, were seen by the Big Four. Deemed belligerent, yet quite obviously without a state, Arab needs were discussed but the needs of an existing country such as Iran were not.

The standards for achieving an equality within an international consensus, which were political, were different to those for membership of the League of Nations which relied on the definition of civilization. Iran was able to tick enough boxes to achieve a very Western definition of civilization, even though, in all probability, it failed to provide proof of being a 'stable government' with 'settled frontiers'.⁷¹ In Mohammad Ali Foroughi's address to the League of Nations, which was not in the event required, he tuned into the league's definition of civilization. He presented Iran as a Western bulwark against Eastern hordes. Iran was not only culturally important to the West but vital:

> The war is over, the Allies have won. The epoch of justice and humanity in political history has begun. What will happen to Iran? Iran's three thousand year old civilisation has alone been the substantial citadel, who in ancient times, resisted the attacks of the Huns and Turanians and protected the Western world from the danger of their barbaric attack – a bright torch which shone through the gloom, illuminating Europe during the Middle Ages through science, art, philosophy and literature.⁷²

And of course, the defenders of civilization were none other than the great dynasties and Iranian Empires of the past.

Shortly afterward Iran's document, itemizing its claims in greater detail, was finally submitted to the Peace Conference. Rooted around the general classification of the political, economic, judicial independence, reparations and the correction of borders, Iran's eight-point programme, *Claims of Persia before the Conference of the Preliminaries of Peace at Paris,* remains the most concise and important of Iran's communications in its endeavour to be admitted to the Peace Conference.

Claims of Persia before the Conference of the Preliminaries of Peace at Paris was split into two sections. The first section, *Claims concerning political, juridical and economic independence,* demanded the following:

1. In seeking independence and sovereignty it annulled all conventions, treaties and precedents. This included the 1907 Anglo-Russian Convention, the Note of 1910 prohibiting the granting of concessions and capitulations contrary to the interests of Russia and Britain and the 1911 Ultimatum which had committed Iran to not hire foreigners without the permission of Britain and Russia.
2. That all other treaties with foreign countries and concessions with foreigners be subjected to revision in line with Iran's political, juridical and economic independence.
3. That foreigners to be taxed as Iranian citizens.
4. That Iran be able to revise and institute her own customs tariff.
5. That foreign powers abstain from extending protection to Iranian subjects and abstain from intervening in Iran's internal affairs and that the armed forces of foreign powers and their consular guards be withdrawn from Iran.

The second section discussed Iran's territorial claims and the revision of its borders in some detail. In the Transcaucasus (see Map 5), it included the return of all Muslim territories above the river Aras lost to Russia in the Treaties of Golestan and Turkmanchai. This corresponded to the 'moderate' demand in the Caucasus. In the Transcaspian, it included the entire territory between the Amou Darya (Oxus River) and the Attrek River. This corresponded with the maximum *desiderata* in the Transcaspian (see Map 4). In the west, all Turkish Kurdistan.

Claims concerning political, juridical and economic independence was no less than a nationalist blueprint to regain Iran's independence and sovereignty whilst retaining Iran's imperial past. Here nationalism is located within an idea of Iranian territory,[73] and a domain of Empire not circumscribed by ethnicity. When the delegates describe that the territorial limits of Iran have 'natural limits' and 'natural frontiers',[74] situated between the 'river Amou Darya, the Caucasus Mountains, the river Tigris and Euphrates and the Persian Gulf',[75] they are describing the territorial imagination of Iranian Empire. Little in fact had changed since John Chardin, a traveller to Iran, who in 1669 described both the real and ethereal frontiers of Iran. At the time he described Iran's borders as

reckoning from *Georgia*, reaches from the 45th degree latitude, which is the farthest Extent on the North side, as far as the 24th Degree along the River *Indus*, on the Southern Side, and from the 77th Degree of Longitude, towards the Mountains of *Ararat*, on the West, as far as the hundred and twelfth Degree over against the *Indies* and *Tartary* on the East.[76]

Moreover, these natural limits operated in a band around the centre which expanded and contracted as the fortunes of Iran's Empire had. John Chardin also comments on the elastic nature of Iran's borders – the Iranians always considered the re-growth of their Empire to 'to the full Extent of its ancient Boundaries … the Black Sea, the Red Sea, the Caspian Sea, and the Gulph of Persica'.[77] Any other description would hinder 'Contests about Limits of Dominion' and that 'Persian Geographers cease not, however to stretch their Empire out, in their most modern Descriptions, as far as those Boundaries'.[78]

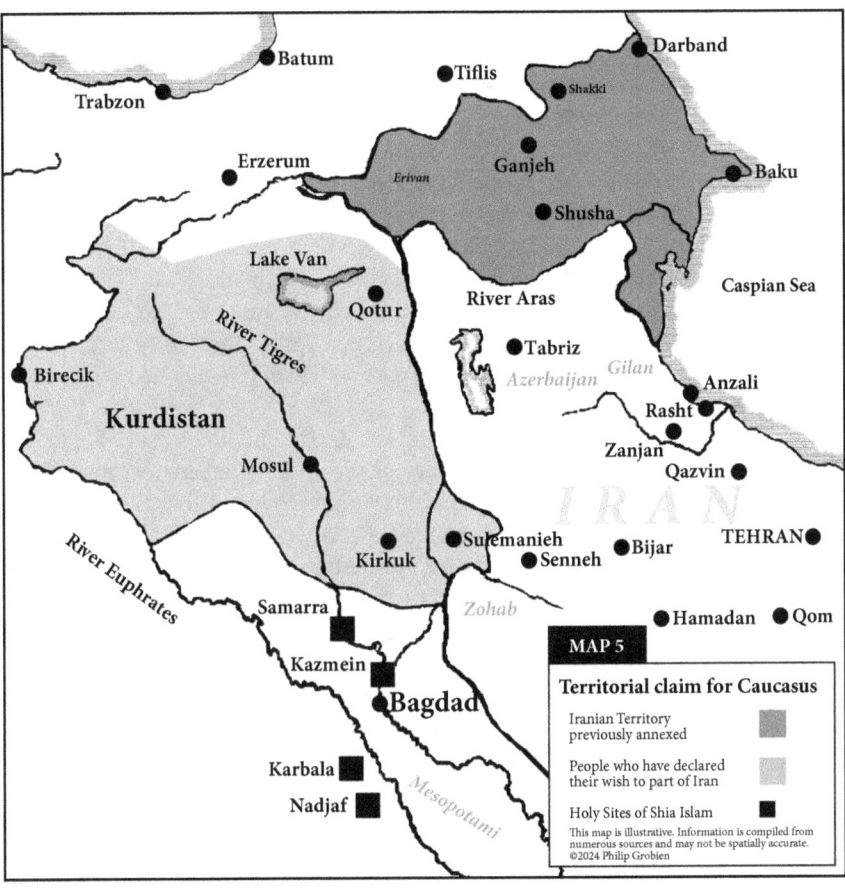

As Iran's Empire, past or present, had a natural feel about it so did the people who occupied the Empire. Fittingly, the definition of the peoples of this Empire was also fluid and flexible. *Claims of Persia before the Conference of the Preliminaries of Peace of Paris* explained: 'The majority of the inhabitants of this region have always been of the Iranian race; the empires founded in this country have always been considered Iranian Empires.'[79] But what constituted the 'Iranian race'?[80] Certainly, as far as these territorial claims went, an 'Iranian race' included ideas of culture, language and religion, though not always at the same time. In amalgamation they approximated to notions of cultural unity described by Marshall Hodgson as *Persianate* and harked back to the cultural paradigm espoused in the *Shahnameh*, hinging on the legends and myths of Iran's imperial past.

In *Claims of Persia before the Conference of the Preliminaries of Peace of Paris*, the demand for the Transcaspian hinged on the 'Persian language' being widely spoken, though it is not clear if this was Persian or another derivative. From a cultural standpoint it was observed that several Iranian poets had come from the region. Where this classification was inadequate, as in the case of the Turkomans for instance, tribes were claimed because they were affiliated to other tribes within Iran. Strangely, the demonstrable link between the Turkic-speaking people of Iran and the Qajars, who were of Turkic descent, was not made.

The Transcaucasus was claimed on the basis of religion, which suitably redefined the Christian Georgian provinces as outside the Iranian Empire. Parts of the Transcaucasus that were to be returned to Iran were claimed based on history, geography, economics and commerce, and culture. Surprisingly, Iran's territorial claims against Turkey were quite limited. It firmly included the territory around Suleimanieh, which Ottoman Turkey had received after the Treaty of Erzerum, and the Kurdish territories under Turkish control which Iran claimed on the basis of language, race and religion.

Iran claimed the religious but not the territorial rights to the holy Shia cities and shrines in Mesopotamia. Whilst annexing more Ottoman territory might have been in keeping with Iranian strategies, they only requested that their 'interests be safeguarded' when the time came to 'adjust the Mesopotamian question'.[81] In practice, this meant that Iran sought a consultative role when it came to the Shia religious shrines. The delegates' reticence to include these territories may have been a nod towards British plans for the region.

The response to *Claims of Persia before the Conference of the Preliminaries of Peace of Paris* was swift, uncompromising, and detailed in a series of internal communications over the next few weeks. Lord Curzon's comprehensive reply to Lord Balfour discounted the methodology the Iranians had used to justify reparations and restitutions as misleading and inaccurate. Curzon was also scathing when it came to describe the issue of border restitution, surmising that they were inflated in such a way as to enable eventual agreement on a smaller scale. This was indeed confirmed in a conversation between Moshaver al-Mamalek and Arthur Moore (1880–1962),[82] who had reported as a journalist in Iran during the Constitutional Revolution and who was returning to Tehran to become the correspondent for *The Times* in the Middle East. The claim to the eastern Transcaspian, based on language and culture, was also disparaged by Lord Curzon on the basis that it was occupied by fanatical Sunni tribes that Russia had barely managed to subjugate and that the Iranians had not the military capacity to contain.

On the Caucasus and the lands lost under the Treaty of Turkmanchai, Lord Curzon argued that the mixed population of Turks, Armenians, Georgians, Tartars and Kurds was out of touch with Shia sympathies. From a political point of view the possibility of oil-rich Baku under Iranian misrule was not a serious question that the British would even countenance. Lord Curzon's points regarding the Caucasus were to be mirrored when it came to the Kurds, who, though of Iranian stock, had no 'vestige of Persian national feeling'. It is likely that Lord Curzon was probably already aligning the Kurds as part of the 'Mesopotamian solution', which was to be a British mandate. The issue of Iranian influence regarding the Shia shrines in Mesopotamia was also dismissed.[83]

The only sliver of hope was that Lord Curzon seemed to approve the return of the Russian Sarakhs to Iran (see Map 4). It is presumed that this did not include new Sarakhs but the immediate region around it. Sarakhs was a village divided by the river Tejen. It lay within a break in the mountains in the north-east of Iran, near a village called *Dahan-e Zulfiqar*, and given its proximity to the town of Mashad gave any army, but in this case the Russians, almost unfettered access to Iran and British interests in Afghanistan. The Russians had in the 1880s taken over eastern Sarakhs and had proceeded to bring in 200 Turkmen families to live there and eventually settled a small colony of Russian families of German descent.[84]

Lord Curzon's criticism of Iran's territorial *desiderata* would have not seemed out of place in any political discussion between British politicians of the time. Commentators, particularly those who had low expectations of Iranian politicians and the Qajar dynasty, could not see past these condescensions. Yes, there were exaggerations and *desiderata* which may have seemed out of place but criticism, in reality, revolved more about covering British motives and Britain's own plans than a realistic appraisal. Even so, as Iran's diplomacy during this period has been marginalized or camouflaged by research heavily weighted towards the Anglo-Persian Agreement, this criticism appears to have lingered.

One renowned historian, Firuz Kazemzadeh, also labelled Iran's claims as 'fantastic' and declared that the claims 'showed a complete lack of understanding of the historical forces which were shaping the destinies of the world'.[85] Yet the same forces, which were, in this case, operating in Azerbaijan, Armenia and Georgia, were also the same nationalist forces that were operating in Iran. Lord Curzon's criticism revolved around an Iran which was making demands that had no foundation in fact. Surely if Iran's *desiderata* utilized opportunistic foundational justifications, then so did Lord Curzon's criticisms.

The British defence towards Iran's *desiderata* was only self-serving and amounted to a well-judged smokescreen to enable Britain to be the only and final arbiter of what would happen to Iran. Only one criticism stands some credibility when one assesses Iran's *desiderata* and that is how Iran could protect new territory when she could not protect what she had. Even here one could argue that none of the nations and would-be nations around Iran could protect themselves either and any protection may not be necessary if European empires had not involved themselves in the region.

In any case the Iranian delegation would have been largely ignorant of the specificity of British inter-governmental criticism as there was little if any communication between the two sides in Paris. In ignorance of the consequences of their programme, they simply continued. Much of Iranian attention continued to be directed towards the Americans. Just a day before the publication of *Claims of Persia before the Conference of the Preliminaries of Peace of Paris,* on 22 March, Moshaver al-Mamalek went to see Robert Lansing and gave a preview of Iran's *desiderata*.[86]

There is no doubt though that the delegation was feeling the pressure and, with reason, was feeling more paranoia. A telegram asking the delegation to desist from forming more concrete ties with the Americans had depressed the delegates'[87] and had led to the assumption that the Iranian government was fully under the British thumb.[88] Towards the end of March one interchange between Moshaver al-Mamalek and Vosuq al-Dowleh was a poignant reminder of the circumstances in which the delegates found themselves and the divisions between the two men. In a rare expression of honesty and directness Vosuq al-Dowleh wrote, using the development of railways and mines as an example,

> We cannot do without their [British] help. That is why your Excellency is not welcome in London. From the beginning they were suspicious of your Excellency and some members of the delegation. I was therefore worried about the chances of success of your Excellency's mission, and I did what I could to remove this suspicion. Recently I have discussed the necessity for Your Excellency to go to London by negotiating with the Ministry of Foreign Affairs, but their answer is that they are ready to assist as long as their advice is considered in good faith; If we know that your officials do not agree with us, how can we help? You say that England cannot use its former power in Iran and that we should not panic. I don't believe this. It is not necessary for England to exercise power in Iran ... if England cuts off financial aid it gives to the [Iranian] government, America or France cannot object; but immediately, the security of the shaky country ... will be disrupted. If it wasn't for British assistance, the government would not have even managed to send a delegation to Paris. I write frankly that the pursuit of a policy that attracts more than this suspicion of the British will not only make your Excellency's mission ineffective, but will also accelerate the risk of disintegration and the disappearance of total independence. I write frankly that the pursuit of a policy that attracts more than this suspicion of the British will not only make Your Excellency's mission ineffective, but will also accelerate the risk of disintegration and the disappearance of total independence.[89]

Vosuq al-Dowleh's assessment of himself as a *realpolitiker* gives us a preview of his motivations for the Anglo-Persian Agreement. Moshaver al-Mamalek's reaction was emotional as he saw this as an attack on his probity:

> So it becomes clear that the opponents and the hypocrites, who have never imagined anything but selfishness and their own interests, have made it appear that I and the members of the delegation have become indiscreet and imprudent in our work, and it is because of this, that we have conceivably attracted British antagonism and brought dangers to the country.[90]

Despite the pessimism the delegates felt, they nevertheless carried on with the job of maintaining Iran's diplomacy in Paris. On 31 March Hossein Ala and Mohammad Ali Foroughi attended a meeting at the *Comité National D'Études Sociales et Politiques,* an intellectual pacifist think tank which promoted international arbitration and the League of Nations post-World War.[91] The meeting was entitled 'The National Aspirations of Iran'.[92] Participating in this meeting, the delegates were, not for the first time, attempting to appeal to intellectuals across the political spectrum. Distinctly left-leaning, the *Comité National D'Études Sociales et Politiques* had been created in 1916 by banker and philanthropist Albert Kahn. The organization sought to provide a forum for intellectuals and others 'to reflect on the organization of the post-war world'.[93]

By early April the delegates' gloom had not lifted. Considering themselves slaves of the British, they continued to feel that their intentions and actions were being circumscribed and restricted.[94] As access to the British was not a possibility the delegates agreed to renew their efforts specifically aimed at the French and Americans.[95] On 3 April the delegates discussed a new telegram from Vosuq al-Dowleh which had just arrived.[96] In it Vosuq al-Dowleh explained that British opposition to Ahmad Shah's trip to Europe had been influenced by the actions of the delegates in Paris.[97] Now, in addition to being told not to firm up political connections with the Americans and being called an unwanted and problematic sideshow, preventing a more open dialogue with the British, they were now accused of making it difficult for their sovereign to travel to Europe.

In truth, much of this was window-dressing and the British had resolved to do what they could to prevent Ahmad Shah from going to Europe anyway. Sir Percy Cox and Lord Curzon had done what they could to dissuade Ahmad Shah from coming to Europe, firstly to prevent collusion with the delegation in Paris and secondly to prevent a magisterial parade to the presentation of the delegations' *desiderata*. However, now that the Iranian delegation seemed even more isolated and moribund, the British were beginning to see that Ahmad Shah's trip to Europe might be beneficial. If the Anglo-Persian Agreement could be finalized, then a reception for Ahmad Shah in Britain could provide the icing on the cake to the agreement.

The last telegram received from Vosuq al-Dowleh had also criticized the foundational basis of *Claims of Persia before the Conference of the Preliminaries of Peace of Paris* which was strange as it was based on Iran's eight-point programme. Vosuq al-Dowleh seemed a man under pressure and took to venting his anxiety by blaming the delegation; how could the delegation put forward a *desiderata* which was at variance to the help that Britain could provide and how could the delegates be so antagonistic to Britain which was keeping Iran financially afloat.

Much of the ire seemed to be based on a meeting held between the long-serving Mehdi Khan Ala al-Saltaneh, minister to Britain, and Lord Curzon. Ostensibly a meeting to ask why Lord Curzon would not meet Moshaver al-Mamalek had turned into a description of the logical conundrum that the delegates found themselves. Once the delegates had either failed in enlisting other countries to their plight or managed to get a mandate, they will have no choice but to come to Britain for help and then Lord Curzon would receive them.[98] As these criticisms were conveyed to Moshaver al-Mamalek, he was forced to defend his mission and his response made a few points. Deprecating the chaos caused by the lack of unity between Tehran and the delegates, he declared that the Iranian delegation was doing exactly what it was asked to do. If Britain was a friend to Iran, then why would it prevent Iran's access to the conference?[99]

Moshaver al-Mamalek's sense of isolation was if anything confirmed when he finally met with Lord Charles Hardinge on 16 April.[100] Lord Hardinge was under secretary to the Foreign Office and worked for Lord Balfour. The discussion, in which Iran's independence and territorial aims were discussed, was frustrated by Lord Hardinge who declared that nothing would be decided until an agreement was achieved in Iran. Moshaver al-Mamalek was told that there was no likelihood of raising the question of their participation again, though Iranian views, however, might be noted if the need arose. When Moshaver al-Mamalek then proposed a more direct negotiation with Britain he was told that such a meeting would depend on the progress of negotiations in Tehran. Moshaver al-Mamalek was simply rebuffed when he asked what those negotiations were about.[101] Beneficially from the British point of view, Lord Hardinge was not able to throw light on these negotiations as they were in the hands of Lord Curzon. One of the delegates notably declared that it seemed the harder they pushed the greater the British pushed back.

There can be little doubt that the British felt that they could control the French and this seemed to be borne out when the delegates decided to influence the French and resubmitted *Claims of Persia before the Conference of the Preliminaries of Peace of Paris*. According to Oliver Bast, the French were not totally against Iranian representation at the peace conference even if they resisted it publicly[102]; nevertheless the re-submission of Iran's *desiderata* had no effect at all.

To what extent the British were able to control the Americans is open to debate. The Americans, once again, proved more receptive than the French and Moshaver al-Mamalek managed to press his claims again directly with Woodrow Wilson.[103] The British had already been concerned by Iranian approaches to the American delegation and these concerns increased further when the subject of a meeting with Secretary of State Robert Lansing (see above) was brought up by Lord Curzon when he met the Iranian minister to Britain on the 23 March. He informed the shocked minister that a 'direct attempt to interest the United States in the financial and administrative future of Persia had been made'.[104]

Indeed, the Americans were open to helping Iran again. On 23 April President Wilson brought up the question of Iran's participation at the Council of Ten meeting and remarked that Iran had appealed to him directly. He complained that Iran had not been admitted nor had their request had even been replied to. Lloyd George responded by temporizing and answered that 'Mr. Balfour was opposed to the admission of Persia' but he did not know the reasons.[105]

In the same month, Hasan Taqizadeh made a speech in the Hague in which he supported Iran's agenda for independence and freedom within a new international order. He declared, 'Persia is still able to contribute to the peaceful progress of civilization, if she is given a chance, which means no more than freedom'.[106] One cannot be certain about ongoing communication between Taqizadeh and the delegates in Paris; however, it is safe to assume that there was some dialogue between Taqizadeh and Mohammad Ali Foroughi. Taqizadeh's speech, therefore, was timely and was probably intended to jump-start Iran's diplomacy in Paris.

Controlling the narrative

Despite the lack of success in overcoming British objections, the Iranian delegation had set out to spread its intentions far and wide in an effort to gain acceptance for their plans. They, and, in particular, Mohammad Ali Foroughi, took every opportunity to speak to both national representatives of countries far away and closer to home, including the Armenians, Kurds and Assyrians. They met with suffragettes, socialists and Russians – both White Russians and Bolsheviks. At the same time, they met with writers and politicians such as Maurice Barres (1862–1923), who had considerable anti-Semitic views and was a proto-fascist.[107] They also met with numerous French academics, such as the archaeologist Marcel-Auguste Dieulafoy (1844–1920), who had worked in Iran and had become helpful as a source of advice.[108]

The eclectic nature of the people that the delegates met was part of the delegates' strategy but belied a broader interest. The delegates showed a voracious appetite for the cultural, educational and political landscape that lay in front of them. They also took the opportunity to introduce themselves to the local masonic lodges, including the small but prestigious lodge, *La Clémente Amitié*, and exchanged membership lists.

They spent a considerable time and effort visiting and reviewing the French educational system, which included various university departments. They were invited and some went to the *Pasteur Institute* and the *Académie des Sciences*. The visit to the *Pasteur Institute* was of considerable interest given the influenza pandemic in 1919 which had also affected Iran. Subsequently, a branch of the *Pasteur Institute* was opened in Tehran in 1921. They went to the obvious museums such as the *Louvre* and *Musée d'Ethnographie* but less obviously to the *Phare de France*. They enjoyed the botanical wonders of the *Jardin des Plantes* and the zoo of the *Jardin Zoologique*.

Mohammad Ali Foroughi and the other delegates spent a great time walking and enjoying the Parisian parks. They had beer at the famous pub and theatre, *La Taverne de l'Olympia*, and went to the famous *Café de la Paix* and *Café Dauphine*. They explored bookshops and even got involved in translating books. They went shopping for clothes and sent postcards home.

They visited numerous churches, including the Notre Dame Cathedral, and spoke to the Grand Rabbi of France. It is, however, their visits to theatres to see plays and operas which show the lengths they went to absorb what Paris had to offer. Operas included *La Traviata*, *Carmen*, *Tosca* and *L'Ami Fritz* [sic], based on the book by Émile Erckmann and Pierre-Alexandre Chatrian.

While the play *L'Aiglon*, based on the life of Napoleon II, was criticized for its acting by Mohammad Ali Foroughi, he was impressed with the dancing in the *Damnation of Faust*. The work of Molière was particularly sought after and they watched his comedies *Tartuffe* and *Les Femmes Savantes* and the satirical *Le Bourgeois gentilhomme*, and the tragedies of *Andromaque* and *Ruy Blas* by Victor Hugo and Voltaire's tragedy play *Zaïre*. In keeping with past and current attitudes towards Greek interpretation of Iranian/Greek history, Foroughi was less than impressed by *Les Perses* by Aeschylus which he considered rather pointless.

Mohammad Ali Foroughi was not averse to seeing plays with a sexual content including *Lysistrata*. They even went to the *Théâtre de l'Athénée* to see the racy and erotic *Le Coucher de la Mariée*, though it's not clear if they saw the play or the film which came out in 1899. Nevertheless, Mohammad Ali Foroughi did not appreciate members of the delegation buying erotic French postcards nor the fashion tastes of Parisian women which showed too much body shape. He does show distaste for the friendship which had developed between Moshaver al-Mamalek and a 'Polish woman'. Individual and personal growth was fundamental to the time they spent in Paris in 1919.

As discussed above, the delegates spoke to French politicians who were members of the *parti colonial*. They also meet journalists from *Le Journal, Petit Parisien* and *Le Petit Journal*, all of which were run by members of the *parti colonial*.[109] One journalist, who worked for *Le Journal*, called Monsieur Barbi, frequently met with the delegates, gave advice and was seemingly prepared to plug Iran's cause. Another, affiliated to the *parti colonial*, was Jean Herbette, a journalist and ambassador who had been to Iran with his wife. Jean Herbette was given Mohammad Ali Foroughi's preliminary work to look over and pushed the idea that the delegates should use social gatherings to aid the dissemination of Iran's *desiderata*.[110] On 8 February they had met with a journalist from *Petit Parisien*.

French newspapers of the time were very influential in promoting policies. However, despite the connections between the delegates and journalists from *parti colonial*, only one article of note was printed that supported Iran's cause. In fact, the ability to control the Iranian narrative in the newspapers of the day was not as effective as the delegates might have liked. In many cases, journalists demanded money to promote Iran's cause and, though likeminded, seemed more intent on meeting the delegates to pick their brains on the Bolshevik threat in the Middle East or the role of the British – both of which might threaten French plans in the region.

In the event, it was one of the heavyweight daily's, *Le Temps*, which jumped to Iran's cause. *Le Temps*, also directed by members of the *parti colonial*,[111] blamed Iran's problems not on its own lack of ability but primarily on Russian, but also British intervention, in the country. Despite Iran's inability to bring any military might to bear, bringing Iran on the side of the Allies would have opened up a better route with which to supply the Russians during the First World War. They note that Moshaver al-Mamalek had made an approach to join the Allies in 1915. Given being let down in the past, *Le Temps* looked on Iran's request to be admitted to the Peace Conference with a great deal of sympathy as a just cause.[112]

The American press for much of the first month of 1919 concentrated on the issues of famine in Iran and the role of the American Relief Commission. The method of newspaper syndication which existed in the United States meant though that many articles were re-published by local newspapers throughout the country, hence bringing the question of Iran's future to a larger audience. Most news and editorials were reported in a neutral manner. However, on 1 January the Evening

Sun had made the perceptive point that though of little interest to other nations, Britain was uniquely interested in Iran's success in Paris.[113] They might have gone on to write that Britain was almost exclusively invested in the lack of success for Iran's delegates. *Claims of Persia before the Conference of the Preliminaries of Peace of Paris* sparked articles in April that discussed Iran's *desiderata*. The only obvious matter of contention mentioned was that Iran's territorial aspirations contrasted with those of the other nations in the Transcaucasus also demanding independence and territory. Armenia and its territorial desires would have to be fulfilled before those of Iran.[114]

British newspapers had noted the arrival of the Iranian delegation to Paris disparagingly but had noted little else in the first few months of 1919. While many newspapers toted the government line, one prominent liberal newspaper, the (Manchester) *Guardian* had taken on board Iran's agenda and written articles in their support.[115] In one article, the *Guardian* agreed with *Le Temps* that it was time for Britain to atone for being Russia's accomplice in Iran's misfortunes and that a place at the Peace Conference was fitting.[116] In March, in reference to *Claims of Persia before the Conference of the Preliminaries of Peace of Paris*, the *Guardian*'s Paris Correspondent declared that he could not see how Britain could object to Iran's *desiderata* since the military threat to Iran and therefore India was now absent and that any prevention of 'Persia's rights … would be a frank and cynical policy of greed or ambition.'[117]

The *Guardian*'s special correspondent in Paris, John Lawrence Hammond (1872–1949), journalist and social historian, was anti-imperialist and very receptive to Iran's wishes. Nevertheless, even he had been critical of a few points in Iran's *desiderata* – unsure whether Iran was ready for the 'abolition of extra-territoriality', i.e. to have foreigners under Iranian court jurisdiction. He was also not sure by what mechanism Iran could receive reparations or the efficacy and extent of its territorial demands. It was Iran's territorial demands that seemed ill-considered and ill-advised, not easily defended under the logic of self-determination and ambiguity.[118]

It was the question of territorial wants, also criticized in an acerbic article in the *London Times*, which had rattled the delegation the most. The Iranians, whose claims were 'fantastic and ridiculous', had demanded 'half the Middle East' while not able 'to keep order in her own capital'. In fact, it was claimed that Iran could have put together a strong appeal if she had concentrated on war damages rather than territorial aggrandizement. The article finished with a flourish of half-truths leading to the argument that Iran should be grateful for what Britain has done for it.[119] The *Times* article prompted Mohammad Ali Foroughi to vent that he had always thought that Iran's territorial claims had been too extensive and a distraction.[120]

In Iran, criticism of the delegation's *desiderata* was repeated in the Iranian press. *Ra῾d* reprinted an article from a British journal regarding Iran's future which argued that the Peace Conference could only deal with facts and not sentimentality. The propriety of such ideas and British commercial and regional aims was not lost on the journalists at *Ra῾d* who issued a rebuttal questioning the framework of the

Peace Conference.[121] In fact, Iranian appreciation of the workings of the Peace Conference was, in hindsight, closer to the truth. The conference was not working on logical lines but riven by the individual political necessities and rivalries of the Big Four. Agendas were created on whims and in truth Iran was a long way down on a list that Lloyd George successfully managed to exclude from discussions.

Conclusion

Despite the pause demanded by Vosuq al-Dowleh, it is likely that Iran's diplomacy in Paris, while retarded, had not been damaged. Iran's delegates had continued to utilize the modern methods in the development of the diplomacy of *imperial nationalism* as they had in its inception. Notwithstanding the suspicions and enmities that existed between delegates and between Moshaver al-Mamalek and Vosuq al-Dowleh, the delegates were able to develop intelligent arguments for reforming Iran as an independent and sovereign state, expressing Iran's *desiderata* through the newspaper media, organizing and attending as many receptions as they could.

The delegates made every effort to target the British, French and Americans directly or through the press. They were only partially successful with the French, making more progress with the *parti colonial* than with George Clemenceau. The delegates were far more successful with the Americans who appeared to embrace their arguments and *desiderata*.

Iran's ability to appeal to the British, over these first few months, can only be characterized as a failure. Lord Balfour saw no reason to countenance the furtherance of Iran's *desiderata* in front of the Big Four as it directly hindered British post-war plans. For good or bad, the British held the custodianship of Iran's progress. British arguments that Iran's *desiderata* were exaggerated and that its nationalistic impulses in an imperial context were too extreme to succeed were disingenuous. Iran's *desiderata* were 'fantastic' because it threatened British plans for Iran. This will become more apparent as we discuss the Anglo-Persian Agreement.

Despite a strategy that had been sanctioned at the highest levels, Iran's progress in determining its independence and sovereignty had been brought to the ground by a contemporary secret deal and old-style imperial hegemonic diplomacy. One could argue, as Mansoureh Ettehadieh has done, that the delegates were naïve to believe that the world had changed. One could also see this argument in reverse; Iran given the new world political outlook could not have produced anything else and that it was the British and the Vosuq al-Dowleh who had not understood that after the First World War, underhand deals which threatened Iran's independence would not be looked upon favourably by the international community.

Chapter 5

THE CAUTERIZATION OF INDEPENDENCE

The Iranian delegates had begun with great hope and had set about their business with both skill and vigour. The delegates were now sure of two political forces operating against them. Firstly, British intransigence was not just covert but was now very evident. Secondly, it was obvious that Vosuq al-Dowleh had been working on another diplomatic initiative that he felt might have greater success, but which was inimical to the work the delegates in Paris were committed to. Nevertheless, the delegates had continued to ply Iran's *desiderata*. Always cognizant that a peace treaty with Germany would signal the beginning of peace negotiations regarding the Ottoman/Turkish question, the delegates would need to be in a favourable diplomatic position before that happened.

May

Yet, the Iranian delegates were feeling increasingly powerless and isolated in Paris. No news, good or bad, was coming from Tehran. Given these circumstances the delegation felt that Vosuq al-Dowleh was merely waiting it out so he could negotiate with the British while the delegation got nowhere. They worried about being blamed whatever they did. They might spend a considerable time in Paris getting nowhere, pilloried for doing nothing, but likewise accused of a dereliction of duty if they left.

Building bridges with the British was discussed but the chances of any rapprochement seemed slim as they did not know what was happening in Tehran.[1] In the vacuum of information, suspicions and paranoia were never far away and the delegates became concerned that the British may even hinder Iran's membership of the League of Nations.[2] What course such an action may have taken was hardly clear. By this point the delegates were meeting prominent individuals who argued that the delegates had made a mistake by irritating the British and that they should do what they could to repair relations. A disrespected Moshaver al-Mamalek didn't see how he could now go to London.[3]

On 7 May President Wilson again brought up the question of Iran's participation. He reported that the Iranians were depressed as a result of not being consulted and that 'their interests were being considered'.[4] Lloyd George replied that Iran would be consulted when Turkey would be discussed in detail. 'He thought that Persia ought then to be heard.'[5] Nevertheless, the Americans seemed less than impressed by this answer. The next day, Henry Morgenthau, erstwhile American ambassador to Turkey, remarked to Mirza Hossein Khan and Moshaver al-Mamalek that the US delegation, including President Wilson, distrusted the Europeans when it came to Iran.[6]

On 9 May Mohammad Ali Foroughi met President Wilson at a social gathering and they discussed the problems Iran faced. It is not known exactly what was discussed but President Wilson had obviously been willing to be seen publicly with a member of the Iranian delegation – a tacit and public show of support.[7] President Wilson was also being courted by small political movements hoping to take advantage of Wilson's perceived affirmation of self-determination principles. Around this time, President Wilson had been sent a telegram from lawyers in Nakhchevan, seeking independence.[8] Nakhchevan, of course, had been part of Iran's previous Empire and had become Russian territory under the Treaty of Turkmanchai and the Iranians wanted it back (see Map 2). Iranian claims relied on their own concept of self-determination. They might have relied on despatches from Nakhchevan and other places for guidance, but these were subject to interpretation and a return to the Iranian fold was not for everyone.[9] Today, Nakhchevan forms part of the Republic of Azerbaijan but, as the Nakhchevan Autonomous Republic, a nod to its separatist tendencies.

Self-determination, on which much of Iran's arguments for sovereignty and *imperial nationalism* relied, was now to be used as a stick to beat Iran with. During May, the British had begun to realize that more cogent arguments against Iran's admittance to the Peace Conference needed to be prepared. For Lord Balfour, it was a question of criteria. How could Iran claim Russian Azerbaijan? The inhabitants of Azerbaijan were not Iranian in language, race or religion, and the whole situation was very different to Denmark's claim to Schleswig.[10] Such facile arguments could not stand up to scrutiny, after all most Azeris were of Shia faith and similar ethnic groups lived in Iran, not least in the Iranian region of Azerbaijan. Also, clearly, if this theory of self-determination was reversed, then one had to ask why Iran should not be broken up into its constituent elements.

Of course, it was not necessary for these arguments to stand up to much scrutiny as, in truth, the French and Americans had even less knowledge about the Middle East than Lord Balfour, or infamously, Lloyd George. Lord Balfour was, of course, simply fabricating layers of excuses that could be trotted out as and when Iran's participation would come up. The internal communication, in which these points were raised, argued that Iran might appeal for access to the Peace Conference if they became a mandate. Lord Balfour correctly surmised that this would never happen but significantly did not suggest by what mechanism territorial restitution could take place under a mandate. The opinion of Lord Curzon, though Balfour's junior in government, carried great weight when it came to Middle-Eastern issues, and he had, of course, already firmly ruled against a mandate for Iran.

And so it was that the buck and in fact any progress stopped with Lord Curzon. He, of course, refused to meet the Iranian delegation. This, even though he had gone to Paris on 20 May. A letter of introduction to no avail. On the four-month anniversary of the delegation residing in Paris, Lord Curzon left after one day expressing regret that an opportunity to meet the Iranian delegation had not arisen. Despite his opposition to much of the Iranian proposals, this lack of etiquette did not pass unnoticed. In fact, even the British press who saw the Iranians as largely a distraction to the important work of the Paris Peace Conference admonished Lord Curzon for not seeing the delegation. 'Discourtesy as a form of diplomacy' would not be tolerated.[11] Nevertheless, the British had decided that as long as he did not meet the delegation, then thorny questions regarding the British view of Iran's *desiderata* would not arise. In a parliamentary debate in the commons on 19 May, the Prime Minister, Lloyd George, having been asked whether the government had received or refused the claim of the Iranian delegates in Paris, replied that as the answer to first part of the question was a negative, the second part of the question did not arise.[12]

Some notable Frenchmen also kept their distance from the Iranian delegation. The outgoing French Minister in Tehran, Raymond Lecomte, had unbeknownst to the delegation, been to Paris and left again without seeking them out. The incoming Minister to Iran, Charles Bonin, was still in Paris and also avoided contact with the principal delegation for the country that he would be the leading minister for.

There was still little communication between the delegation in Paris and Vosuq al-Dowleh in Tehran. Finally, on 21 May, Vosuq al-Dowleh responded to a telegram from Moshaver al-Mamalek who had described the dire financial state of the delegates. Vosuq al-Dowleh explained that he had not replied earlier because the telegrams from Paris were not couched in terms that merited a reply and that money was short.[13] Nevertheless, Moshaver al-Mamalek did reason that money was needed for the delegation not just to live in Paris but also to promote Iran's *desiderata*, whatever that may be at this point. If the delegation could get in front of the Peace Conference, then what should he say?[14] An anxious Moshaver al-Mamalek wanted to be prepared as it had been clear for some time that the delegation's window of opportunity was fast closing, as the fates of the German and the Austro-Hungarian Empires had been decided.

The British vision

In the meantime, Vosuq al-Dowleh had been negotiating exclusively with the British – a negotiation which he told Moshaver al-Mamalek in February had been merely about the hire of advisors and which by this point had led to no agreement.[15] The British, led exclusively by Sir Percy Cox and Lord Curzon, had opted for the modernization and transformation of Iran under British control. The same memorandum, of December 1918, in which Sir Percy Cox had described practical initiatives to prevent the delegation in Paris from being successful, also formed the basis for a very British modernization of Iran.[16] In this memorandum, Sir Percy Cox reiterated his proposal outlined in early November 1918 to obtain a mandate for Iran.[17]

The idea for an Iranian mandate was roundly condemned by both the Foreign Office and the Government of India, a rare case of unanimity between the capital and India. The mandate question is important, not because anybody else other than Sir Percy Cox wanted one, but because it remained the fountainhead for the Anglo-Persian Agreement. Because, undaunted from being turned down, Sir Percy Cox issued another proposal, which he called 'extremely generous' but which was still remarkably similar to that of a mandate. Broadly, he proposed the reiteration of Iran's independence, abrogation of the 1907 Anglo-Russian Convention, the creation of a uniform military force, the appointment of a financial advisor and finally the withdrawal of British troops at the earliest opportunity.[18]

As Sir Percy Cox began discussions with Vosuq al-Dowleh, and two other cabinet members, Nosrat al-Dowleh and Sarem al-Dowleh (1885–1975), known as the Triumvirate, more detail was put forward by Sir Percy Cox expected an

> English financier with adequate powers together with staff including Treasurer-General, Adviser for Ministries of Interior, Public Works, and Agriculture and for Education and Law ... If possible we had much better have advisors associated with governor each major Province to advise Administration and supervise expenditure ... we must supply officers for internal force of thirty thousand men with head mission working nominally under Ministry of War but with practically independent Administration powers.[19]

Vosuq al-Dowleh's response has not been recorded. Lord Curzon voiced his approval. India, however, was far from impressed. The Viceroy, Lord Chelmsford (1868–1933), believed that the reforms were too comprehensive, went too far and 'may well prove too strong meat' even for the Triumvirate. Moreover, the deployment of British advisors had been ill-thought-out and smacked of a protectorate. He also saw problems with officering the new uniform force.[20] Sir Hamilton Grant (1872–1937), secretary of the Foreign Office for India, in a clear and concise memorandum that seemed to be at odds with Sir Percy Cox's almost hysterical desire to stamp British authority over Iran, discussed the options and strategies available to the British. Ultimately as those responsible for India had done many times before, he opted for a policy of limited assistance.[21]

Sir Hamilton Grant's opposition was, from someone who was part of the Foreign Office apparatus, stunning. Others also opposed Sir Percy Cox's plans which had the approval of Lord Curzon. Lord Montagu, secretary of State for India, had also objected to these proposals and would not contribute financially to a policy of which the Government of India and India Office did not approve. Though Lord Montagu's opposition was eventually softened by Lord Curzon, the point had been made.[22] All in all, the Indian side of the debate felt that assisting Iran on a more limited scale satisfied the overarching objective of keeping India commercially and militarily safe.

A more limited role for Britain in Iran would also soften the financial repercussions. Britain's financial debt following the First World War was considerable and it was clear that Britain could not go on spending as before. John

Maynard Keynes, in a memorandum, suggested that British expenditure in Iran was unsustainable.[23] But there were other, more parochial, considerations. The onus for paying for policies regarding India's security had frequently been on India whether they agreed with the policy or not. The India government repeatedly had to balance unexpected financial outlay with its own finance department.[24] Now, the Government of India was faced with paying for an extensive policy commitment, which was not only un-costed, but seemed like it would necessitate a huge financial outlay.

Lord Curzon had been 'taken aback by Mr. Keynes' note' which suggested that expenditure in Iran was exceeding 30 million pounds a year.[25] Most of which was spent on British military presence,[26] though this did include the monthly payment of approximately 350,000 tumans a month to the Iranian government. Still, Lord Curzon feared the political and commercial repercussions of a British withdrawal from Iran even more than financial overreach. He described any such idea to leave Iran as 'immoral, feeble, and disastrous'.[27] As Iran's financial plight had reached a point where it could not be ignored, in May, the India Office declared that India would not be content to send further payments to Iran unless they were secured on an interest-bearing loan which 'was adequately secured upon Persian public revenues'.[28] A subsequent meeting of the Eastern Committee appeared to cement this idea.[29] This now meant that any agreement between Iran and Britain could be secured by a loan on customs revenues.

Financing the current financial arrangements and future reforms in such a way was by no means unprecedented. Loans to Iran had been frequently secured on customs receipts. Britain had also determined such an arrangement as good practice. Where possible, colonial practice had been that financial assistance was to be self-financing.[30] Naturally, whilst the financing of Britain's extensive plan by this method meant that Iran would pay for it, in one way it also seemed to emphasize limited help – after all, the only person needed was a financial controller, who could make sure that Britain would get its loan paid back and who would facilitate all other reforms. Or as the Viceroy declared before the end of January, 'financial reform is the *all quo* of Persia regeneration'.[31] Now that Iran would foot the bill completely for British endeavours in Iran, despite his original concern, Lord Curzon had become quite relaxed with the financial implications of the agreement. Just a few weeks before, Lord Curzon had noted on a treasury memorandum that he believed he would be thanked by the Treasury when his plans were put in place.[32]

Lord Curzon's role in sanctioning such an elaborate scheme for Iran remains, at least for this writer, a point of contention. In his memorandum informing the rest of the government of the need for such an agreement, he declared that Iran's geographical position, British interests in the country and the safety of Britain's Eastern Empire all formed the basis for such a large intervention in the country. In addition, Britain could not permit 'between the frontiers of our Indian Empire in Baluchistan and those of our new Protectorate, of a hotbed of misrule, enemy intrigue, financial chaos, and political disorder'.[33] Peace and order were to be the backbone of both commercial and political security.

This does not explain why Lord Curzon was willing to go to such great lengths rather than a more limited scale of intervention, which the Government of India proposed. Why would a person so intrinsically bound into the fabric of Empire and the belief in the sanctity of Britain's Empire seek a root-to-branch reform of Iran? The quick answer would be that Lord Curzon did not think a limited intervention in Iran could be successful and that any person employed to become a 'financial controller' would fail much as Morgan Shuster had done. The logic would further go on to argue that at its root, the nature of the Iranian government, the various power centres and pervasive corruption would prevent further progress in the direction of reform.

The fuller answer lies in several related issues. Lord Curzon was a conceited man and was a believer in a paternalistic imperialism.[34] He believed that Iran could not be re-vitalized without British help. His hubris made him believe that he was the man to do this and that this was to be his legacy. If widespread reform could be achieved with no harmful effects to the British Empire, then how could it not be tried? Issues raised by India concerning the comprehensive nature of Britain's proposed involvement in Iran fall away when one understands that re-vitalization may have been one of Lord Curzon's primary aims.

In truth, Lord Curzon and Sir Percy Cox's 'vision' for Iran was only new in that it confirmed an over-arching and complete plan to finally resolve the 'Persian question'. Parts of the agreement were in one way, or another, discussed with Iran over the previous years and decades. These included the reform of the military forces in Iran, the supply of experts, and the provision of communication and transport infrastructure. All these issues had been caught up in the imperial politics of Britain and Russia and the *Great Game*. The withdrawal of Russia from Iranian politics had taken away an important obstacle to deal with these issues and had made a root-to-branch reform as possible.

The Triumvirate

One of the criticisms of the Anglo-Persian Agreement has been that it had somehow come out of nowhere and that Iran could suddenly be thrown into a new and new-fashioned paradigm. In truth, Britain and Iran had in fact been working towards such an association for years, though it had been a bumpy ride. This was especially the case from the turn of the century onwards. An association with Russia and Russian policies, cemented by the Anglo-Russian Convention, had painted the British in a bad light – an unfavourable situation, which the British and Sir Edward Grey, the foreign secretary at the time, had done little to ameliorate. Not for the first time, or the last, British policy towards Iran was defined by European exigencies and the view that it was necessary to keep Russia onside with the rise of an enemy, now not France, but Germany. Indeed, the Iranians had been perplexed and angry that a liberal Britain may have played such a negative role during the Constitutional Revolution.

The years during the First World War had done nothing to change these views. Yes, a diplomatic relationship with Britain had continued but it had been soured by Britain's close collaboration with the Russians – a collaboration that had embarked on joint financial control over Iranian finances and latterly, given the Russian revolution, after 1917, the sole prerogative of the British government. The British went out of their way to prevent Iran from borrowing from financial institutions, even British ones, and gradually built up financial control over Iran by owning its debt.

Arthur Hardinge had spent some time as a member of the British government as did the previously mentioned, but not related, Lord Charles Hardinge. A member of the British Legation in Tehran, his perceptions of British financial control over Iran are damning though may not have been representative of British policy. As the Indian government was contemplating a loan to Iran, in 1903, three years into his tenure in Tehran, Arthur Hardinge wrote to Lord Lansdowne, foreign secretary of the time, and described the importance of a financially penitent Iran: 'We must get Persia a little more into our debt and under our influence before we can negotiate for substantial gains.'[35]

Iran, which had lost control and revenues from many of its northern-western provinces because of the war, looked to the Anglo-Persian Oil Company (APOC) for royalty payments. However, during the First World War, Bakhtiari tribesmen, working on behalf of German agents, had blown up several oil pipelines. The APOC considered the Iranian government responsible and withheld royalty payments between 1916 and 1917. The disingenuous methods by which the APOC had derived their figures of damage and avoided arbitration called for by the contract have been discussed elsewhere. However, as these royalty payments dried up, the Iranian government had to beg for handouts from the very government which could and should have brought the APOC to heel and in which it was the largest shareholder.

Iran was caught between the British rock and the APOC hard place. Britain may have explained its 'help' to Iran as pompously intended to save the Iranians from themselves and a possible alignment with Germany. However, by the end of the war, the result as far as the Iranians were concerned was the inception of another foreign army, the South Persia Rifles, operating in Iran, a recalcitrant APOC, and complete British control of Iran's purse strings.

It was for these reasons that when the Iranian delegation was accused of being ungrateful as their very presence in Paris had been paid for by the British government, they were able to reason that funds from the British government were only replacing those from the APOC, which had been disingenuously withheld. British efforts to make Iranians, and the delegation in particular, feel beholden to the British were spurious – a situation that was even more unlikely to succeed since, though Iran's financial position was poor, Iran was far from insolvent.[36]

Despite these problems there existed a functioning relationship with Britain and it is natural that some in the higher echelons of Iran's government imagined Britain as Iran's saviour. Not only was Britain the only game in town, but in

Britain, Iran had a passable diplomatic relationship with a European power that had the administrative and institutional expertise of running foreign countries and had a military presence in the region. In truth, a closer association between the two countries had been articulated for years and Britain's association with Iran might have been much closer if it had not been for the Russians. A theoretical basis for such a relationship had been established back in the mid-1880s when the aforementioned Malkam Khan had begun to actively think about a greater involvement in Iran for Britain.

As discussed, Malkam Khan's only practical method put forward to accelerate the progress of modernity in Iran was to give concessions to foreign powers on whatever terms necessary to attract capital.[37] This naturally meant even greater involvement of European imperial powers in Iran and, in particular, Britain. In 1882, Malkam Khan had a meeting with Lord Hartington in which he discussed his recall to Tehran and not wanting to return empty handed wanted to take with him a proposal from the British government that would help it during its current difficulties with the Russians.[38] At the time, the Russians had annexed huge swathes of what the Iranians considered Iranian territory and were establishing a new border on the Attrek River. Malkam Khan expressed the view that Britain was being left behind by Russian use of force and diplomacy, which the British were not prepared to counter. What is particularly striking is his bemoaning the lack of reform in Iran and that 'in order to effect useful and beneficial reforms the aid of Europeans would be required'.[39]

Malkam Khan was prepared to go further and in March 1885, in a conversation with Ronald Thomson, minister to Iran, set out his vision for an increased British presence in Iran.[40] He declared that he had for some time working out how to 'make England mistress of Persia [sic] the situation without responsibility'.[41] The draft further records, 'The administration of Persia would be engaged on the same principles as has been done in Tunis and Egypt, but without any sacrifice of independence on the part of Persia or any assumption of open responsibility on the part of England.'[42] Ministers were to be given European assistants and England was to 'exercise as much direct or indirect influence over Persia as she thought fit' and 'Persia would organise her own internal affairs, including finance, army, public works, and general administration exactly on the same principles and nearly in the same forms as those which had been introduced by France in Tunis, and which we were endeavouring to introduce in Egypt'.[43]

This 'protectorate', Malkam Khan argued, had the backing of the Shah and certain Iranian ministers. There is, however, no evidence that Naser al-din Shah had seen or would have entertained such a plan in any shape or form. Nevertheless, in substance, these plans were to dovetail with those of Lord Curzon. Lord Curzon would have been in London during some of the periods in which Malkam Khan had been minister. It is compelling to suggest that Malkam Khan and Lord Curzon might have discussed these plans at some length. However, though it is probable that they both might have met, there is no evidence that they ever communicated with each other in any form. Also, Lord Curzon's ideas regarding Iran's future may not have reached such definitive reasoning at that point. Nonetheless, Lord

Curzon had regretted British passivity during the 1880s regarding Russia and had considered the 1907 Anglo-Russian Convention as a betrayal of the Iranian people.[44]

The Constitutional Revolution had implemented a constitutional system that was still incomplete. It has become a habit to view Iran between 1911 and 1918 as unfit to carry out further reforms. Yet, though incapable, successive Iranian governments made efforts to implement reforms. Even during the First World War, these discussions took place between the British government and Iran. Other countries were not considered by Iran's political elite. In June 1917 Britain was 'informed of the Iranian desire to institute financial and other reforms'.[45] An agreement to set up the South Persia Rifles in 1916 provoked great opposition in Iran and was contested by Iranian nationalists,[46] and was followed in December 1917 by an Iranian announcement to develop a uniform army force.[47] This was followed by an appeal from the Iranian government which included the abrogation of the 1907 Convention and the revision of the Customs Tariff.[48]

Despite a 'natural' pre-disposition towards the British for reform, the Triumvirate was inclined to take negotiations slowly and at the beginning wanted to utilize the British without losing Iranian oversight over reforms. They wanted the undertaking of railways, transport infrastructure and public works to remain under Iranian control.[49] The Triumvirate also specified a guarantee of independence from the Allies, a revision of the customs tariff and territorial restitution on the lines of those presented in Paris. It may come to surprise some that the intentions of the Triumvirate were no different from the *desiderata* being plied by the Iranian delegates in Paris. Such was the widely accepted *imperial nationalism* that the Triumvirate was only utilizing another route to the same objective.

It is therefore of no surprise that Vosuq al-Dowleh had asked the delegation in Paris to secure the hiring of French advisors and professors to be sent to Iran. Vosuq al-Dowleh's interpretation of any deal with Britain was, therefore, in this respect, much more liberal. As many previous Iranian governments before them, the Triumvirate, rather than being beholden to the British, was still intent on using other nations.[50] This was despite the intervention of Sir Percy Cox who felt forced to ask the Iranian cabinet not to take on any foreign advisors in January 1919.[51] Thereafter, attempts to hire advisors and teachers from other nations were to test Lord Curzon's patience over the next few months. By June, Iran was requesting eleven professors from the French. On 5 July the introduction of French Lycées into Iran was also mooted.[52]

Lord Curzon replied to the Triumvirate's stance on the agreement a few days later. As he saw it, any projects such as those for railways, transport infrastructure and public works that remained under Iranian control would be doomed to failure. Britain would not guarantee Iran's independence with its allies and dismissed territorial restitution which may be used by Iran to lever itself into the Peace Conference.[53] In view of the British attitude towards any agreement, the hiring of non-British nationals completely missed the point and in any case teachers and professors had the unfortunate ability to 'develop into advisers'.[54] But the issue which would irritate Lord Curzon the most was Iranian endeavours in Paris to enlist a non-British financial advisor – one of the primary motivations for the agreement as far as he was concerned.[55]

Specifically, the Triumvirate had asked for the return of territory taken by Russia in the Treaty of Turkmanchai, especially Nakhchevan, and the return of the Sarakhs. They also asked for Turkish Kurdistan.[56] It is here, where Lord Curzon made a diplomatic mistake. Apart from the Sarakhs on which he thought that Iran may have had a claim he was against any territorial restitution at all. Lord Curzon never understood the necessity for Iran to either ameliorate the shadow of the despised Treaty of Turkmanchai or show a modicum of success in either Paris or Tehran. Even a glimmer of a territorial renaissance would have gone a long way to show Iran's revitalization, its political sovereignty and its emergence as an international player. Any territorial restitution would have gone a long way to legitimize the Anglo-Persian Agreement.

Sir Percy Cox, operating in Tehran, seemed at first to understand the importance of reclaiming territory for both the Triumvirate and the public at large. The cover sheet to a letter Sir Percy Cox sent to Lord Curzon makes it clear that Sir Percy Cox felt unable to brush off the inclusion of 'an increase in Persian territory' being 'an essential point' of the Triumvirate wishes.[57] In the letter, Sir Percy Cox went on to suggest that territorial issues should be addressed in a separate document rather than the agreement itself and certain issues could also be addressed to 'humour Persian aspirations'.[58] Sir Percy Cox suggested that some territorial rectification, possibly around 'Kotor' (Qotur) or 'Zohab',[59] could take place on the basis of a gap in the frontier and on racial lines (see Map 6). With regard to Iran's interest in the Sarakhs, Iran might be done a good turn 'when the boundaries of Georgia, Armenia, Turkestan and Azerbaijan come up for decision' in Paris. Finally, Sir Percy Cox suggested that the transfer of territories could be made on the basis of self-determination, or a present *in lieu* of reparations from either Turkey or Iraq.

These solutions to Iranian irredentism, which Sir Percy Cox proposed, trampled on many long-held views and policies of British governments towards Iran. If Sir Percy Cox was being serious, then it is hard not to be critical of his suggestions. The British had for years suggested that the issue of the Ottoman-Iranian border was closed. At the same time, it is unclear on what basis self-determination could be granted. The idea of a present *in lieu* of reparations cut a swathe through British-Iranian diplomacy for the last hundred years and it would have also established a precedent for Iran as a non-belligerent nation to receive reparations.

Nevertheless, Arnold Wilson, at the time Sir Percy Cox's assistant, also developed some possible modifications of frontiers to keep the Iranians happy.[60] They were all concerned with the delimitation of the Ottoman/Iranian boundary. He suggested that following the ratification of the work of the 1913/14 Boundary Commission, they could make some modifications based on 'the desires of the local inhabitants and local considerations of expediency'. In the 'Pusht-i-Kuh', at the foothills of the Alborz mountains to the east of present-day Kermanshah, he suggested that the delimitation could be adjusted to run along the foothills of the

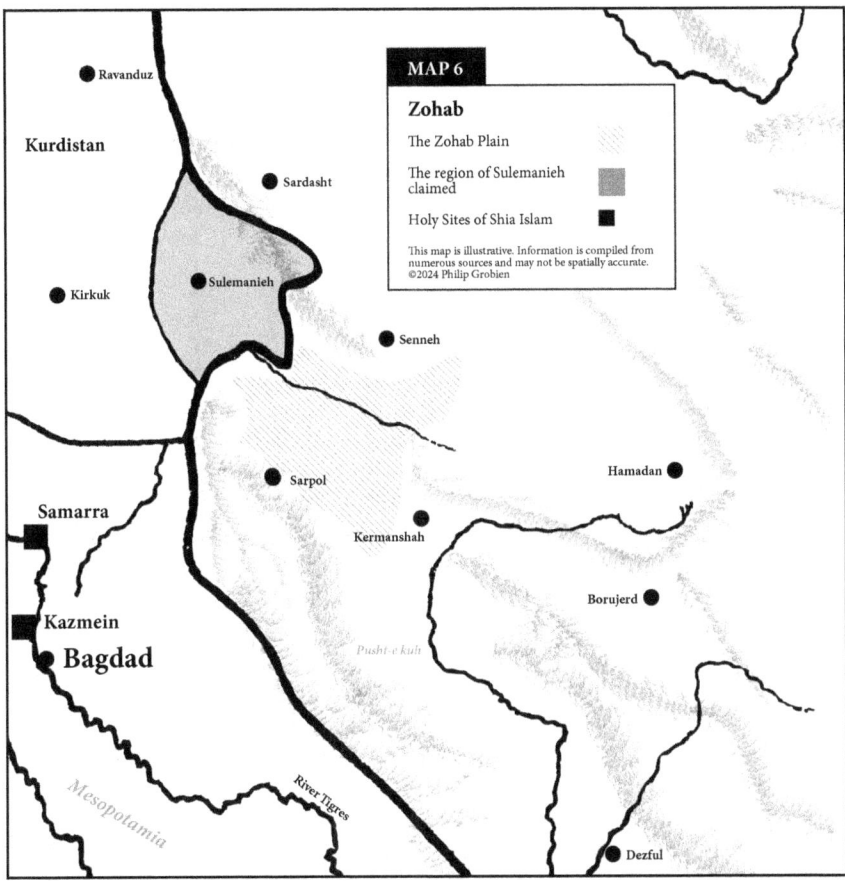

Turkish side rather than the mountain crests. Whereas the crests of mountain ranges had been a usual method of delimitation as shown in Europe in the Treaty of the Pyrenees in 1795, where the Pyrenees was delimited between France and Spain, the general practice had become to delimit along the mountain watershed. Iranian tribes in the 'East of Halebja' in Turkish Kurdistan could be handed over as they were 'Persian by race and patriotic', though unlikely to pay Iran any taxes. Wilson went on to express the view that the British could not help north of latitude 36° on the Turkish frontier and suggested that the existence of oil in the Mendeli-Zohab region made it impossible to suggest any rectification there. All recommendations were made on the basis that these changes would 'do us no harm'.

By May the Triumvirate were still sticking to their guns and expected a guaranteed commitment from the British regarding the revision of treaties, compensation for war damage and rectification of frontiers. They also wanted this commitment to be made public. A British promise would go a long way in assuaging the doubters of such a close association with the British.⁶¹ Lord Curzon had no wish to be lumbered by such commitments and Sir Percy Cox looked to providing the wording to any agreement which might keep the Triumvirate happy but at the same time to keep the British free of any entanglements. Lord Curzon had long opined that Britain had never developed a consistent plan or policy with regard to Iran that had come close to answering the 'Persian question'. His answer, like those who went before him, baulked at any answer to the 'Persian question', which necessitated a guaranteed commitment.

The Anglo-Persian Agreement

In fact, as Sir Percy Cox negotiated in Tehran, the initial points on which the negotiations had begun had been watered down. The revision of treaties, compensation for war damage and the rectification of frontiers were not to be included in the main agreement but to be included in a letter to accompany the agreement.⁶² This letter was to be kept secret. The Triumvirate were unlikely to be happy with this arrangement, as they not only wanted some guarantee that these issues would be addressed but also would have seen a public affirmation that there were considerable upsides to the agreement. Unfortunately, the agreement without these points was far easier to criticize.

There were to be two letters that accompanied the Anglo-Persian Agreement. The first stated that 'in the event of the agreement ... being concluded', Britain would 'co-operate with the Persian Government with a view to the realization of the following desiderata':

1. The revision of the treaties actually in force between the two powers.
2. The claim of Persia to compensation for material damage suffered at the hands of other belligerents.
3. The rectification of the frontier of Persia at the points where it is agreed upon by the parties to be justifiable.⁶³

The second letter emphasized that the British would not claim the cost of the maintenance of British troops and the Iranians would not claim damages against the British military during the First World War.⁶⁴

The preamble to the Anglo-Persian Agreement remarked on the 'close ties' and 'friendship' between Britain and Iran and the 'conviction' of their 'mutual interests' and that the 'progress and prosperity of Persia should be promoted to the utmost'.⁶⁵ The agreement was split into two sections. The first dealt with a political and military agreement. This part detailed six points:

1. A reiteration of the British undertaking 'to respect absolutely the independence and integrity of Persia'.
2. The supply of expert advisors to the government of Iran.

3. The supply of military officers and equipment necessary for the formation of 'a uniform force' for 'the establishment and preservation of order in the country and on its frontiers'.
4. A loan agreement to finance the 'reforms' listed above.
5. British cooperation to extend trade and 'Anglo-Persian enterprise in this direction, both by means of railway construction and other forms of transport'.
6. To set up a committee to examine and revise the existing customs tariff.

The second section dealt with the loan of £2,000,000 sterling at 7 per cent to carry out the political and military agreement. The loan was to be paid off by revenues and custom receipts.

As we will see, the Anglo-Persian Agreement was to provoke considerable backlash. What has been seldom discussed, however, is whether, if imposed, it might have been successful. From the British point of view the most important part of the agreement called for a supply of expert advisors to the government of Iran. Despite objections from the Government of India, the agreement clearly assumed numerous advisors. Sir Percy Cox's view, based as it was on a mandate for Iran, proposed an array of advisors in key positions in the Iranian government, and defined as follows: an 'English financier with adequate powers together with staff including Treasurer-General, Advisor for Ministries of Interior, Public Works and Agriculture and for Education and Law. The latter two might well be of Egyptian experience as needs and circumstance are much the same'.[66]

Given Sir Percy Cox's predilection to a mandate-style re-organization of Iran we can see that the responsibilities of the financial advisor may have been extensive and called for the advisor to be responsible for 'all financial arrangements, the formation of budget, the collection of revenue and control of expenditure, and for arranging loans'. The department would also have a foreign deputy advisor and controller responsible for the organization, administration and efficiency of the department.[67] As Sir Percy Cox had pointed out, the financial advisor had to have extensive powers and be the focal point of the agreement. 'Purely advisory powers will obviously not suffice', he had earlier written to Lord Curzon in November 1918.[68] Indeed, he saw other departments such as Agriculture, Public Works and Treasury, reporting to the financial advisor. Sir Percy Cox also intended to go further and develop a system of British advisors in each major province. The viceroy of India questioned the 'wisdom' of such an idea on the grounds of confusion and whether these advisors would 'supplement' or 'supercede' the Consuls.[69]

The problems with such a plan were Iranian expectations. The Triumvirate had asked for the immediate appointment of a financial advisor.[70] They had also gone further and asked for the British to help appoint a British Municipal Administrator to run Tehran.[71] Yet, despite being asked by Sir Percy Cox not to take on any foreign advisors in January 1919,[72] they made many representations for French advisors and professors to be sent to Iran. In effect, they did not expect the agreement to be so all-encompassing.

British and Iranian eagerness to put the agreement into action allows us to make more tangible judgements. Despite other candidates such as H Maclean, who was already in Tehran as Commercial Attaché,[73] Sidney Armitage-Smith (1876–1932) took up his post in October 1919 as financial advisor and arrived in Tehran in April 1920. He was to be assisted by James Balfour. Other advisors also arrived in Tehran. These included Mr Watkins, tasked with reforming the Customs Tariff,[74] and two advisors to the Ministry of Public Works.

Sidney Armitage-Smith was never to have a chance to carry out his duties. When he arrived in Tehran, the agreement was in stasis and already overcome by criticism. Instead, he was put to work negotiating for the Iranian government with the Anglo-Persian Oil Company and went back to London to do so. In concluding a revision to the original D'Arcy concession on which the Anglo-Persian Oil Company operated in Iran, he was to uncover significant irregularities amounting to fraud.[75] Seen as a triumph at the time, Sidney Armitage-Smith had in fact exceeded his instructions and had made unwanted concessions to the British.[76]

How successful could he have been? His role was of unquestioned necessity, but his role would have encountered significant opposition and suffer from structural concerns. For one thing though he did not have to put up with the rivalry between Russia and Britain, which led to Morgan Shuster being sacked as financial advisor in 1911, it was likely that he would still have to put up with the different factions within Iran's government and society. In a sign of difficulties to come Sidney Armitage-Smith was locked out of his office on the command of Iran's finance minister and he later commented that he and his staff were treated 'as pariahs'.[77] As James Balfour described without 'despotic powers', Sidney Armitage-Smith would have failed, caught between Iranian resentment and active resistance to reform.[78]

In theory the role of a financial advisor at the heart of government would have been beneficial to Iran, bringing to Iran modern methods of monetary management, budgets and taxes. However, as a British subject, Sidney Armitage-Smith would ride two horses. Needing time to balance the budget, he needed the monthly payments to continue for a while. He, however, might have been more intent on forestalling Iran going to another country for finance. There can be no doubt that one of the reasons Britain had been so insistent on a British financial advisor was to consolidate and establish a lien on the advances and loans that Britain had financed.[79]

This introduced another conflict of interest. The Imperial Bank of Persia had developed two roles and functions. It served as a central and state bank serving the government, and, at the same time, a commercial bank. As a commercial bank it was responsible to shareholders who were mostly British. The bank was also registered in Britain and subject to British regulations. The bank also made commercial loans to the Iranian government. The 'inherent ambiguities' therefore offered a 'considerable scope for conflict of interest'.[80] Almost immediately, Sidney Armitage-Smith found himself caught between the banks' lending duties to the Iranian government, a Foreign Office who saw the bank as a facilitator of its policy and a financial advisor who expected the bank to act as he saw fit.[81] Lord Curzon, in particular, became frustrated by the bank whose lending policy to the Iranian government did not either coincide with, or was determined by, British policy towards Iran and the Anglo-Persian Agreement.[82] From the Iranian point of view the bank had increasingly been seen as 'Lord Curzon's Bank of Persia'.[83]

Forming a new modern army for Iran under the Anglo-Persian Agreement was also fraught with difficulties. The view of the Eastern Committee as early as January 1919 was that the South Persia Rifles was to provide the nucleus of the new Iranian Army.[84] The independence of the army was, therefore, brought into question almost immediately. Iranian nationalists who had been opposed to the South Persia Rifles would have seen this army as nothing more than an army of occupation. The merging of the Cossack Brigade into the new force would have been beneficial as it removed, once and for all, a sometime volatile but always omnipresent variable in Iranian politics, since it was formed in 1879.[85] However, in reality, the Cossack Brigade was being dissolved into Iran's new army and Colonel Starosselski (1875–1935), the Russian commander of the Cossack Brigade, was working against its demise and was to provide a stumbling block to the implementation of the new army.[86]

In addition, Sir Percy Cox envisioned far more than the paltry supply of a British officer corps and imagined a force of thirty thousand.[87] The army would be split into ten brigades – each brigade to include three infantry, one cavalry along with two mountain and two field batteries.[88] Sir Percy Cox also envisaged the army 'working nominally under Ministry of War but with practically independent administration powers'.[89] Actually, Sir Percy Cox expected the army to be controlled through the Ministry of War. Likewise, the Ministry of War itself was to be staffed by British advisors which meant British control over the new army. As early as December 1918 the minutes of the Eastern Committee recorded that Lord Curzon and other members of the committee believed that the leading military man had to be British.[90] Plans for the development of the new army were accorded to the Mixed Military Commission, which was set up very quickly after the agreement was signed. Sir Percy Cox asked for permission to fill the Mixed Military Commission as he saw fit and set out to use political, medical, artillery, quartermaster professionals in addition to General Staff officers. The War Office was happy to oblige him.[91]

The resulting Military Commission Report detailed an army that had a British Officer in overall command and obviously as chief of staff to the Iranian Army, and the division of Iranian territory into seven zones, each commanded by a British Officer.[92] The British Officer in overall command was to be Major-General William Dickson, a Persian speaker and no stranger to Iran, having served as the inspector-general of the East Persia Cordon during the First World War.

There can be little doubt that the British were intent on developing an Iranian Army that would be directed by them and which would owe its operational fealty to them. The Government of India opined the obvious and questioned the wisdom of an exclusive British officered force and felt that it would be counterproductive. They proposed the enlistment of 'harmless' officers, such as French Swiss, to make the agreement more palatable.[93] The Military Commission Report invited criticism from the viceroy who saw it as the 'Egyptianisation of Persia'.[94] The report was not accepted by the Iranians on the Mixed Commission, and the Iranian secretary to the commission, Colonel Fazlullah Khan Aq-Evli of the Iranian Gendarmerie, apparently committed suicide rather than sign.[95]

Had the British approach to military reform in Iran prevailed, it would have added to the sense of injustice felt by most Iranians and provide succour to those who felt that the agreement meant nothing else than the existence of Iran as a British protectorate. In this way, had the report of the Mixed Military Commission been accepted and put into action, the fundamental basis of the army was such that it was, in time, doomed to failure. Not enough care and understanding had been taken in producing a blueprint for an Iranian Army which would have been acceptable. Britain's proposal for military reform in Iran was, therefore, one of the more problematic points in the agreement.

In the background, there existed other issues which would have come to the fore. Sir Percy Cox had certainly imagined that the army, commanded by the British, would be able to operate independently and aloft from febrile Iranian politics. Yet, as Major-General William Dickson remained in Tehran, he involved himself in local politics, earning himself a rebuke from his superior General Ironside.[96] This episode exemplified how the 'Iranian Army', commanded by the British, would be buffeted and tarnished by the differing factions in Iranian society.

There were no 'operating plans' of any note, a recipe for failure. More problematically, the Mixed Military Commission included representation from the Royal Air Force.[97] As early as January 1919, Sir Percy Cox had become convinced that the use of military aircraft was to be an 'important factor in restoration and maintenance of security'.[98] The use of air power in Iraq and throughout the British Empire[99] was indicative of how it may be used in Iran. The bombing to quell tribal uprisings might have been effective in the short term and an economical and 'a moral instrument of social control', but was ultimately only a 'blunt weapon', 'despotic',[100] and in the longer term likely to be resented by Iranians.

In the final analysis, we are left unsure as to how Iran's new army might have helped the Iranian government effect control and defence without accumulating considerable ill feeling amongst the populace. Moreover, as reported by James Balfour, since Britain was not to be able to prevent the Bolshevik landings at Anzali,[101] its military reputation would take a severe knock and there were now doubts as to Britain's military abilities.

June, July and August

Back in Paris the delegates had made do and continued working in anticipation of being called to the Peace Conference. The deafening silence from Vosuq al-Dowleh was finally broken when he again asked the delegates to investigate hiring French teachers. After a month of silence, the delegates were even more puzzled by this request.

In the meantime, the delegates met with John Caldwell who had gone to the United States but had now returned to Paris on the way back to Tehran where he would, once again, take up his post as minister to Iran. While in the United States, Caldwell had clearly been surprised how much the American public had become aware of Iran.[102] Even the much-revered Morgan Shuster, a victim of Anglo-Russian rivalry, had declared how he would be delighted to return to Iran if called upon. Caldwell had also met Robert Lansing who reiterated American support for Iran and his suspicions of British imperial goals.[103] All of which was a far cry from Momtaz al-Saltaneh, who, presumably at the request of Vosuq al-Dowleh, had been feeding the delegates a different narrative of American ambivalence towards Iran.

On 15 June the delegates received a telegram from Vosuq al-Dowleh.[104] In this telegram he repeated how upset the British were with the delegation and how disturbed they were that the delegates were involved in anti-British propaganda which was funded by the monthly stipend given to the Iranian government. Vosuq al-Dowleh also declared that while still hopeful no agreement had, at this point, been reached with the British. In truth, the delegation had not acted against the British though presumably opening diplomatic dialogue with the Americans counted as treachery according to the British. At the same time as establishing the delegations' credentials as a failure and a nuisance, Vosuq al-Dowleh was not being truthful; certainly, by this point the Anglo-Persian Agreement had been largely agreed.

Later in July Moshaver al-Mamalek was finally received by Georges Clemenceau. Apparently, Iran's claims had not been seen by him and they were re-presented. With a comment that Iran should remind him if they do not hear anything after a few days, the meeting ended.[105] A reminder was duly written but Momtaz al-Saltaneh took his time and did not deliver it promptly.

Of note, however, was the information that Ahmad Shah was to come to Europe and that this trip was to begin sooner rather than later.[106] Nosrat al-Dowleh was to accompany the Shah and it was not clear to the delegates what this might mean, if anything.[107] The more the delegates spoke amongst themselves the more they feared that they, and particularly, Moshaver al-Mamalek, would be made redundant with the arrival of Nosrat al-Dowleh. Much of this paranoia was fuelled by the preparation the delegates were making for their own departure, something that seemed unavoidable given that they were running out of funds and that Tehran had said little on providing further funds. Not having instructions, the delegates planned their own departures.

On 11 August Moshaver al-Mamalek received the telegram that on the one hand held the instructions the delegates urgently needed but on the other hand was a communication they had dreaded. In the telegram Vosuq al-Dowleh declared that the agreement with the British had been finalized. For once, the description of the agreement, while not full, was accurate. Extending the life of the Iranian delegation in Paris was now no longer necessary and the telegram went on to explain what would happen to the delegates. Nosrat al-Dowleh was to become foreign minister and Moshaver al-Mamalek was to leave Paris and to take up his post as the new minister in Istanbul. Mirza Hossein Khan Ala would go to London as he requested and Entezam al-Molk and Mohammad Ali Foroughi were to stay in Paris.

The Anglo-Persian Agreement had been all that the delegates in Paris had been dreading – fealty to one nation. Despite relying on bits of information the delegates had been correct in their assumptions regarding the nature of the negotiations in Tehran. Mohammad Ali Foroughi had expressed a sense of foreboding in his diary entries. With a sense of inevitability, he noted in the aftermath of hearing of the agreement *'Tehran ham nokar-e englisi-ha ast'* (Tehran is also England's vassal).[108]

Criticism of the agreement

While the tribulations of the Iranian delegation had received some press in Paris and around the world over the first few months of 1919, it was nothing compared to the deluge of articles published in newspapers around the world that criticized the agreement. These articles, reports and editorials were all studied in detail by the delegation and reinforced the overriding notion that Iran had given up what was left of its independence, rather than what the delegation had set out to do, which was to secure it.

The Anglo-Persian Agreement provoked criticism in France and in America, though the articulation of their condemnation was still to an extent circumscribed by the fact that they remained allies of Britain. The French government, far from happy with an agreement that had been negotiated while they were getting nowhere on Syria with the British government, remained largely silent. What active resistance there was to the agreement was focused on helping Iran find teachers, lawyers and advisors. Official actions against the agreement by the French were focused on Tehran.

The French Minister to Iran, Charles Bonin, in contrast to his government's public insouciance, actively worked against the agreement. An apparently indignant Charles Bonin remonstrated with a newly installed Nosrat al-Dowleh before he made his way to Paris.[109] Charles Bonin's actions to 'disparage and belittle the agreement' had not gone unnoticed by the British.[110] This provoked a complaint to the chastened chargé d'affaires in London who admitted it was not French government policy.[111] In September, Lord Hardinge again questioned 'the active campaign of hostile propaganda' carried out by Charles Bonin against the agreement in the face of a French government policy of 'political disinterestness' in Iran.[112]

John Caldwell, just returned to Tehran after one month's leave in which he had met Iranian delegates in Paris, was also caught up in the growing British resentment. Praising Moshaver al-Mamalek, he declared that the 'Persian Government allowed him a free hand to negotiate any amount of money and other assistance [which] would have been forthcoming from America'.[113] Though in reality Caldwell's utterings had concerned Iran's *desiderata* in Paris, a defensive Sir Percy Cox asked that when the French and American governments were made aware of the agreement, they should be asked, if they were not supportive, to at least not 'propaganda against it'.[114]

5. The Cauterization of Independence

As has been detailed by Homa Katouzian, the US government was to be more vocal, though it would take time for their criticism to be voiced. Both in Washington and in Tehran, the Americans seemed to have been caught flat-footed by the announcement of the agreement. Lord Curzon had informed the Americans about the negotiations in Tehran and on 18 August had, in a despatch, confirmed that the agreement had been finalized.[115] The import of this agreement was seemingly missed by the US government. But in a matter of weeks, a communique issued in Tehran designed to dispel notions that America had misled, abandoned and had put Iran under the protection of Britain only managed to have the effect of criticizing the agreement; America had not been supported in backing Iran's representation in Paris and that the agreement appeared to be the result of this lack of support.

Lord Curzon, taken aback by the American reaction to the agreement, had felt surprised that the agreement had taken them by surprise.[116] In response, Lord Curzon was forced to ask the Americans to clarify their stance and 'to inform the Persian Government and the Persian press that the communiqué ... was intended not to cast any aspersion on the Anglo-Persian Agreement'.[117] Lord Curzon had, unrealistically, believed that his notification of the finalized agreement to the US ambassador to Britain would be accepted and merely acknowledged.[118] However, Secretary Lansing and President Wilson were angry with the nature and secrecy in which the agreement had come about.[119] The American perception of what was becoming a diplomatic incident hardened when Lord Curzon had drawn similarities between Britain's desire to help Iran and the American response to a call for protection from the Republic of Liberia. Secretary Lansing made the point that the US relations with, and interest in, Liberia were not similar.[120]

This diplomatic spat was a symptom of the sensitivity with which the British and Lord Curzon in particular were now viewing the criticism of the agreement. This fact is supported by the extensive archiving of public criticism of the agreement. The British archives contain clippings and references to newspaper articles that discussed the Anglo-Persian Agreement. British newspapers, largely in favour of the agreement, were of great interest, stored and commented on by George Churchill, an Iranian specialist at the Foreign Office.[121]

Mostly, however, the analysis and appraisals were addressed to French newspapers that explored limits of criticism that their governments could or would not. Sir George Grahame wrote to Lord Curzon, outlining his thoughts on the critical article which had appeared in *Le Temps*, 'Le cas de la Perse', mentioned above. Foreign Office officials were certainly concerned if not becoming paranoid. Describing one article in *La Liberté* as 'pernicious', George Churchill identified the unknown interviewed 'Persian diplomat' as Moshaver al-Mamalek. Of course, it could have been anyone of the delegates, except for Momtaz al-Saltaneh.

The French newspapers mostly attacked the agreement on the basis that it violated Iran's independence. *L'Écho de Paris*, *Journel Des Débats* and *Les Temps* had drawn comparisons with British and Russian protestations of respecting Iranian integrity and independence in the 1907 Anglo-Russian Convention, and determined logically that Iran's independence was over.[122] In reality, the wording in the Anglo-Persian Agreement which called to 'respect absolutely the independence and integrity of Persia' was remarkably similar to that used in the Anglo-Russian Convention of 1907.[123] This was despite the fact that the agreement's original terminology of 'Convention' had been changed to prevent just such an association.[124]

The American press likewise took a similar tack, and assailed Britain for its treatment of Iran, considering the agreement 'the establishment of a British Persia'.[125] Some reports drew the comparison that while other nations in Paris were willing to hear from the Iranian delegates, the British had vetoed such an approach while consolidating their own monopoly over Iran. Other reports questioned the role and the usefulness of the League of Nations when Britain could run roughshod over several of its foundational cores. One was Article 8 which required the reduction of national armaments,[126] but the more fundamental point was that the agreement was in contravention of Article 10 – respecting 'the territorial integrity and existing political independence of all Members of the League'.

Charges that the Anglo-Persian Agreement violated Iran's independence under Article 10 emanated not only independently but also from Moshaver al-Mamalek. Though he had a few days to digest the agreement and had waited for confirmation from Tehran, Moshaver al-Mamalek was soon to begin to brief against his own government.[127] He reasoned that the League of Nations was a 'sham' if Britain was allowed to violate the League's most important principle, that of independence.[128]

Mohammad Ali Foroughi was also reported as saying that 'the text of the Anglo-Persian treaty shows that it embraces all points which our commission was sent from Tehran to Paris to demand abrogated'. His main point was as follows:

> Persia wants her hands left free to seek aid from the foreigners she chooses, not to be forced to rely upon the English for everything. Persia would like American financiers to handle her fiscal arrangements and American railroad experts to arrange her transportation and American engineers to develop her mining industry and American oil interests to examine her petrol deposits ... America is a long way from Persia, but British interests are all around us, with Afghanistan on the east and Mesopotamia on the west. The British are interested in developing these territories at our expense unless we too become a British colony, pure and simple. We do not know what just happened, as we had no inkling of the negotiations of the Anglo-Persian treaty. The first we heard was that Mamalek was superseded by Prince Firouz [Nosrat al-Dowleh] as Minister of Foreign Affairs, the English treaty was signed and the Shah was en route to Constantinople ... The Persian government undoubtedly was coerced, as British troops are scattered everywhere over Persia and in the Caucasus, Afghanistan and Mesopotamia. But the Persian Chamber of Deputies refused to sign the treaty to make it effective and I do not think they ever will.[129]

It is perhaps a wonder that given Mohammad Ali Foroughi's broadside against the agreement, he was retained in his position in Paris.

On 4 September 1919 Hasan Taqizadeh who was still in Berlin, along with others, published an attack on the Anglo-Persian Agreement. The *Berliner Tageblatt* published what the British considered a 'violently worded manifesto'. The article described the agreement 'as a mockery of the principle preached during the war' and pointed out that Iran's *Majles* had not been consulted. The article appealed to the United States, France and the 'liberals' in Britain to protest.[130]

The question of the role of the League of Nations in Iran's claims in Paris and in the Anglo-Persian Agreement is interesting. Iran's *desiderata* was aiming to establish Iran's independence and sovereignty in reality rather than premise. Iran's membership of the League of Nations relied on that; otherwise, they might be treated as a mandate. In terms of the Anglo-Persian Agreement, Lord Curzon viewed the role of the League of Nations as rubber-stamping the agreement as the agreement was to be filed there. This was despite legal advice which though broadly in agreement with Lord Curzon's approach also mentioned some important qualifications. Lord Curzon, never flexible in thought, did not see how the agreement might have been helped by involving the League of Nations in the agreement itself, something that others, Sir Arnold Wilson in particular, saw more clearly.

In a book on Iran, Sir Arnold Wilson recalled that Sir Edward Grey had suggested how the acceptance of the agreement could have been made much sweeter with the League's involvement prior to publication.[131] This idea had certainly appealed to Sir Edward Grey who had been quoted as saying, 'Here was a case of helping a weak country where the League of Nations ought to have been brought into the matter, and it was a great pity that the League was not brought in.'[132] As Sir Percy Sykes noted, such a move would have made a better impression on the American and French.

Sir Edward Grey's criticism, and his attempt to show the folly in Lord Curzon's concerted effort to prevent any internationalizing of the agreement, must be taken with a pinch of salt. He certainly believed that Lord Curzon was needlessly antagonizing the Americans, whose help in the region they might have to draw upon in the future.[133] Yet, his viewpoint was coloured by the fact that he had always been a proponent of Anglo-American friendship and cooperation as sound diplomacy and that he was, at this point in his career, ambassador to the United States.

He was also the architect of the Anglo-Russian Convention of 1907, and his view was that policies towards Iran were to be suborned to the realities of European politics. Lord Curzon, on the other hand, had criticized the Anglo-Russian Convention. He, however, did not argue that the convention was detrimental to the Iranians, but that 'we have thrown away to a large extent the efforts of our diplomacy and our trade for more than a century'.[134] Lord Curzon had no wish to lose the time and effort put into Iran. Sir Edward Grey had no wish to resolve the 'Persian question'.

Disagreements between the two statesmen over Iran exemplify the differences between the two contemporaries. Lord Curzon, the Conservative steeped in the culture and mechanics of the British Empire, was the expert on the region. The self-styled expert in Iran had also been viceroy of India. Sir Edward Grey, the Liberal, was never interested in details or in travelling as Curzon was. He was the armchair foreign policy expert who rarely ventured abroad. He had also appreciated the usefulness of broadening the base of Britain's foreign policy in the run-up to the First World War.

As the architect of the Anglo-Russian Convention, the importance of keeping Russia on-side in the strategic game of alliances was to suborn Iran to the realities of European politics. It is worth noting, however, that this was not always the case and it is worth pointing out that, in one example, his role in the saga of the Ottoman/Iran border, he was at pains to avoid any oversight by another international organization, The Hague Tribunal.

The American press was also concerned with how the British could make this agreement right under their noses. Not only was President Wilson caught out but Caldwell also had no idea until it was made public. On 18 August, Mohammad Ali Foroughi met with a journalist from the *Chicago Times* who explained that the agreement had given President Wilson a political headache. He said that questions were being asked of Wilson as to how he had not seen the agreement coming given the hours he had spent in the presence of Lloyd George.[135] On the other hand, there was a certain *schadenfreude* in seeing the similarly tarnished imperialists, the French, squirm. It was reported, for example, that the French were concerned that this agreement may only have been the tip of the iceberg and wondered how many other secret agreements the British had entered into.[136] Such paranoia was not without precedent, as the French had been frequently concerned that British plans had been designed to exclude France from the Middle East.

While President Wilson was angry with the British, he kept his own counsel. Nevertheless, the newspapers of the day eagerly reported the American anger towards the agreement. It was reported that the United States had declined to recognize the agreement,[137] when asked to comment by the British. Some politicians, in the United States Senate, were more outspoken and demanded that America should 'insist that the right of self-determination of Persia be maintained'.[138]

Conclusion

The period between May and August had been difficult as the optimism and excitement felt by the delegates in the previous months had worn off. They were now sure of a few conclusions. The first was that their chances of success had come and gone. There was still a possibility that they might be called to give their view on items of interest to the Allies but the diplomacy which they had embarked upon lay moribund. It was also now obvious that Vosuq al-Dowleh, who they always believed had been working against them, had now actually negotiated a deal with the British. The delegates now realized that they had been fighting an internal battle for Iran's future and an external battle against the unmoving force of British imperialism. Also clear was that while French help had been neutralized by their own imperial ambitions, the Americans had been, and were still, showing their support.

How useful was American support? It is a difficult question to give a definitive answer to. Their support seemed unwavering and the Americans seemed more and more appreciative of Iran's *desiderata* as they seemed less and less enamoured by British intransigence, and secretive imperial arrangements. The Americans may have been duped by the British but their support also had limits. The American delegation in Paris, under President Wilson, was only one part of the American political spectrum and he lacked support in Congress, so much so that America's membership of the League of Nations was never ratified. In the final analysis, American support had little inherent value.

Chapter 6

THE PERSISTENCE OF NOSRAT AL-DOWLEH

Iran's mission in Paris had come to an abrupt juncture with the finalizing of the Anglo-Persian Agreement. The agreement with Britain replaced the broader *desiderata* presented by the delegates in Paris. It had not, however, changed the *imperial nationalism* which remained the basis for Iranian policy in 1919. While it is true that the substitution of Moshaver al-Mamalek, with Nosrat al-Dowleh, one of the Triumvirate and a noted Anglophile, marked a public change, Iran's political ambitions remained remarkably similar.

Notably, the re-constituted Iranian delegation in Paris was to follow its *desiderata* against the background of the Anglo-Persian agreement. Not only would the delegation in Paris not dissolve, as Lord Curzon had expected, but Nosrat al-Dowleh's policy goals would broadly remain the same. Between August 1919 and January 1920 Nosrat al-Dowleh used the diplomatic space facilitated by the Anglo-Persian Agreement to pester Lord Curzon regarding Iran's *desiderata*.

Nosrat al-Dowleh

On 15 August Moshaver al-Mamalek received a letter from the British Embassy in Paris inviting him to London.[1] Lord Curzon had decided that now that the agreement had been completed it would be possible to meet with Moshaver al-Mamalek. Lord Curzon had long opposed meeting Moshaver al-Mamalek as negotiations were ongoing in Iran. Though a change of policy had been discussed on several occasions, Lord Curzon could not see past his emotional reaction to meet someone who, in his eyes, had helped retard his policy towards Iran.

The delegates had seen Lord Curzon's stance towards Moshaver al-Mamalek, who had been Iran's foreign minister throughout Iran's representation in Paris, as a slap in the face. Now any meeting seemed pointless, much as lord Curzon had probably expected. Moreover, the delegates in discussing this invitation saw it as nothing more than a poisoned chalice. After all, meeting Lord Curzon after being ignored for so long would only have helped validate the Anglo-Persian Agreement in the eyes of many Iranians, which, under these circumstances, the delegates were loath to do. Diplomatically the invitation was turned down on the basis that Moshaver al-Mamalek was not the Iranian foreign minister anymore.

On the same day, Mohammad Ali Foroughi noted in his diary that *L'Écho de Paris* had written that the concluded agreement had been tantamount to the sale of the government of Iran to Britain.[2] Despite not listing any of the specifics covered by the agreement, the article argued that Iran had become a British protectorate much like Egypt. Furthermore, it was suggested that such an agreement should have been presented to the League of Nations.[3] Another newspaper noted the fact that a protectorate had seemingly been employed in a country that was part of the League of Nations and should have been protected by its covenant.[4]

For the next ten days Mohammad Ali Foroughi and the other delegates absorbed whatever articles they could find regarding the agreement. They discussed the agreement in the knowledge that they were powerless to effect any change. In the meantime, Mohammad Ali Foroughi continued his work in recruiting teachers to go to Iran and concentrated on teachers in physics, chemistry and history – an endeavour that was supported, as already mentioned, by the French government. Mohammad Ali Foroughi, who had been told to remain in France, took a few days off and went with Entezam al-Molk to the town of Deauville in Normandy. Enjoying the seaside, Foroughi mused how nice it would be to replicate the local casino in Shemiran in northern Tehran.

Back in Paris on 26 August Mohammad Ali Foroughi was advised that he would lead the delegation to the League of Nations along with Sadegh al-Saltaneh and Ehtesham Homayoun.[5] Given the Anglo-Persian Agreement, Mohammad Ali Foroughi was hard-pressed to see the point in becoming a delegate to an organization, which had so far failed to rein in Britain. Lord Curzon was far from impressed by these appointments. They had been, after all, part of the maligned delegation to Paris and he considered taking up the issue with Nosrat al-Dowleh at a suitable opportunity.[6] This was despite Vosuq al-Dowleh's vain attempt to reassure Sir Percy Cox and Lord Curzon that Mohammad Ali Foroughi did not hold with Moshaver al-Mamalek's views 'and could be trusted'.[7]

Nosrat al-Dowleh arrived in Paris on 15 September. Mohammad Ali Foroughi did not see him on his arrival but Entezam al-Molk did and his retelling of his discussion with Nosrat al-Dowleh surprised Mohammad Ali Foroughi. Nosrat al-Dowleh had declared that the Anglo-Persian Agreement was far from perfect and that work should take place to correct its 'bad' points.[8] This was confirmed the next day when Nosrat al-Dowleh asked, 'How much of the agreement would it be possible or necessary to cancel or modify.'[9] Mohammad Ali Foroughi reports in his diary that they agreed on what could be improved on in the agreement but sadly does not fully record the discussion. This turn of events was surprising to all the delegates. It was also an amazing admission given that the agreement had only just been concluded. No doubt it might also have come as a surprise to Lord Curzon and Sir Percy Cox.

Now using the diplomatic space that had opened up as a result of the Anglo-Persian Agreement, Nosrat al-Dowleh decided to go to Britain to discuss Ahmad Shah's impending visit, the agreement and other Iranian *desiderata*. He took Mohammad Ali Foroughi and Entezam al-Molk with him. Also in the entourage were Qolam Hossein Khan and Jahanbaksh Mirza. They arrived in Folkestone and made their way to London.

Nosrat al-Dowleh's stop-over in Paris had only lasted a matter of days. Much longer than the British had wanted, who had requested that he go straight to London. Lord Curzon and Sir Percy Cox had felt that there was little to be gained by Nosrat al-Dowleh's exposure to public anti-agreement sentiment circulating in Paris. He had already been much 'perturbed' by the campaign in the Swiss press against the Anglo-Persian Agreement.[10] The few days spent in Paris affected Nosrat al-Dowleh as had been feared. Nosrat al-Dowleh was now in no ignorance of the antagonistic sentiment towards the agreement in Paris and Europe in general nor the more specific issues concerning the incompatibility of the agreement vis-à-vis the League of Nations and other matters.[11]

In London, an agitated Nosrat al-Dowleh was now keen to find out more about the American reaction to the Anglo-Persian Agreement. Sadegh al-Saltaneh

Figure 8 A young Nosrat al-Dowleh. ©Public Domain.

disclosed that *Ra'd* had reported that Iran had been forced to sign the agreement with Britain because no other government was interested and that the Americans had announced that Britain had prevented the issue of Iran from being raised at the Peace Conference in Paris.[12]

As we will see, defending Iran and Britain against criticism of the agreement was one of the items at the forefront of Nosrat al-Dowleh's mind. Whilst European criticism was disconcerting, it was criticism from the US press which was to be more worrying. Keeping an open dialogue with countries who may be able to help Iran in the near future was not only anticipated, but crucial to Iran's reading of the agreement. Amending the Anglo-Persian Agreement now revolved around two interlinked points: ensuring that the agreement was not seen as a *de facto* protectorate and that Iran's independence was both optically and actually secured and that other countries such as France and the United States were not put off offering their services. Despite the agreement, Iran remained open to continual dialogue with other countries. After all, Mohammad Ali Foroughi had continued to interview academics for positions in Iran during much of August and early September.

For Mohammad Ali Foroughi the issues regarding the Anglo-Persian Agreement revolved, and stemmed entirely, from the centrality of independence. He listed several faults and possible remedies to the agreement: To what extent the British would make decisions entirely in their interest and how differences in strategy could be resolved turned on the extent of Iran's ability to stay independent. Only independence, either enshrined in the contracts that would have to be drawn up for each official position, or by the League of Nations or by the strength of Iranian politicians, could limit the influence of the British.[13]

The only option which presented itself now was to effect change to the agreement itself. The approach which Nosrat al-Dowleh took was to see the agreement as a commercial agreement, viewing the agreement as a 'Heads of Terms', rather than a binding agreement which was to be administered by the British government. In a discussion with Naser al-Molk, Nosrat al-Dowleh discussed tactics that avoided specifics concerning British help and instead saw the hiring of British officials and administrators as a private contractual issue and not part of an agreement that had not yet been approved by parliament.[14] In further preparation for a meeting with Lord Curzon, Nosrat al-Dowleh, Mohammad Ali Foroughi and Mehdi Khan Ala al-Saltaneh, minister to Britain, discussed asking the British to re-affirm Iran's independence in view of its membership of the League of Nations and that the status of Iran as an independent nation would remain despite the Anglo-Persian Agreement.[15]

Unable to affect a meeting with Lord Curzon who was away, Nosrat al-Dowleh met, in the first instance, with Sir John Tilley (1869–1952) who was assistant secretary at the Foreign Office.[16] Much of the discussion revolved around the timing of Ahmad Shah's impending visit to Britain. Not wishing to get into too deep a discussion with Sir John Tilley, he did however make the point that he felt that the wide-ranging opposition to the Anglo-Persian Agreement in France had made him think that the opportunity should be taken to change the narrative.

They agreed that a 'supplementary agreement of an explanatory nature' might be useful if Lord Curzon's upcoming pronouncement on the agreement would fail to answer the criticisms of the agreement.

Following his meeting Nosrat al-Dowleh met with Lancelot Oliphant, another assistant secretary at the Foreign Office.[17] Oliphant had spent two years in Iran and had a better grasp of Iranian affairs. This meeting was to be more productive and Nosrat al-Dowleh listed a few points that would be useful in ameliorating the criticism which the agreement was attracting and which he thought Lord Curzon should include in his speech. The first was to counter the narrative that Iran's independence would be lost under this agreement and that Iran was to become a protectorate. The second was to support Iran's position in the League of Nations. The third was for the British government to deliver on Iran's *desiderata* at the Peace Conference, in particular Iran's reparation claims and territorial claims.

In addition to the items that Nosrat al-Dowleh felt should be addressed in Lord Curzon's speech was a list of items that would directly help Vosuq al-Dowleh in his fight to legitimize the Anglo-Persian Agreement in Iran. Firstly, to take over Russian ships on the Caspian, man them with British crews and once again fly the 'Persian flag' on the Caspian. The obvious incongruity of this iteration of sovereignty and independence made possible by the British Navy was not something that had occurred to Nosrat al-Dowleh. Secondly, to resolve the questions regarding oil and to settle the negotiation between the APOC and Iranian government regarding the payment of royalties. Thirdly, that the contracts of the Belgium officials who were running the Iranian Customs would be respected. Fourthly, that the hiring of French academics could take place as this would help to ameliorate the criticism of Iran coming under the cosh of the British. Fifthly, to appoint a joint committee as soon as possible to examine and revise Iran's customs tariff.

In relaying the content of Nosrat al-Dowleh's meeting with Lancelot Oliphant to Sir Percy Cox in Tehran, Lord Curzon was to encapsulate the paradigm in which the Iranians had been caught. He said:

> He hoped [Nosrat al-Dowleh] that I [Lord Curzon] would state publicly that His Majesty's Government were prepared to support at the Peace Conference such claims as the Persian Delegates would put forward, it being, of course, fully understood that they would not put forward any claims regarding which they had not come to a previous understanding with His Majesty's Government.[18]

In doing so it would appear that Nosrat al-Dowleh had also voiced the obvious stumbling block, colloquially a 'Catch-22'. Iran had been told that these issues were to be addressed by the Peace Conference, precisely what Lord Curzon did not want; however, Iran needed the support of Britain to put their wishes forward, which was obviously not to be forthcoming.[19]

The first time Nosrat al-Dowleh and the Iranian entourage met with Lord Curzon was at a banquet at the Carlton Hotel given in Nosrat al-Dowleh's honour on 18 September. Lord Curzon made a speech welcoming Nosrat al-Dowleh. Broadly, he described the agreement in the context of a logical symbiosis between

British and Iranian interests. It was in the best interest of Britain to have a 'peaceful and prosperous Persia' and it was natural that Iran should turn to Britain for its security, administration, financial needs, development of Iran's resources and better communication (transport infrastructure). More specifically, he made a point to jettison the much-hated Anglo-Russian Convention of 1907 (and its revision in 1915). He also addressed the immediate criticism of the agreement. He argued that the agreement had been misconstrued as a 'Protectorate by Great Britain over Persia' but that Britain was fully invested in Iran's independence, and, as if to emphasize that point, Britain did not have, and would not accept, a mandate for Iran. In a specific rejoinder to those who claimed that the agreement 'was a disparagement or deliberate neglect of the League of Nations', he argued that Britain had unreservedly accepted Articles 10 and 20 of the charter.

Nosrat al-Dowleh was able to go into greater detail in a private meeting with Lord Curzon on 23 September. This meeting, which followed on from those with Sir John Tilley and Lancelot Oliphant, and the banquet, was arranged to discuss arrangements to execute the Anglo-Persian Agreement.[20] Nosrat al-Dowleh argued that the British officials and officers sent to Iran should be of the highest class and that none of them should be Indian officials, re-enforcing a long-standing antipathy to Indian officials because of their perceived attitude towards Iranians. He therefore also wanted to keep the British Legation in Tehran, which were partial to Indian officials, out of decision-making loop.[21]

The discussion around finding a financial advisor led to Lord Curzon asking why Iran was in Paris still hiring French teachers to fill academic positions and why they were asking for French legal experts to go to Iran. Despite Sir Percy Cox attempting to persuade the Iranian cabinet to not take on any more French advisors during negotiations for the Anglo-Persian Agreement,[22] the Iranian delegation had continued to do so with some vigour, and these requests were to try Lord Curzon's patience. In May Iran had asked France to send six legal experts. By June Iran was requesting eleven professors from the French. On 5 July the introduction of French Lycées into Iran also been mooted.[23] In fact in a meeting in October in Paris with a worried French Foreign Minister, Nosrat al-Dowleh had reiterated that there was no restriction under the agreement in hiring French teachers.[24]

Nosrat al-Dowleh's response was that French professors were being hired to replace other Frenchmen who had left Iran. He might also have mentioned that Iran's Dar al-Fonun had been founded on French lines. He did explain, however, that Iran's legal system had been largely based on the French one and had been established by Adolphe Perni, a long-term advisor to Iran. Lord Curzon had earlier declared that the hiring of French legal experts had been 'entirely unacceptable' and had also been determined to stop their appointment. Nevertheless, he only said that he was worried that sending so many may result in 'the prospect of a dozen discontented Frenchmen' working against the agreement and the British. Lord Curzon did not, however, mention what had irked him the most in recent months, which was Iranian endeavours in Paris to enlist a non-British financial advisor – one of the primary motivations for the agreement.[25]

Nosrat al-Dowleh also raised the question, which he had brought up in his meeting with Lancelot Oliphant, the desire that some ships on the Caspian Sea could be requisitioned from the Russians and to fly the Iranian flag. To Nosrat al-Dowleh's disappointment, he was told that all the ships had been put at the disposal of General Denikin. He was by now leading the only effective White Russian Army against the Bolsheviks. Lord Curzon attempted to justify this decision by explaining that the ships were mostly useless and in a naval contest between the Bolsheviks and General Denikin, the latter would lose. He saw no point in having an Iranian Navy of a few useless vessels. With this rationalization Lord Curzon missed the point; such a gesture would have been a visual confirmation that Iran was achieving something out of the agreement and that the issue of sovereignty was being taken seriously.

Nosrat al-Dowleh touched on the reconstitution of the Iranian delegation in Paris under himself and to see if there was a way to receive reparations from Turkey and Russia. Lord Curzon made the point that reparations from Turkey could only be made possible through the peace treaty with Turkey but in the case of Russia, whose obligations Britain had already written off as bad debts, he was not sure against whom the claims could be made. Iran could write off some of its debts to Russia though. Lord Curzon's broader reaction to the reconstitution of the Iranian delegation in Paris appears not to have been discussed but it is interesting to speculate what they may have been. He had earlier felt that any discussion on Iranian *desiderata* should take place after the dissolution of the Paris Peace Conference.[26] He would have been forewarned regarding the persistence of these questions as Sir Percy Cox had informed him that journalists in Tehran were already asking when the alterations to the frontiers were to take place.[27] There can be little doubt that he would not have wanted the delegation in Paris to continue working.

Apart from the banquet, Nosrat al-Dowleh had not involved anyone else from either his entourage or the Iranian Legation in London. His objective was to keep negotiations close to his chest. Mohammad Ali Foroughi records his feelings that he and Nosrat al-Dowleh were not on the same page.[28] It was perhaps a result of Mohammad Ali Foroughi's feelings at the time that this banquet passed with little mention in his diary. The night seemed only memorable as he was able to meet with Edward Browne who subsequently invited him to stay in Cambridge for a few days.[29] On the same day that Nosrat al-Dowleh was to meet with Lord Curzon, Mohammad Ali Foroughi left London for Cambridge.[30] While there he received a telephone call that he could spend some time in Cambridge, come back to London and then go back to Paris. In the meantime, Nosrat al-Dowleh had gone back to Paris and Mohammad Ali Foroughi was left to wonder whether he had been brought to Britain to be put on ice.[31]

Back in London, Mohammad Ali Foroughi, invited to a club by Ghaffar Khan, secretary to the Legation in London, had a chance meeting with Winston Churchill.[32] The meeting turned into lunch but sadly the nature of the conversation was not recorded in Foroughi's diary. Winston Churchill was still secretary of State for War at this point and it is likely that Mohammad Ali Foroughi brought up an approach made to him by members of Churchill's staff in Paris in July. An unnamed British official and a general, presumably mischief-making at Churchill's request, had suggested that the War Ministry had better ideas than the Foreign Office when it came to Iran. At the time, Mohammad Ali Foroughi had not put much in store in this encounter.[33]

Winston Churchill's approach speaks to the limitations of Lord Curzon's character by another political heavyweight. For Churchill there was much to be admired. He found Lord Curzon charming, highly intelligent, with a huge work ethic. Yet, like Sir Edward Grey, he felt there had always been something lacking. Erudite to a fault, Lord Curzon, he argued, 'thought too much about stating his case, and too little about getting things done'.[34] Lord Curzon had the qualifications but though '[he often domineered, but at the centre he never dominated'.[35] There can be little doubt that Churchill believed that he might be able to offer Iran more substantive advice.

In the meantime, in Paris, Nosrat al-Dowleh had given a statement to *Les Temps* which was also run in British newspapers:

> We shall submit the Anglo-Persian Agreement to the approval of our Parliament as soon as it meets, which cannot be long, as the elections are over in most provinces and have been held freely, as it proved by the success of our opponents in various places. This Agreement has provoked concern, which, in my opinion, is unjustified. We can only live if we reform, and we cannot reform without the friendly support of a great European Power. Have we obtained exactly all we desire? I cannot assert it, for negotiation implies compromise, but there is nothing in the Agreement affecting Persia's independence, nothing constituting a permanent right of Great Britain or a monopoly of any kind to the advantage of the British Government. We can fix for ourselves the attributes of the advisors and military instructors we like to choose in England, as well as the duration of their contract. We can take them from elsewhere, as in the past. At this moment we are appointing French law professors, a French magistrate, &c., and the contract of our Belgian Customs officials have been renewed. Lastly, the Agreement will be submitted to the League of Nations.[36]

His statement, which likely put Lord Curzon off his breakfast as he read it in his daily paper, is noteworthy for several reasons. At the same time as justifying the agreement as the only deal possible and viable for Iran, he expressed the view that Iran could pick and choose elements of the agreement. As far as Lord Curzon and Sir Percy Cox saw the agreement, Britain's involvement was all or nothing. As Sir Percy Cox would remark, the last thing they wanted was a 'salade russe' of foreign advisors.[37]

Nosrat al-Dowleh had also made the point that the agreement had to have the approval of Iran's *Majles*. This was true given Iran's constitution,[38] but had been of apparently no concern to Lord Curzon, who had seemingly never considered the importance of ratification. Both Sir Harold Nicolson and Sir Percy Sykes had considered the importance of pushing for immediate ratification and had found fault in Curzon, for either not demanding immediate ratification or inserting a further clause overriding the approval of the *Majles*.³⁹ There is no proof that Lord Curzon and indeed Vosuq al-Dowleh had forgotten that such an agreement necessitated *Majles* approval. Vosuq al-Dowleh had certainly not, using it as a backstop to the agreement itself, as he laid out in his speech defending his actions in 1926.⁴⁰ Lord Curzon, a man of tremendous eye for detail, was likewise aware. A reiteration of the Iranian Constitution had been dug up and available in the Foreign Offices files of 1919. It is far more likely that Lord Curzon had simply not been concerned with ratification, either considering it a *fait accompli* or of no consequence. To what extent Lord Curzon's supposition that Nosrat al-Dowleh's visit to London had 'cleared the air',⁴¹ given this statement, was not evident.

Countering the narrative

In Iran, the agreement was made public by Vosuq al-Dowleh in the newspaper *Iran* on 10 August 1919. He explained the reasons behind it and the necessity and practicality of working with Britain to resolve Iran's intractable problems.⁴² A broke, and broken, Iran was not able to defend itself not least because it was riven by rebellions and famine.⁴³ In what can be seen as an attempt to pre-empt criticisms of the agreement, Vosuq al-Dowleh explained how Britain's help remained the only option for Iran. Engaging one country, Britain, forestalled the habitual use, and failure, of using many countries to reform Iran.⁴⁴ Seeking the help of another single country, such as the United States, was likewise not a realistic option, as America did not have the 200 years of experience in running an Empire, that Britain had.⁴⁵ Moreover, it was the solution borne out of logic and dealing with facts rather than emotive desires for an independent strategy, which excluded Britain.

The semi-official newspaper, *Iran*, was edited by Mohammad Taqi Bahar who was a friend and supporter of Vosuq al-Dowleh. Vosuq al-Dowleh was to use this newspaper to good effect and embarked on a press campaign that included a series of articles, letters and editorials, discussing the agreement between August and September 1919.⁴⁶ They emphasized Iran's dire state of affairs, applauded that Vosuq al-Dowleh was the man committed to change,⁴⁷ that opposition to the agreement was based more on emotion and a visceral reaction rather than logical thought,⁴⁸ and that only two countries can be party to such an agreement and Britain rather than the US was the better choice.⁴⁹ However, running through all the articles were two themes: Firstly, that most ideas for Iran's reform were utopian and illusory, and as one article put it, 'Iran's national aspirations cannot match the daily wishes and needs of this country'.⁵⁰ Secondly, that Iran's problems were so extensive that an association with just one foreign power made more sense and that 'true patriots who attribute great misery to the lack of civilization, territorial administration and universal poverty, must admit that the Iranian government was compelled to commit to a plan with one foreign government'.⁵¹

Vosuq al-Dowleh did not directly tackle the accusations of consigning Iran's independence to Britain until March 1920 when another article in defence of the agreement was published.[52] The article argued that the agreement would actually secure Iran's independence rather than lose it. Vosuq al-Dowleh stated that 'true' independence could only be achieved by good governance and the generation of wealth. If one accepts the veracity of Vosuq al-Dowleh's arguments for negotiating and entering the Anglo-Persian Agreement, then one must doubt the much-trodden accusation of the man who had sold Iran's independence. Certainly, a case can be made that a sincere and thoughtful man had seen no other way out of Iran's predicament than such an agreement. In this way, I don't believe that Vosuq al-Dowleh was in any way less of a nationalist than those who argued for outright independence. He simply believed that independence was not possible given the means at Iran's disposal and could not be achieved without modernization.

Other support for the agreement in the press came from two other newspapers – *Ra'd* and *Rahnama,* edited by Seyyed Zia al-din Tabataba'i and 'Abdolrahim Rahnama respectively. Both editors were also supporters of the agreement. In particular, Seyyed Zia al-din Tabataba'i (1889–1969) became closely affiliated with Vosuq al-Dowleh and the agreement. Tabataba'i was to become more famous as one of the original leaders of the coup in 1921, in which he became prime minister.

In this way, Vosuq al-Dowleh was able to control the narrative. In a country where government communications and meetings of the *Majles* were sporadic, newspapers remained the only way for government policy to be articulated. Otherwise, it is difficult to determine the extent of support for the agreement in Iran. It is therefore almost impossible to substantiate Homa Katouzian's claim that the agreement may only have had a handful of supporters in Iran and that those who did support the agreement did so for personal benefit.[53]

Nevertheless, despite Vosuq al-Dowleh's impressive public relations strategy, criticism in Iran began almost immediately. Opposition to the agreement appeared to permeate most parts of Iranian society, including the *Ulema*, nationalists and constitutionalists, journalists, the Gendarmerie and members of the Cossack brigade.[54] The idea that Iran had become a British protectorate was hard to shake.

In the months that followed, Vosuq al-Dowleh continued to rely on the pen to defend his policy towards the agreement but also began to rely on more draconian means. Controlling the press narrative, to some extent, was not enough. Mohammad Ali Foroughi, following the news from Iran, noted that the exile from Tehran of five distinguished men, including Momtaz al-Dowleh, previously the speaker of the *Majles*, was only the tip of the iceberg and that at least twenty people had been accorded the same fate. Foroughi was far from convinced by either Vosuq al-Dowleh's intentions or rationale for doing so.[55]

Squaring the circle

Many nationalist politicians in Iran were to take their cue from, and be emboldened by, the international criticism of the agreement. The dominant criticism, both abroad and in Iran, was that, under this agreement, Iran would become a British vassal state. British protestations that 'independence and integrity' would be protected by this treaty were a particularly hard pill to swallow. Lord Curzon had no choice but to counter these accusations but he was to struggle. He argued that, under this agreement, Iran would not become a protectorate and sought to resolve the 'misunderstandings of the treaty' and explain that 'there were no grounds for suspicion'.[56] He declared that Britain would not have taken a mandate for Iran if offered, nor would it assume a protectorate of Iran. He affirmed:

> We have, or shall have, as a result of this war, enough to do in the Eastern parts of the world. If a nation assumes a protectorate, it also assumes certain responsibilities which have a tendency to attain the weight of a heavy burden. Above all, it is compelled to give financial assistance on a scale which may ultimately be overwhelming.[57]

In truth, Lord Curzon was, however, walking a nuanced and tight line; Britain had discussed taking a mandate and this was originally to be Sir Percy Cox's favoured route.[58] Moreover, as one can see his definition of a 'protectorate' relied on a financial litmus test and the amount of the British government's financial exposure. As Iran was, however, required to take out a loan to pay for the agreement, it could be argued that Iran was not becoming a protectorate.

The question of control was missing from this definition and such a tenuous argument was unlikely to satisfy those who disagreed with British policy towards Iran. But Lord Curzon's reaction, rather than proposing concrete or even optical changes to the agreement, was simply to dig in his heels. Lord Curzon was simply unwilling or temperamentally unable to modify his intentions for the agreement. His obstinacy was obvious, not only in his lack of being able to appreciate the similarity between the agreement and a protectorate, in words and deeds, but in guarding sole British participation in the agreement. It seemed he did not really understand the criticism the agreement faced. Would it have been different if the French and Americans had been invited to be part of Iran's regeneration? Certainly, neither Lord Curzon, nor Sir Percy Cox, thought so. After all, they had reasoned that it had been Iran's predilection of employing various nations in various capacities in the past, which lay at the root of its problems.[59]

What Lord Curzon might have been avoiding was to draw similarities between plans for Iran and Britain's role in Egypt. Egypt had become a salutary lesson on the pitfalls of how a simple intervention had, over the years, become a policy of occupation and control. The British had occupied Egypt in 1882 and, in time, had exercised military and political control through the Egyptian government. By the beginning of the First World War, Britain had declared Egypt a protectorate. By the end of the war, there were calls to annex Egypt, a move the British were disinclined to take. As the Eastern Committee discussed the Anglo-Persian Agreement in May 1919, a contemporary Egyptian insurrection in 1919 was clearly on their minds.[60] Both Lord Montagu, secretary of State for India, and Lord Curzon were able to equivocate; Iran was dissimilar to Egypt and, in any case, it was the Iranians who had asked for help.[61]

It was to be a fine line on which the Anglo-Persian Agreement was to be rationalized. If the agreement could be made to look different from British involvement in Egypt, then it could be claimed that Iranian independence had been preserved. However, in the final analysis, the words 'to respect absolutely the independence and integrity of Persia' were remarkably similar to those used in the Anglo-Russian Convention of 1907.[62]

Lord Curzon had throughout based the foundation of the agreement on the narrow edifice of his knowledge of Iran. A visit for a few months, many years before, had been enough for him to construct a plan for Iran. He had not understood the development of nationalist sensitivities in Iran. In the meantime, in this, his ignorance he was abetted by Sir Percy Cox. Time and time again, Sir Percy Cox supported claims that the agreement would have deep support within Iran. This occurred during the negotiations for the agreement,[63] and in its aftermath.[64] It may be that Sir Percy Cox sincerely believed that support for the agreement was deep-rooted. It is certainly the case that he had made a similar assumption for the greater involvement of Britain in Mesopotamia,[65] claiming wrongly, as it turned out, that Britain was welcome. When Sir Percy Cox did fight his corner, when he pushed for Iran's *desiderata*, he was not able to make Lord Curzon see how important these issues were. These items were to be pushed into a separate and secret letter (see above) when their public articulation was vital. Despite suggestions such as the restitutions of territory,[66] Sir Percy Cox seemed unable to make Lord Curzon see the necessity of these commitments to counter subsequent criticism.

Nevertheless, while Lord Curzon's hand in the construction of the Anglo-Persian Agreement is clear, so is the hand of Vosuq al-Dowleh. Vosuq al-Dowleh legacy as a traitor and British lacky appears to have emanated solely from his role in negotiating the agreement in 1919. Accusations made easier, because he was disliked by his colleagues and not trusted by Ahmad Shah. However, before working with Sir Charles Marling to become first prime minister and then to negotiate the agreement with Marling's successor Cox, one cannot discern any proclivities towards the British.

There is some doubt, therefore, whether Vosuq al-Dowleh was wedded to the British for any other reason than pragmatism. Proclivities either towards the Russians or the British and, during the war years, the Germans, were a natural by-product of an Iran competed over by foreign powers. In fact, William Olson has suggested that Vosuq al-Dowleh had been considered pro-Russian at some point before 1919.[67] Vosuq al-Dowleh's politics appear to have been pragmatic. He simply assumed that Iran's regeneration could not happen without a significant role of the major power in Iran, the British.

Traitorous accusations were made easier by his role in thwarting Iran's programme in Paris. Despite arguments to the contrary,[68] there can be no doubt that Vosuq al-Dowleh obstructed the work of the Iranian delegates in Paris. As the delegates pressed for entry to the conference, Vosuq al-Dowleh incurred the ire of the British who saw no reason to engage with the Iranian delegates. However, Iranian diplomacy did, at times, serve a useful role in pushing the British towards the agreement with Vosuq al-Dowleh. Nevertheless, the delegates in Paris,

Figure 9 The Guildhall, London, 1919: Right to left, prominent British representatives: Lord Curzon, Prince Albert, Sir Horace Brookes Marshall (London Lord Mayor). Right to left, prominent Iranians representatives: Ahmad Shah, Nosrat al-Dowleh, Mohammad Ali Foroughi. ©Public Domain.

pursuing a programme for independence and nationalism, carried the hopes of the nation, something which an agreement with the British could not do.

The agreement was also to be marred by two specific issues: secrecy and fraud. An agreement, seemingly thrust on Iran, appeared more sinister as it had been negotiated in secrecy. The agreement had seemingly been unleashed without any inkling that negotiations had, in fact, taken place. While it is true that the delegation would unlikely have kept such a secret for long, rumours of these negotiations undercut Iranian diplomacy in Paris. In the febrile politics of post-war Iran, such ominous beginnings for an agreement seemed to signal yet another agreement that would be detrimental to Iran. The list of previous such agreements was long, the most recent example had been the 1907 Anglo-Russian Convention. Iranians feared the lack of agency which seemed the result of secret negotiations.

Lord Curzon's view on secrecy was driven by necessity. In the Triumvirate they had found Iranians with which they could do business. Keeping the negotiations secret, rather than broadening them, would have stopped the negotiations in their tracks. The problem was that in also demanding that the delegation in Paris be kept in the dark,[69] Curzon was to further doom the Anglo-Persian Agreement, as it needlessly positioned the British as sabotaging the delegates in Paris.

Vosuq al-Dowleh's demand for secrecy was multi-faceted. He did not want to contradict, at least until the agreement was finalized, the work of the delegation in Paris. Whilst there was a chance of success in Paris, the negotiations with the

British had to remain secret. When it was obvious that success in Paris was unlikely, then a completed Anglo-Persian Agreement would serve as a last-ditch attempt to reform Iran. It is worth noting that most diplomacy, then as now, takes place within reasonable confidentiality. Nevertheless, Ahmad Shah did know the negotiations were taking place, though he was in all probability a reluctant participant. The delegates in Paris were also informed that these negotiations were taking place, though they found out through the British not their own government. On hearing that negotiations were taking place in Tehran behind their backs, the delegates in Paris feared the worst. Vosuq al-Dowleh was culpable in not informing the head of the delegation, Moshaver al-Mamalek, what separate negotiations had been going on in Tehran. Apart from that though, it is difficult to see what Vosuq al-Dowleh could have done. It is probable that he would have reasoned, correctly, that any further openness would have led to enough front-end opposition from politicians and Iranians to render the negotiations, let alone an agreement, impossible. Vosuq al-Dowleh, however, was playing a difficult hand. On the one hand secrecy was important in the success of the negotiations; on the other hand, he must have known that secrecy would help to sink the agreement.

The most damning indictment of the Triumvirate was the agreement to 'fund' them to get the agreement over the line. In total, 400,000 tomans (£131,000) was sent to the three ministers. Ostensibly this money had been intended to 'oil the wheels' and to be used to promote the agreement amongst recalcitrant politicians. The actual disposal, amongst the Triumvirate, remains foggy but it can be, and was not, considered anything more than a bribe. It is doubtless that Lord Curzon or Sir Percy Cox saw it as anything other than a bribe. Lord Curzon was evidently concerned about these payments and would have not made them unless necessary, Sir Percy Cox less so.[70] The Triumvirate, however, seemed to view it as danger money. They evidently assumed that they may have had to leave the country in a hurry.

Of course the use of money to further agreements in Iran was not new but, given the nature of this agreement, it was to be highly suggestive that Iran had been 'sold' to the British. Despite Sir Percy Cox's assertion that Vosuq al-Dowleh had not been the prime motivator but 'was doubtless not in strong enough position to risk a split with them [Nosrat al-Dowleh and Sarem al-Dowleh] over it,'[71] he was implicated. Though rumours existed at the time, the issue of bribery only became public in November 1920, months after the fall of Vosuq al-Dowleh's government and the agreement's ratification and implementation grinding to a halt. This element of the agreement therefore had not led to its demise but did enhance its dubious recollection.

Some of these accusations were quite intractable and would sink the agreement. Opposition to the agreement in and outside Iran, the sudden invasion of the Russians and opposition of the British politicians to the agreement, rendered it moribund.[72] However, there is one point which has been hitherto not emphasized. Both the Anglo-Persian Agreement and the proposals that the Iranian delegation took to Paris included similar *desiderata* that Lord Curzon and to a lesser extent Sir Percy Cox had seen as an irrelevancy. These concerned the issue of sovereignty and independence.

Iran's diplomatic approach in Paris and the Anglo-Persian Agreement has been grist to those who believed that Iran's approach had been haphazard. In truth, it was remarkably consistent and the only difference was the wholesale involvement of the British. The replacement of Moshaver al-Mamalek by Nosrat al-Dowleh had only replaced one diplomat working within the restrictions of not being able to negotiate directly with the British, with another who knew he had their ear. As we will see, this is borne out by Nosrat al-Dowleh's attempts to revive the *desiderata* that the delegates had attempted to present in Paris.

Round two

By 10 October, Mohammad Ali Foroughi was back in Paris and saw Nosrat al-Dowleh briefly before he went back to Britain. Nosrat al-Dowleh had asked Mohammad Ali Foroughi to stay in Paris even though he had expressed the preference to return to Tehran. In Britain, Nosrat al-Dowleh once again met with Lord Curzon and asked that the 'rectification of the Persian frontier', agreed as a letter and part of the Anglo-Persian Agreement, be put on the agenda for when he returned to London with Ahmad Shah to sign the agreement.[73] Nosrat al-Dowleh wanted to know, in particular, what Lord Curzon's reaction would be if the question of Turkestan, mainly concerning the Sarakhs, and Kurdistan was raised. A non-committal Lord Curzon instead asked for a more specific list of *desiderata*, in order of preference.

On 31 October Ahmad Shah and Nosrat al-Dowleh travelled to London. The Shah arrived in Dover on the royal yacht Alexandra and was met by Prince Albert (later George VI) and in London by the King. The fanfare for the young monarch was a far cry from how he had entered and left Paris, mostly incognito, because of the antipathy towards the Anglo-Persian Agreement. The parade put on for him and his inspection of British Airforce planes was undoubtedly put on to impress Ahmad Shah with Britain's military prowess and no doubt arranged to bolster the case for the agreement. Iran could now look forward to developing such a military through closer ties with Britain.

That night a banquet was put on at Buckingham Palace and the next day Ahmad Shah travelled from Buckingham Palace to Guildhall for a huge luncheon in the Shah's honour. In Lord Curzon's speech at Guildhall, he outlined what the Anglo-Persian Agreement would bring to Iran and symbolically saw in the Iranian flag the juxtaposition of the lion and the sun – the lion, the 'the proud and valiant champion of the rights and liberties of Persia', and the sun, a rising orb 'of the steadily increasing progress and prosperity of Persia itself'.[74] Ahmad Shah's response was far less lyrical and far more general in his assessment of the Anglo-Persian Agreement which he did not specifically mention. In his speech he set out a role for Iran in international relations that would prove favourable to the Europeans, but independent of them.[75]

Whether Lord Curzon was disappointed in Ahmad Shah's speech we don't know. He was, however, irritated when Nosrat al-Dowleh resumed Iran's *imperial nationalism* and wished to discuss territorial re-adjustments. Downgraded to letters in the agreement, pointless discussions, at least to Lord Curzon, only diverted negotiations from the meat of the Anglo-Persian Agreement. Lord Curzon had not replied to the question of Turkestan and Kurdistan raised by Nosrat al-Dowleh and was 'somewhat startled' when Ahmad Shah and Nosrat al-Dowleh produced a map showing the border rectifications that the Iranians still wanted to press at the Paris Peace Conference.[76] It is not clear which map was being presented to Lord Curzon but, as there is no evidence another map was produced, it was probably the same map that formed part of *Claims of Persia before the Conference of the Preliminaries of Peace of Paris*.

Two specific issues were discussed. The first showed an annexation of a considerable amount of Kurdish territory. Lord Curzon argued that this region had been under Turkish occupation for a long period and went far beyond the delimitation of the Ottoman-Iranian boundary concluded before the First World War. He saw no point in a proposal that ate 'right into the heart of Kurdish Country'.[77] Nosrat al-Dowleh's response revolved around the habit of the nomadic Kurdish tribes to cross the present border at will and that this change to the border would prevent this. This was, of course, a notable symptom of the implementation of borders through nomadic pasture lands. Lord Curzon was unlikely to approve the loss of Kurdish territory just as Britain was to receive the mandate for Mesopotamia.

The second issue was the return of a sizeable territory north of the Aras River, much of it lost to the Russians under the Treaty of Turkmanchai. Arguably, this alone would have done much for the success of the Anglo-Persian Agreement and Iran's nationalist fervour. After all, the Treaty of Turkmanchai had remained a sore and long-standing bugbear in the modern history of Iran. The region Iran claimed was likely similar to the minimum demand which they had formulated nearly a year ago in Tehran and likely included, in addition to the 'watershed of the River Aras', the repatriation of Talesh and a small part of Armenia (see Map 2). Lord Curzon hinted that such a change might not go down well with Iran's neighbours.[78]

A third rectification was noticed by Lord Curzon on the map but not discussed. It concerned extending Iranian territory to include Turkmenistan, the Sarakhs up to Merv and the Murghab River. Lord Curzon seemed less than impressed by these *desiderata* and expected them to be looked upon unfavourably by the British government. It is, however, unclear what he expected. The Iranians wanted major changes, yet the British had only given in to discussing rectifications as long as they were minor refinements.

More to Lord Curzon's liking would have been the discussion about the development of Iran's railway system which had been neglected. The question of developing a railway system in Iran was crucial to its transport infrastructure and one of the virtues of the Anglo-Persian Agreement. Despite the importance of deciding on a methodological structure for the railway, Lord Curzon had resolved little in the comparative merits of railways which were either owned and run by the state, owned and run by companies, or constructed by companies and run by the state.[79]

The Iranians had already come up with a plan for implementing a railway in Iran and had drawn up a prioritized list. Much of these plans had been determined by the necessity of producing a transport infrastructure to help develop greater trading opportunities, for example, linking northern Iran to the Bagdad railway and ports on the Caspian Sea. As the implementation of railways would take some time, they had also agreed to plan roads, which could be developed in a shorter time frame. Here a road from Bagdad to Tehran took priority.[80] It is curious given Lord Curzon's objection to allowing other Europeans or the Americans a piece of the Anglo-Persian Agreement pie, that he seemed contented with discussing French interest in Iran's future railway.

At the same meeting, Ahmad Shah also gave Lord Curzon an undated memorandum in French which was not discussed.[81] The memorandum specified a methodology for territorial acquisition, which differed from before in terms of complexity. Iran's irredentist argument had become augmented and had become more complex. The foundational basis now, in addition to the usual points of analogous *Persianate* attributes and previous title, included a greater consideration for the nomadic movement of tribes and military considerations. As the memorandum referred to the map which was shown to Lord Curzon, one can only guess at the specific regions Iran wanted to re-appropriate.

In the west, Iran claimed a 'tongue of land' to help the movement of nomadic tribes, presumably based on similar discussions regarding the movement of Kurdish tribes. Neither the tribes nor the 'tongue' was defined. The only significant plain and break in the Zagros mountains was the tract known as Zohab and the memorandum probably referred to this region. Iran's new claim included providing an access point through the mountains for nomadic tribes to pass, providing natural mountain irrigation and the cessation of border violations (see Map 6). Iran's assertions aside it is likely that this claim was playing towards Britain's own interests. The Zohab had long been contested territory between Iran and the Ottoman Empire. It was also a point where the natural defences of Iran were broken. As early as 1844, the British had considered that giving Zohab back to the Ottomans would remove the natural defence of the Zagros from Iran and would 'inflict a deep blow on the interests and security' of Iran.[82] Now, in the early twentieth century, it was also a region that had provided the APOC with its first oil strike. Nosrat al-Dowleh was clearly pandering to British security and commercial concerns.

In the north-west, the Iranians proposed the annexation of a small part of Erivan, Nakhchevan, and the area up to the Moghan Steppe. The security of Iranian Azerbaijan was mooted as a reason for the repatriation of these territories. In the north-east, the document argued for Iranian territory to be extended to the Murghab River (presumably to extend dominium over the Sarakhs) and northwards following the Attrek River to Merv. Merv was, therefore, to be the town on the eastern corner of Iran's domain. These changes would ameliorate the real problems that the Protocols agreed with Russia had created in the provision of water for the Iranian villages.[83] In terms of security, the changes would also help to protect Iran from Turkmen incursions.

The document went on to discuss some wide-ranging and bewildering corrections to the Sistan Boundary based on the need to safeguard water supplies and the natural limits of Iran. This would include making changes to the Iranian-Afghanistan border which had been negotiated with the British. It also specified the exact route an altered delimitation of Iran's borders would take if the British would agree with the changes. The detail was both extensive and exhaustive, and provided a roadmap for Iran's *imperial nationalism*. It was also testament to Iran's ability to employ modern methods of examination and argument.

Attached to the memorandum was a separate enclosure that detailed the wishes of the new 'Azerbaijani Republic'.[84] Nosrat al-Dowleh was now following a policy of dialogue with the independent Azeri Republic which had been transformed from Iran's previous strategy. Moshaver al-Mamalek had largely ignored Azeri entreaties to open a political dialogue with the Iranian delegation both on the way to, and in, Paris. Nosrat al-Dowleh had begun negotiations with the Azeri delegation which Mohammad Ali Foroughi took over when Nosrat al-Dowleh went to Britain. The Azeri memorandum was the result of these discussions and represented a political partnership between Iran and what used to be Russian Azerbaijan.

The enclosure specified the birth of a democratic Azerbaijani Republic on 28 May 1918, elected by universal suffrage. Its territorial sovereignty was to be within the limits indicated by the map submitted as part of the *Claims of the Peace Delegation of the Republic of Caucasian Azerbaijan Presented to the Peace Conference in Paris* (see Map 1). It also proposed a political and economic link between the two countries in the shape of a confederation and a unified foreign policy. Thus, the Azerbaijani delegation in Paris had concluded that its very existence would be more precarious without an umbilical cord with Iran. Moreover, they expected Britain to protect its fledgling democracy and to help 'develop its political, economic, cultural and military forces, similar to those granted to Persia'. Though a much-maligned agreement, at least the Azeris were enticed by the advantages of the Anglo-Persian Agreement.

The Azeris were of course fearful of a revitalized Russia and its re-incorporation in another Russian Empire. This fear was of course not misplaced as by the end of spring 1920 Azerbaijan's democracy had first been cast aside by the Bolsheviks and its territory was soon after invaded by the Red Army.[85] The inability of the new Transcaucasian Republics to remain independent when menaced by the Red Army has echoes in the collapse of the Anglo-Persian Agreement and indeed Iran's military inadequacy.

Nosrat al-Dowleh saw fit to follow the memorandum left with Lord Curzon on 13 November with two further memorandums issued in quick succession and received by Lord Curzon on 18 and 19 November. Nosrat al-Dowleh had become desperate to achieve some success on the issue of territorial rectification, as he was also coming under pressure from Vosuq al-Dowleh who feared that the Peace Conference in Paris could be wrapped up without Iran being heard. A threat he had shared with Lord Curzon. Both memoranda display a development in Iran's argument for territorial rectification as well as an increased sophistication of it.

The first memorandum sought to add substance and clarification to Iran's *desiderata* already put to Lord Curzon.[86] In addition to the general tenets behind Iran's territorial rectifications such as previous possession, *Persianate* attributes, consideration for the nomadic movement of tribes and military considerations, it now included something new – bringing certain groups who lacked the wherewithal to form independent states under Iran's territorial umbrella and the claims of some of those groups to join Iran.

Inchoate states, particularly in the Caucasus, whose independence hung by a thread would, the Iranians believed, be better off as Iranian provinces. These states were threatened by the Red Army and Bolshevik activity that they found hard to counter. The Western powers had shown themselves unwilling or unable to protect them. The United States had not picked up the mandate for Armenia and Britain saw no reason to take any mandate other than that of Mesopotamia. Ultimately, though, Britain's military presence in the region was too small to afford any protection for these states.

While this methodology seemed sound, Nosrat al-Dowleh also claimed that both the inhabitants of Nakhchevan, the Sarakhs and Kurds, had claimed they wanted to 'return to the mother country'. Here, Iranian claims relied on despatches from Nakhchevan and other places.[87] Kurdish appeals to come under Iran's imperial umbrella were symptomatic of the tenuous links the Iranians were claiming. Sharif Pasha had discussed a more permanent inclusion of Kurdistan under Iranian sovereignty. However, he had been in Paris since 1910 and 'had no constituency in Kurdistan' and it was said that no one took him seriously.[88]

Yet, in both arguments, the Iranians were cleverly alluding to and applying the principles of self-determination. Either in that groups of various ethnicities were choosing to be part of Iran or calling into question the viability of the existence of nationalist entities given the territorial patchwork of ethnicities, which made territorial sovereignty almost impossible. Where Kurds were discussed, Nosrat al-Dowleh played both cards and pointed out that Kurds had a long-standing attachment to Iran and pointed out that they would never tolerate Armenian domination. The basis for another *desideratum* in the Caucasus and the Transcaspian was further extended. For example, in Transcaucasus, Iran suggested that out of 3.2 million inhabitants 1.2 million were of 'pure Iranian origin' and that the others were Muslim. In an obvious alliteration of Empire, Iranian arguments were becoming more political and strategic rather than primordial.

The second memorandum referred to the memorandum concerning the new Azeri Republic, which had been left with Lord Curzon, but not discussed.[89] Nosrat al-Dowleh's intention was to illuminate the paradox of an independent Azerbaijan, yet closely linked politically and economically with Iran. He proposed that as Lord Curzon had no obvious wish to get involved in Caucasian affairs, and that Azerbaijan's independence was somewhat tenuous, Iran could operate a measure of control over Azerbaijan. This would help Iran in defending its northern borders. The Iranians had already had discussions with the Azeris in early November. They had even earlier concluded a treaty of friendship and commerce in April; now, looking towards issues of security, they concluded a four-point treaty whereby in recognition of Azeri independence, certain political and economic relations could be normalized.[90]

Though Lord Curzon suggested that it was wise for Iran to enter negotiations with the Azeris, he queried what they might have thought if they knew that Iran also wanted to annex and absorb so much of pre-Russian Armenia and Azerbaijan. However, by December 1919 it was the Azeris, who, following the advance of Russian troops, had advocated Iranian annexation.[91] Lord Curzon was not able to square this circle, though Nosrat al-Dowleh was pushed to find an ambiguity, only claiming that he doubted that the Azeris would be opposed to such a prospect. Nosrat al-Dowleh must have known that conversations were taking place in this context. Nevertheless, the subject ended when Lord Curzon pointed out that the new Azeri government had not yet been recognized and the conversation was, therefore, moot.[92]

Nosrat al-Dowleh had left many issues for Lord Curzon to reflect on and wanted Lord Curzon to voice his opinion on these issues – seemingly before Iran could submit its more nuanced arguments for territorial restitution at the Paris Peace Conference. Lord Curzon's response was detailed in a memorandum to Sir Percy Cox following 'a final discussion' of Iran's territorial *desiderata*.[93] In 'absolute frankness', Nosrat al-Dowleh was told that most of the claims could not be supported and that any chance of success had been wrecked by the original claims that Moshaver al-Mamalek had included in the *Claims of Persia before the Conference of the Preliminaries of Peace of Paris*. If Iran were to present these, albeit lesser *desiderata*, to the Peace Conference, then Britain would not block it but would not support it either.

In truth, Lord Curzon's assertions were curious and at the very least misleading. Iran's claims in Paris had never made it to either the Big Four or even the Council of Ten and it is not clear how Moshaver al-Mamalek's actions had 'wrecked all chances of success'. After all it was the British who had blocked Iran's representations in Paris and it was the British, who were effectively blocking them now. It was probable that Lord Curzon had been irritated by the constant level of demands coming from the Iranians for territorial restitutions which were also continuously changing. Nevertheless, Lord Curzon's response was disingenuous.

Lord Curzon was on firmer ground, however, when he pointed out the essential irrelevancy of Iran's *desiderata* when Nosrat al-Dowleh asked why Iran could not recover lost territories if other nations could. Lord Curzon told him that other countries had the military force to defend new territories and that other countries had not professed neutrality during the First World War and 'now sought a wide extension of its territory, as a reward for its inaction'. This was a stinging rebuke for Nosrat al-Dowleh, but not the end of it.

As Lord Curzon had replied in the negative to all of Nosrat al-Dowleh's *desiderata* over the last few weeks, a disconsolate Nosrat al-Dowleh was forced to ask how Iran could achieve any satisfaction. He was urged to take matters to the League of Nations. Nosrat al-Dowleh was right in this regard to be dubious of this course of action and was to be proved right. One of the first and most enthusiastic members of the League of Nations and described as one of the 'champions of the small states',[94] Iran was also one of the first to put a grievance to the League of Nations, only to be rebuffed.[95]

More final, perhaps, was the feeler that Nosrat al-Dowleh next put out. Why could not Iran come to an agreement directly with the Bolsheviks, and one assumes others in Transcaucasia and the Afghans to re-fashion and protect Iran's borders. Lord Curzon was said to answer that given British enmity towards the Bolsheviks such entreaties would result in the evacuation of British forces in north-western Iran.

Lord Curzon was not to budge. In the final analysis, he had once again proved two points that would work against the Iranians as they pursued their *desiderata* under the contemporary state of affairs: Iran lacked the military wherewithal to take what it believed was theirs or wanted, and that Iran would not receive any help from the British. Lord Curzon would not even give an indication for future rectifications, which he could not see would have helped the Iranian government, the Anglo-Persian Agreement and help neutralize the anti-British sentiment. Lord Curzon had made a crucial mistake in brushing off the Iranian Peace Delegation and Iran's *desiderata*.

There can be no doubt that, reading the runes of these negotiations, Nosrat al-Dowleh was also becoming frustrated with the government in Tehran, which had pushed for wide-ranging territorial restitutions which Lord Curzon would not sanction. Nosrat al-Dowleh knew he was asking for the moon and it was unlikely, left to his own devices, that he would have pushed for such extensive *desiderata*. Still, Nosrat al-Dowleh, pushed by the government in Tehran to get results, was not about to give up and went to see Lord Curzon again.

In late November, Nosrat al-Dowleh saw Lord Curzon. He wanted to discuss the items brought up in the meeting with Ahmad Shah. Though clearly under duress to achieve something before the Peace Conference ended, he asked if the British government had considered Iran's *desiderata*, before it was to be put forward in Paris. This was soon followed by another meeting with Lord Curzon in which Nosrat al-Dowleh explained his fear of sending a telegram of a 'very discouraging nature' to Iran and had been considering how he 'could possibly furnish any encouragement to the Prime Minister'.[96] Though Nosrat al-Dowleh accepted Lord Curzon's reasons for opposing changes to Iran's borders, he did ask if there was some mileage in the Azerbaijan question. He suggested that Lord Curzon link further 'sympathy and support' only if a 'working understanding' with Iran could be reached.

Lord Curzon's reply, in the middle of December, to Nosrat al-Dowleh's entreaties reiterated the position of the British government and declared that the Iranian territorial wish list was so comprehensive in character, and 'so ancient in nature', that it could not hope to be supported by the British. He then went on to reinforce the two methods by which Iran could get access to the Paris Peace Conference, either to offer 'a more moderate assertion of Persian desiderata backed by the support of His Majesty's Government' or to go ahead on their own responsibility.[97] The memorandum went on to explain that the proposed Iranian resolution, which Iran wanted to be proclaimed at the Peace Conference, which declared, 'the Conference recognizes that the territorial claims of Persia in Transcaspia are well-founded, but that the whole of the question, depending as it does upon the solution of the Russian problem, cannot be decided at present',[98] could for the same reasons not be supported by the British. At no point, however, were the Iranians contemplating trying to get access to the Peace Conference without British support and Nosrat al-Dowleh rather meekly asked what a 'moderate assertion' might be.[99]

The night before Nosrat al-Dowleh left for Paris, he discussed Lord Curzon's last crushing memorandum with Lancelot Oliphant.[100] During this discussion, Nosrat al-Dowleh hoped that Britain could support more limited *desiderata*. He re-argued the points regarding Nakhchevan and juxtaposed the notion of Armenians forcing the Azeris to leave Nakhchevan with the wishes of the Azeris of Nakhchevan to be incorporated in Iran. Nosrat al-Dowleh was proposing nothing less than a plebiscite to decide the fate of the Azeris. The obvious utility of plebiscites was not lost on the Iranians when the need arose; however, even given ideas of self-determination, Britain was loath to help establish a precedent in the Middle East.

Nosrat al-Dowleh seemed at no point willing to give up pressing for Iran's territorial *desiderata*, and communications between the Iranian and British governments were to continue towards the end of December 1919 and early January 1920. These communications show that Iran now considered any border modifications as confirmation of the success of the Anglo-Persian Agreement, as they had always intended it to be. As the same issues were brought up by Nosrat al-Dowleh, the British put up the same resistance. Lord Hardinge did not see any of Iran's territorial *desiderata* as minor rectifications and suggested that British troops would be needed to be sacrificed to achieve these aims as Iran had no troops to hand. Lord Curzon felt simply that all the Iranian proposals were 'utterly unreasonable'.[101]

Vosuq al-Dowleh, in a telegram between himself and Nosrat al-Dowleh, rationalized that he did not understand why the British, who always strove for tranquil border regions, did not understand the dangers of delay in settling these questions. Conflicts caused by the breakup of the Russian Empire meant 'tolerating the existence in the Transcaspian provinces of a hotbed of anarchy and unrest which threatens to spread and extend to all the neighbouring countries'.[102] Clearly, though Turkestan and Nakhchevan were not lands that the Peace Conference felt were within their remit, Vosuq al-Dowleh pointed out that other similar exceptions had been made, such as Finland and Poland. The Iranians simply did not understand why the British did not consider that border modifications might help to mitigate some of the opposition to the Anglo-Persian Agreement in Iran.

Russia and the endgame

Iran's irredentist pursuits had begun when she had lost considerable territory to the Russian Empire under the terms of the Treaty of Turkmanchai in 1828. It seemed almost appropriate that Russia would have the last word in ending Iran's irredentist diplomacy in 1920. Iran's diplomatic policy to re-invent itself as both an Empire and a modern state ended when they firstly could not get a hearing at the Peace Conference in Paris and when it was obvious that the Anglo-Persian Agreement, which also carried territorial hopes, had become hopelessly mired in controversy and unable to succeed.

The Allies had not agreed to allow a Russian delegation to be invited to Paris, even though Russia was a factor in decisions concerning the emerging Baltic states, eastern Europe, and the Caucasus. President Wilson and Lloyd George had been broadly in favour of engaging with the Russians, but Georges Clemenceau had felt that Russia had betrayed the Allies and, given his rabid hatred of Bolshevism, saw no part for them in the peace process. Of course, it was impossible to know who to deal with. Who really represented Russia, the White Russians or the Soviets?

Iran was caught in the same bind. Without a firm understanding as to whether the Russian Empire or a Bolshevik Republic would emerge from the rubble of revolution, it was safer to keep both at arms-length. The Iranian delegation did their best, therefore, to not engage with the various unofficial Russian delegates and agents milling around Paris. There were good reasons for this. Iran, just as in Georgia, Azerbaijan, Armenia and other parts of the Russian Empire, was also facing a Bolshevik menace of their own.

Towards the end of 1919 Bolshevik forces had begun to exert supremacy over the disintegrating forces of the Russian Empire. General Denikin's forces, the only available barrier to Bolshevik success, had begun to crumble. By April 1920 Bolshevik Red Army troops entered Baku. Many British politicians, including Lloyd George and Winston Churchill, had arrived at the conclusion that an ultimate Bolshevik victory could not now be prevented. As the British now considered alternate military scenarios intended to protect its dominions, it was obvious that they did not have the wherewithal to resist any sustained attack by the Red Army. Little had changed since Sir Charles Marling had been forced to make do in April 1918 with meagre military support.

In January 1920 Vosuq al-Dowleh asked Britain to provide military reinforcements. Fearing that the Anglo-Persian Agreement had only tied Iran to British politics and Bolshevik ire,[103] he was, at the very least, also hoping that Britain would help to protect Iran under the agreement. As Nosrat al-Dowleh wrote to Lord Curzon on 30 December:

> No one knew better than Lord Curzon and Sir Percy Cox that Britain lacked necessary means and forces. The object of the agreement was to help Persia to restore internal order, recover her prestige, and acquire a strong position in the Middle East.[104]

Significantly, the agreement did not call for Britain to defend Iran from aggression but Britain's inaction on this request was to be yet another black event in the diplomatic relationship between the two countries, somewhat reminiscent of Britain's efforts to get out of its responsibilities under the Definitive Treaty of 1814, when they also did little to prevent Russian aggression.

Lord Curzon's plans for Iran had finally been curtailed by those who had been opposed to the Anglo-Persian Agreement and neither the cabinet nor the War Office could justify any greater military defence to the Bolshevik threat than was already available.[105] Yet, Curzon did not seem overly concerned that Iran was in fact in any immediate danger.[106] Certainly he seemed startled when Nosrat al-Dowleh had, a month earlier, gone to see him to discuss the efficacy of Iran establishing direct relations with Soviet Russia.[107] Steadfastly anchored to the agreement, Lord Curzon was in no way moved to see the efficacy of such a diplomatic move – a move which others, including Lord Montagu, thought eminently sensible.

Almost while Lord Curzon had dismissed Russian threats to Iran and had rebuffed Iranian wishes to take the bull by the horns and open a dialogue with the Russians, the Russians landed at the Iranian port of Anzali on the shores of the Caspian on 18 May. Notwithstanding the immediate shock of the landing, it was not clear for the next few weeks if the Russian force was to stay in Anzali, or even whether it was part of a much broader military intervention in Iran. Two things happened which were to change British attitudes towards the landing. The first was the landing of fresh troops rather than the repatriation of the original landing force, and the second was the proclamation of the Soviet Republic of Gilan, the result of an alliance between the noted revolutionary Kuchik Khan, his Jangali guerrillas and Bolshevik troops.

The exploits of Kuchik Khan (1880–1921), which had begun during the First World War, exhibit several parallels to Iran's more recent general history. Kuchik Khan's revolutionary activities would follow multiple iterations. He had begun as a *mojahed* (constitutional combatant) during the Constitutional Revolution. In 1915, he formed the *Jangali* Movement, named for being forest dwellers, to fight the Russian occupation of Gilan. At the time he allied his movement to Ottoman's pan-Islamism, which formed much of pan-Turkism and was therefore affiliated with the Central Powers. Kuchik Khan was soon wooed by the Bolsheviks in 1919 and was involved in the formation of the Gilan Socialist Republic.

While these activities also helped to heighten fears of Bolshevism in Iran, Kuchik Khan's separatist and socialist credentials are in serious doubt. He was a staunch Muslim, but not a committed socialist nor looking to separate Gilan from Iran. Another, Mohammad Khiabani (1880–1920), who led a revolt in Azerbaijan, was equally not a separatist but sought to 'establish a strong autonomous rule in Azerbaijan as part of Iran'.[108] Both are examples of revolutionary activity in Iran which flirted with Bolshevism and pan-Islamism but which were not separatist.

The landing in Anzali by the Bolsheviks was the effective end of the Anglo-Persian Agreement. James Balfour, not a fan of it or Lord Curzon, had declared that the agreement was dead from the moment that the Bolsheviks had landed at Anzali.[109] Yet, in truth, the agreement was on life support, caught between Lord Curzon, who was still reluctant for it to die, and Iranian politicians, who were reluctant to ratify it through the *Majles*. For Iranians it was clear that though Britain was not, under the agreement, obliged to protect Iran, the agreement had little use if Britain could not. The prevailing mood was that British forces would be evacuated in the north and leave the approaches to Tehran open.[110] Sir Percy Cox had to remind Lord Curzon that he had himself emphasized 'the advantages of the agreement against Bolshevism'.[111]

Only one month after the landing of Bolshevik forces, Vosuq al-Dowleh resigned. Tired, isolated and unable to do his job effectively, he had only waited for Ahmad Shah to come back to Iran from Europe to see if he would support him.[112] With one of the architects of the agreement out of the picture, Moshir al-Dowleh, the likely replacement, wanted to suspend the Anglo-Persian Agreement pending the convening and agreement by the *Majles*. He subsequently only put it into 'abeyance'. This confirmed Lord Curzon's 'grave misgivings' of Moshir al-Dowleh who he considered 'a weak character and inspires no confidence'.[113]

By this time, Herman Norman (1872–1955) had replaced Sir Percy Cox in Tehran. Coincidently, he had been part of the British delegation to the Peace Conference. Sir Percy Cox, whose overly sanguine reports had contributed so much to Lord Curzon's denial, had gone to take up his new post as High Commissioner in Iraq. Norman, taking stock of the *realpolitik* in Tehran, not only supported Moshir al-Dowleh but was also to be more realistic towards the survival of the agreement. This was, unfortunately, to put him at loggerheads with Lord Curzon.

Moshir al-Dowleh found the difficulties Iran faced too intractable. The question of ratifying the Anglo-Persian Agreement still existed. It hinged, however, on the continuation of elections that had taken place under Vosuq al-Dowleh or to call new ones, all in a country where governmental control was hardly complete.[114] The Bolshevik threat still existed as well as did the revolts discussed above. The diplomatic pressure which Lord Curzon brought to bear on ratifying the agreement was equally a problem and so Moshir al-Dowleh's government was only to last four months. Crucially though, he opened a diplomatic dialogue with the Bolsheviks.

In November 1919, Nosrat al-Dowleh had proposed that Iran should reach out to the Bolshevik government and come to an agreement concerning relations between the two. Still in Europe, Nosrat al-Dowleh had gone to Lord Curzon on numerous occasions to ask for his consent.[115] Lord Curzon had shut this idea down abruptly, but the idea had much going for it, not least that it might facilitate the evacuation of the Red Army from Iranian soil. Norman, like Lord Curzon, resisted this plan but Moshir al-Dowleh, who also believed in its efficacy, went ahead anyway. To Lord Curzon's added discomfort, Moshir al-Dowleh asked Moshaver al-Mamalek to head the delegation to Moscow and recalled him from Istanbul.

Moshaver al-Mamalek's negotiations with the Bolsheviks were painfully slow and the results would only see light in February 1921, the same month that Iran underwent a military coup and Reza Khan and Seyyed Zia al-din Tabataba'i were forced onto Ahmad Shah. In fact, February 1921 was to be a crucial month in Iran's history. It was the beginning of the end of the Qajar dynasty, which would limp on in name only until 1925, and it also saw the emergence of Reza Khan, who epitomized a uniquely Iranian solution to 'the Persian problem'. For Iranian nationalists, Reza Khan 'would be the Enlightened Despot rescuing the floundering Iranian Revolution [Constitutional Revolution], providing the necessary force to implement the policies of centralisation and modernisation'.[116]

Under Reza Khan, territorial issues were to be more about protection than irredentist pursuits. Reza Khan believed that the reclaiming of territory was not consistent with his brand of nationalism. He was also to understand that, even though borders were integral to a bourgeoning nationalism, you had to be able to defend them. Reza Khan saw the Iranian Army not only 'as the symbol of Iran's independence and integrity, but also as the principal instrument of his country's administrative centralization and viability',[117] and vital to protect Iran's borders.

Iran would, during Reza Shah's reign, complete much of the reform programme which formed part of Iran's *imperial nationalism*. Despite accusations that he had been brought to power by a coup that was either organized or assisted by the British, Iran would, under his rule, be noticeably more independent. The question of Empire, on which *imperial nationalism* depended, ceased to be irredentist but Iran's Empires of the past, their territories, history and myths remained a strong element in the Pahlavi dynasty, which would include his son, Mohammad Reza Shah. Like other shahs before them, they extracted their legitimacy from the past and absorbed themselves in the idea of Iran.

It was Reza Khan who, through military intervention, ultimately resolved the revolutionary activity in Azerbaijan and tribal unrest elsewhere in Iran. He would also benefit from the negotiations with the Bolsheviks. The 'Treaty of Friendship', signed with Bolshevik Russia in February, was a curious amalgam of socialist camaraderie, goodwill and hard diplomacy.[118] The island of Ashuradeh, and the village and environs of Firouzeh were given back to Iran 'in view of the repugnance which the Russian Federal Government feels to enjoying the fruit of the policy of usurpation of the Tsarist Government'. Russian goodwill did not extend to the question of the Sarakhs, the Turkmen lands or indeed the Caucasus.

What it did do was to reset Iran's diplomacy with its nearest and largest neighbour, and it has been seen as a success for Iran in which it received most of what it wanted. Despite Bolshevik Russia being granted the right to send its military to Iran, in the event of third-party 'armed intervention', Iran gained much. All conventions and treaties with Tsarist Russia were annulled, which included the 1907 Anglo-Russian Convention. Loans were cancelled, and communication and transport infrastructure built by Russia was passed to the Iranian government. All concessions, capitulations and economic interests were also cancelled, and Iran was to have equal rights to navigate the Caspian Sea, which had been lost under the Treaty of Turkmanchai.

Encouraged by negotiations with the Bolsheviks, Moshaver al-Mamalek was asked to negotiate similar treaties with Azerbaijan, Armenia and Georgia.[119] Their nationalism and state-building attempts had been brought to an end as Russia, now Soviet rather than Tsarist, sought to regain control of these territories. The opportunity to set a new relationship with Afghanistan, recently independent, was taken up and a 'Treaty of Friendship' was negotiated between Iran and Afghanistan.

Lord Curzon had also been against the approach to the Afghanis, as he had the Bolsheviks. It was left to Norman to describe Iran's predicament:

> If Persian Government are reproached for negotiating a treaty with Bolsheviks, they can reply that His Majesty's Government did not forbid despatch of a mission

to Moscow when proposed by late Cabinet, that they have kept His Majesty's Government fully informed of discussions, and are being alone guided by their adviser, that weakness of Persia's geographical and military position obliges them to make such an agreement, more especially since they have more than once been told that Great Britain cannot defend her against serious invasion, and since they [now] learn that British troops are to be withdrawn in the spring; and, finally, that His Majesty's Government are themselves negotiating with Soviet [the Soviets].[120]

Homa Katouzian noted that had Iran been able to negotiate earlier with the Bolsheviks, as they had wanted, then the Red Army might not have invaded.[121] By this point, confused by the many memoranda from Norman who was reacting to shifting circumstances, Lord Curzon took his frustrations regarding the Anglo-Persian Agreement out on Norman. His response that Norman was still hoping that the agreement would be ratified was one of indifference. Moreover, he blamed Norman for installing the government of Moshir al-Dowleh, which had put the agreement in abeyance.

In truth, all the short-term governments since the fall of Vosuq al-Dowleh had been unable or unwilling to ratify the agreement. Lord Curzon's attitude to carrying on, while hostile to all who did not see the benefits of the agreement, even though hanging on to it seemed to obstruct rather than help British diplomacy in Iran, was one of denial. In the event, the agreement was finally put out of its misery with the coup of 1921. By this point, despite the state of political flux in Iran, it had reset Iran's diplomacy with some of its nearest neighbours.

Conclusion

Iran's diplomacy after the announcement of the Anglo-Persian Agreement was distinguished by the fact that Iran's Foreign Minister, Nosrat al-Dowleh, had unfettered access to Lord Curzon, unlike Moshaver al-Mamalek, his predecessor. Against the background of both internal and international criticism of the agreement, the delegation would continue to push for achieving success in Iran's original eight-point programme.

Despite the agreement, Iran sought an independent future which was not exclusively bound to the British. They still pursued the internationalizing of Iran's reform and they still pursued the restoration of Iranian territory. Taken as a whole, Nosrat al-Dowleh's communications and meetings with Lord Curzon and others in the British government show the disconnect between British and Iranian strategies for Iran, despite an increase in friendship between the two countries.

The Triumvirate continued to do what they could to counter the criticism of the Anglo-Persian Agreement. They also attempted, and failed, to make Lord Curzon appreciate that much could have been gained by some flexibility on the part of the British. The British could have opened the agreement to other countries and could have involved the League of Nations. Lord Curzon could have understood the vital importance for the Iranian government of the day to show tangible and visible optics of success. Lord Curzon's rationalization of the agreement failed to obviate criticism of the agreement.

Nosrat al-Dowleh will always be associated with the Anglo-Persian Agreement and the bribes that he, as part of the Triumvirate, exhorted out of Lord Curzon and Sir Percy Cox. Under his tenure, Iran's claims for territorial restitution, however, became more complex. The methods by which Iran claimed its previous Empire, such as regional security, involved a greater understanding of British strategies in the region. Nevertheless, like Moshaver al-Mamalek before him, he was also not to be successful.

The death of the agreement now brought to a close Iran's programme of *imperial nationalism*. The more time it had taken for the Anglo-Persian Agreement to be ratified, the more it had been apparent that it was ill-suited to the politics and development of nationalism in Iran. Other factors had also come into play. Iran had begun to look towards its own security by treaties with nations who shared its borders. The military coup in 1921, led primarily by Reza Khan, also demonstrated a more muscular answer to Iran's considerable problems. Irredentism for a greater Iran would be put aside, though the echoes of Iran's great dynasties and empires would continue to loom large in the nationalist narratives in Iran.

CONCLUSION: A REASSESSMENT

This study has set out to dispel some of the lingering interpretations that the period between the end of the First World War and the Pahlavi dynasty had been characterized by a weak, unguided Iranian government, which lacked foresight or the ability to govern effectively. Using Persian archive material, as well as Mohammad Ali Foroughi's diary entries, it has been possible to show that this period was a particularly vibrant and febrile chapter in Iran's nationalist historiography. The modern methods the Iranians had used, to prepare and organize the delegation to the Paris Peace Conference, were nothing more than remarkable. Against a backdrop of a war-torn country, they were able to develop the structure of a cogent nationalist plan which would be further refined in Paris. After many years of deference to Western attitudes and modernism, they were to adapt and use modern methods in pursuing their own *desiderata*.

Iranian sources suggest that Ahmad Shah may have been more involved in planning for peace than previously appreciated. In the final analysis, the make-up of Iran's delegation was very much his. His role in the diplomacy during the First World War and in the immediate aftermath should be open to revision. The delegation, led by Moshaver al-Mamalek, left Iran with a brief that had been fully discussed and tailored in a series of meetings. These meetings had been foregrounded by research into the damages inflicted on Iran during the First World War. In Paris, in the first few months of 1919, the delegation embarked on a programme in which they met with a multitude of statesmen, politicians and other agents as they promoted Iran's *desiderata*. The delegation published numerous documents in support and enlisted the help of various journalists. No stone was left unturned in their efforts to be heard.

So why did Iran's *imperial nationalism* fail? There was no fault in its planning. Despite considerable headwinds, Iran was able to plan for, and deliver, a delegation to Paris with a defined pathway. It has been claimed that Iran's claims were unrealistic and, even if sensible, that the Peace Conference was not the forum in which to voice these concerns. The territorial claims were unrealistic, as Mohammad Ali Foroughi himself suggested. The negotiation ploy of asking much to achieve lesser gains was also obvious to Lord Curzon. This leads us to one of the most important facets of Iran's failure in Paris; Iran did not have the wherewithal to protect the additional territories it had asked for. It would have been far simpler for Iran to take the territories by military force and then, as other European states had done, come to the Peace Conference and have their gains ratified.

It is also unlikely that a different delegation would have succeeded. British opposition would have taken place against all but Vosuq al-Dowleh and Nosrat al-Dowleh. In the event even Nosrat al-Dowleh failed. However, had they gone then only the Anglo-Persian Agreement would have been negotiated. The narrative in this book has suggested that the end of the Qajar era was distinguished by greater energy, planning and proactive diplomacy than first thought. Some may argue that the narrative has also touched on the missed opportunities of the delegation and the suspicions and antagonism between delegates. Nevertheless, it should be noted that the delegates did broadly pull in the same direction and that disagreements amongst delegates of all nations at the Peace Conference were sometimes fractured and difficult. As Lord Curzon showed, even his plan for Iran did not have all-encompassing approval.

Was Paris the correct forum in which to discuss Iran's *desiderata*? Paris was the only international outlet available for resolving Iran's problems, and other nations, and would-be nations, were doing the same. In fact, given that the future of the Ottoman Empire needed to be resolved, and that the Armenians, Georgians, Kurds and Azeris had all sent delegations, then would it have not been strange if Iran had not. If Iran had not cared enough to send a delegation, then it might have conceded political capital to its neighbours.

Many of the accusations concerning Iranian overreach in Paris stem from the British who did not want their plans for the Middle East and Iran to be part of a wider discussion amongst their Allies. Lord Curzon long argued that Iran's *desiderata* could have, and should have been, dealt with away from the Peace Conference. The problem was, as the negotiations towards the Anglo-Persian Agreement have shown, that he never really seemed willing to do so.

One cannot disassociate Britain's scepticism for Iran's programme of *imperial nationalism* from British plans in the regions and borders contiguous to both Iran and India. Iran was already bordered by India in the south and in the north by the buffer state of Afghanistan and was, therefore, a factor in India's security. Now, Britain had the chance to control the region of Mesopotamia through a mandate. A weak and chaotic Iran may have been permissible before, but now it would serve only as a bad apple within a cordon of British imperial management.

This now informed two consequences. The first, as Lord Curzon had noted, was that it was now time for Britain to once and for all come up with a complete plan for the resurrection and management of Iran. The second was that despite allusions to the contrary, such management could only be constructed as something akin to a mandate. One cannot separate British plans for Iraq under a mandate and Lord Curzon's plans for the Anglo-Persian Agreement. The roles of, and methods of, Sir Percy Cox and Lord Curzon in Iraq and Iran were intertwined.

British opposition to Iran's participation in the Peace Conference was as extensive as Iran's plans had been. Despite early on countenancing Iran's participation at the Conference, British opposition was to slowly gather steam. Disparate notes between Foreign Office officials were to be solidified in Sir Percy

Cox's memorandum which was sent the very day that the delegation left for Paris.[1] Thereafter, hurdles to Iranian participation were frequently discussed in Foreign Office memoranda and in the meetings of the Eastern Committee.

Were Iran's ruling elite therefore naïve to believe that the opportunity for change had followed the end of the First World War? Had they not sufficiently realized that little had changed and that world politics would continue to be dominated by imperial powers and their exigencies? There is some truth in this. Iran had embraced concepts such as internationalism and self-determination without fully understanding that the world really had not changed significantly. Britain still held sway in that part of the Middle East and British imperialism was far from dead.[2] However, as Nosrat al-Dowleh's later discussions with Lord Curzon showed, the Iranians were learning quickly and adapting their methodologies to the international paradigm.

Iran had fully engaged in the 'Wilsonian moment'[3] and ideas of self-determination. They believed these ideas would serve to both sanctify and justify Iran's independence and sovereignty. They had done this only to discover the intellectual paucity of these ideas. Despite a strategy that had been sanctioned at the highest levels, Iran's progress in determining its independence and sovereignty had been brought to a halt by a contemporaneous secret deal and old-style imperial hegemonic diplomacy. But we can turn the question of Iranian naivety on its head; Iran, given the new world political outlook, could not have produced anything else and that it was the British and the Vosuq al-Dowleh who had not understood that after the First World War underhand deals which threatened Iran's independence would not be looked upon favourably by the international community.

Yet, these judgements are made with considerable hindsight and do not consider the immense sense of change that was possible. It also does not take into account another important factor: Iran had no choice. Iran was a failing state in today's vernacular and many of Iran's elite were forced to look to the future. There was little else they could do. In declaring what 'What will happen to Iran?',[4] Mohammad Ali Foroughi was giving voice to what many had thought. Iran's plight could not get much worse and they simply did not have any alternatives left.

Most, if not all, of Iran's elite, and I would also argue, Ahmad Shah, by their actions saw the necessity of economic and political reform. Participants in the Constitutional Revolution, they hoped that the achievements needed to be both consolidated and to be further extended. The development of a constitution and constitutional monarchy now necessitated institutional and economic reform to safeguard those gains. For many, this goal was to be routed through the path of independence and practical sovereignty. Looking back, this elite saw the political and economic development of Iran held back by the exigencies of British and Russian imperialism.

Yet it was obvious that Lord Curzon, Sir Percy Cox and others in the British government did not believe that Iran's elite were capable of developing a competent or efficient government. The British frequently pointed to successive Qajar shahs as weak, duplicitous and venal. There is much truth to this characterization, but it does ignore the role of Britain and its various policies over the long eighteenth century in this paradigm.

Ahmad Shah was certainly weak and ineffectual in his early years, yet his abilities had been much sharpened towards the end of the First World War. I would suggest that British criticism of his weakness was partly a result of Ahmad Shah's antipathy towards British efforts to control him. At what point did the British expect a 'strong' ruler within the context of Iran's Constitutional Monarchy? Actually, Ahmad Shah stands accused, rightly, of exceeding his authority.

Similarly, British attitudes towards the delegation were also coloured by the fact that Britain could not control them. Committed nationalists all, they stood for an independent Iran – an outlook which British officials believed was either a flight of fancy, did not fit into their plans, or both. In at least two respects British dismissal of their abilities was not valid. Moshaver al-Mamalek, downgraded to the ambassadorship in Turkey after his removal as foreign minister, would make a remarkable comeback when he negotiated the Treaty of Friendship with Soviet Russia which concluded in part the repatriation of Iranian territory. Though largely symbolic, the transfer of territory showed exactly the symbolism that had been entirely lost on the British. Mohammad Ali Foroughi, second in command under both Moshaver al-Mamalek and Nosrat al-Dowleh, would go on to a considerable political career which would culminate in the Premiership under the reign of Reza Khan Pahlavi. In addition, he stands as an important but sometimes largely overlooked Iranian nationalist, who worked diligently and quietly for Iran.

So why did Lord Curzon and Sir Percy Cox gravitate towards Vosuq al-Dowleh? He was, after all, also a nationalist weaned on the Constitutional Revolution. It was Sir Charles Marling who had identified Vosuq al-Dowleh as someone the British could deal with. This was somewhat unsurprising as it was Vosuq al-Dowleh who was the only one willing to deal with the British. However, the tendency of the British to have Iranian interlocutors who were like-minded meant that Lord Curzon and Sir Percy Cox were only getting one side of the Iranian narrative. Overlooked was the growth in Iranian nationalism, nationalist politics and a changing country.

In truth, the British also misinterpreted Vosuq al-Dowleh's cooperation. Modernization was a means to an end, the end being independence. In this way, Vosuq al-Dowleh's compliance went only so far. Even he was unable to completely discard the long-held diplomatic method of hiring teachers and advisors from other nations. Feelers were consistently put out for French and American nationals to come and work for Iran's government. In fact, as shown by the diplomacy of Nosrat al-Dowleh, the Triumvirate obviously believed that the agreement, whilst agreed, had not been completed, and could yet be improved.

A blinkered Lord Curzon had made two crucial mistakes. Firstly, he had ignored the Iranian delegation in Paris and secondly, he never considered the necessity for dealing with Iran's territorial wishes at any level. Lord Curzon never once appreciated the need for the Iranians to show even a modicum of success in their dealings with the British. Dealing with the Triumvirate directly, Lord Curzon was ignorant of the wider political concerns of Iran's political elite. Obstinately, he simply ignored reports of Iranian nationalist sympathies because they did not gel with his own ideas about Iran, which he had formed many years previously and still maintained.

British antagonism and opposition towards the Iranian delegation were at times hysterical. The barriers that were discussed to prevent the delegation in Paris from being heard before the Big Four or even the Council of Ten seemed excessive. One cannot see a large downside to the interests of the British government, save the pathological intention for Britain's views and plans for Iran not to be aired in public, or in an arena in which the discussions could not be controlled. Sir Percy Sykes, a critique of both Iran's *desiderata* and its delegation in Paris, decided it was a shame that Iran's wishes had not been aired so that Iran's fantastic claims could not blow up in public.[5]

Iran's delegation wrote and published several documents in favour of their *desiderata* in Paris. The main document, *Claims of Persia before the Conference of the Preliminaries of Peace of Paris*, remains the most complete exposition of Iran's claims at the Paris Peace Conference. Based on the eight-point programme, it described a plan to secure an independence in name and reality through political, economic and judicial means. It sought reparations from Russia and Turkey and for Germany to be held responsible for 'its clandestine and subversive conduct of her agents'.[6] Arguments describing Iran's territorial claims obscured the very valid argument that Iran had due reparations for damages through no fault of their own.

Would Iran's claims have been better received if the delegates had concentrated on arguing Iran's case purely on the grounds of reparations? Adolphe Perni had certainly told Mohammad Ali Foroughi that Iran was making a mistake in not arguing the case for economic damage more forcefully. It might not have made a difference. The claims for reparations, unquantified in *Claims of Persia before the Conference of the Preliminaries of Peace of Paris*, would rely on judgements by the Big Four. They were not willing to countenance giving reparations to a country labelled non-belligerent in the conflict. The British likely would also have followed the line, mentioned by Lord Curzon, that they did not see how reparations could be recovered from a Russian Tsarist government that had ceased to exist.

In truth, there was another reason why the British did not want to discuss reparations. How would they answer accusations that they might also owe Iran reparations? Lord Curzon had negotiated to keep any British reparations off the table. One of the secret letters accompanying the Anglo-Persian Agreement had dealt with the question of British compensation for war damage. The letter agreed:

> His Majesty's Government will not claim from the government of His Majesty the Shah the cost of the maintenance of British troops which His Majesty's Government were obliged to send to Persia owing to Persia's want of power to defend her neutrality, and that on the other hand the Persian government will not claim from the British Government an indemnity for any damage which may have been caused by the said troops during their presence in Persian territory.[7]

Britain had, rather deftly, ensured that it would not be held responsible for its actions during the First World War. But, had the issue of reparations come up at the conference, British actions in Iran during the war might also have garnered greater scrutiny.

Lord Curzon could not support Iran's *desiderata* while working towards the Anglo-Persian Agreement. Together with Vosuq al-Dowleh, Lord Curzon and Sir Percy Cox would develop this agreement in isolation. The discussions towards the agreement were carried out in great secrecy. However, there were always damaging rumours. The delegations' approach to the Peace Conference was to be undercut by these rumours. In truth, the results of the agreement might have been very different if Vosuq al-Dowleh had achieved what he had set out to attain – an agreement that included the repatriation of territory.

Might Iran's diplomacy have been more successful with greater French or American backing? This is hard to say but probably unlikely. The delegates met with Georges Clemenceau, Poincaré and others, but the French, despite some verbal support for Iran, were largely uncommitted and supported British plans to keep Iran off the peace agenda. This tacit support continued when the Anglo-Persian Agreement was announced. Despite a vociferous anti-agreement campaign in the French press, French leaders remained unmoved. At the highest levels of the French government keeping on the good side of an ally appeared more important. Georges Clemenceau neither knew nor cared much about French interests in the Middle East. France had no huge political or commercial pull towards Iran and Iran was largely only a factor as a bargaining chip in terms of Syria, which was only important because of public opinion and the *parti colonial*. It was they who carried the torch against British imperialism. In Tehran, it was left to the Minister, Charles Bonin, to provide an unwelcome nuisance to British diplomacy.

The Americans were largely supportive of Iran's *desiderata* and felt that Iran should be at least heard. In this, they were supported by the Italians. Whilst they encouraged the Iranians, their own efforts were largely ineffectual and it should therefore be asked how important Iran's *desiderata* was to them. It should be remembered that whilst Iran's *desiderata* seemed vital to the Iranians, it came far down the list of important issues that the Peace Conference was meant to resolve. It was also linked to the Ottoman question, which was also not as vital.

Nevertheless, the Americans had found British intransigence with regard to Iran a nuisance. The seeds of American disapproval towards British views on Iran had been set as the delegation promoted its diplomacy. It bloomed when the Anglo-Persian Agreement was announced. Publicly reticent to voice their disapproval, President Wilson felt let down. There can be little doubt that President Wilson and his entourage and indeed Minister to Iran, Caldwell, were against the agreement. It was left to the American press to be more strident.

Tellingly, American support for Iran had been substantially no greater than the goodwill for many of the local ethnicities who attempted to garner their support. They had, after all, been sympathetic to Armenian claims for independence, as indeed the British and French had been. Long-established links through regional education projects and the work of missionaries had propelled American interest in the problems that Christian Armenians faced in the culturally and religiously diverse region. Further impacted by reports of Turkish savagery towards Armenians, President Wilson had actively begun to investigate an American mandate for Armenia. However, as time went on, it began to be clear to both Wilson and indeed other allies that 'all the promises made to the Armenians, especially the principle of self-determination, were devoid of all national and inter-state realities'.[8] Ultimately, the patchwork nature of ethnic distribution was too great for the level of support the Americans felt they could give. How far, therefore, were the Americans willing to go to support Iran if they could not support Armenia?

It should be noted that President Wilson was operating and making decisions in Paris both for Europe and outside Europe which were largely not supported back home. They may have been but Wilson had jealously guarded the work he was doing. To such an extent that no Republicans had been invited to Paris and he did little to keep either his own party or Congress informed.[9] In the end, Congress could not see a path to ratifying the League of Nations, the very edifice that President Wilson had put so much store by. If the League could not be ratified by Congress, then what chance was there for the United States to undertake the mandate for Armenia?

The Anglo-Persian Agreement was both part of Iran's *imperial nationalism* and responsible for the demise of Iran's programme in Paris. It is therefore reasonable to ask whether the agreement might have delivered some of Iran's *desiderata*. Could it have modernized Iran's ailing bureaucracy, army and helped Iran's economy grow? Unfortunately, there has been very little research into this. Yet, as the agreement was partially implemented, it is possible to suggest a few points. The introduction of a British financial advisor may have been largely positive and could have resulted in a modern and streamlined department, which might have introduced a workable tax regime. The improvement and development of transport and communication infrastructure would certainly have helped develop Iranian trade and grow the economy. The modernization of Iran's army, though seemingly a straightforward operation, would probably have failed. Ultimately, seen as an army of occupation, it would not have been supported by the wider population.[10]

It is also very likely that the agreement which had begun badly would likely have ended badly. Ignoring the Iranian delegation had done Britain no favours amongst either the growing polity in Iran or Iran's political elite. It came on the back of many perceived slights, including the Anglo-Russian Convention, but more recently Britain's role in the First World War – still collaborating with the Russians, disputing the responsibility of sabotaged oil pipelines and having control over Iran's purse strings. Pursuing a secret negotiation was never likely to endear the British to Iran. Then there was opposition from the Americans, French and Russians against the agreement, grist to local Iranian opposition. Finally, the military landings by Russia in northern Iran at Anzali exposed the paucity of British backing for the agreement. This was before rumours of the Triumvirate's malfeasance had gained traction. When the agreement ran into trouble, both the India government, always lacklustre in its support, and a stretched War Department had finally stopped supporting the agreement.

In truth, Lord Curzon had dragged many parts of the wider British government, sometimes willingly, but always with some reticence towards an agreement. The Eastern Committee, Lord Curzon's vehicle to mould British foreign policy in the Middle East as he saw it, likewise trampled on the Foreign Office's and India government's turf. He, like President Wilson, had ploughed ahead with policy agendas which tottered on narrow acceptance. As Wilson found out when he returned to the United States and Curzon when the Anglo-Persian Agreement came under pressure, policies developed in isolation from others were not to inspire support.

Lord Curzon's tunnel vision was also a problem when it came to the ratification of the Anglo-Persian Agreement. The agreement was always to be subject to ratification by the *Majles*, an action which was ignored by Lord Curzon or one that he had assumed was simply a *fait accompli*. The *Majles* had not reconvened since 1915, but when it did, it was fully expected that the agreement was not to be ratified. Given the post-war political climate in Iran, ratification of the agreement by the *Majles* was not even considered after the fall of Vosuq al-Dowleh's government. Vosuq al-Dowleh's resigned as prime minister in June 1920, a casualty of an increasingly moribund agreement.

Vosuq al-Dowleh remains a much-vilified figure. His role as the principal Iranian politician engaged in both the negotiation and finalizing of the Anglo-Persian Agreement has established him as a man willing to sell Iran's independence and establish Iran as a vassal state. In the round, however, he was a committed Iranian nationalist who seemed sincere in his desires. Critics quite rightly point to the bribes that were paid to the Triumvirate as a point that cannot be argued away. Despite his reticence to take the money, he did little to oppose Nosrat al-Dowleh and Sarem al-Dowleh who pushed for financial recompense. In this he was culpable, though curiously, he himself did not spend the money.

The argument that Vosuq al-Dowleh was also behind Iran's strategy at the Peace Conference in Paris cannot be substantiated. His only involvement was to direct the delegates in the pursuit of teachers and advisors from other countries. Otherwise, he did not believe in the strategy of sending a delegation to Paris. When he did intervene, it was to disrupt Moshaver al-Mamalek's considered plan of action. There is little doubt that Vosuq al-Dowleh used the delegation as a bargaining ploy with the British. Pressure for a deal was helped by the stopping or unleashing of the delegates. I do not believe, however, that both the work of the delegation in Paris and the negotiations for the Anglo-Persian Agreement were part of a consolidated plan under the direction of Vosuq al-Dowleh.

Lord Curzon had put a lot of store in the Anglo-Persian Agreement. The agreement was to be a resounding finale to his involvement in Iran. In a letter to his second wife, Grace, Lord Curzon wrote:

> The papers give a good reception to my Persian Treaty, which I have been negotiating for the past year, and which is a great triumph as I have done it all alone. But not a single paper as much as mentions my name, or has the dimmest perception that, had I not been at the F.O., it would never have been done at all.

I only wonder that they do not attribute it to the superhuman skill and genius of Ll.G. [Lloyd-George][11]

As the agreement began to crumble, he fought against various departments in an attempt to keep the agreement going.

When the agreement failed, he blamed others. Very few were spared his criticism. Lying in bed for a number of weeks attempting to ease his ailing back, Lord Curzon wrote a letter to Sir Percy Loraine, the latest Minister to Iran, in 1922.[12] In it he described, in a mixture of anger and sadness, the amount of money and time that had been sacrificed to Iran and the ultimate loss of British prestige. He thought that Sir Percy Cox, like Sir Percy Loraine, one of his confidants, might have, along with the Triumvirate, 'deceived us'. He blamed Herman Norman, minister to Iran, after Sir Percy Cox. He blamed the British Cabinet, Prime Minister Lloyd George and Winston Churchill for not having the foresight to stay the course and for withdrawing troops when they could have stood firm. He blamed the *Majles* and the 'incomparable, incurable and inconceivable rottenness of Persian politicians', and the 'desperate and colossal incapacity of the Shah'.

In all this, Lord Curzon took none of the blame upon himself. He was, however, correct in one respect; British prestige had taken a beating. In this way, the end of the First World War was a defining moment in Anglo-Persian relations. It tentatively marks the beginning of the end of British involvement in Iran. The war and Iran's *imperial nationalism* were also, I believe, the precursor to what was to come rather than the end of a turbulent period in Iran's history. The considerable changes that were to be put into place by Reza Shah Pahlavi had in fact begun during this period.[13]

Iran's nationalist policy was tethered to an imperial past, but still looked to the future. The initiatives for independence, sovereignty and reform, which began in 1919, were to be taken forward by Reza Shah, albeit not in the context of a territorial empire but in a nationalized state. Again, it would be an Iranian state suborned to one man's power, but a state more complete than ever before. However, though the elements were in place for the rise of Reza Shah, or someone like him, such a result had not been inevitable. The period under investigation shows that other options did exist, options which Iran was exploring – in Paris at the Peace Conference, with other nations and with the British.

Suitably the final word regarding Iran's experiences in Paris should be left to Mohammad Ali Foroughi and his thoughts articulated in two letters to Iran. His sombre assessments of Iran's inability to galvanize the imagination of the United States, France and Britain in their *imperial nationalism* were based on the foundational knowledge that despite protestations of rights, justice and fairness, the larger nations wanted to keep the world in its 'old form' at the expense of weaker countries. Nevertheless, in pointing to the success of Britain in the Middle East, Asia and Africa, Foroughi also noted how these successes were to be transitory and would ultimately fail.

In the meantime, Iran should not wait but reform itself. It was incumbent on Iran to make the reforms necessary to protect itself from known powers and other powers on the rise, which may seek to dominate it. Protection would also come from the development of Iranian nationalism. After all, would the Anglo-Persian Agreement have been contemplated or possible if 'the Iranian nation existed, if there was public opinion in Iran, would the Iranian government have dared to conclude this recent agreement with Britain?'[14]

Mohammad Ali Foroughi's reference to the immediate dominance of powers, such as Britain, also tempered his appreciation of the League of Nations. Joining the League was perhaps the most tangible success for the Iranian delegation but Foroughi was not sure it would even sit. After all, the US Congress did not seem to be on board with the project. If it did sit, would it not, despite its declaration to guarantee each other's independence and sovereignty, succumb to the wishes of powerful countries? What place was there for the League of Nations when Britain controlled Egypt and under the Anglo-Persian Agreement was to control Iran?

Critics of Iran's immediate post-war diplomacy will point to Iran's failure to be heard, and, because of its weakness, the imposition of the Anglo-Persian Agreement. Still, the Iranian delegation had significantly raised Iran's status in world politics. The delegation had met with presidents, politicians and other people of influence. Iran, never a backwater but dealt with at arm's length, was now, in the twentieth century, part of global diplomacy. In Foroughi's words, 'we made a lot of noise … we took a lot of specific measures that will be beneficial to the country'.[15]

APPENDIX

Claims of Persia before the Conference of the Preliminaries of Peace at Paris

I. - Claims concerning Political, Juridical and economic independence.
II. - Right to territorial Restorations.
III. - Right to Reparations.

Paris, March 1919.

I

Claims concerning political juridical and economic independence

The importance of Persia is a matter of universal knowledge, and the glorious part she has played during the past ages and centuries is not denied. Those endowed with accurate information regarding Eastern matters recognize the Persians to be an intelligent race, having always produced great scholars and thinkers. The Persian People have possessed one of the loftiest ranks amongst nations. This is exemplified by their contributions to the literature, philosophy, arts, sciences and civilization of the world.

This ancient nation has, unfortunately, been weakened for more than one century, and its march towards progress arrested by the fact that when it desired to adopt the new methods of European Civilization, it found itself face to face with stronger neighbours who only thought of weakening her and suppressing her independence.

However, the principle of Persia's independence and integrity has been confirmed, time and again, by the Powers which have always pledged themselves to respect it. But unfortunately certain amongst the Powers have, in practice, violated that principle, directly or indirectly, and by so doing, they have not only committed an injustice, but they have thereby prevented the development of Persia, both from the view point of administrative reforms and that of developing her natural wealth.

This is why, to-day [sic], the Persian Government requests of the Peace Conference that the Conventions, Treaties and precedents in contravention of Persia's independence be recognized null and void and that guarantees be given her for the future.

It is necessary to set forth here in brief the violations committed upon the independence of Persia, in order that the motives supporting the claims of the Persian Government may be better understood.

The attacks directed upon Persia have violated her independence from three points of view: Political, Economic and Juridical[sic]. These assaults have been in certain cases made in writing and in others by actual acts. The majority of these attacks owe their origin to Russian initiative. Although on the one hand, British policy was opposed to the Russian and England desired, as much as possible, to mitigate the effects of the oppressive policy of her rival, yet, on the other hand, in her eagerness not to be outdone by Russia, England often followed the former's example, and she found it at times opportune to act in agreement with Russia.

The independence of Persia has suffered the following violations:
I. - *From the political point of view*

a) In 1907 a Convention was made between Russia and England dividing Persia into a Russian 'Sphere of Influence' in the North, and a British 'Sphere of Influence' in the South, with a neutral zone in the middle. This arrangement was announced to the Persian Government which rejected it; but the two Powers, using the same pressure which effected the dismissal of the Shuster financial Mission, compelled Persia in 1912 to recognize and to comply with the principles of the said Convention.

After the fall of the old Russian regime which had imposed upon Persia treaties, conventions and agreements contrary to her independence, the Persian Government taking note of the declarations and assurances on the part of the liberal regime which immediately succeeded Tsarism and which had declared itself in favor of the liberty and independence of peoples, - denounced the treaties, conventions and concessions which had bound Persia to autocratic Russia and which had been invariably exacted by force. Among these conventions was the agreement of 1907, to the cancellation of which the British Government, as a party thereto, has since adhered.

b) ln 1910 the Governments of Russia and Great Britain imposed, as a condition essential to Persia's acquisition of loans from foreign countries, that no concessions which they might consider as contrary to their political and strategic interests shall be granted by Persia to any other Powers or their subjects. As this stipulation was obviously incompatible with the political and economic independence of Persia, it was rejected by the Persian Government. Nevertheless the two Powers would not withdraw their pretentions to this effect.

c) When, in 1911, the Russian Government found that Mr. Shuster, engaged for the reorganization of the Persian finances, was doing effective work, which would result in delivering Persia financially from the Russian yoke, - it, in accord with England, lodged an ultimatum with Persia compelling her to dismiss Mr. Shuster and his Mission, and in addition, to undertake never to employ for her services any foreign officials without the previous consent of Russia and Great Britain.

Thus, due to these forcibly imposed restrictions and obstacles, the Persian Government was prevented from reorganizing its finances and reforming its other administrative Departments.

d) For ten years, Russia, animated by enmity towards the liberal Persian Regime, and desirous to increase her authority in that country, adopted, under various pretexts, the policy of extending protection to Persian subjects. The Russian Consular agents did not spare any effort in expanding the circle of this protection to such dimensions that even Persian rebels and outlaws were always sure of being given refuge and thus enabled to evade justice. Thus were real difficulties created for the Government and public peace was disturbed.

e) The neighboring Powers, always anxious to see that Persian affairs should follow a course in complete harmony with their own interests and aims, meddled in purely internal matters, such as the appointment or recall of Governors and other high officials, the administration of finance, the organization of military forces, the posts and telegraphs, etc-, etc.

By so doing, they paralysed the efforts of the Persian Government, and caused it many annoyances highly prejudicial to its prestige as well as to the orderly course of affairs.

f) The foreign subjects, supported by their Legations, refused to pay the taxes legally imposed upon the Persian subjects. This created an unjust discrimination against the Persians who suffered in competition with foreigners and who, contrary to every usage, were in their own country, treated less favorably than strangers.

g) Certain foreign Powers would, now and then, enter into direct negociations [sic] with the chiefs of Persian tribes and conclude arrangements with them without the knowledge of the Persian Government whose sovereignty and prestige were thus put in jeopardy.

h) The Foreign Legations, consulates and firms have always enjoyed great consideration and most perfect security in Persia. Nevertheless, the Russian Government, and then later, the British, introduced into Persia armed escorts under the title of Consular guards, while, as a matter of fact, the Persian Government has always protected the Russian and British Legations and consulates, equally with the other foreign Missions, none of which has ever had any cause for complaint.

i) Similarly, the life and property of foreign subjects have always been respected, even during the most troubled times. Nevertheless, the Russian Government with a view to strengthening its position, intimidating the Persian Liberals, and, finally, achieving her object of suppressing the independence of Persia and occupying her territory - introduced troops into that country, and maintained them there for ten years, first in Azerbaidjan and, little by little, in the other northern provinces and constantly threatening the capital, realized the majority of its illegitimate aims. This process naturally hampered the Persian Government, lowered its prestige in the provinces and prevented it from devoting itself to necessary reforms. By so doing, Russia encouraged the turbulent and reactionary elements in the country. In response to the repeated protests of Persia, Russia invariably promised to evacuate Persian territory, but far from fulfilling this promise, she increased the number of her forces. This state of affairs continued until the advent of the war in

1914. At that time, Russia's refusal to respect Persian neutrality and to withdraw her troops from Persian territory, furnished the Turks, with the pretext to invade Azerbaidjan and the provinces of the west. It likewise gave the Germans the chance to disturb the country and to the British the opportunity to land forces in the South, and following the example of Russia, to occupy Persian territory and bring their 'Sphere of Influence', as well as the neutral zone, under military occupation. Thus Persia became a theatre of conflicts which she had desired to avoid at any price, and her populations suffered the horrors of the war to the same degree as the most tried belligerent Powers.

j) Russia had always endeavored [sic] to prevent in Persia the formation of a national force capable of assuring order and tranquillity. She had been even opposed to the gendarmerie and police forces penetrating the northern provinces. Specially during recent years, Russia set herself to restricting the Persian army to the 'Cossack Brigade', a force organized by Russian officers and only serving the Russian cause and aiming at the invasion of the country. Finally, during the European war, Russia profiting by the occasion, and bringing England again to share her point of view, demanded of the Persian Government to transform the 'Cossack Brigade' into a Division in the north under the command of Russian officers, and to create a similar force in the south under the command of British officers. The above measure, which had always provoked protests on the part of the Persian Government - who had in mind the organization of a uniform force for the whole Empire - ended in the Government of His Britannic Majesty's willingness to meet this Persian desire with favor. They recently addressed a note to the Teheran cabinet declaring their readiness to deliver to the Persian Government the force which they had organized in the South.

II. - *From the Juridical point of view*

a) The first attack upon the juridical independence of Persia was delivered by the Treaty of Turkomantchai, made between Russia and Persia in 1828, wherein in the article seven, it is stipulated that law suits affecting the subjects of Russia and the Persians should be tried in the presence of Russian representatives.

b) Later, in practice, these foreign representatives intervened in the cases, and this intervention was especially mentioned in the subsequent treaties made between Persia and certain Powers such as Germany and Austria.

c) Moreover, by virtue of the same treaties and on account of the improper interpretation put upon them, foreign subjects in Persia are almost beyond the reach of the police and Persian courts, so that they can commit all kinds of offenses and crimes without being prosecuted by the Persian authorities. Even in civilian matters it often comes to pass that Persians find themselves in a state of inferiority compared to foreigners, because of the priviledged [sic] position conferred upon the latter.

Meanwhile, for a number of years, the Persian Government have entered resolutely in the path of judicial reforms. With the aid of foreign advisers, they have engaged in the organization of justice, taking France as a model. The work of codification is being actively pursued and Persian justice will shortly offer all the guarantees of justice as in the European States. Consequently, there is no reason to continue indefinitely the peculiar situation created in favor of foreigners in Persia and the time has come to terminate it.

III. - *From the economic point of view*

a) We have already pointed out the effort continually put forth by Russia to check the economic development of Persia and to control all her resources. With this object in view, Russia opposed the construction of railways in that country. This opposition has been the more effective in view of the fact that Persia by herself could not create a railway system without the cooperation of foreigners in the matters of capital, material and technical aid. In this direction, Russia went as far as to obtain from the Persian Government, concessions which she has never utilized. The British Government on its part, could not remain indifferent on this point, and acted in the south of Persia in the same fashion as its rival in the north. The result is that Persia has remained, to this day, without railways and is deprived of the most essential means for her economic development.

b) Persia being forced to submit to the terms of the Convention of 1907, and to the Note of 1910, has been deprived of the means of attracting foreign capital and initiative for the development of her economic resources. Moreover, for some years, foreign Governments or subjects have wrested from the Persian Government industrial, commercial and agricultural concessions with conditions entirely incompatible with the economic interests of Persia, and even often contrary to the fundamental laws of the country.

The Persian Government being in need of foreign capital and instrumentalities for the development of her economic resources, is, as a matter of fact, desirous to profit, as much as possible, by the financial and technical cooperation of foreigners; but the majority of concessions thus far acquired by foreigners involve political aims and have therefore failed to aid in the economic progress of Persia. To enable the country to develop its resources, it is absolutely necessary that all existing concessions shall be revised to the end that the clauses prejudicial to the economic interests of Persia be eliminated.

c) The Customs Convention concluded between Russia and Persia in 1901 has been conceived with the double object of suppressing the export of Persian-made commodities and barring Persia from the commerce of other countries.

Persian industry has thereby declined more and more and the Russians have succeeded in their policy of Persia's economic isolation to such an extent that they would not even permit the transit of goods through the Caucasus. The latest Customs tarif [sic] was so prejudicial to foreign trade in Persia that Great Britain could not consent to its application to British goods. She, therefore, in concert with the Persian Government, established a new tarif which rectified the situation from the British point of view. Now, however, the Persian Government, in conformity with the Principles of Mr. Wilson, desiring the open door and the equality of treatment for all Nations in Persia, is anxious to revise its Customs tarif and to conclude treaties of commerce with foreign countries based on Persia's economic freedom.

This brief summary will allow an appreciation of the attempts hitherto made with the object of restricting the political, juridical and economic independence of Persia, and will show how the Persians have been oppressed and placed in their own country in a state of inferiority to foreigners, and how the economic development of that country has been checked.

The new Era of Justice and Equity which is dawning in every country and which adumbrates the advent of the reign of Humanity and Justice under the aegis of the League of Nations, gives Persia the firm conviction that the attacks until now directed upon her political, juridical and economic independence shall be atoned for and that she shall be enabled to consecrate herself, unhampered, to necessary reforms and to the development of her natural wealth, on the basis of her complete independence and sovereignty.

CONCLUSIONS

The Persian Government therefore claims:

a) That the Anglo-Russian accord of 1907 be definitely considered as void, as regards the signatory powers, as regards Persia and as regards all and any powers which might have adhered to it, or recognized, in part or in whole, the situation created by it;

b) That the Note of 1910 prohibiting the granting of concessions of a political and strategical nature to foreigners, be declared null and void;

c) That the Ultimatum of 1911 compelling Persia to bind herself not to take into her service foreigners without the previous consent of Russia and England, and the consequent effects which that Ultimatum might have entailed, or may entail, shall be recognized as null and void;

d) That the foreign powers abstain from extending protection in Persia to Persian subjects;

e) That the foreign powers abstain from intervening in the internal affairs of Persia;

f) That foreigners be placed on the same footing with Persians in all matters affecting the payment of taxes;

g) That the armed forces of foreign powers and their consular guards be withdrawn from Persian territory;

h) That the treaties made between Persia and foreign countries be subjected to a revision, to the end that all clauses contravening the political, juridical and economic independence of Persia be eliminated;

i) That the concessions acquired by foreigners be revised and all stipulations made therein prejudicing the economic interests of Persia be eliminated;

j) That Persia's right to freely frame or revise her Customs tarif be recognized, and all ban against the free transit of goods to Persia be removed.

II

The right to territorial restitutions

Persia is a country which has natural frontiers. In following the course of her history, even though beginning only from the time of Cyrus, one finds that for 25 centuries, the numerous empires which succeeded one another in that country generally attained her natural limits. These comprised the territories situated between the river Amou Darya, the Caucasus Mountains, the rivers Tigris and Euphrates and the Persian Gulf. The majority of the inhabitants of this region have always been of the Iranian race; the empires founded in this country have always been considered as Iranian Empires. If certain portions of these territories have at times been wrested from Persia, they have been rapidly reconquered by the Persians. Without desiring to recall the grandeur of the Persian Empires of the remote past and considering only the modern times, it will be found that at the periods of the Sefevides, of Nadir Shah and even under the first Kadjars, that is, during the 16th, 17th and 18th centuries, Persia attained her natural limits, and defended her territories against all invaders.

In the early years of the 19th century, Persia, weakened by a long period of civil wars, and conflicts against foreigners, found herself face to face with neighbours who had become great and strong, and who did not fail to invade her territories, She could not defend herself as she had done in the past. A portion of her patrimony was thus wrested from her.

The attacks directed upon the integrity of Persia have had for their authors the Russians in the North and the Turks in the West.

The Russians first began in the Caucasus. During two wars which they made upon Persia, they took possession, in 1813 and 1828, of an important portion of Persian territory. Later on, the Russians, profiting by the fact that Persia had become exhausted by these wars, as well as by those against the Turks, advanced in the direction of the Transcaspian Province. Finally, in 1881, the Persian Government felt obliged to enter into negociations [sic] with the Government of the Tzar in order to fix a frontier line and put an end to Russian invasions. As a consequence of this delimitation of frontier, a great portion of Persian territory was again cut off. That was the region comprised between the rivers Amou-Darya and Atrek.

The wresting of these provinces from Persia constituted by itself an act of iniquity; but Russia did not stop even at that and, in the course of territorial negociations and arrangements made with Persia, she committed still many other injustices. As an instance, we will cite the case of the delimitation of frontier made in Transcaucasia. It was agreed that in that direction the Araxes river would separate Russia from Persia, but in the eastern section of that region the Russians departed from this natural frontier and occupied a portion of the territories situated on the south of the river, thus creating an arbitrary frontier. In this fashion, they appropriated a large portion of the two provinces of Moghan and Talish, separating, without any legitimate reason, populations which had been used to living in unison and in constant relations. On this account, the Russians occasioned for themselves as well as for Persia, perpetual embarrassments. Moreover, as it was impossible to fix a natural limit in these regions, they always found the means to push into Persian territory and to provoke frontier quarrels.

On the coast of the Caspian Sea, and in the direction of Khorassan Persia has met with the same difficulties and the same violation of her rights. Besides, the Russians have imposed upon her conditions notoriously unjust. In certain regions in the proximity of the frontier, they forbade the inhabitants of the Persian villages to utilize the water of rivers whose sources were in Persia and which flowed into the territory annexed by Russia. They exacted that the Persian villagers should not extend the limits of their farming, in order that the waters of the rivers would not be absorbed by Persian irrigation and that the entire bulk of the waters should flow into Russian territory. As a consequence of these impositions vast and rich properties of Persians have been destroyed or left uncultivated.

Turkish aggressions were not any less in the West. Turkey took possession of great territory which belonged to Persia, and, during the last centuries, she has always sought quarrels with Persia on the subject of frontiers. The Persian Government has always shown itself very conciliatory. In 1847, by virtue of the Treaty of Erzeroum, she ceded the region of Suleymanieh to Turkey in order thus to cut short that country's pretentions to Mohammerah. Turkey, however, remained difficult and unreasonable, and in 1907, she invaded a section of the contested territory which she did not evacuate until 1914, while still retaining a portion of the territory which served as summer resort to the different Persian tribes.

This brief expose clearly shows how Persia has been oppressed by Russia and Turkey from the territorial point of view. Now that it has been decided that the injustices done to the peoples should be redeemed, and that the countries subjected to the Turks and Russians will be liberated in order that they may be constituted upon logical and just foundations, Persia asks, in the name of Right and Equity, that the territory taken from her by force and unjustly be restored to her. She demands that her frontiers be fixed in conformity with the rules of right and nature, so that she may, henceforth, be secured against invasion by her neighbours.

The following embodies, in brief, the territorial claims of Persia:

1st. *In the North-East, The Transcaspian Province.*

This province has always formed part of Persia and it is even considered one of the centers of Persian nationality. A great number of illustrious Persians - poets, men of letters, savants, philosophers - have had their origin in this province. The Persian language is widely diffused there, and is spoken even beyond as far as Bokhara and Samarkand. The inhabitants of this region are largely Persian (Kurds, Tadjiks, Persian emigrants). The rest of the population consists of Turkomans; that is to say, they belong - to the same tribes which inhabit the Astrabad region, - a province which is actually Persian - and which entertain with their campatriots [sic] of the other side of the frontier the most intimate and close relations. Moreover, when recently, following the Russian Revolution, troubles broke out in Russia, the inhabitants of the Transcaspian Province, and particularly the Turkomans of the Steppes and the inhabitants of Sarakhs, finding themselves exposed to pillage and

Bolshevik massacres, appealed to Persia for help, and expressed the wish to return to the mother country, the Persian Government did not fail to respond to their appeal and to send forces who protected them by suppressing the Bolshevik incursions.

2nd. *In the North, the cities and provinces wrested from Persia after the Russian wars. We will cite Bacou, Chirvan, Derbent, Chakki, Chemakha, Guendja (Elisabethpol), Karabagh, Nakhdjevan, Erivan.*

These provinces must be returned to Persia, for they had already made part of Persia. The large majority of their inhabitants are Musulmans, and the generality of them are Persian in origin and race. In fact, from every point of view, - historic, geographical, economical, commercial, religious, cultural - they are attached to Persia. Furthermore, a large portion of the inhabitants of these provinces have lately appealed to the Government of Teheran, to protect them, and they have expressed the wish to be restored to Persia.

3rd. *In the West, that portion of Kurdistan which formed part of the Turkish Empire.*

Kurdistan is a territory inhabited by a people Persian in race and language, professing lslamism. That country has been divided between Persia and Turkey. The Turkish part comprises:

a) The region of Suleymanieh wrested from Persia by the Treaty of Erzeroum mentioned above, and which, in all justice, should be restored to her;

b) The rest of Turkish Kurdistan which for ethnic, geographical, religious and other reasons, is bound to Persia and which should naturally be joined to that country, more especially because its religious chiefs and notable Kurds have declared themselves desirous to be re-united to Persia.

4th. The ties existing between Persia and the Holy Places situated in Mesopotamia, are innumerable and incontestable. The inhabitants of these places, Kerbela, Nedjef, Kazemein, Samerah, are, in large numbers, Persian in origin, or are Persian emigrants. These cities constitue [sic] the nucleus of the Shiite religion which is the official religion of Persia, and which is professed by all the Persians. The great spiritual leaders of Persia reside in those cities, and many thousands of Persians visit them annually as pilgrims. It may be stated that these cities whose commerce and industry are in large part, in Persian hands, live on the money and activity of Persia. Consequently, the Persian Government is extremely interested in the disposition of these Holy Places and asks that, when the time comes to adjust the Mesopotamian question, Persia's important interests be safeguarded.

III

The Right to Reparations

Persia, although a neutral country, suffered by the war greater losses than those sustained by certain belligerent countries. Her special position as a country invaded by foreign armies, her devastated provinces, her decimated population, in equity and by analogy give her the right to reparations and indemnifications due the belligerent countries.

In fact, her neutrality has been violated first by Russia, and then by the other neighbouring countries.

To better explain the position of Persia, it would be necessary to give a brief historical sketch of the facts, in order to prove how certain foreign Powers have deviated from the path of Justice and Equity in their relations with Persia, and how they have sacrificed that country's interests to their own aims.

In the beginning of the war, soon after the Turkish mobilization, Russia and England expressed the desire to see Persia remain neutral in that conflict, and to declare her neutrality. Russia, whose policy had always been hostile to Persia, unlawfully retained at that time her troops in Azerbaidjan, in spite of the protests of the Persian Government. The latter proposed to the Russian Government to withdraw their troops, in order not to give pretexts to the Turks to invade Persia and convert it into a theatre of the war. It added that if after the departure of the Russian troops the Turks attempted to transgress the Persian frontier, the Persian Government would not fail to defend itself against Turkish aggression with all the means at its disposal. The representative of England wholly shared the point of view of the Persian Government, but his Russian colleague showed himself opposed thereto. Meanwhile, the Persian Government, realizing that England and France were in accord with Russia in their desire for Persian neutrality, would not, in spite of lack of goodwill on the part of Russia, act contrary to the wishes of England and France.

Shortly afterwards, the Russian Minister at Teheran advised the Persian Government that Russia was going to increase the number of her effectives in Azerbaidjan in order that they might be able to confront the Turks. In reply to the protests of the Persian Government, who declared that warlike operations on Persian territory constituted a violation of their neutrality which would not fail to entail the country's ruin, the Russian Minister undertook on behalf of his Government to make amends for all damages which might be occasioned to Persia.

Thus the provinces of Hamadan, Kermanschah, Kurdistan and Azerbaidjan, which constitute the richest and the most fertile regions of Persia, became fields of battle between the Russians and the Turks who pillaged, burned, massacred and committed rapine and rape in those parts. Cities and villages were bombarded, forests were destroyed to facilitate military operations and to furnish firewood, thousands of women and children driven from their homes sought shelter in the fields and mountains where they died of cold and hunger. One of the richest cities of Azerbaidjan, Oroumiah, was pillaged and burned on several occasions. Each time that the troops of one of the belligerents would take possession of some locality, the officers of the victorious force would reduce to extreme misery the inhabitants who had been fortunate enough to escape the exactions and cruelty of the retreating forces. The population suffered from the soldiers tyranny, not only in the regions of actual battles, but also in places where troops were stationed who had no enemies to oppose, such as in the provinces of Khorassan and Ispahan, where the Russian soldiers maltreated the inhabitants. At Ispahan, the Russian authorities confiscated the belongings of the notables in the interest of the Imperial Russian crownlands; in the province of Khorassan the Russian Cossaks destroyed dwellings with their cannon and compelled the inhabitants everywhere to accept their much depreciated paper-money for its face value.

After the change of regime in Russia, when it was decided to evacuate Persia, the brutality of the Russian troops who had lost all discipline increased in violence. Cities, towns, villages, farms, in fact, everything found on their way, was pillaged, and nothing was spared. Hamadan and Kazvin were sacked, and the Russian officers confessed themselves incapable of controlling their men.

Not content with being themselves the authors of so much wrong to Persia, the Russians assisted in causing them other misfortunes. They distributed arms to the Djelou tribes who had sought refuge in Persia to escape the tyranny of the Turks. These tribes, armed by the Russians were encouraged to combat the Turks; and once started, they abandoned themselves to the worst excesses. Before leaving Persian territory, instead of disarming the Djelous, the Russians gave them still more arms, leaving them thirty cannons and a number of officers as instructors. Thus the Djelous could continue their depredations at Ourumieh, Salmas and elsewhere, and massacred the inhabitants by thousands, including religious leaders. These proceedings immediately furnished a pretext to the Turks to return, for a last time, to Azerbaidjan and subject that unfortunate country to new aggressions.

One of the principal reasons of the great famine which raged last year in Persia, and which cost the life of thousands of the poor, was precisely the presence of foreign troops and the atrocities which they committed. The everyday food of the majority of Persians is bread. In the provinces where there were sanguinary conflicts, farmers either perished, or were prevented from sowing and cultivating the land. Their oxen and their seeds were seized either for export or for feeding the foreign troops on the spot.

Even though Germany was not a neighbour of Persia, she had a large share of responsibility for the miseries suffered by that country. She encouraged Turkish encroachements [sic], and her agents intrigued everywhere, sowed the seeds of corruption and fomented political troubles.

To resume: the losses suffered by Persia during the war are subdivided into three categories:

    I. - Losses from the acts of Russia.
    II. - Losses from the acts of Turkey.
    III. - Responsibilities of Germany.

I. - LOSSES FROM THE ACTS OF RUSSIA:
  A. - IN PERSIA:
  1st. - *Damages caused to the State*:
a) The death of many thousands of Persians who perished during the battles fought in Persia by foreign armies;
b) Losses and deteriorations caused to public property - domain of the State, buildings, telegraphic and telephone equipment destroyed, or requisitioned, forests burnt or felled, etc;

c) Obstacles which handicapped the working of the food administration, the postal service, etc, by the seizure of the beasts of burden, waggons and other vehicles of transport;

d) Expenditure of millions of tomans by the Persian Government to mitigate the effects of the famine caused largely by military operations;

e) The seizure and wastage of arms and ammunition belonging to Persia;

f) The collection of taxes was hindered by the occupation of territory and by the disorders thereby occasioned;

g) The free importation by military authorities of considerable quantities of merchandise, which deprived the customs department of its revenues.

2nd. - *Losses caused to individuals*:

a) The bombardement [sic], destruction and burning of houses, farms, villages, properties, etc. etc.

b) The pillage and confiscation of goods belonging to individuals;

c) The requisitioning of food-stuffs;

d) The forced currency given to Russian paper-money;

e) The seizure and destruction of great quantities of cereal and cattle, serving, respectively, as food to the population and for agricultural work, have caused the ruin of peasants and hindered the tilling of the fields.

B. - OUTSIDE OF PERSIA:

1st. - *Losses to the State*:

The massacre of thousands of Persian subjects during the troubles which followed the struggle between the Russian and Turkish troops at Bacou and the outbreak of Bolchevism in Transcaspia and in the interior of Russia.

2nd. - *Losses to individuals*:

a) The enormous losses suffered by Persian merchants and subjects whose merchandise and belongings were pillaged in the circumstances mentioned above in the 1st;

b) Many millions of tons of Persian rice were confiscated at Bakou by the Russian authorities before the Revolution, without its price having as yet been paid.

II. - LOSSES FROM THE ACTS OF TURKEY:

A. - IN PERSIA:

The same damages as those occasioned by Russia to the State and to individuals, and, besides, forced contributions collected in the occupied towns.

B. - OUTSIDE OF PERSIA:

Contrary to international law, Persian merchants and subjects resident in Turkey, were drafted by the Sublime Port for military service and suffered by this act considerable losses besides material and moral coercion.

III. - RESPONSIBILITIES OF GERMANY:

A. - IN PERSIA:

By the clandestine and subversive conduct of her agents who constantly created difficulties for the Government and disturbed the country.

B. - OUTSIDE OF PERSIA:

For the unrestricted submarine warfare which caused the death of Persian subjects on the "Lusitania" and the "Sussex", notably the death of Prince Bahram, son of Prince Zill-es-Soltan. The Persian Government duly protested against these German acts and in their note of April 14-1916, reserved the right to demand reparations.

CONCLUSION

The above-mentioned losses which have caused an enormous prejudice to the Persian State and People, necessitate sufficient reparations, in order that Persia may be enabled to reconstruct herself and to resume her normal life. It is, therefore, with confidence that the Persian Government appeal to the spirit of equity and justice of the Peace Conference; and they are persuaded that by virtue of the principles proclamed [sic] by the Allied and Associated Powers, the Conference will recognize that Persia has a right to just and legitimate reparations for her devastated territories and her massacred populations.

While leaving the means of reparation to the judgment of the Conference, the Persian Government venture to make the following suggestions:

1st. - *As regards Russia*, but a very small portion of the losses caused by her could be covered by

a) The cancellation of Persia's debts to Russia;

b) The cancellation of the concessions obtained by the Russian Government and subjects;

c) The seizure of the property of the Russian State in Persia.

2nd. - *As regards Turkey*, the amount of the damages she has caused Persia could be assigned to her general debt.

3rd. - *As regards Germany*, the Persian Government would ask to receive a part of the general indemnity which will be collected from her.

Lastly, it is to be noted that foreign Powers have asserted that during the war their subjects as well as their industrial and commercial institutions have suffered losses in Persia. The Persian Government hold, however, that losses of this kind are the consequence of the violation of Persian neutrality, and that none but the authors of that violation should be held responsible for them.

MOCHAVER-OL-MEMALEK,
Minister for Foreign Affairs of Persia.

Paris, March 1919.

NOTES

Prologue: The Paris Peace Conference

1. See declaration of neutrality (no. 41) and circulation to foreign legations (no. 44) in Empire de Perse, Ministère Des Affaires Étrangéres, *Neutralité Persane*, Documents Diplomatiques, 30 Septembre 1914–22 Mars 1915 (Paris: Georges Cadet,1919).
2. Ibid.
3. Emile Joseph Dillon, *The Inside Story of The Peace Conference* (New York; London: Harper and Bros, 1920), p.9.
4. H. W. V. Temperley, *A History of the Peace Conference of Paris*, Volume 1 (London: Hodder & Stoughton, 1920) Introduction, p.xxx.
5. Recent and pertinent monographs include Margaret Macmillan, *Peacemakers, The Paris Conference of 1919 and Its Attempt to End War* (London: John Murray, 2002), and Leonard V. Smith, *Sovereignty at the Paris Peace Conference of 1919* (New York: Oxford University Press, 2018).
6. Macmillan, *Peacemakers*, p.6.
7. Erez Manela, *The Wilsonian Moment: Self-Determination and the International Origins of Anticolonial Nationalism* (Cary: Oxford University Press, 2007).
8. The Secretary of State to the Ambassadors and Ministers in Belligerent Countries, Washington, 18 December 1916. Washington, DC: US Government Printing Office. (FRUS), 1916 Supplement, The World War, pp.97–9.
9. Woodrow Wilson, Address to a Joint Session of Congress on the Conditions of Peace ['The Fourteen Points'] Online by Gerhard Peters and John T. Woolley, The American Presidency Project https://www.presidency.ucsb.edu/node/206651.
10. Rosa Luxemburg, *The National Question – Selected Writings by Rosa Luxemburg*, in Horace B. Davies (ed) (Monthly Review Press, 1976), chapter 1 'The Right of Nations to Self-Determination'.
11. Macmillan, *Peacemakers*, p.21.
12. Ibid., p.20.
13. Ibid., p.66.
14. Requoted from Arnulf Becker Lorca, 'Petitioning the International: "A Pre-History" of Self Determination', *The European Journal of International Law*, Vol. 25, No. 2 (2014), p.509.
15. Ibid., p.514.
16. Taken from Brett Bowden, *The Empire of Civilization: The Evolution of an Imperial Idea* (Chicago: University of Chicago Press, 2014), p.16.
17. James Barr, *A Line in the Sand: Britain, France and the Struggle for the Mastery of the Middle East* (London: Simon & Shuster, 2011).
18. Committee of Imperial Defence, Report of a Committee, Asiatic Turkey, July 1915, CAB 42/3/12.
19. Ibid., Preliminary Considerations, points 1 and 3.

20 Woodrow Wilson, 'Democracy and Efficiency', *Atlantic Monthly*, March, 1901.
21 Saad Zaghloul, *The Egyptian National Claims: A Memorandum Presented to the Peace Conference by the Egyptian Delegation Charged with the Defence of Egyptian Independence* (Paris: Imprimerie artistique Lux, 1919).
22 Nikoloz Chkheidze and Irakli Tsereteli, MEMORANDUM presented to the Peace Conference (political claims-frontiers) followed by THE ACT OF INDEPENDENCE OF GEORGIA AND A MAP (Paris: Impr. M.Flinikowski, 1919).
23 A. Aharonian and Boghos Nubar, *THE ARMENIAN QUESTION before the Peace Conference, A Memorandum Presented Officially by the Representatives of Armenia to the Peace Conference at Versailles, on February 26th, 1919* (New York: Press Bureau, The Armenian National Union of America).
24 Metin Atmaca, 'Sherif Pasha's "Memorandum on the Claims of the Kurd People" to the Conference of Peace in Paris on February 6, 1919', in Sebastian Maisel (ed), *The Kurds: An Encyclopedia of Life, Culture, and Society* (Santa Barbara, California: ABC-CLIO, 2018), pp.328-30.
25 E. Joel Werda, and Cap. A.K. Yoosuf, M.D., *The claims of the Assyrians before the Conference of the preliminaries of Peace at Paris* (Paris: Imp. Ph.Rosen, 1919).

Introduction: Iran at the crossroads

1 Mochaver-Ol-Memalek, *Claims of Persia before the Conference of the Preliminaries of Peace at Paris* (Paris: Cadet, March, 1919), p.1.
2 Oliver Bast, 'Disintegrating the "Discourse of Disintegration": Some reflections on the historiography of the Late Qajar period and Iranian cultural memory', in Touraj Atabaki (ed), *Iran in the 20th Century: Historiography and Political Culture* (London: I.B. Taurus, 2009), pp.55–68.
3 For a contemporary narrative of Iranian bureaucracy, see Abdollah Mostowfi, *Sharh-e zendegani-ye man ya tarikh-e ejtema'i va edari-ye dowreh-ye Qajariyeh*, volume III (Tehran: Zovar, 1384).
4 Edward Ingram, *The Beginning of the Great Game in Asia 1824–1834* (Oxford: Clarendon Press, 1979).
5 The Transcaucasus relates roughly to the territory which encompasses modern-day Georgia, Azerbaijan and Armenia. The Transcaspian relates to the oblast and territory reaching from modern-day Iran up to the Aral Sea and the Amu-Darya River.
6 Ali M. Ansari, *Modern Iran since 1797: Reform and Revolution, 3rd Edition* (London; New York: Routledge, 2019), chapter 5.
7 Jürgen Habermas (translated by Thomas Burger), *The Structural Transformation of the Public Sphere: An Inquiry into a Category of Bourgeois Society* (Cambridge, MA: The MIT Press, 2001), p.65.
8 Ehsan Yarshater, 'The Qajar Era in the Mirror of Time', *Iranian Studies*, Vol. 34, No. 1/4 (2001), 187–94, p.191.
9 Re-quoted in Maryam Ekhtiar, 'Nasir al-Din Shah and the Dar al-Funun: The Evolution of an Institution', *Iranian Studies*, Vol. 34, No. 1–4 (2001), 153–63.
10 Abbas Milani, 'Nasir al-din Shah in Farang', in Abbas Milani (ed), *Lost Wisdom: Rethinking Modernity in Iran* (Washington, DC: Mage Publishers, 2004), p.52.
11 Consider the ability of Naser al-Din Shah to play the British and Russians against each other and arguably secure the viability of Iran. See Abbas Amanat, *Pivot of the Universe* (London; New York: I.B. Taurus, 2008).

12 Ernest Gellner, *Nations and Nationalism*, Second Edition (Malden: Blackwell, 2006).
13 Ansari, *Modern Iran since 1797*, p.15.
14 John Breuilly, *Nationalism and the State*, Second Edition (Manchester: Manchester University Press, 1995).
15 Gellner, *Nations and Nationalism*.
16 Benedict Anderson, *Imagined Communities: Reflections on the Origin and Spread of Nationalism* (London; New York: Verso, 2006).
17 Yael Tamir, 'Review: The Enigma of Nationalism: Imagined Communities by Benedict Anderson, Nationalism: Five Roads to Modernity by Liah Greenfeld, National Identity by Anthony D. Smith', *World Politics*, Vol. 47, No. 3 (1995), 418–40, p.421.
18 Ibid., p.44.
19 More recent monographs on Iranian nationalism include Meir Litvak (ed), *Constructing Nationalism in Iran: From the Qajars to the Islamic Republic* (Abingdon, Oxon: Routledge, 2017); Afshin Matin-Asgari, *Both Eastern and Western: An Intellectual History of Iranian Modernity* (Cambridge, UK: Cambridge University Press, 2018); Reza Zia-Ebrahimi, *The Emergence of Iranian Nationalism: Race and the Politics of Dislocation* (New York: Columbia University Press, 2016).
20 See introduction by Kamran Scot Aghaie and Afshin Marashi, in Kamran Scot Aghaie and Afshin Marashi (eds), *Rethinking Iranian Nationalism and Modernity* (Austin: University of Texas, 2015).
21 Elie Kedourie, *Nationalism* (Malden; Oxford: Fourth edition, Blackwell Publishers, 2000).
22 Richard W. Cottam, *Nationalism in Iran* (Pittsburgh: Pittsburgh Press, 1979).
23 Firoozeh Kashani-Sabet, *Frontier Fictions: Shaping the Iranian Nation, 1804–1946* (London; New York: I.B.Tauris, 2000).
24 Kashani-Sabet, *Frontier Fictions*, p.7.
25 See introduction and chapter 8, David B. Knight 'Self-determination for indigenous peoples: The context for change', in R.J. Johnston, David B. Knight and Eleonore Kofman (eds), *Nationalism, self-determination and political geography* (London; New York: Croom Helm, 1988).
26 Anthony D. Smith, *The Ethnic Origins of Nations* (Oxford: Blackwell, 1988), pp.22–30.
27 Marshall Hodgson, *The Venture of Islam: Conscience and History in a World Civilization* (Chicago: University of Chicago Press, 1974).
28 This is a summation of the historical tenets of a Civilizational State as presented in Christopher Coker, *The Rise of the Civilizational State* (Cambridge; Medford: Polity, 2019). See also Martin Jacques, *When China Rules the World: The End of the Western World and the Birth of a New Global Order* (London: Penguin Books, 2012), and the more polemic Zhang WeiWei, *The China Wave: Rise of the Civilizational State* (Hackensack: World Century, 2012).
29 Anja Pistor-Hatam, 'Progress and Civilization in Nineteenth-Century Japan: The Far Eastern State as a Model for Modernization', *Iranian Studies*, Vol. 29, No. 1/2 (Winter–Spring, 1996), pp.111–26.
30 Coker, *The Rise of the Civilizational State*, see p.93 in particular, pp.92–6.
31 The concepts of pan-Turkism and pan-Turanism have been used interchangeably in academic writing. While similar they differ in terms of scope. Turan reflects a more esoteric and mythical understanding, notably covering a larger territory.
32 Describing and analysing Iran as a Civilizational State over a longer period, including the Pahlavi dynasty and the Islamic Republic of Iran, is beyond the scope of this book;

however, it may provide a better framework for understanding Iran's evolving national identity.
33 David Fromkin, *A Peace to End All Peace: The Fall of the Ottoman Empire and the Creation of the Modern Middle East* (New York: A Holt paperback, 2009), p.385.
34 Fromkin, *A Peace to End All Peace*, p.391.
35 'Major-general Sir Percy Zachariah Cox', *The Geographical Journal*, Vol. 90, No. 1 (July, 1937), pp.1–5.
36 See the moqadameh by Mohammad Afshin Vafaie and Pejman Firouzbakhsh, *MAF*, p.19.
37 Mansoureh Ettehadieh, 'Les illusions et les faits: l'Iran et la Conférence de Versailles', in Oliver Bast (ed), *La Perse et La Grande Guerre*, Bibliothéque Iranienne 52 (Tehran; Louvain: Peeters, 2002) p.428.
38 Kashani-Sabet, *Frontier Fictions*, pp.9–10.
39 See chapters 4 and 5 in Homa Katouzian, *State and Society in Iran: The Eclipse of the Qajars and the Emergence of the Pahlavis* (London; New York: I.B Tauris, 2006).
40 Houshang Sabahi, *British Policy in Persia 1918-1925* (London; Portland: Frank Cass, 1990).
41 Shaul Bakhash, 'The Origins of the Anglo-Persian Agreement of 1919', *Asian and African Studies: Journal of the Israel Oriental Society*, Volume 25, Number 1, March 1991.
42 William J. Olson, 'The Genesis of the Anglo-Persian Agreement of 1919', in Elie Kedourie and Silvia G. Haim (eds), *Towards a Modern Iran* (London: Routledge, 2016), and William J. Olsen, *Anglo-Iranian Relations during World War 1* (London; New York: Routledge, 2013).
43 Olivier Bast, 'Les « buts de guerre » de la Perse neuter pendant la Première Guerre Mondiale', in *Relations Internationales*, Hiver 2015 (janvier-mars), No. 160, États neutres et neutralité dans la Première Guerre mondiale – II (Hiver 2015 (janvier-mars)) 95–110.
44 Oliver Bast, 'Putting the Record Straight: Vosuq al-Dowleh's Foreign Policy in 1918/19', in Touraj Atabaki and Erik J. Zürcher (eds), *Men of Order: Authoritarian Modernization under Ataturk and Reza Shah* (London: I.B. Tauris, 2004), p.275.
45 Sohail Rohani, 'Qarardad-e 1919 (Qarardad-e Vosuq al-Dowleh)', *Ayandeh*, sal-e 13 Aban ta Esfand, 1366, shomareh-ye 8 ta 12, 651–664, pp.654.
46 See in particular Moqadameh in Kaveh Bayat and Reza Azari Shahrzayee, *Amal-e Iraniyan az konferans-e solh-e Paris ta qarardad-e 1919 Iran va Engelis* (Iran: Pardise Danesh, 1392). Henceforward shortened to *AI*. Ahmad Ali Sepehr, *Khaterate-e siyasi-e Movarekhaldowleh Sepehr* (Iran: Namak, 1374). Alireza Mollai Tavani, 'Negahi-e dobareh be qarardad-e 1919', *Faslnameh-ye Tarikh-e ravabet-e khareji*, Bahar va Tabestan, 1388, shomareh-ye 38 va 39, 113–45. Saeed Jahangiri, Ebrahim Mottaqi and Shahrokh Ashja Mahdavi, ''Vakavi-ye sharayat-e dakhely va beynolmelali eneghad-e qarardad-e 1919 (aba´ad va roykerd-ha)', *'Ulum-e siyasi: nashreyeh-ye rahbord-e siyasi*, Paiz, 1398 shomareh-ye 10. 1–18.
47 Bayat, Shahrzayee, *Amal-e Iraniyan az konferans-e solh-e Paris ta qarardad-e 1919 Iran va Engelis*.

Chapter 1

1 Sir Antony Sherley, *His Relation of His Travels into Persia* (London: Forgotten Books, 2018).

2   Sir John Chardin, *Travels in Persia* (London: The Argonaut Press, 1927).
3   Chardin, *Travels in Persia*, p.89.
4   See Geographical and Historical Background in Charles Issawi, *The Economic History of Iran 1800-1914* (Chicago; London: University Chicago Press, 1971).
5   Elena Andreeva, *Russia and Iran in the Great Game: Travelogues and Orientalism* (London; New York: Routledge, 2007), p.11.
6   See Denis Wright's note of de Gobineau's description of India government agents in chapter 11, *The English Amongst The Persians: During the Qajar Period 1787-1921* (London: Heinemann, 1977). This chapter also serves as excellent general background for the British who came to Iran.
7   John Malcom, *History of Persia, Vol.2* (London: John Murray, 1815), p.628.
8   F. Kazemzadeh, 'Iranian relations with Russia and the Soviet Union, to 1921', in Peter Avery, Gavin Hambly and Charles Melville (eds), *The Cambridge History of Iran, Volume 7* (Cambridge: Cambridge University Press, 2003), p.331.
9   Muriel Atkin, *Russia and Iran, 1780-1828* (Minneapolis: University of Minnesota Press, 1980), p.70.
10 Atkin, *Russia and Iran*, p.92.
11 Stephanie Cronin, 'Building a new army: Military reform in Qajar Iran', in Roxane Farmanfarmaian (ed), *War and Peace in Qajar Iran: Implications Past and Present* (London; New York: Routledge, 2008), p.52.
12 Nikki R. Keddie, *Qajar Iran and the Rise of Reza Khan 1796-1925* (Costa Mesa: Mazda Publishers, 1999), p.21.
13 Stanford Shaw, 'Iranian relations with the Ottoman Empire in the eighteenth and nineteenth centuries', in Peter Avery, Gavin Hambly and Charles Melville (eds), *The Cambridge History of Iran, Volume 7* (Cambridge: Cambridge University Press, 2003), p.313.
14 Tadeusz Swietochowski, *Russia and Azerbaijan: A Borderland in Transition* (New York: Columbia University Press, 1995), p.6.
15 C. U. Aitchison, *A Collection of Treaties, Engagements, and Sanads relating to India and Neighbouring Countries*, Vol. X (Calcutta: Office of the Superintendent of Government Printing, India, 1892), pp.37-41.
16 Ouseley to Buckingham, Tehran, 17 February 1814, FO60/9, pp.43-7.
17 Draft letter Willock to Foreign Office, 10 November 1826, FO60/27, p.8.
18 Willock to Canning, Camp Sultanieh, 13 January 1826, FO60/27, p.15.
19 Confidential Notes on the progress of Russia to the Eastward, John Malcolm, 18 November 1826, FO60/29, pp.129-42.
20 See Instructions to Sir Gore Ouseley His Majesty's Ambassador Extraordinary and Plenipotentiary at the Court of Persia, London, 13 July 1810, FO60/4, pp.81-96.
21 Ingram, *The Beginning of the Great Game in Asia, 1824-1834*, p.31.
22 Ibid.
23 Castlereagh to Cathcart, Secret Enclosure No.3, Foreign Office, 2 February 1819, FO181/17, unnumbered.
24 Canning to Mirza Abdul Wahab, His Persian Majesty's Minister for Foreign Affairs, Foreign Office, 27 May 1823, FO60/23, pp.1-2.
25 After the Indian Mutiny which ended in 1859, the British government took control of India's administration from the East India Company. The administration was split between the India Office, based in London, and the Government of India, run by the British governor in India. I use the term India government to refer to the totality of Indian administration in Britain and India which was separate to British government's functions.

26 Edward Ingram, *Britain's Persian Connection, 1798-1828: Prelude to the Great Game in Asia* (Oxford: Clarendon Press Oxford, 1992), p.6.
27 Ibid., p.195.
28 Rose Greaves, *Persia and The Defence of India, 1884-1892* (London: University of London, 1959), p.194.
29 Elizabeth Monroe, *Britain's Moment in the Middle East, 1914-1956* (London: Chatto & Windus, 1963), p.12.
30 Ingram, *The Beginning of the Great Game*, p.2.
31 Hadi Enayat, *Law, State and Society in Modern Iran: Constitutionalism, Autocracy, and Legal Reform, 1906-1941* (New York: Palgrave Macmillan, 2013), p.24.
32 H. Lyman Stebbins, 'British Imperialism, Regionalism, and Nationalism in Iran, 1890-1919', in Abbas Amanat and Farzin Vejdani (eds), *Iran Facing Others: Identity Boundaries in a Historical Perspective* (New York: Palgrave Macmillan, 2012).
33 Ibid.
34 Aitchison, *A Collection of Treaties*.
35 Issawi, *The Economic History of Iran*, p.73.
36 Ibid.
37 Charles Issawi, 'Iranian Trade, 1800-1914', Iranian Studies, Vol. 16, No. 3/4, Studies on the Economic and Social History of Iran in the Nineteenth Century (Summer-Autumn, 1983), 229-41, p.235.
38 Andrew Porter, *European Imperialism, 1860-1914* (Studies in European History, Macmillan, 1994), p.40.
39 Issawi, 'Iranian Trade', p.235.
40 Nikki Keddie, 'The Economic History of Iran, 1800-1914, and Its Political Impact: An Overview', Iranian Studies, Vol. 5, No. 2/3 (Spring-Summer, 1972), 58-78, p.64.
41 Nikki Keddie has pointed out that the economic engagement with the West was not entirely negative. See Keddie, *Qajar Iran*, p.36.
42 For a synopsis of concessions in Iran see Issawi, *The Economic History of Iran*, and Wilhelm Litten, *Persien, Von der 'pénétration pacifique' zum 'Protektorat'* (Berlin: Berlin und Leipzig, 1920), pp.2-222.
43 Arthur Herbert, Report on present state of Persia and her Mineral Resources, 7 May 1886, FO60/482, pp.110-64.
44 Drummond Wolf to Salisbury, Tehran, 21 April 1888, FO60/492, unnumbered.
45 Soli Shahvar, 'Iron Poles, Wooden Poles: The Electric Telegraph and the Ottoman: Iranian Boundary Conflict, 1863-1865', British Journal of Middle Eastern Studies, Vol. 34, No. 1 (April, 2007), 23-42, p.24.
46 Ekhtiar, 'Nasir al-Din Shah and the Dar al-Funun'.
47 'The Persian Question', The Times, 24 July 1873, p.7.
48 George N. Curzon, *Persia and the Persian Question, Vol. 1* (London; New York: Longmans, Green and Co, 1892).
49 'The Persian Concession to Baron Reuter', The Times, 5 July 1873, p.7.
50 'The Persian Question', The Times, 24 July 1873, p.7.
51 'Reuters Concession', The New York Times, 29 July 1873, p.5.
52 John S. Galbraith, 'British Policy on Railways in Persia, 1870-1900', Middle Eastern Studies, Vol. 25, No.4 (1989), 480-505, pp.486-7.
53 Amanat, *Pivot of the Universe*, p.425.
54 Keddie, 'The Economic History of Iran, 1800-1914', p.74.

55 For articles see John S Galbraith, 'British Policy on Railways in Persia, 1870–1900'. Excellent primary sources include the substantive IOR/L/PS/18/C122, Memorandum on Persian Railways, 20 June 1911, and shorter IOR/L/PS/18/C124, Note on Persian Railways, 3 July 1911.
56 Amanat, *Pivot of the Universe*, pp.422–3.
57 For text of this convention and reaction to it, see Negin Nabavi, *Modern Iran: a History in Documents* (Princeton: Markus Wiener, 2016), pp.25–9.
58 Zahra Alizadehbirjandi, 'Avamel-e mo'aser bar ravabet-e Iran va usmani dar doreh-ye Qajarieh', *Mahnameh-ye andeshe va Tarikh-e siyasi-ye Iran mo'aser*, sal-e 5, eshareh-ye 50, Aban, 1380. 39–42.
59 Sir John Malcolm, 'Notes on the Invasion of India by Russia', re-quoted in Ingram, *The beginning of the Great Game*, p.69.
60 Kenneth Bourne, *The Foreign Policy of Victorian England, 1830–1902* (London: Clarendon Press, 1970), p.3.

Chapter 2

1 Ansari, *Modern Iran since 1797*, pp.57–8.
2 See in particular introduction by Abbas Amanat in Edward G. Browne, *The Persian Revolution 1905–1909* (Washington: Mage, 2006).
3 Hamid Algar, 'An introduction to the History of Freemansory [sic] in Iran', *Middle Eastern Studies*, October, 1970, Vol. 6, No. 3 (October, 1970), pp.276–96.
4 Hassan Bashir, 'The Iranian Press and Modernization Under the Qajars', unpublished thesis, University of Leicester, p.64.
5 Iraj Afshar, 'Book Translations as a Cultural Activity in Iran 1806–1896', *Iran*, Vol. 41 (2003), pp.279–89.
6 Some foreign books were translated into Persian for use at the Dar al-Fonun.
7 Thomas M. Wilson and Hastings Doonan (eds), *Border Identities: Nation and State at international frontiers* (New York: Cambridge University Press, 1998), and Peter Sahlins 'Natural Frontiers Revisited: France's Boundaries since the Seventeenth Century', *The American Historical Review*, Vol. 95, No. 5 (December, 1990).
8 Edith Sheffer, *Burned Bridge: How the East and West Germans Made the Iron Curtain* (Oxford; New York: Oxford University Press, 2014).
9 Hamid Algar, *Mirza Malkum Khan: A Biographical Study in Iranian Modernism* (Los Angeles; London: University of California Press, 1973), p.112.
10 Ansari, *Modern Iran since 1797*, p.74.
11 Shaul Bakhash, 'The Evolution of Qajar Bureacracy [sic]: 1779–1879', *Middle Eastern Studies*, Vol. 7, No. 2 (May, 1971), pp.139–68.
12 See chapters 1 and 2 in Shaul Bakhash, *Iran: Modernity, Bureaucracy & Reform under the Qajars: 1858–1896* (Oxford: Ithaca Press London, 1978).
13 Mirza Malkam Khan, *Ruznameh-ye Qanun*, edited by Homa Natiq (Tehran: Amir Kabir, 2535).
14 Nikki Keddie, *An Islamic Response to Imperialism: Political and Religious Writings of Sayyid Jamal ad-Din 'al-Afghani'* (Los Angeles; London: University of California Press, 1983).
15 Mostafa Elm, *Oil, Power, and Principle: Iran's Oil Nationalization and Its Aftermath* (Syracuse; New York: Syracuse University Press, 1994), p.9.

16 Ibid., Elm, *Oil, Power, and Principle*.
17 Memorandum by Lord Curzon, Mss Eur F112/274, Eastern Committee, 30 December 1918, in Papers of the War Cabinet's Eastern Committee, 13 March 1918–7 January 1919, pp.2–3.
18 Ibid, Memorandum by Lord Curzon.
19 See Sabahi, *British Policy in Persia 1918–1925*, pp.2–3.
20 Letter from Captain Lorimer to Sir Cecil Spring Rice, Teheran, 14 September 1907, FO248/923, pp.297–8.
21 Browne, *The Persian Revolution 1905–1909*, Appendix A.
22 Enayat, *Law, State, and Society*, p.24.
23 O'Beirne to Grey, St. Petersburg, 1 September 1910, FO416/164, no.339, p.251.
24 See Firuz Kazemzadeh, *Russia and Britain in Persia: Imperial Ambitions in Qajar Iran* (London; New York: I.B.Tauris, 2013), chapter 9.
25 W. Morgan Shuster, *The Strangling of Persia* (New York: The Century Co, 1912), p.123.
26 Abbas Amanat, *Iran: A Modern History* (Newhaven; London: Yale University Press, 2017), p.370.
27 Cronin, 'Building a new army: Military reform in Qajar Iran', p.68.
28 See chapter 9, 'The Strangling of Persia' in Kazemzadeh, *Russia and Britain in Persia*.
29 Reprinted in Kazemzadeh, *Russia and Britain in Persia*, p.500.
30 No.27 of 1904, Government of India, Foreign department, Secret, Frontier, 4 February 1904, in 'Persia: Anglo-Russian Agreement (1907)', IOR/L/PS/10/122, pp.182–4.
31 Harold Nicholson, *Curzon: The Last Phase 1919–1925* (London: Constable & Co, 1934), pp.125–9.
32 'British Diplomacy in Persia', article from *The Economist* re-printed in *The Living Age*, 13 January 1912, 116–18.
33 Kazemzadeh, *Russia and Britain in Persia*, p.501.
34 Nicholson, *Curzon: The Last Phase*, p.127.
35 The Russians in Akhal in IOR/L/PS/20/MEMO22/N, p.55.
36 The Russians in Akhal, p.59.
37 Ibid., p.61.
38 Ibid.
39 Sabri Ateş, *The Ottoman-Iranian Borderlands: Making a Boundary, 1843–1914* (Cambridge: Cambridge University Press, 2013), p.230.
40 Marling to Grey, Constantinople, 23 August 1912, FO416/168, no.309, p.185.
41 Lowther to Grey, Constantinople, 5 April 1913, FO416/171, no.54, p.59.
42 William Edward David Allen and Paul Muratoff, *Caucasian Battlefields: A History of the Wars on the Turco-Caucasian Border 1828–1921* (New York: Cambridge University Press, 2010), pp.495–6.
43 'A Manual on the Turanians and Pan-Turanianism', November, 1918, Naval Staff Intelligence, British Library, IOR/L/MIL/17/16/25.
44 Cypher, Marling, 11 May 1918, FO371/3259, p.537.
45 Swietochowski, *Russia and Azerbaijan*, p.61–7.
46 Cypher, Marling, 19 April 1918, FO371/3259, p.440.
47 War Office Memorandum, War Office, 2 November 1918, FO371/3262, p.523.
48 Hedley Bull, Benedict Kingsbury and Adam Roberts (eds), *Hugo Grotius and International Relations* (Oxford: Clarendon, 2002), p.71.
49 Bull, *Hugo Grotius and International Relations*, pp.75–6.
50 Danilo Zolo, 'The Rule of Law: A Critical Reappraisal', in Pietro Costa and Danilo Zolo (eds), *The Rule of Law: History, Theory and Criticism* (Netherlands: Springer, 2007), p.7.

51 Koskenniemi, *The Gentle Civilizer of Nations*, pp.70–1.
52 Ibid., p.72.
53 Ibid., pp.73–4.
54 Ibid., pp.34.
55 Gotelind Müller, 'Versailles and the Fate of Chinese Internationalism: Reassessing the Anarchist case', in Urs Matthias Zachmann (ed), *Asia after Versailles: Asian Perspectives on the Paris Peace Conference and the Interwar Order, 1919–33* (Edinburgh: Edinburgh University Press, 2017).
56 Printed in: The Right Honourable Ameer Ali, *The Rights of Persia* (London: Chapman Hall, 1919).
57 Ibid., p.20.

Chapter 3

1 Oliver Bast, 'La mission persane à la Conférence de Paix en 1919: Une nouvelle interprétation', in Oliver Bast (ed), *La Perse et La Grande Guerre*, Bibliothéque Iranienne 52 (Tehran; Louvain: Peeters, 2002), p.375.
2 Sir Percy Sykes, *A History of Persia, Volume II*, Second Edition (London: Macmillan and Co, 1921), pp.518–20.
3 Balfour to Marling, Tehran, 10 January 1918, FO371/3262, p.179.
4 *Iran* newspaper, 28 December 1916.
5 The Secretary of State to the Ambassadors and Ministers in Belligerent Countries, Washington, 18 December 1916. Washington, DC: US Government Printing Office. (FRUS), 1916 Supplement, The World War, pp.97–9.
6 Firuz Kazemzadeh, *The Struggle for Transcaucasia (1917–1921)* (London: Anglo Caspian Press Ltd, 2008), p.57.
7 Moqadameh, *AI*, p.11.
8 Homa Katouzian, 'Sayyed Hasan Taqizadeh: Three Lives in a Lifetime', *Comparative Studies of South Asia, Africa and the Middle East*, Vol. 32 (1, April 2012).
9 Seyyed Hasan Taqizadeh, *Zendegi-ye Tufani* (Tehran: Ferdowsi, 1379), p.195.
10 For an interesting discussion of the Berlin Circle, see Afshin Matin-Agari, 'The Berlin Circle: Iranian Nationalism Meets German Countermodernity', in Kamran Scot Aghaie and Afshin Marashi (eds), *Rethinking Iranian Nationalism and Modernity* (Austin: University of Texas, 2015).
11 Timothy Nunan, 'Persian Visions of Nationalism and Inter-Nationalism in a World at War', in Marcus M.Payk and Roberta Pergher (eds), *Beyond Versailles: Sovereignty, Legitimacy, and the Formation of New Polities after the Great War* (Bloomington, Indiana: Indiana University Press, 2019), pp.174–5.
12 'Dad khahi-ye mellat-e Iran' in *Kaveh*, shomareh-e 22, 26 Shavval, 1335. pp.2–4.
13 Mehdi Khan to Robert Lansing, Washington, 15 January 1917, FRUS, 1917, Supplement 1, The Great War, p.14.
14 2, Vezarat-e Omur-e Kharejeh be He'at-e Dowlat, 12 Safar-e 1337, *AI*, pp.94–5.
15 50, Reasat-e Vowzara be sefaratkhaneh-haye Iran dar Landan va Paris, pp.160–1, *AI*.
16 51, Vazir-e Omur-e Kharejeh be He'at-e Vowzara, 22 Moharram-e 1337, pp.161–3, *AI*.
17 See 19, Sefarat-e Iran dar Washington be Vezarat-e Omur-e Kharejeh, 23 Rabiolakhar-e 1336, *AI*, p.117.
18 5, Sefarat-e Iran dar Paris be Vezarat-e Omur-e Kharejeh, avval-e Rabiolavval-e 1336, *AI*, pp.98–9.

19 Behruz Qotbi (ed), *Asnad-e jang-e avval-e jahani dar Iran* (Tehran: Nashr-e Qarn/Sazman-e Chap va Entesharat-e Vezarat-e Farhang va Ershad-e Eslami, 1370), pp.276-7.
20 Bast, 'Putting the Record Straight', p.261.
21 Ibid.
22 Green Books are political diaries produced by countries wishing to diarize, account for policies and to provide diplomatic guidance. See Reza Qoli Nezam Mafi, *Ketab-e Sabz* (Tehran: Nashr-e Tarikh, 1363).
23 Peter Avery, *Modern Iran* (London: Ernest Benn Limited, 1965), p.201.
24 J. W. Wheeler-Bennett, *Brest-Litovsk: The Forgotten Peace, March 1918* (London: Macmillan, 1971), pp.403-8.
25 'Proceedings of the Brest-Litovsk Peace Conference: The Peace Negotiations Between Russia and the Central Powers', 21 November 1917-3 March 1918, *Washington Government Printing Office*, 1918.
26 Mr Lindley memorandum, 29 January 1918, FO371/3265, p.392.
27 The decision was made on the 27th July but seems to have been formally communicated in October. See Nadjaf Gholi, Persian Legation, London, 24 October 1918, FO371/3262, p.470.
28 7, Vezarat-e Omur-e Kharejeh, *AI*, pp.100-2.
29 11, Sefarat-e Iran dar Landan be Vezarat-e Omur-e Kharejeh, 17 Rabiolavval-e 1336, *AI*, pp.106-7.
30 See FO371/3260, pp.34-6 and p.37.
31 Persian Azerbaijan Memorandum, Sir Percy Cox, Foreign Office, 14 October 1918, FO371/3262, p.351.
32 Secretary of State India Office to Foreign Office, 10 September 1918, FO371/3262, p.58.
33 Marling to Foreign Office, 5 September 1918, FO371/3262, p.51.
34 Eastern Committee Memorandum, Political Department, India Office, 30 September 1918, FO371/3262, p.244.
35 Cox to Foreign Office (assumed), 1 October 1918, FO371/3262, p.257.
36 Memorandum Oliphant, 18 October 1918, FO371/3262, p.385.
37 *Iran* newspaper, 13 November 1918.
38 56 to 62, *AI*, pp.167-75.
39 Bast, 'Putting the Record Straight', p.262.
40 57, Komisiyun-e amal, jalaseh-ye avval, 12 Safar-e 1337, *AI*, p.169.
41 60, Vezarat-e Omur-e Kharejeh be Vezarat-e Post va Telgraf, 18 Safar-e 1337, *AI*, pp.173-4.
42 59, Komisiyun-e amal, jalaseh-ye sevom, 18 Safar-e 1337, *AI*, pp.172-3.
43 58, Komisiyun-e amal, jalaseh-ye dovom, 14 Safar-e 1337, *AI*, pp.170-2.
44 Ibid.
45 66, Gozareshi az va'zeyat-e marzi-ye Iran, *AI*, pp.180-2.
46 46, 47 and 48, *AI*, pp.156-8.
47 61, Komisiyun-e amal, jalaseh-ye chaharom, 22 Safar-e 1337, *AI*, pp.174-5.
48 48, Arfa al-Dowleh be Reasat-e Vowzara, 12 Zeq'adeh-ye 1336, *AI*, p.158.
49 68, Komisiyun-e amal be Vezarat-e Omur-e Kharejeh, 4 Rabiolavval-e 1337, *AI*, pp.184-6.
50 Some are more commonly known as ... Derbent, Qobbeh ... Shirvan and Shakki.
51 69, Komisiyun-e amal, jalaseh-ye nohom, 4 Rabiolavval-e 1337, *AI*, pp.186-7.
52 Marling to Mushar es Saltaneh, 2 August 1918, FO371/3262, p.551.

53. Marling to Persian Minister for Foreign Affairs, 2 August 1918, FO371/3262, p.552.
54. Mohammad Lashkari, 'dar neemeh rah-ye konferans-e solh-e Paris', Aban, 1393, *Goftigu*, no.65.
55. 'Entekhab-e nemayandeh-ye solh, az taraf-e Iran', *Iran* newspaper, 22 November 1918.
56. Hossein Makki, *Zendegani-ye siyasi-ye Ahmad Shah Qajar* (Tehran: Amir Kabir, 1357), p.70.
57. Cox to Foreign Office, 6 December 1918, FO371/3263, pp.290–1.
58. Makki, *Zendegani-ye siyasi-ye Ahmad Shah Qajar*, p.70.
59. William J. Olson, *Anglo-Iranian Relations during World War 1* (London; New York: Routledge, 2013), p.166.
60. A point raised by the French who believed that Moshaver al-Mamalek had openly collaborated with the Germans during the war. See Bast, 'Putting the Record Straight', p.266.
61. Afshin Parto, 'Peyman-e 1919 va vakonesh-haye barkhaste dar barabar-e an', *Ettela'at siyasi-eqtesadi*, Khordad va Teer, 1377, No 129, 130, 86–101, p.88.
62. Adolphe Perni was engaged to help organize the Ministry of Justice in 1911 and presented the first Iranian Penal Code to the Majles in 1912. See Avery, *Modern Iran*, p.151.
63. Mohammad Ali Foroughi, *Hoquq-e assasi-e (ya'ni) adab-e mashrutiat-e doval* (Iran: Koyer, 1382).
64. Baqer Aqeli, *Shahr-e hal-e rajel-e siyasi va nezami-ye mo'aser-e Iran (2)* (Tehran: Goftar, 1380), p.1011.
65. 'Appointed Consul General', *New York Times*, 22 September 1915, p.22.
66. Cox to Foreign Office, 14 January 1919, FO371/3858, p.65.
67. 'Iran dar 1919', letter to Ebrahim Hakimi, *MAF*, pp.458–69. Also, in *Maqalate-e Foroughi, jeld-e avval* (Tehran, Tus, 1384) pp.61–79.
68. Cox to Foreign Office (assumed), 31 October 1918, FO371/3262, p.496.
69. Cox to Foreign Office (assumed), 18 November 1918, FO371/3263, pp.101–3.
70. Cox to Foreign Office (assumed), 20 November 1918, FO371/3263, pp.132–3.
71. See Cypher, Cox to Foreign Office, 26 November 1918, FO371/3263, pp.187–8.
72. The Persian Foreign Minister (Aligoli) to the Persian Chargé (Ali-Kuli Khan), Tehran, 18 November 1919. FRUS, 1919. The Paris Peace Conference, Vol.1, pp.258–9.
73. Cox to Foreign Office (assumed), 18 November 1918, FO371/3263, pp.105–6.
74. The Chargé in Persia (White) to the Acting Secretary of State, Tehran, 7 January 1919. FRUS, 1919, Vol.1, p.263.
75. The Persian Chargé (Ali-Kuli Khan) to Acting Secretary of State, Tehran, 18 December 1919. FRUS, 1919, Vol.1. pp.261–2.
76. 'Memorandum Regarding the Policy of His Majesty's Government towards Persia at the Peace Conference', 17 December 1918, IOR/L/PS/18/C193.
77. Annex, Shorthand notes of a Meeting of the Committee held in Lord Curzon's Room at the Privy Council Office, on Thursday, 19 December 1918, at 3 pm, Eastern Committee, 30 December 1918, in Papers of the War Cabinet's Eastern Committee, 13 March 1918–7 January 1919, Mss Eur F112/274, pp.241–8.
78. Ibid.
79. Ibid.
80. Ibid.
81. Bakhash, 'The Origins of the Anglo-Persian Agreement', pp.14–16.
82. Bast, 'Putting the Record Straight', p.263.
83. 'Annex, Shorthand notes of a Meeting of the Committee', pp.241–8.

84 For a fuller analysis of French reactions, see page 383 in Oliver Bast, 'La mission persane', p.92.
85 Marie-Louise Chaumont, 'iv. RELATIONS WITH PERSIA SINCE 1918', *Encyclopaedia Iranica*, X/2, pp.136–41, available online at http://www.iranicaonline.org/articles/france-iv-relations-with-persia-since-1918 (accessed on 11 October 2022).
86 Bast, 'Putting the Record Straight', p.264.
87 The Minister in Persia (Caldwell) to the Secretary of State, Tehran, 15 November 1918. FRUS, 1919, Vol.1, p.256.
88 Cox to Foreign Office, 20 November 1918, FO371/3263, pp.133–4.
89 The Minister in Persia (Caldwell) to the Secretary of State, Tehran, 15 November 1918. FRUS, 1919, Vol.1, p.256.
90 Cox to Foreign Office, 26 November 1918, FO371/3263, pp.185–6.
91 The Secretary of State to the Persian Chargé (Ali-Kuli Kahn), Washington, 2 December 1919. FRUS, 1919, Vol.1, p.261.
92 21, Moqadarat-e qat´at-e az dast rafteh-ye Iran, *AI*, pp.120–3.
93 Cox (assumed) to Rodd (Rome) Foreign Office, 18 January 1919, FO371/3858, p.59.
94 For Mohammad Ali Foroughi's diary entries on this, see pp. 20–3. For a more in-depth discussion of the *Mohajeran's* activities during the war, see Mansoureh Ettehadieh, 'The Iranian Provisional Government', in Touraj Atabaki (ed), *Iran and the First World War: Battleground of the Great Powers* (London; New York: I.B Taurus, 2006).
95 Chahar shanbeh, bist-o hashtom-e Rabiolavval, *MAF*, p.15.
96 Do shanbeh, dahom-e Rabiolsani, *MAF*, p.26.
97 Chahar shanbeh, bist-o yekom-e Rabiolavval, *MAF*, pp.8–10.
98 Se shanbeh, yazdahom-e Rabiolsani, *MAF*, p.27.
99 Manela, *The Wilsonian Moment*.
100 'Memorandum Regarding the Policy of His Majesty's Government Towards Persia at the Peace Conference', 17 December 1918, IOR/L/PS/18/C193.

Chapter 4

1 Dillon, *The Inside Story of The Peace Conference*, p.4.
2 Ibid., pp.5–7.
3 See entry for Jom´eh, bist-o yekom-e [Rabiolsani], *MAF*, pp.35–6.
4 Chahar shanbeh, bist-o sheshom-e [Rabiolsani], *MAF*, p.38.
5 Authors translation of 84, Reasat-e Vowzara be Moshaver al-Mamalek, 25 Rabiolsani-ye 1337, *AI*, p.203.
6 86, Moshaver al-Mamalek be Reasat-e Vowzara, 27 Rabiolsani-ye 1337, *AI*, pp.205–6.
7 88, Moshaver al-Mamalek be Reasat-e Vowzara, selkh-e Rabiolsani-ye 1337, *AI*, p.207.
8 90 and 91, *AI*, pp.208–9.
9 91, Moshaver al-Mamalek be Reasat-e Vowzara, 5 Jammadiolavval-e 1337, *AI*, pp.208–9.
10 Jom´eh, panjom-e [Jammadiolavval], *MAF*, pp.44–5.
11 'Abdol-Hossein Ma´sud Ansari in *Zendegani-ye man va negahi be tarikh-e mo´aser-e Iran va jahan, jeld-e avval* (Tehran: Chap Aftab, undated), p.264.

12 Panj shanbeh, bist-o haftom-e [Rabiolsani], *MAF*, p.39.
13 Jom'eh, panjom-e [Jammadiolavval], *MAF*, pp.44–5.
14 Shanbeh, shesh-e [Jammadiolavval], *MAF*, p.46.
15 92, Moshaver al-Mamalek be Reasat-e Vowzara, 7 Jammadiolavval-e 1337, *AI*, pp.209–10.
16 93, Reasat-e Vowzara be Moshaver al-Mamalek, 8 Jammadiolavval-e 1337, *AI*, pp.210–11.
17 98, Reasat-e vowzara be Moshaver al-Mamalek, 12 Jammadiolavval-e 1337, *AI*, p.216.
18 88, 91, 92, *AI*, pp.207–9.
19 Oliver Bast, 'British imperialism and Persian diplomacy in the shadow of World War I (1914–1921)', in Nick Wadham Smith and Danny Whitehead (eds), *Didgah: New Perspectives on UK-Iran Cultural Relations* (London: British Council, 2015), pp.83–124.
20 For a summation see Moqadameh [introduction], *AI*.
21 Ibid., *AI*, p.21.
22 Do shanbeh, hashtom-e [Jammadiolavval], *MAF*, pp.47–8.
23 Jom'eh, bist-o hashtom-e [Rabiolsani], *MAF*, p.40.
24 Cox to Foreign Office (assumed), 14 February 1919, FO371/3858, p.384.
25 Balfour to Curzon, 10 May 1919, FO371/3860, p.316.
26 Foreign Office to Balfour, Astoria, Paris, 13 February 1919, FO371/3858, p.347.
27 Yek shanbeh, haftom-e [Jammadiolavval], *MAF*, pp.46–7.
28 Ansari, *Zendegani-ye man va negahi be tarikh-e mo'aser-e Iran va jahan*, pp.261–2.
29 Panj shanbeh, chahar-e [Jammadiolavval], *MAF*, p.44.
30 Ansari, *Zendegani-ye man va negahi be tarikh-e mo'aser-e Iran va jahan*, p.262.
31 C. M. Andrew and A. S. Kanya-Forstner, 'The French "Colonial Party": Its Composition, Aims and Influence, 1885–1914', *The Historical Journal*, Vol. 14, No. 1 (March, 1971), pp.99–128.
32 L. Abrams, D. J. Miller, 'Who Were the French Colonialists? A Reassessment of the Parti Colonial, 1890–1914', *The Historical Journal*, Vol. 19, No. 3 (September, 1976), pp.685–725.
33 This interpretation relies on an examination of the colonial party in Bast, 'La mission persane', pp.396–7. Bast more generally makes the point that given Franco-British tensions concerning the partition of the Ottoman Empire, Iranian affairs simply disappeared off the agenda when the Ottoman Empire ceased to be discussed.
34 Panj shanbeh, bist-o haftom-e [Rabiolsani], *MAF*, p.39.
35 Ansari, *Zendegani-ye man va negahi be tarikh-e mo'aser-e Iran va jahan*, p.261.
36 The Minister in Persia (Caldwell) to the Secretary of State, Tehran, 15 November 1918, FRUS, 1919, Vol.1. p.256.
37 Panj shanbeh, chaharom-e [Jammadiolavval], *MAF*, p.44.
38 Shanbeh, shesh-e [Jammadiolavval], *MAF*, p.46.
39 Jom'eh, bist-o hashtom-e [Rabiolsani], *MAF*, p.40.
40 Ansari, *Zendegani-ye man va negahi be tarikh-e mo'aser-e Iran va Jahan*, p.267.
41 See FO371/3859, p.316, pp.51–4.
42 100, Vezarat-e Omur-e Kharejeh be Moshaver al-Mamalek, 15 Jammadiolavval-e 1337, *AI*, p.219.
43 Bast, 'Putting the Record Straight', pp.266–7.
44 I have used the rough exchange rate of 3 tomans to the pound.
45 'Persia to Claim Indemnity', *New York Times*, 11 June 1919, p.1.

46 Mr Sonnino, The Italian representative brought this up on a Council of Ten meeting on 19 February 1919. FRUS, 1919, Vol.4. p.57.
47 *Iran* Newspaper, 5 March 1919.
48 George Brandes, *The World at War* (New York: Macmillan, 1917), pp.250–9.
49 'Persia, Handbooks prepared under the direction of the historical section of the foreign Office, no.80 (Confidential)', June 1919.
50 104, Moshaver al-Mamalek be Vezarat-e Omur-e Kharejeh, 19 Jammadiolavval-e 1337, *AI*, p.230.
51 Chahar shanbeh, hefdahom-e [Jammadiolavval], *MAF*, p.53.
52 Shanbeh, bistom-e [Jammadiolavval], *MAF*, p.55.
53 See chapter 17 in Kazemzadeh, *The Struggle for Transcaucasia (1917–1921)*.
54 Kazemzadeh, *The Struggle for Transcaucasia*, pp.121–2.
55 111, Moshaver al-Mamalek be Vezarat-e Omur-e Kharejeh, 25 Jammadiolavval-e, 1337, *AI*, p.237.
56 Pier Patton, *Why The Peace Conference Should Requite Persia's Wrongs* (Paris: Cadet, 1919).
57 Patton, *Why The Peace Conference*, p.5.
58 Shanbeh, Panjom-e Jammadiolakhar-e 1337, *MAF*, p.68.
59 'Iran dar 1919', letter to Ebrahim Hakimi, *MAF*, pp.458–69. Also, in *Maqalate-e Foroughi, jeld-e avval* (Tehran, Tus 1384), pp.61–79.
60 'Persia Wants Your Help, 8 March 1919', *New York Times*, p.12.
61 118, Moshaver al-Mamalek be Vezarat-e Omur-e Kharejeh, 6 Jammadiolsani-ye 1337, *AI*, pp.245–6.
62 Shanbeh, Panjom-e Jammadiolakhar-e 1337, *MAF*, pp.68–9.
63 This fact has been repeated often. See Mohammad Ali Foroughi's entry for Shanbeh, panjom-e Jammadiolakhar-e 1337, *MAF*, pp.68–9.
64 123, Reasat-e Vowzara be Moshaver al-Mamalek, 15 Jammadiolsani-ye 1337, *AI*, p.253.
65 Cox to Curzon, 18 March 1919, FO371/3859, pp.430–1.
66 Panj shanbeh, dahom-e [Jammadiolakhar], *MAF*, pp.71–2.
67 Ibid., *MAF*.
68 Ibid., *MAF*.
69 Curzon to Cox, Foreign Office, 12 March 1919, FO371/3859, p.364.
70 128, Moshaver al-Mamalek be Vezarat-e Omur-e Kharejeh, 24 Jammadiolsani-ye 1337, p.258, *AI*, p.258.
71 See prologue, pages xi–xvii.
72 Mohammad Ali Foroughi, 'Notgh-e Foroughi dar konferans-e solh-e Paris dar 1919, Va′z-e keshwar-e Iran qabl az jang – heyn-e jang- va ba′d as jang', Yagma, Farvardin 1342 – no.177, p.15.
73 As suggested in Kashani-Sabet, *Frontier Fictions*.
74 *Claims of Persia*, p.7.
75 Ibid., *Claims of Persia*.
76 Chardin, *Travels in Persia*, p.126.
77 Ibid., p.125.
78 Ibid.,
79 Ibid., *Claims of Persia*.
80 Ibid.
81 Ibid., p.9.
82 Moore to Oliphant (Foreign Office), 12 May 1919, FO371/3860, p.354.
83 Curzon to Balfour, Foreign Office, 1 May 1919, FO371/3860, p.107.

84 Lieutenant Colonel C.E Yate, *Khurasan and Sistan* (Edinburgh: W. Blackwood, 1900), pp.33–5.
85 Kazemzadeh, *The Struggle for Transcaucasia,* p.267.
86 Shanbeh, nuzdahom-e [Jammadiolakhar], *MAF,* p.79.
87 Se shanbeh, bist-o dovom-e [Jammadiolakhar], *MAF,* p.83.
88 Panj shanbeh, bist-o chaharom-e Jammadiolakhar, *MAF,* p.84.
89 127, Reasat-e Vowzara be Moshaver al-Mamalek, 21 Jammadiolsani-ye 1337, *AI,* pp.256–8.
90 129, Moshaver al-Mamalek be Vezarat-e Omur-e Kharejeh, 26 Jammadiolsani-ye 1337, *AI,* pp.259–60.
91 Jom´eh, panjom-e [Jammadiolavval], *MAF,* pp.44–5.
92 See page 775, *AI.*
93 Florence Prévost-Grégoire, 'Pacifisme et universalisme: le cas du Comité national d'études sociales et politiques (1916–1931)', *Matériaux pour l'histoire de notre temps,* Vol. 129–130, No. 3–4 (2018), pp.42–7.
94 Panj shanbeh, dovom-e [Rajab], *MAF,* p.89.
95 Jom´eh, sevom-e [Rajab], *MAF,* p.89.
96 Shanbeh, chaharom-e [Rajab], *MAF,* pp.90–1.
97 133, Reasat-e Vowzara be Moshaver al-Mamalek, 2 Rajab-e 1337, *AI,* pp.310–11.
98 Curzon to Cox, Foreign Office, 12 March 1919, FO371/3859, p.364.
99 134, Moshaver al-Mamalek be Reasat-e Vowzara, 9 Rajab-e 1337, *AI,* pp.312–14.
100 Chahar shanbeh, panzdahom-e [Rajab], *MAF,* pp.99–100.
101 Balfour to Curzon, Paris, 23 April 1919, FO371/3860, p.192.
102 Bast, 'Putting the Record Straight', p.269.
103 Ibid., Bast, 'Putting the Record Straight', p.269.
104 Curzon to Cox, 26 March 1919, FO371/3859, p.462.
105 The Paris Peace Conference, FRUS, 1919, Vol.5. p.153.
106 S. H. Taqizadeh, Member of the Persian parliament for Teheran, 'Memorandum on Persia's wishes and her Aspirations addressed to the Peace Conference of Paris', The Hague, April 1919, reprinted in *Maqalat-e Taqizadeh, Volume VII,* edited by I. Afshar (Tehran: Shokufan, 1977), pp.722–8, p.724.
107 Do shanbeh, hashtom-e [Jammadiolavval], *MAF,* p.47.
108 Chahar shanbeh, nohum-e [olakhar], *MAF,* p.70.
109 Abrams and Miller, 'Who Were the French Colonialists?' p.715.
110 Do shanbeh, gharatolejammadiavval ya doyum, *MAF,* p.42.
111 Abrams, Miller, 'Who Were the French Colonialists?' p.715.
112 'Bulletin De Jour, Les Droits de la Perse', *Le Temps* (Paris), 17 February 1919, p.1.
113 'Persia Now Problem: What Will Happen to Her At Peace Conference Is Vital to England', *The Evening Sun,* 1 January 1919, p.3.
114 See 'Persia', 13 April 1919, *New York Times,* p.37 and a letter to the editor 'Persia's Claims', 16 April 1919, *New York Times,* p.12.
115 'Persia and the World Settlement', *The Manchester Guardian,* 12 February 1919, p.4.
116 'Persia and the Peace Conference', *The Manchester Guardian,* 20 February 1919, p.6.
117 'England and Persia: The sufferings and claims of a neutral', *The Manchester Guardian,* 22 March 1919, p.10.
118 'Persia's Wrongs', *The Manchester Guardian,* 11 April 1919, p.6.
119 'Persia and the Conference', *The Times,* 23 April 1919, p.13.
120 Panj shanbeh, bist-o sevom [Rajab], *MAF,* p.106.
121 144, Ateye-e Iran, *AI,* pp.323–30.

Chapter 5

1. Se shanbeh, bist-o hashtom-e [Rajab], *MAF*, pp.111.
2. Shanbeh, dovom-e Sha'ban, *MAF*, pp.113–14.
3. Do shanbeh, chaharom-e [Sha'ban], *MAF*, pp.115–16.
4. Paris Peace Conference, FRUS, 1919, Vol.5, p.498.
5. FRUS, 1919, Vol.5, p.498.
6. Panj shanbeh, haftom-e [Sha'ban], *MAF*, pp.117–18.
7. Jom'eh, hashtom-e [Sha'ban], *MAF*, pp.118–19.
8. 138, Vokala-ye nakhjavan be Rais Jomhuri-ye Ayalat-e Motahedeh, 6 Sha'ban-e 1337, *AI*, pp.316–17.
9. See, 139, Kargozari-ye Maku be Kargozari-ye kol-e Azerbaijan, 15 Rajab-e 1337, pp.318–19, *AI*.
10. Balfour to Foreign Office, Astoria Paris, 2 May 1919, FO371/3860, p.270.
11. 'Persia', *The Times*, 30 May 1919, p.13.
12. Parliamentary Question, 19 May 1919, FO371/3860, p.463.
13. 160, Reasat-e Vowzara be Moshaver al-Mamalek, 20 Sha'ban-e 1337, *AI*, p.363.
14. 167, Moshaver al-Mamalek be Reasat-e Vowzara, *AI*, pp.368–9.
15. 184, Reasat-e Vowzara be Moshaver al-Mamalek, 16 Ramazan-e 1337, *AI*, p.404.
16. Memorandum Regarding the Policy of His Majesty's Government towards Persia at the Peace Conference, 17 December 1918, IOR/L/PS/18/C193.
17. Cox to Foreign Office, 14 November 1918, FO371/3263, pp.60–2.
18. Cox to Foreign Office, 11 January 1919, FO371/3858, pp.11–12.
19. Cox to Foreign Office, 13 January 1919, FO371/3858, pp.70–4.
20. Viceroy, 28 January 1919, FO371/3858, pp.282–3.
21. Grant, The Persian Question, 20 December 1918, FO371/3858, pp.3–4.
22. Nicholson, *Curzon: The Last Phase*, pp.132–4.
23. Keynes, 31 December 1918, FO371/3263, pp.558–60.
24. For some of these tensions see Greaves, *Persia and the Defence of India*, pp.12–13.
25. Ibid.
26. Olson, 'The Genesis of the Anglo-Persian Agreement of 1919', p.197.
27. Eastern Committee, 30 December 1918, in Papers of the War Cabinet's Eastern Committee, 13 March 1918–7 January 1919, Mss Eur F112/274, 266–9.
28. India Office to Foreign Office, 3 May 1919, FO371/3860, p.285.
29. Inter-departmental Conference on Middle Eastern Affairs, 7 May 1919, FO371/3860, pp.478–82, p.6.
30. D. W. Stammer, 'British Colonial Finance', *Social and Economic Studies*, June, 1967, Vol. 16, No.2 (June, 1967), pp.191–205, p.195.
31. Viceroy to Foreign Office, 28 January 1919, FO371/3858, pp.282–3.
32. Curzon handwritten note, 21 April 1919, FO371/3860, pp.167–8.
33. Memorandum by Earl Curzon on the Persian Agreement, *Documents on British Foreign Policy 1919–1939* (DBFP), First Series, Volume iv, no.710, p.1121.
34. Ali Ansari, *The Politics of Nationalism in Modern Iran* (Cambridge: Cambridge University Press, 2012), p.70.
35. Hardinge to Lansdowne, 28 March, PERSIAN LOAN. TELEGRAMS, 20TH JANUARY – 1ST APRIL, 20 January 1903–1 April 1903, IOR/L/PS/18/C108A, p.8.
36. Sabahi, *British Policy in Persia*, p.23.
37. Algar, *Mirza Malkum Khan*, p.112.

38 Lord Hartington memorandum, 4 February 1882, FO60/450, pp.196–203.
39 Ibid., p.197.
40 Thomson draft, Foreign Office, 11 March 1885, FO60/468, pp.35–46.
41 Ibid., p.39.
42 Ibid., p.41.
43 Ibid., pp.43–4.
44 Nicholson, *Curzon: The Last Phase*, pp.125–9.
45 Bakhash, 'The Origins of the Anglo-Persian Agreement of 1919', p.4.
46 Cronin, 'Building a new army', pp.72–3.
47 Enclosure Marling of October 12, 10 October 1917, FO371/3265, p.207.
48 Mushavar-ul-mamalik [sic] to Marling, 1 February 1918, FO371/3265, pp.227–8.
49 Cox to Curzon, 25 February 1919, FO371/3859, p.12.
50 In fact, the Iranian government had asked for two French professors to teach administrative and commercial law in 1911. See Grey to Cambon, 4 April 1919, FO371/3861, p.33.
51 Cox to Curzon (assumed), 14 January 1919, FO371/3858, p.84.
52 Paris Embassy to Curzon, 5 July 1919, FO371/3861, p.448.
53 See correspondence, FO371/3859, pp.10–13.
54 French Ambassador, 25 June 1919, FO371/3861, pp.288–90.
55 Curzon to Derby, 5 March 1919, FO371/3859, p.77.
56 Cox to Curzon, 25 February 1919, FO371/3859, p.12.
57 Cox to Curzon, 10 April 1919, FO371/3860, pp.61–2.
58 Ibid., p.62.
59 Kotor [qotur] and the region of Zohab, which included references to 'Pusht-i-Kuh' [pushte-kuh], Mendeli and aforementioned Qasr-e Shirin were all regions which had been contested between the Ottomans and Iranians.
60 Wilson memorandum, 16 April 1919, FO371/3860, p.149.
61 Cox to Curzon, 13 May 1919, FO371/3860, p.378.
62 Cox to Curzon, 13 May 1919, FO371/3860, p.378.
63 No.3. Separate Letter No. 1, addressed by His Majesty's Minister at Tehran to the Persian Prime Minister, p.6, Persian Agreement, 12 August 1919, FO371/3862, pp.225–8.
64 No.4. Separate Letter No. 2, addressed by His Majesty's Minister at Tehran to the Persian Prime Minister, p.6, Persian Agreement, 12 August 1919, FO371/3862, pp.225–8.
65 Nabavi, *Modern Iran,* pp.114–16.
66 Cox to Foreign Office, 13 January 1919, FO371/3858, pp.70–4.
67 Ibid., p.187.
68 Cox to Curzon, 10 November 1918, no.842, DBFP, p.1224.
69 Viceroy to Foreign Office, 28 January 1919, FO371/3858, pp.282–3.
70 Cox to Curzon, 11 August 1919, no.713, DBFP, p.1124.
71 Tilley to Treasury, 10 April 1919, FO371/3859, p.489.
72 Cox to Curzon (assumed), 14 January 1919, FO371/3858, p.84.
73 Board of Trade memorandum, 1 August 1919, FO371/3862, p.103.
74 Board of Trade, 30 August 1919, FO371/3863, p.219.
75 Elm, *Oil, Power, and Principle,* pp.19–22.
76 Ibid.
77 Sabahi, *British Policy in Persia*, p.19.

78 Hon J. M. Balfour, *Recent Happenings in Persia* (Edinburgh, London: William Blackwood, 1922), p.155.
79 Sabahi, *British Policy in Persia*, 23.
80 Frances Bostock, 'State Bank or Agent of Empire? The Imperial Bank of Persia's Loan Policy 1920–23', *Iran*, 1989, Vol. 27 (1989), pp.103–13, p.103.
81 Bostock, 'State Bank or Agent of Empire?'
82 Ibid.
83 Ibid., p.111.
84 Foreign Office to Cox, 11 January 1919, FO371/3858, pp.13–4.
85 Curzon to Cox, 21 October 1919, no.822, DBFP, p.1209.
86 Stephanie Cronin, 'Britain, the Iranian military and the rise of Reza Khan', in Vanessa Martin (ed), *Anglo-Iranian Relations since 1800* (London; New York: Routledge, 2005), p.116.
87 Cox to Foreign Office, 13 January 1919, FO371/3858, pp.70–4.
88 Viceroy to Foreign Office, 28 January 1919, FO371/3858, pp.282–3.
89 Cox to Foreign Office, 13 January 1919, FO371/3858, pp.70–4.
90 Annex to Eastern Committee, 30 December 1918, Papers of the War Cabinet's Eastern Committee, 13 March 1918–7 January 1919, Mss Eur F112/274, 532–44.
91 War Office memorandum, 21 August 1919, FO371/3863, p.23.
92 For a more concise report covering the main points see FO371/4911, Confidential Supplement to the Report of the Anglo Persian Military Commission by the British Members, pp.79–85.
93 Viceroy to Foreign Office, 28 January 1919, FO371/3858, pp.282–3.
94 Sabahi, *British Policy in Persia*, p.46.
95 Ibid., pp.45–6.
96 C. J. Edmonds, *East and West of Zagros: Travel, War and Politics in Persia and Iraq 1913–1921* (Leiden; Boston: Brill, 1920), p.345.
97 Cox to Curzon, Tehran, 11 August 1919, no.713, DBFP, p.1124.
98 Cox to Foreign Office, 22 January 1919, FO371/3858, p.193.
99 David Omissi, *Air Power and Colonial Control: The Royal Air Force, 1919–1939* (Manchester: Manchester University Press, 1990).
100 Toby Dodge, *Inventing Iraq: The Failure of Nation-building and a History Denied* (London, UK: Hurst, 2003), pp.131–56.
101 Balfour, *Recent Happenings in Persia*, p.131.
102 Do shanbeh, dahom-e [Ramazan], *MAF*, p.143.
103 Chahar shanbeh, davazdahom-e [Ramazan], *MAF*, pp.144–5.
104 184, Reasat-e Vowzara be Moshaver al-Mamalek, 16 Ramazan-e 1337, *AI*, p.404.
105 Shanbeh, bistom-e [Shavval], *MAF*, pp.172–3.
106 Panj shanbeh, bist-o panjom-e [Shavval], *MAF*, p.176.
107 Jom'eh, bist-o sheshom-e [Shavval], *MAF*, p.177.
108 Panj shanbeh, selkh-e [Rajab], pp.112–13, *MAF*. 'nokar' can be literally translated as servant but needs to be read as slave or vassal.
109 Cox to Curzon, Tehran, 13 August 1919, no.716, DBFP, p.1126.
110 Curzon to Lindsay (Washington), Foreign Office, 18 August 1919, no.727, DBFP, p.1135.
111 Curzon to Cox, Foreign Office, 19 August 1919, no.728, DBFP, p.1136.
112 Cox to Foreign Office (assumed), 25 September 1919, IOR/L/PS/10/736 pt.6, pp.66–7.
113 Cox to Foreign Office (assumed), 14 August 1919, FO371/3862, p.326.
114 Ibid.

115 Curzon to Lindsay (Washington), Foreign Office, 18 August 1919, no.727, DBFP, p.1135.
116 Curzon to Lindsay, 18 August 1919, no.727, DBFP, p.1135.
117 Curzon to the American Ambassador in London, Foreign Office, 11 September 1919, no.774, DBFP, pp.1163–5.
118 Curzon to Lindsay, 18 August 1919, no.727, DBFP, p.1135.
119 Secretary of State to the Ambassador in Great Britain, 20 August 1919, FRUS, Vol.2, p.700.
120 Secretary of State to the Ambassador in Great Britain, 4 October 1919, FRUS, Vol.2, pp.714–17.
121 See FO371/3862, pp.345–76.
122 'Le cas de la Perse', Bulletin De Jour, *Le Temps* (Paris), 16 August 1919.
123 For text of this convention and reaction to it, see Nabavi, *Modern Iran*, pp.25–9.
124 Foreign Office to Cox, 5 August 1919, IOR/L/PS/10/736 pt.5, pp.177–8.
125 'Imperialism Proceeds', *Chicago Tribune*, 19 August 1919, p.8.
126 'Britain blocked Persia in Paris', *New York Herald*, 18 August 1919, p.6.
127 'Persian Mission in Paris refuse to discuss the British Agreement', *The Courier*, 18 August 1919, p.5.
128 'Persians see loss of independence', *New York Herald*, 20 August 1919, p.3.
129 'Persians claim treaty unfair', *The Los Angeles Times*, 20 August 1919, p.6.
130 In addition to Hasan Taqizadeh, the list of signatories to the article included some of the *Komiteh-ye Melliyun*. See IOR/L/PS/10/736 pt.6, Foreign Office to Cox, 30 September 1919, 55–6.
131 Sir Arnold T. Wilson, *Persia* (London: Ernest Benn Limited, 1932), p.142.
132 Sykes, *A History of Persia*, p.522.
133 Grey to Foreign Office, 17 October 1919, IOR/L/PS/10/736 pt.6, pp.30–1.
134 Earl of Ronaldshay, *The Life of Lord Curzon, Volume Three* (London: Ernest Benn Limited, 1932), p.43.
135 Do shanbeh, bist-o yekom-e Zeq´adeh, *MAF*, p.198.
136 'Anglo-Persian pact stirs French political circles', *The Baltimore Sun*, 22 August 1919, p.2.
137 'Said to oppose Persian treaty', *The New York Times*, 30 August 1919, p.3.
138 'Britain after Persia', *The Dallas Express*, Dallas Texas, 20 September 1919, p.11.

Chapter 6

1 Panj shanbeh, shanzdah-e [Zeq´adeh], *MAF*, p.194.
2 Panj shanbeh, hefdahom, [Zeq´adeh], *MAF*, pp.194–6.
3 'L'Angleterre en Perse et en Syrie', *L'Écho De Paris*, 15 August 1919, p.1.
4 'Un accord anglo-persan', *Journal Des Débats*, 15 August 1919, p.1.
5 Se shanbeh, bist-o nohom [Zeq´adeh], *MAF*, pp.203–4.
6 Curzon to Cox, Foreign Office, 8 September 1919, no.762, DBFP, p.1158.
7 Cox to Curzon, Foreign Office, 24 August 1919, no.735, DBFP, p.1142.
8 Panj shanbeh, panzdahom-e [Zehajeh], *MAF*, p.212.
9 Jom´eh, shanzdahom-e [Zehajeh], *MAF*, pp.212–13.
10 Rumbold (Berne) to Curzon, Foreign Office, 6 September 1919, no.760, DBFP, pp.1156–57.

11 Cox to Curzon, Tehran, September 1919, no.784, DBFP, pp.1170–1.
12 Do shanbeh, panzdahom-e septambr, nuzdahom-e Zehajeh, *MAF*, pp.215–17.
13 Chahar shanbeh, hefdahom-e [septambr], biste-e yekom-e Zehajeh, *MAF*, pp.218–19.
14 Do shanbeh, panzdahom-e septambr, nuzdahom-e Zehajeh, *MAF*, pp.215–17.
15 Se shanbeh, shanzdahom-e [septambr], bistom-e Zehajeh, *MAF*, pp.217–18.
16 Curzon to Cox, Foreign Office, 24 September 1919, no.790, DBFP, p.1178.
17 Curzon to Cox, Foreign Office, 24 September 1919, no.791, DBFP, p.1180.
18 Ibid., p.1181.
19 Ibid.
20 Note by Earl Curzon of a conversation with the Persian Minister for Foreign Affairs, no.789, DBFP, p.1175.
21 Sanad-e 33, in Ettehadieh, *Nosrat al-Dowleh*, pp.130–1.
22 Cox to Curzon (assumed), 14 January 1919, FO371/3858, p.84.
23 Paris Embassy to Curzon, 5 July 1919, FO371/3861, p.448.
24 Sanad-e 48, in Ettehadieh, *Nosrat al-Dowleh*, p.149.
25 Curzon to Derby, 5 March 1919, FO371/3859, p.77.
26 Earl Curzon to Sir P. Cox, Foreign Office, 2 September 1919, no.753, DBFP, p.1152.
27 Cox to Curzon, Tehran, 22 September 1919, no.787, DBFP, p.1173.
28 Panj shanbeh, bist-o dovvom-e Zehajeh, *MAF*, p.220.
29 Jom'eh, nuzdahom-e septambr, 23 Zehajeh, *MAF*, p.220.
30 Se shanbeh, bist-o sevom [septambr], 27 Zehajeh, *MAF*, pp.223–4.
31 Panj shanbeh, sheshom-e [Moharram], *MAF*, pp.231–2.
32 Se shanbeh, sihom-e [septambr], chaharom-e Moharram, *MAF*, p.230.
33 Jom'eh, bist-o sheshom [Shavval], *MAF*, p.177.
34 Winston S. Churchill, *Great Contemporaries* (London: The Reprint Society London, 1941), p.243.
35 Churchill, *Great Contemporaries*, p.240.
36 'Persia's need for help, Prince Firuz on the Agreement', *The Times*, 13 October 1919, p.11.
37 Cox to Curzon, 30 April 1919, FO371/3860, p.264.
38 Ratification had to take place in accordance with Article 24 of the Iranian Constitution.
39 See Sykes, *A History of Persia*, p.522 and Nicholson, *Curzon: The Last Phase*.
40 'Notgh-e Vosuq al-Dowleh', in Hossein Makki, *Tarikh-e bistsale-ye Iran, jeld-e chaharom* (Tehran: Kaveyan, 1361), pp.178–90.
41 Curzon to Cox, Foreign Office, 29 September 1919, no.795, DBFP, p.1185.
42 209, Bayaneyeh-e Reasat-e Vowzara, 13 Zeq'adeh-ye 1337, *AI*, pp.437–46.
43 A small English precis of this article can be found in Katouzian, *State and Society in Iran*, pp.108–9.
44 Major H Thorburn, Persia's position in the League of Nations, January 1919, FO371/3859.
45 Ansari, *Zendegani-ye man va negahi be tarikh-e mo'aser-e Iran va jahan*, p.325.
46 213 to 223, Dar atraf-e bayaneyeh-e Rais Alvowzara, *AI*, pp.457–518.
47 213, Dar atraf-e bayaneyeh-e Rais alvowzara, 14 Zeq'adeh-ye 1337, *AI*, pp.457–61.
48 216, Dar atraf-e bayaneyeh-e Rais alvowzara, 21 Zeq'adeh-ye 1337, *AI*, pp.473–6.
49 218, Dar atraf-e bayaneyeh-e Rais alvowzara, 24 Zeq'adeh-ye 1337, *AI*, pp.482–9.
50 214, Dar atraf-e bayaneyeh-e Rais alvowzara, 17 Zeq'adeh-ye 1337, *AI*, pp.461–6.
51 Ibid.,
52 254, Bayaneyeh-e Reasat-e Vowzara, 10 Rajab-e 1338, *AI*, pp.692–703.

53   Katouzian, *State and Society in Iran,* pp.109–10.
54   Katouzian, *State and Society in Iran,* p.122.
55   Yek shanbeh, shanzdahom-e [Moharram], *MAF*, pp.240–2.
56   'Curzon Denies British Grab in Persian Treaty', *The New York Tribune,* 21 September 1919, p.11.
57   Ibid.
58   Cox to Foreign Office, 14 November 1918, FO371/3263, pp.60–2.
59   Thorburn, Persia's position in the League of Nations, FO371/3859, p.159.
60   Inter-departmental conference on Middle Eastern Affairs, 7 May 1919, FO371/3860, pp.478–82, p.3.
61   Ibid.
62   For text of this convention and reaction to it see Nabavi, *Modern Iran,* pp.25–9.
63   Grant, The Persian Question, 20 December 1918, FO371/3858, pp.3–4.
64   Cox to Foreign Office (assumed), 1 September 1919, IOR/L/PS/10/736 pt.6, pp.95–6.
65   Cox to Foreign Office (assumed), 14 February 1918, IOR/L/PS/10/686, p.133.
66   Cox to Curzon, 10 April 1919, FO371/3860, p.62.
67   Olson, *Anglo-Iranian Relations,* p.66.
68   Bast, 'Putting the Record Straight'.
69   Katouzian, *State and Society in Iran,* p.127.
70   Cox to Curzon, 13 May 1919, FO371/3860, p.378.
71   Cox to Curzon, 14 August 1919, no.720, DBFP, p.1131.
72   Katouzian, *State and Society in Iran,* p.89.
73   Curzon to Derby, Washington, 25 October 1919, no.825, DBFP, p.1213.
74   'The Shah's visit to the City', *The Times,* 3 November 1919, p.43.
75   Ahmad Shah's speech was widely syndicated throughout Britain, the reference used here is from *The Scotsman,* Monday, 3 November 1919.
76   Curzon to Cox, Foreign Office, 13 November 1919, no.845, DBFP, p.1225.
77   Ibid., no.845, DBFP, p.1226.
78   Ibid., no.845, DBFP.
79   Ibid., no.845, DBFP.
80   Sanad-e 60, Ettehadieh, *Nosrat al-Dowleh,* pp.164–5.
81   Persian Memorandum, no.846, DBFP, p.1228.
82   Justin Sheil to Lord Aberdeen, Tehran, 12 July 1844, Enclosure 1 in No.6, in R. N. Schofield (ed), *The Iran-Iraq Border 1840–1958* (Farnham Common: Archive Editions, 1989), Vol.1.
83   Water protocols, agreed between Iran and Russia, in the 1880s formed part of the delimitation of frontier in the Transcaspian. These are detailed in Wolff to Salisbury, 10 May 1888, FO60/492, unnumbered.
84   Enclosure in No. 846, DBFP, p.1231.
85   See chapter 18 in Firuz Kazemzadeh, *The Struggle for Transcaucasia*.
86   The Persian Minister for Foreign Affairs to Earl Curzon, Londres, le 17 novembre, 1919, no.849, DBFP Vol.iv, p.1235.
87   See, 139, Kargozari-ye Maku be Kargozari-ye kol-e Azerbaijan, 15 Rajab-e 1337, pp.318–19, *AI*.
88   David McDowall, *A Modern History of the Kurds* (London; New York: I.B. Taurus, 2004), p.121.
89   The Persian Minister for Foreign Affairs to Curzon, Londres, le 17 novembre, 1919, no.850, DBFP, p.1239.
90   Ettehadieh, 'Les illusions', p.434.

91 Ibid.
92 Curzon to Cox, Foreign Office, 28 November 1919, no.854, DBFP, p.1245.
93 Ibid.
94 Lorca, 'Petitioning the International', p.514.
95 Iran lodged a complaint with the League when the Russians landed in Anzali in 1920. The subsequent meeting of the Council of the League of Nations between 14 and 16 June 1920 only threw the complaint back to the Iranians, expecting them to directly ask the Russians to evacuate Anzali but it did affect their withdrawal. See Mansoureh Ettehadieh, 'Les illusions'.
96 Curzon to Cox, Foreign Office, 6 December 1919, no.865, DBFP, p.1256.
97 Curzon to the Persian Minister for Foreign Affairs, Foreign Office, 19 December 1919, no.871, DBFP, p.1262.
98 Ibid., 871, p.1263.
99 The Persian Minister for Foreign Affairs to Curzon, Carlton Hotel, le 20 décembre, 1919, no.872, DBFP, p.1265.
100 Note by Mr Oliphant of a conversation with the Persian minister for Foreign Affairs, Foreign Office, 20 December 1919, no.872, DBFP, p.1263.
101 Curzon to Cox, Foreign Office, 30 December 1919, no.877, DBFP, p.1268.
102 Enclosure in No.877, Translation of a cable received by Prince Firuz from the Persian prime minister, DBFP, p.1270.
103 Sabahi, *British Policy in Persia*, p.69.
104 Enclosure in No.877, Translation of a cable received by Prince Firuz [Nosrat al-Dowleh] from the Persian Prime Minister, DBFP, p.1270.
105 Sabahi, *British Policy in Persia*, p.67.
106 Eastern Committee, 26 May 1920, in Papers of the War Cabinet's Eastern Committee, 7 January 1919–7 December 1920, Mss Eur F112/275, pp.256–68.
107 Sabahi, *British Policy in Persia*, p.70.
108 Katouzian, *State and Society in Iran*, pp.149–53.
109 Balfour, *Recent Happenings in Persia*, p.131.
110 Norman to Curzon, 18 June 1920, no.468, DBFP XIII, p.522.
111 Cox to Curzon, 21 February 1920, no.375, DBFP XIII, p.438.
112 Norman to Curzon, 14 June 1920, no.463, DBFP XIII, p.515.
113 Curzon to Norman, 23 June 1920, no.481, DBFP XIII, p.535.
114 Katouzian, *State and Society in Iran*, pp.195–6.
115 See no's 401 (p.462), no.406 (p.466) and no.407 (p.469) in DBFP XIII.
116 Ansari, *Modern Iran since 1797*, p.129.
117 Alvin J. Cottrell, 'Iran's Armed Forces under the Pahlavi Dynasty', in George Lenczowski (ed), *Iran under The Pahlavis* (Stanford: Hoover Institution Press, 1978), p.389.
118 G. Tchitcherin, L. Karakhan Mochaverol-Memalek, *Persia and the Russia Socialist Federal Soviet Republic, Treaty of Friendship*, signed at Moscow, 26 February 1921, Vol. 9, No 268, League of Nations, Treaty Series, pp.384–413.
119 Norman to Curzon, 14 January 1920, no.649, DBFP XIII, p.694.
120 Norman to Curzon, 11 December 1920, no.609, DBFP XIII, p.660.
121 Katouzian, *State and Society in Iran*, p.178.

Conclusion: A reassessment

1. 'Memorandum Regarding the Policy of His Majesty's Government Towards Persia at the Peace Conference', 17 December 1918, IOR/L/PS/18/C193.
2. Ettehadieh, 'Les illusions', p.428.
3. Manela, *The Wilsonian Moment*.
4. Foroughi, 'Notgh-e Foroughi dar konferans-e solh-e Paris dar 1919', p.15.
5. Sykes, *A History of Persia*, p.520.
6. *Claims of Persia before the Conference of the Preliminaries of Peace of Paris*, p.14.
7. No.4. Separate Letter No. 2, addressed by His Majesty's Minister at Tehran to the Persian Prime Minister, p.6, Persian Agreement, 12 August 1919, FO371/3862, pp.225-8.
8. Mim Kemâl Öke, *The Armenian Question 1914-1923* (Oxford: K. Rustem & Brother, 1988), p.171.
9. MacMillan, *Peacemakers*, pp.161-3.
10. For a discussion on the issues concerning the implementation of the Anglo-Persian Agreement, see 'The Politics of Economic Development: The Anglo-Persian Agreement, 1919', *Iran*, forthcoming.
11. Leonard Mosley, *CURZON: The End of an Epoch* (London: Longmans, Green and Co, 1961), p.202.
12. Gordon Waterfield, *Professional Diplomat: Sir Percy Loraine* (London: John Murray, 1973), pp.61-3.
13. See Bert G.Fragner, 'World War 1 as a Turning point in Iranian History', in Bast (ed), 'La mission persane à la Conférence de Paix en 1919', pp.441-7.
14. Letter to Mahmoud Vasal (Vaqar al-Saltaneh) from Paris, 17 Decembr 1919, *MAF*, pp.471-7.
15. 'Iran dar 1919', letter to Ebrahim Hakimi, *MAF*, pp.458-69.

SELECTED BIBLIOGRAPHY

British archives

Cabinet Office Records (CAB):
CAB 42/3/12, Committee of Imperial Defence, Report of a Committee, Asiatic Turkey, July 1915.
Foreign Office Files (FO):
FO60/9, FO60/23, FO60/27, FO60/29, FO60/4, FO60/450, FO60/468, FO60/492, FO181/17, FO371/3259, FO371/3260, FO371/3262, FO371/3263, FO371/3265, FO371/3858, FO371/3859, FO371/3860, FO371/3861, FO371/3862, FO371/4911, FO248/923, FO416/168, FO416/171.
British Library, India Office Records:
L/PS/10, L/PS/18, L/PS/20, L/MIL/17 and Mss Eur F112.
Documents on British Foreign Policy:
1919–1939, First Series, Volume IV, 1919, Her Majesty's Stationery Office, 1952.
1919–1939, First Series, Volume XIII, Her Majesty's Stationery Office, 1963.

United States archives

Papers relating to the foreign relations of the United States, 1916. Supplement, The World War.
Papers relating to the foreign relations of the United States, 1919. The Paris Peace Conference, Washington, DC: US Government Printing Office. Volume 1, Volume 4, and Volume 5.
'Proceedings of the Brest-Litovsk Peace Conference: The Peace Negotiations Between Russia and the Central Powers', 21 November 1917–3 March 1918, *Washington Government Printing Office*, 1918.
Woodrow Wilson, Address to a Joint Session of Congress on the Conditions of Peace ['The Fourteen Points'] Online by Gerhard Peters and John T. Woolley, The American Presidency Project, https://www.presidency.ucsb.edu/node/206651

Persian primary sources

Ansari, 'Abdol-Hossein Ma'sud, *Zendegani-ye man va negahi be tarikh-e mo'aser-e Iran va jahan, jeld-e avval* [My life and a look at the contemporary history of Iran] (Tehran: Chap-e Aftab, undated).
Bayat, Kaveh, and Reza Azari Shahrzayee (eds), *Amal-e Iraniyan az konferans-e solh-e Paris ta qarardad-e 1919 Iran va Engelis* [Iranian activity from the Conference at the Peace of Paris to the Anglo-Iranian Agreement of 1919] (Iran: Pardise Danesh, 1392).

Ettehadieh, Mansoureh, and So'ad Pira (eds), *Nosrat al-Dowleh, Majmu'eh-ye mokatebat-e, asnad-e, khaterat-e ... Firuz Mirza Firuz* [Nosrat al-Dowleh, collection of correspondence, documents, memoirs and effects of Firuz Mirza Firuz] Chap-e avval (Tehran: Siamak, 1378).

Foroughi, Mohammad Ali, 'Notgh-e Foroughi dar konferans-e solh-e Paris dar 1919, Va'z-e keshwar-e Iran qabl az jang – heyn-e jang – va ba'd as jang' [Foroughi's address to the Conference of the Peace of Paris in 1919, condition of the country before, during, and after the war] *Yagma*, Farvardin, 1342 – no.177.

Mafi, Nezam, and Reza Qoli, *Ketab-e Sabz* [Green book] (Tehran: Nashr-e Tarikh, 1363).

Qotbi, Behruz (ed), *Asnad-e jang-e avval-e jahani dar Iran* [Documents of the First World War] (Tehran: Nashr-e Qarn/Sazman-e Chap va Enteshat-e Vezarat-e Farhang va Ershad-e Eslami, 1370).

Vafaie, Mohammad Afshin, and Pejman Firouzbakhsh (eds), *Yaddashtha-ye ruzaneh-ye Mohammad Ali Foroughi az safar-e konferans-e solh-e Paris* [A daily memoir of Mohammad Ali Foroughi's trip to the Paris Peace Conference] (Desambr-e 1918–Ut-e 1920) Requested by Iraj Afshar, Chap-e panjom (Tehran: Sokhan, 1394).

Other primary sources

Aharonian, A., and Boghos Nubar, *THE ARMENIAN QUESTION before the Peace Conference, A Memorandum Presented Officially by the Representatives of Armenia to the Peace Conference at Versailles, on February 26th, 1919* (New York: Press Bureau, The Armenian National Union of America).

Aitchison, C. U., *A Collection of Treaties, Engagements, and Sanads relating to India and Neighbouring Countries*, Volume X (Calcutta: Office of the Superintendent of Government Printing, India, 1892).

Ali Mardan Bek Topchibashev, *Claims of the Peace Delegation of the Republic of Caucasian Azerbaijan, Presented to the Paris Peace Conference* (Paris: Imp. Robinet-Houtain, 1919).

Aligholi Khan, Mochâver-el-Menâlek, *Requête adressée par le Gouvernement Persan à la Conférence des Préliminaires de Paix á Paris afin d'être admis à y participer* (Paris: Cadet, February 1919).

Empire de Perse, Ministère Des Affaires Étrangéres, *Neutralité Persane*, Documents Diplomatiques, 30 Septembre 1914–22 Mars 1915 (Paris: Georges Cadet, 1919).

Khan, Mirza Malkam, *Ruznameh-ye Qanun*, in Homa Natiq (ed) (Tehran: Amir Kabir, 2535).

Lieutenant Colonel Yate, C. E., *Khurasan and Sistan* (Edinburgh: W. Blackwood, 1900).

Mochaver-Ol-Memalek [Moshaver al-Mamalek], *Claims of Persia before the Conference of the Preliminaries of Peace at Paris* (Paris: Cadet, March, 1919).

Nikoloz Chkheidze and Irakli Tsereteli, MEMORANDUM presented to the Peace Conference (political claims-frontiers) followed by THE ACT OF INDEPENDENCE OF GEORGIA AND A MAP (Paris: Impr. M.Flinikowski, 1919).

Pasha, Shérif, *Memorandum on the claims of the Kurd people* (Paris: Imprimerie A.-G. L'Hoir, March 1919).

Patton, Pier, *Why The Peace Conference Should Requite Persia's Wrongs* (Paris: Cadet, 1919).

Taqizadeh, S. H., Member of the Persian Parliament for Teheran, 'Memorandum on Persia's wishes and her Aspirations addressed to the Peace Conference of Paris', The Hague, April 1919, reprinted in *Maqalat-e Taqizadeh, Volume VII*, in Iraj Afshar (ed) (Tehran: Shokufan, 1977).

Tchitcherin, G., L. Karakhan, Mochaverol-Memalek, [Moshaver al-Mamalek], *Persia and the Russia Socialist Federal Soviet Republic, Treaty of Friendship*, signed at Moscow, 26 February 1921, Vol. 9, No 268, League of Nations, Treaty Series, pp.384–413.

Werda, E. Joel, and Cap. A.K. Yoosuf, M.D., *The claims of the Assyrians before the Conference of the preliminaries of Peace at Paris* (Paris: Imp. Ph.Rosen, 1919).

Zaghloul, Saad, *The Egyptian National Claims: A Memorandum Presented to the Peace Conference by the Egyptian Delegation Charged with the Defence of Egyptian Independence* (Paris: Imprimerie artistique Lux, 1919).

Newspapers

Britain: *The Times, The Evening Sun, The Manchester Guardian, The Scotsman.*
United States: *The New York Times, Chicago Tribune, New York Herald, The Los Angeles Times, The Baltimore Sun, The Dallas Express, The Courier, The New York Tribune.*
Iran: *Iran, Kaveh, Ra´d, Rahnama.*
France: *Le Temps, L'Écho De Paris, Journel Des Débats.*

Secondary sources

The Peace Conference

Dillon, Emile Joseph, *The Inside Story of The Peace Conference* (New York; London: Harper and Bros, 1920).

Fromkin, David, *A Peace to End All Peace: The Fall of the Ottoman Empire and the Creation of the Modern Middle East* (New York: A Holt paperback, 2009).

Lorca, Arnulf Becker, 'Petitioning the International: "A Pre-History" of Self Determination', *The European Journal of International Law*, Vol. 25, No. 2 (May 2014), pp.497–523.

Luxemburg, Rosa, *The National Question – Selected Writings by Rosa Luxemburg* in Horace B. Davies (ed) (New York: Monthly Review Press, 1976), chapter 1 'The Right of Nations to Self-Determination'.

Macmillan, Margaret, *Peacemakers, The Paris Conference of 1919 and Its Attempt to End War* (London: John Murray, 2002).

Manela, Erez, *The Wilsonian Moment: Self-Determination and the International Origins of Anticolonial Nationalism* (Cary: Oxford University Press, 2007).

Smith, Leonard V., *Sovereignty at the Paris Peace Conference of 1919* (New York: Oxford University Press, 2018).

Temperley, H. W. V., *A History of the Peace Conference of Paris*, Volume 1 (London: Hodder & Stoughton, 1920).

Wilson, Woodrow, 'Democracy and Efficiency', *Atlantic Monthly*, March, 1901.

Post-war diplomacy and the Anglo-Persian Agreement

Anon, 'British Diplomacy in Persia', article from *The Economist* reprinted in *The Living Age*, 13 January 1912, 116–18.

Bakhash, Shaul, 'The Origins of the Anglo-Persian Agreement of 1919', *Asian and African Studies: Journal of the Israel Oriental Society*, Vol. 25, No. 1 (March, 1991).

Balfour, Hon. J. M., *Recent Happenings in Persia* (Edinburgh, London: William Blackwood, 1922).

Bast, Olivier, 'Les « buts de guerre » de la Perse neuter pendant la Première Guerre Mondiale', *Relations Internationales*, Hiver 2015 (janvier-mars), No. 160, États neutres et neutralité dans la Première Guerre mondiale – II (Hiver 2015 (janvier-mars)) 95–110.

Bast, Olivier, 'British imperialism and Persian diplomacy in the shadow of World War I (1914–1921)' in Nick Wadham Smith and Danny Whitehead (eds), *Didgah: New Perspectives on UK-Iran Cultural Relations* (London: British Council, 2015), 83–124.

Bast, Olivier, 'Disintegrating the "Discourse of Disintegration": Some Reflections on the Historiography of the Late Qajar Period and Iranian Cultural Memory' in Touraj Atabaki (ed), *Iran in the 20th Century: Historiography and Political Culture* (London: I.B. Taurus, 2009), 55–68.

Bast, Olivier, 'Putting the Record Straight: Vosuq al-Dowleh's Foreign Policy in 1918/19' in Touraj Atabaki and Erik.J Zürcher (eds), *Men of Order: Authoritarian Modernization under Ataturk and Reza Shah* (London: I.B. Tauris, 2004).

Bast, Olivier (ed), *La Perse et La Grande Guerre*, Bibliothéque Iranienne 52 (Tehran; Louvain: Peeters, 2002).

Bast, Olivier, 'La mission persane à la Conférence de Paix en 1919: Une nouvelle interprétation' in Oliver Bast (ed), *La Perse et La Grande Guerre*, Bibliothéque Iranienne 52 (Tehran; Louvain: Peeters, 2002).

Dodge, Toby, *Inventing Iraq: The Failure of Nation-building and a History Denied* (UK: Hurst, 2003).

Edmonds, C. J., *East and West of Zagros: Travel, War and Politics in Persia and Iraq 1913–1921* (Leiden; Boston: Brill, 1920).

Ettehadieh, Mansoureh, 'Les illusions et les faits: l'Iran et la Conférence de Versailles' in Oliver Bast (ed), *La Perse et La Grande Guerre* Bibliothéque Iranienne 52 (Tehran; Louvain: Peeters, 2002).

Evans, Luther Harris, 'The Emancipation of Iraq from the Mandates System', *The American Political Science Review*, December, 1932, Vol. 26, No. 6 (December, 1932), 1024–49.

Farhoody, Hossein, 'Iran va konferens-e solh-e Paris' [Iran and the Paris peace Conference] *Irannameh*, Bahar, 1367, shomareh-ye 23.

Grobien, Philip Henning, 'The Origins and Intentions of the Anglo-Persian Agreement 1919: A Reassessment', *Iran*, DOI: 10.1080/05786967.2022.2080581. 2022.

Grobien, Philip, 'Iran and imperial nationalism in 1919', *Middle Eastern Studies*, Vol. 57, No. 2 (2021), 292–309.

Grobien, Philip Henning, 'The Politics of Economic Development: The Anglo-Persian Agreement, 1919', *Iran*, forthcoming.

Jahangiri, Saeed, Ebrahim Mottaqi, and Shahrokh Ashja Mahdavi, ''Vakavi-ye sharayat-e dakhely va beynolmelali eneghad-e qararad-e 1919 (aba'ad va roykerd-ha)' [Analysing the domestic and international effects of the 1919 contract (approaches and scope)] *'Ulum-e siyasi: nashreyeh-ye rahbord-e siyasi*, Paiz, 1398 shomareh-ye 10. 1–18.

Kashani-Sabet, Firoozeh, *Frontier Fictions: Shaping the Iranian Nation, 1804–1946* (London; New York: I.B. Tauris, 2000).

Katouzian, Homa, *State and Society in Iran: The Eclipse of the Qajars and the Emergence of the Pahlavis* (London; New York: I.B. Tauris, 2006).

Lashkari, Mahmood, 'dar neemeh rah-ye konferans-e solh-e Paris', [Midway through the Paris Peace Conference], Aban, 1393, *Goftigu*, no.65.

Louis, Roger, 'The United Kingdom and the beginning of the Mandates System, 1919–1922', *International Organization*, Winter, 1969, Vol. 23, No. 1 (Winter, 1969), 73–96.

Malkasian, Mark, 'The Disintegration of the Armenian Cause in the United States, 1918–1927', *International Journal of Middle East Studies*, Vol. 16, No. 3 (1984), 349–65.

Mollai Tavani, Alireza, 'Negahi-e dobareh be qarardad-e 1919' [Another look at the 1919 Agreement] *Faslnameh-ye Tarikh-e ravabet-e khareji*, Bahar va Tabestan, 1388, shomareh-ye 38 va 39, 113–45.

Müller, Gotelind, 'Versailles and the Fate of Chinese Internationalism: Reassessing the Anarchist case' in Urs Matthias Zachmann (Ed), *Asia after Versailles: Asian Perspectives on the Paris Peace Conference and the Interwar Order, 1919–33* (Edinburgh: Edinburgh University Press, 2017).

Nayeri, Loghman Dehghan, Morteza Nooraei, and Farhad Puryanejad, 'Konferens-e solh-e Versailles va ed'eha-ye arzi-ye Iran darbareh-ye manateq-e Irani-e shomal-e rud-e aras' [The Versailles Peace Conference and Iran's territorial claims north of the Aras river] *Jestarha-ye Tarikhi*, sal-e 1, shomareh-ye 2, Paiz va Zemestan, 1389.

Nunan, Timothy, 'Persian Visions of Nationalism and Inter-Nationalism in a World at War' in Marcus M. Payk and Roberta Pergher (eds), *Beyond Versailles: Sovereignty, Legitimacy, and the Formation of New Polities after the Great War* (Bloomington, IN: Indiana University Press, 2019).

Öke, Mim Kemâl, *The Armenian Question 1914–1923* (Oxford: K. Rustem & Brothers, 1988).

Olson, William J., 'The Genesis of the Anglo-Persian Agreement of 1919' in Elie Kedourie and Haim Silvia G (eds), *Towards a Modern Iran* (London: Routledge, 2016).

Olson, William J., *Anglo-Iranian Relations during World War 1* (London; New York: Routledge, 2013).

Omissi, David, *Air Power and Colonial Control: The Royal Air Force, 1919–1939* (Manchester: Manchester University Press, 1990).

Parto, Afshin, 'Peyman-e 1919 va vakonesh-haye barkhaste dar barabar-e an' [The 1919 treaty and reactions to it], *Ettela'at siyasi-eqtesadi*, Khordad va Teer, 1377, No 129, 130, 86–101.

Rohani, Sohail, 'Qarardad-e 1919 (Qarardad-e Vosuq al-Dowleh)' [Agreement of 1919 (Vosuq al-Dowleh's agreement)] *Ayandeh*, sal-e 13 Aban ta Esfand, 1366, shomareh-ye 8 ta 12, 651–64.

Sabahi, Houshang, *British Policy in Persia 1918–1925* (London; Portland: Frank Cass, 1990).

Safaei, Ebrahim, *Vosuq al-Dowleh 1254–1329* (Tehran: Ketab-e Sera, 1374).

Waterfield, Gordon, *Professional Diplomat: Sir Percy Loraine* (London: John Murray, 1973).

Intellectual foundations

Aghaie, Kamran Scot and Afshin Marashi (eds), *Rethinking Iranian Nationalism and Modernity* (Austin: University of Texas, 2015).

Anderson, Benedict, *Imagined Communities: Reflections on the Origin and Spread of Nationalism* (London; New York: Verso, 2006).
Ansari, Ali, *The Politics of Nationalism in Modern Iran* (Cambridge: Cambridge University Press, 2012).
Atabaki, Touraj, 'Pan-Turkism and Iranian Nationalism' in Touraj Atabaki (ed), *Iran and the First World War: Battleground of the Great Powers* (London; New York: I.B Taurus, 2006).
Bowden, Brett, *The Empire of Civilization: The Evolution of an Imperial Idea* (Chicago: University of Chicago Press, 2014).
Breuilly, John, *Nationalism and the State*, Second Edition (Manchester: Manchester University Press, 1995).
Bull, Hedley, Benedict Kingsbury, and Adam Roberts (eds), *Hugo Grotius and International Relations* (Oxford: Clarendon, 2002).
Coker, Christopher, *The Rise of the Civilizational State* (Cambridge; Medford: Polity, 2019).
Cottam, Richard W., *Nationalism in Iran* (Pittsburgh: Pittsburgh Press, 1979).
Ekhtiar, Maryam, 'Nasir al-Din Shah and the Dar al-Funun: The Evolution of an Institution', *Iranian Studies*, Vol. 34, No. 1-4 (2001), 153-63.
Gellner, Ernest, *Nations and Nationalism*, Second Edition (Malden, MA: Blackwell, 2006).
Habermas, Jürgen (translated by Thomas Burger), *The Structural Transformation of the Public Sphere: An Inquiry into a Category of Bourgeois Society* (Cambridge, MA: The MIT Press, 2001).
Hodgson, Marshall, *The Venture of Islam: Conscience and History in a World Civilization* (Chicago: University of Chicago Press, 1974).
Jacques, Martin, *When China Rules the World: The End of the Western World and the Birth of a New Global Order* (London: Penguin Books, 2012)
Johnston, R.J., David B. Knight, and Eleonore Kofman (eds), *Nationalism, self-determination and political geography* (London; New York: Croom Helm, 1988).
Kedourie, Elie, *Nationalism* (Malden; Oxford: Fourth edition, Blackwell Publishers, 2000).
Koskenniemi, Martti, *The Gentle Civilizer of Nations: The Rise and Fall of International Law 1870-1960* (Cambridge: Cambridge University Press, 2008).
Litvak, Meir (ed), *Constructing nationalism in Iran: From the Qajars to the Islamic Republic* (Abingdon, Oxon: Routledge, 2017).
Matin-Asgari, Afshin, *Both Eastern and Western: An Intellectual History of Iranian Modernity* (Cambridge, UK: Cambridge University Press, 2018).
Milani, Abbas, *Lost Wisdom: Rethinking Modernity in Iran* (Washington, DC: Mage Publishers, 2004).
Mirsepassi, Ali, *Intellectual Discourse and the Politics of Modernization: Negotiating Modernity in Iran* (Cambridge: Cambridge, 2000).
Pistor-Hatam, Anja, 'Progress and Civilization in Nineteenth-Century Japan: The Far Eastern State as a Model for Modernization', *Iranian Studies*, Winter–Spring, 1996, Vol. 29, No. 1/2 (Winter–Spring, 1996), 111–26.
Smith, Anthony D, *The Ethnic Origins of Nations* (Oxford: Blackwell, 1988).
Tamir, Yael, 'Review: The Enigma of Nationalism: Imagined Communities by Benedict Anderson, Nationalism: Five Roads to Modernity by Liah Greenfeld, National Identity by Anthony D. Smith', *World Politics*, Vol. 47, No. 3 (April, 1995), 418–40.
WeiWei, Zhang, *The China Wave: Rise of the Civilizational State* (Hackensack: World Century, 2012).
Yarshater, Ehsan, 'The Qajar Era in the Mirror of Time', *Iranian Studies*, Vol. 34, No. 1/4 (2001), 187–94.

Zia-Ebrahimi, Reza, *The Emergence of Iranian Nationalism: Race and the Politics of Dislocation* (New York: Columbia University Press, 2016).

Historical research

Abrams, L. and D. J. Miller, 'Who Were the French Colonialists? A Reassessment of the Parti Colonial, 1890–1914', *The Historical Journal*, Vol. 19, No. 3 (September, 1976), 685–725.
Afshar, Iraj, 'Book Translations as a Cultural Activity in Iran 1806–1896', *Iran*, Vol. 41 (2003), 279–89.
Ahmadinejad, Taher, 'negahi be zendegi va fa'aleyat-e deplomatik-e Ali Qoli Ma'sud Ansari, Moshaver al-Mamalek yek 'omr-e deplomat' [a look at the life and diplomatic activity of Ali Qoli Ma'sud Ansari, Moshaver al-Mamalek – a lifetime diplomat] *Ruznameh-e Ettela'at*, shomareh-ye 23610.
Alder, G. J., 'Britain and the Defence of India – The Origins of the Problem 1798–1815', *Journal of Asian History*, Vol. 6, No. 1 (1972), 14–44.
Algar, Hamid, *Mirza Malkum Khan: A Biographical Study in Iranian Modernism* (Los Angeles; London: University of California Press, 1973).
Algar, Hamid, 'An introduction to the History of Freemansory [sic] in Iran', *Middle Eastern Studies*, October, 1970, Vol. 6, No. 3 (October, 1970), 276–96.
Alizadehbirjandi, Zahra, 'Avamel-e mo'aser bar ravabet-e Iran va usmani dar doreh-ye Qajarieh' [Factors effecting Iran-Ottoman relations in the Qajar period] *Mahnameh-ye andeshe va Tarikh-e siyasi-ye Iran mo'aser*, sal-e 5, eshareh-ye 50, Aban, 1380, 39–42.
Allen, William Edward David and Paul Muratoff, *Caucasian Battlefields: A History of the Wars on the Turco-Caucasian Border 1828–1921* (New York: Cambridge University Press, 2010).
Amanat, Abbas, *Pivot of the Universe* (London; New York: I.B Taurus 2008).
Amanat, Abbas and Farzin Vejdani (eds), *Iran Facing Others: Identity Boundaries in a Historical Perspective* (New York: Palgrave Macmillan, 2012).
Andreeva, Elena, *Russia and Iran in the Great Game: Travelogues and Orientalism* (London; New York: Routledge, 2007).
Andrew, C. M., and A. S. Kanya-Forstner, 'The French "Colonial Party": Its Composition, Aims and Influence, 1885–1914', *The Historical Journal*, Vol. 14, No. 1 (March, 1971), 99–128.
Anon, 'Major-general Sir Percy Zachariah Cox', *The Geographical Journal*, July, 1937, Vol. 90, No. 1 (July, 1937), 1–5.
Ansari, Ali M, *Modern Iran since 1797: Reform and Revolution, 3rd Edition* (London; New York: Routledge, 2019)
Aqeli, Baqer, *Shahr-e hal-e rajel-e siyasi va nezami-ye mo'aser-e Iran (2)* [Biography of contemporary and distinguished Iranian political and military figures] (Tehran: Goftar, 1380).
Aqeli, Baqer, *Nosrat al-Dowleh Firuz, Az ruya-ye padeshahi ta zendan-e Reza Shahi* [Nosrat al-Dowleh Firuz, from the dream of a kingdom to Reza Shah's jail] (Tehran: Korsheed, 1373).
Atabaki, Touraj (ed), *Iran and the First World War: Battleground of the Great Powers* (London; New York: I.B. Tauris, 2006).
Ateş, Sabri, *The Ottoman-Iranian Borderlands: Making a Boundary, 1843–1914* (Cambridge: Cambridge University Press, 2013).

Atkin, Muriel, *Russia and Iran, 1780–1828* (Minneapolis: University of Minnesota Press, 1980).
Avery, Peter, *Modern Iran* (London: Ernest Benn Limited, 1965).
Bakhash, Shaul, *Iran: Modernity, Bureaucracy & Reform under the Qajars: 1858–1896* (Oxford: Ithaca Press London, 1978).
Bakhash, Shaul, 'The Evolution of Qajar Bureaucracy: 1779–1879', *Middle Eastern Studies*, Vol. 7, No. 2 (May, 1971), 139–68.
Barr, James, *Lords of the Desert: Britain's Struggle with America to Dominate the Middle East* (London: Simon & Shuster, 2018).
Barr, James, *A Line in the Sand: Britain, France and the Struggle for the Mastery of the Middle East* (London: Simon & Shuster 2011).
Bashir, Hassan, 'The Iranian Press and Modernization Under the Qajars', unpublished thesis, University of Leicester.
Bigdeli, Ali, 'fahm-e roshanfekran-e mashrutehkhah az mafhoom-e modernite' [Constitutional intellectual's understanding of the concept of modernity] *Human Sciences*, No. 51 (Autumn 2006), 85–208.
Bostock, Frances, 'State Bank or Agent of Empire? The Imperial Bank of Persia's Loan Policy 1920–23', *Iran*, 1989, Vol. 27 (1989), 103–13.
Bourne, Kenneth, *The Foreign Policy of Victorian England, 1830–1902* (London: Clarendon Press, 1970).
Brandes, George, *The World at War* (New York: Macmillan, 1917).
Browne, Edward G., *The Persian Revolution 1905–1909* (Washington: Mage, 2006).
Chardin, Sir John, *Travels in Persia* (London: The Argonaut Press, 1927).
Churchill, Winston S., *Great Contemporaries* (London: The Reprint Society London, 1941).
Clarke, John, *British Diplomacy and Foreign Policy 1782–1865: The National Interest* (London: Unwin Hyman, 1989).
Cottrell, Alvin J., 'Iran's Armed Forces under the Pahlavi Dynasty' in George Lenczowski (ed), *Iran under The Pahlavis* (Stanford: Hoover Institution Press, 1978).
Cronin, Stephanie 'Building a New Army: Military Reform in Qajar Iran', in Roxane Farmanfarmaian (ed), *War and Peace in Qajar Iran: Implications Past and Present* (London; New York: Routledge, 2008).
Cronin, Stephanie, 'Britain, the Iranian Military and the Rise of Reza Khan' in Vanessa Martin (ed), *Anglo-Iranian Relations since 1800* (London; New York: Routledge, 2005).
Curzon, George N., *Persia and the Persian Question, Vol. 1* (London; New York: Longmans, Green and Co, 1892).
Elm, Mostafa, *Oil, Power, and Principle: Iran's Oil Nationalization and Its Aftermath* (Syracuse; New York: Syracuse University Press, 1994).
Enayat, Hadi, *Law, State and Society in Modern Iran: Constitutionalism, Autocracy, and Legal Reform, 1906–1941* (New York: Palgrave Macmillan, 2013).
Fragner, Bert G., 'World War 1 as a Turning point in Iranian History' in Oliver Bast, 'La mission persane à la Conférence de Paix en 1919: Une nouvelle interprétation' in Oliver Bast (ed), *La Perse et La Grande Guerre*, Bibliothéque Iranienne 52 (Tehran; Louvain: Peeters, 2002).
Foroughi, Mohammad Ali, *Hoquq-e assasi (ya'ni) adab-e mashrutiat-e doval* [Fundamental rights, namely the conduct of constitutional states] (Iran: Koyer, 1382).
Galbraith, John S., 'British Policy on Railways in Persia, 1870-1900', *Middle Eastern Studies*, Vol. 25, No. 4 (October, 1989), 480–505.

Greaves, Rose, *Persia and The Defence of India, 1884–1892* (London: University of London, 1959).
Ingram, Edward, *Britain's Persian Connection, 1798–1828: Prelude to the Great Game in Asia* (Oxford: Clarendon Press Oxford, 1992).
Ingram, Edward, 'Approaches to the Great Game', *Middle Eastern Studies*, Vol. 18, No. 4 (October, 1982), 449–57.
Ingram, Edward, *The Beginning of the Great Game in Asia 1824–1834* (Oxford: Clarendon Press, 1979).
Issawi, Charles, 'Iranian Trade, 1800–1914', *Iranian Studies*, Vol. 16, No. 3/4, Studies on the Economic and Social History of Iran in the Nineteenth Century (Summer–Autumn, 1983), 229–41.
Issawi, Charles, *The Economic History of Iran 1800–1914* (Chicago; London: University Chicago Press, 1971).
Katouzian, Homa, 'Sayyed Hasan Taqizadeh: Three Lives in a Lifetime', *Comparative Studies of South Asia, Africa and the Middle East*, Vol. 32 (1, April 2012).
Kazemzadeh, Firuz, *Russia and Britain in Persia: Imperial Ambitions in Qajar Iran* (London; New York: I.B. Tauris, 2013).
Kazemzadeh, Firuz, *The Struggle for Transcaucasia (1917–1921)* (London: Anglo Caspian Press Ltd, 2008).
Kazemzadeh, Firuz, 'Iranian Relations with Russia and the Soviet Union, to 1921' in Peter Avery, Gavin Hambly, and Charles Melville (eds), *The Cambridge History of Iran, Volume 7* (Cambridge: Cambridge University Press, 2003).
Keddie, Nikki, *Qajar Iran and the Rise of Reza Khan 1796–1925* (Costa Mesa: Mazda, 1999).
Keddie, Nikki, *An Islamic Response to Imperialism: Political and Religious Writings of Sayyid Jamal ad-Din 'al-Afghani'* (Los Angeles; London: University of California Press, 1983).
Keddie, Nikki, 'The Economic History of Iran, 1800–1914, and Its Political Impact: An Overview', *Iranian Studies*, Vol. 5, No. 2/3 (Spring–Summer, 1972), 58–78.
Litten, Wilhelm, *Persien, Von der 'pénétration pacifique' zum 'Protektorat'* (Berlin: Berlin und Leipzig, 1920).
Makki, Hossein, *Tarikh-e bistsale-ye Iran, jeld-e chaharom* [Twenty years of Iranian history, volume 4] (Tehran: Kaveyan, 1361).
Makki, Hossein, *Zendegani-ye siyasi-ye Ahmad Shah Qajar* [The political life of Ahmad Shah Qajar] (Tehran: Amir Kabir, 1357).
Malcom, John, *History of Persia*, Volume 2 (London: John Murray, 1815).
McDowall, David, *A Modern History of the Kurds* (London; New York: I.B. Taurus, 2004).
Monroe, Elizabeth, *Britain's Moment in the Middle East, 1914–1956* (London: Chatto & Windus 1963).
Mosley, Leonard, *CURZON: The End of an Epoch* (London: Longmans, Green and Co, 1961).
Mostowfi, 'Abdollah, *Sharh-e zendegani-ye man ya tarikh-e ejtema'i va edari-ye dowreh-ye Qajariyeh*, [My life story: The administrative and social history of the Qajar period] volume III (Tehran: Zovar, 1384).
Nabavi, Negin, *Modern Iran: a history in documents* (Princeton: Markus Wiener, 2016).
Nicholson, Harold, *Curzon: The Last Phase 1919–1925* (London: Constable & Co, 1934).
Prévost-Grégoire, Florence, 'Pacifisme et universalisme: le cas du Comité national d'études sociales et politiques (1916–1931)', *Matériaux pour l'histoire de notre temps*, Vol. 129–130, No. 3-4 (2018), 42–7.

Sahlins, Peter, 'Natural Frontiers Revisited: France's Boundaries since the Seventeenth Century', *The American Historical Review*, Vol. 95, No. 5 (December, 1990).

Sepehr, Ahmad Ali, *Khaterate-e siyasi-e Movarekhaldowleh Sepehr* (Iran: Namak, 1374).

Shahvar, Soli, 'Iron Poles, Wooden Poles: The Electric Telegraph and the Ottoman: Iranian Boundary Conflict, 1863–1865', *British Journal of Middle Eastern Studies*, Vol. 34, No. 1 (April, 2007).

Shaw, Stanford, 'Iranian Relations with the Ottoman Empire in the Eighteenth and Nineteenth Centuries' in Peter Avery, Gavin Hambly and Charles Melville (eds), *The Cambridge History of Iran, Volume 7* (Cambridge: Cambridge University Press, 2003).

Sheffer, Edith, *Burned Bridge: How the East and West Germans Made the Iron Curtain* (New York: Oxford University Press, 2014).

Sherley, Sir Antony, *His Relation of His Travels into Persia* (London: Forgotten Books, 2018).

Shuster, W. Morgan, *The Strangling of Persia* (New York: The Century Co, 1912).

Stammer, D. W., 'British Colonial Finance', *Social and Economic Studies*, June, 1967, Vol. 16, No. 2 (June, 1967), 191–205.

Stebbins, H. Lyman, 'British Imperialism, Regionalism, and Nationalism in Iran, 1890–1919' in Abbas Amanat and Farzin Vejdani (eds), *Iran Facing Others: Identity Boundaries in a Historical Perspective* (New York: Palgrave Macmillan, 2012).

Swietochowski, Tadeusz, *Russia and Azerbaijan: A Borderland in Transition* (New York: Columbia University Press, 1995).

Sykes, Sir Percy, *A History of Persia, Volume II*, Second Edition (London: Macmillan and Co, 1921).

Taherahmadi, Mahmood, 'Ali Qoli Ma´sud Ansari, Moshaver Al-Mamalek', *Nameh-ye Anjoman*, Paiz, 1384, shomareh-ye 19.

Wheeler-Bennett, J. W., *Brest-Litovsk: The Forgotten Peace, March 1918* (London: Macmillan, 1971).

Wilson, Sir Arnold T., *Persia* (London: Ernest Benn Limited, 1932).

Wilson, Thomas M., and Hastings Doonan (eds), *Border Identities: Nation and State at International Frontiers* (New York: Cambridge University Press, 1998).

Wright, Denis, *The English Amongst The Persians: During the Qajar Period 1787–1921* (London: Heinemann, 1977).

Yate, Lieutenant Colonel C.E., *Khurasan and Sistan* (Edinburgh; London: W. Blackwood, 1900).

Yazdi, Mahmood Afshar, 'Iran va konferans-e solh-e Paris' [Iran at the Paris Peace Conference], 1358, www.rasekhoon.net.

Zolo, Danilo, 'The Rule of Law: A Critical Reappraisal' in Pietro Costa and Danilo Zolo (eds), *The Rule of Law: History, Theory and Criticism* (Netherlands: Springer, 2007).

Zuqi, Iraj, 'Chegunegi-ye shekast: ma´muriyat-e nemayandegan-e Iran dar konferens-e solh-e Paris (Versailles 1919)' [How the mission of the Iranian delegation to the Paris Peace Conference failed] *Baressiha-ye tarikhi*, 1354, No 60, 65–90.

INDEX

Abbas Mirza, Prince 5, 21
'Abol-Qasim Khan Qarazuglu, Naser al-Molk 55, 62
academics *See* teachers
Afghanistan 23, 26, 48, 57, 61, 69, 118
Agha Muhammad Khan 20
Aharonian, Avetis xvi
Ahmad Shah Qajar xi, 5, 10, 14, 52, 55, 147, Anglo-Persian Agreement 136–7, Britain 93, 115, 124, 126, character 14, 154, *imperial nationalism* (role in) 3, 14, 59, 62, 67–8, 74, 77, 138–9, 143, 151, 153, Moshaver al-Mamalek 62–3, 78, sovereignty/Peace Note 52, US 52, 84–5, Vosuq al-Dowleh, 62, 134
Akhundzadeh, Mirza Fath Ali 37–8
al-Afghani, Jamal al-Din 38–9
al-Saltaneh, Adib 73
al-Saltaneh, Ashjeh 63
al-Saltaneh, Mehdi Khan Ala 93, 126
al-Saltaneh, Momtaz 55, 70, 78–9, 85, 115, 117, 132
al-Saltaneh, Nezam 73
al-Saltaneh, Sadegh 124–5
al-Saltaneh, Samsam 61
al-Saltaneh, Sho'a' 42
Ala, Hossein Khan 59, 63, 65–6, 75, 80, 84, 92, 100, 115
Albert, Prince (George VI) 137
Alborz mountains 108
Allenby, Field Marshall Edmund 59
Allies/Allied xii, xiv, xvi–xvii, 12, 14, 16, 23, 33, 52, 54, 67–8, 70, 80, 86, 96, 107, 116, 120, 145, 152, 157
Amanat, Abbas 31, 42
Ameer Ali 49–50
America *See* United States
American Relief Commission 70, 71, 96
Anglo-Persian Agreement 1–2, 16, 17, 98, 110, 115, 123–4, 128, 137, 140, 150, 152, 157, 160, agreement end 145–7, 149, 158, 159, British plans 1, 3, 12, 93, 102, 113, 133–5, 138–9, 143, 146, 152, 155–6, criticism 91, 104, 108, 111, 116–19, 125–6, 134, 144, 149, 156, 158, delegation 123, 124, 126, 156, Iranian plans 3, 77, 92, 126–8, 130, 132, 136–9, 144, 149, 154, 156, League of Nations 118–19
Anglo-Persian Military Commission 113–14
Anglo-Persian Oil Company (APOC) 40–1, 105, 127, 139
Anglo-Russian Convention 1907 (1915) xv, 31, 39, 43, 47, 49, 54, 57, 59, 69, 87, 102, 104, 107, 117, 118–20, 128, 134, 135, 148, 157
Anjoman 9
anti-Semitism 30, 90
Anzali 72, Anglo-Persian Agreement 146, 157, Bolshevik landing 114, 146
APOC *See* Anglo-Persian Oil Company
Aq-Evli, Colonel Fazlullah Khan 114
Armenia xvi, 20, 60, 75, 82–3, 90, 108, 138, 145, 157, 156–7, claims xvi–xvii, 82–3, 91, 97, delegation xvi, 152, First World War 47–8, 52, 82–3, Iran 73, 95, 141–2, 144, 148, mandate 141, 157, Transcaucasian Federation 83
Armitage-Smith, Sydney 112
Army 33, 47, 129, 140–1, 145, 147, 149
Army (Iranian) 5, 10, 21, 60, 106–7, 113–14, 148, 157
Articles 8, 10, 22 *See also* League of Nations xiv 118, 128
Aryanism xiv
Ashuradeh 148
Assyrians xvii, 75, 95
Austro-Hungarian Empire 7, 101
Azerbaijan xii–xiii, xvi–xvii, 72, 100, 108, 145, claims 91, 100, 108, 140, 143–4, delegation 82, 152, First World War xii,

48, Iran 108, 140–2, Transcaucasian Federation 83
Azerbaijan (Iran) 41–2, 44–5, 47–8, 58, 60, 81, 139, 146, 148

Bagdad xv, 13, 139
Bahar, Mohammad Taqi 131
Bakhash, Shaul 16, 37
Bakhtiari 41, 105
Baku 21, 47, 58, 60, 72, 90, 145
Balfour, Arthur (Lord) 12, 52, 76–8, 81, 90, 94, 98, 100
Balfour, James 112, 114, 146
Baluchistan 26, 61, 103
Barbi, Monsieur 96
Barres, Maurice 95
Basra xv
Bast, Oliver 2, 16, 17, 77, 94
Batum 72, 83
bazaars 5, 70
Belgium xii, 55, 68, 81–2, 127
Belligerent(s) xi, xvi, 52, 81, 110, 170
Berlin 53, 57, 119
Berliner Tageblatt (newspaper) 119
Big Four 10, 86, 98, 142, 155
Black Sea xv, 24, 32, 48, 83, 88, 145
Boghos Nubar Pasha xvi
Bolsheviks/Bolshevism xv, xvii 53, 58, 129, 145, 147–8, Anzali 114, 146, 157, Brest-Litovsk 57–8, 61, 63, Iran 52, 59, 79, 96, 140, 146–7, 149, Paris xvii, 95, self-determination 52, 57, Transcaucasus 141, 145, Treaty of Friendship 143, 148
Bonin, Charles 70, 101, 116, 156
Borchalo 83
borders xi, xv, xvii, 2, 4, 7–8, 10, 26, 29, 31–2, 36, 44–5, 47–8, 60–1, 68, 72, 75, 83, 87–8, 90, 106, 108, 120, 138–41, 143–4, 148, 150, 152
Bosphorus xv, 25
Brandes, George 81–2
Bravin, Karl 58
Brazil 81
Britain xii, xv–xvi, 4, 13, 38, 54, 65, 104, Anglo-Persian Agreement 103–4, 107, 110, 112, 114, 116–19, 123–4, 126, 128, 130–1, 133–4, 137, 145–6, 152, 155, 157, 160, Anzali 145, 149, attitudes towards Iran/Iranians xvi, 19, 23–3, 39–45, 61, 70, 106–7, 154, during/post-war in Middle East/Iran xii, xv, 1, 3, 12, 14, 16, 40, 43, 45–50, 52–3, 58–9, 61, 82, 84, 86, 91, 104–5, 120, 141, 152–3, 156–7, 159, financing 102–3, 112, India 20, 16, 70, 97, 103, 152, Iran/Peace Conference 55, 68–70, 74, 79, 87, 91, 93–4, 97, 126–7, 129, 137–40, 142, 144
British xi, xiii, xv–xvi, 1–6, 9–14, 16–17, 19–21, 35–6, 39–45, 47–8, 50–6, 58, 61–3, 65–82, 84–6, 90–121, 123–8, 130, 132–40, 142–5, 146–50, 152–9
Browne, Edward 35, 51, 129
buffer *See also* Britain/India and masterly activity/inactivity)14, 25–6, 31, 61, 152
Bushire 29

Caldwell, John 12, 71, 120, 156, Iranian claims 11, 70, 80, 114–16
Canning, George 25
capitulations 6, 27–8, 58–9, 67, 87, 148
Caspian Sea 23, 30, 58, 88, 127, 129, 139, 146, 148
Castlereagh, Robert 25
Catherine the Great 4, 20
Caucasus *See also* Transcaucasus xvii, 4, 20, 23, 32, 45, 47, 60, 68, 71, 82–3, 87, 90, 118, 141, 145, 148, Maps 1/2/5/6
Cecil, Lord Robert 69
Central Powers xii, 33, 48, 57, 73, 146
Chardin, Sir John 87–8
chargé d'affaires 24, 41, 53, 55, 65, 116
Chelmsford, Lord 102
China 8, 81
Chkheidze, Nikoloz xvi
cholera 21
Churchill, George 117
Churchill, Sir Winston 40, 129–30, 145, 159
civilization/civilizing *See also* Article 22 xv, 12, 20, 29, 87, 94, 13, standard xiv, 86
Civilizational State 8–9
Claims of Persia before the Conference of the Preliminaries of Peace at Paris 8, 10, 84, 87, 89, 90–1, 93–4, 97, 138, 142, 155
Claims of the Peace Delegation of the Republic of Caucasian Azerbaijan

Presented to the Peace Conference in Paris 140
Clemenceau, George 10–1, 79, 98, 115, 145, 156
colonialism xii, xiv, xv, 10, 49, 75, 79, 103, colony(ies) xiii, xiv, 91, 118, semi-colonial xii, xiii, 1, 14, 27, 33, 35, 39, 50–1, 61
Comité National D'Études Sociales et Politiques 92–3
concessions 5–6, 27–31, 36, 38–40, 54, 57–9, 61–2, 67, 87, 106, 112, 148
Constitution (Iranian) 41, 130–1, 153
Constitutional Revolution 5, 7, 9, 10, 28, 35, 41–2, 44–5, 47, 49–50, 53, 63–6, 80, 90, 104, 107, 146–7, 153–4
consuls/consular 26–7, 42, 57, 59, 61, 65, 87, 111
conventions 67, 87, 148
Cossack Brigade 42, 113, 132
Council of Ten 81, 94, 142, 155
coup (1921) 14, 132, 147–50
Cox, Sir Percy 13, 93, 124, 147, 159, Anglo-Persian Agreement 3, 14, 101–2, 104, 107–8, 110–1, 113–14, 116, 124–5, 127–9, 130, 133–4, 136, 142, 145–6, 150, 152–4, 156, claims 66–7, 68, 70, 76, 78, 85
Curzon, George Nathanial (Lord) xvi, 12, 30, 120, 154, Anglo-Persian Agreement 3, 33, 94, 102–4, 106, 107–8, 110–13, 117, 119, 123–31, 133–50, 152, 154, 156, 158–9, Anglo-Russian Convention 43–4, 107, background/outlook 12–14, 100–1, Eastern Committee 40, 68–9, Iranians Paris 70, 85, 90–1, 93–4, 101, 108, 123, 151, 153, 155
customs 37, 41, 54, 59–60, 67, 87, 103, 107, 111–2, 127, 130

Dahan-e Zulfiqar 91
Dar al-Fonun 29–30, 128
Darband 21, 60
D'Arcy Oil Syndicate 41
D'Arcy, William Knox 30, 40, 112
Dashnak Party xvi
de Bunsen committee xv
debt(s) 27, 57, 102, 105, 129
Definitive Treaty 1814 24–5, 27, 145

delegate(s) xvii, 7–8, 15–17, 39, 54–5, 57, 60–3, 66, 72–8, 80–2, 84–5, 87, 90, 92–9, 101, 107, 114–18, 120, 123–4, 127, 134–7, 145, 152, 155–6, 158
delegation(s) xi, xvi–xvii, 1–3, 12, 14, 16–17, 49, 50, 52–3, 59, 61–3, 65–80, 82–6, 91–7, 99, 100–1, 105, 107, 115–16, 121, 123–4, 128–9, 135–6, 140, 143, 145, 147, 149, 151–8, 160
delimitation(s) 7–8, 31, 45, 47, 61, 108–9, 138, 140
Denekin, Anton General 129, 145
Denmark 100
desiderata (Iranian) 3, 19, 28, 53–5, 57, 67–8, 70, 74, 76, 79, 83–4, 86–7, 91, 93–4, 96–9, 101, 107, 110, 116, 119, 121, 123–4, 127, 129, 134, 136–8, 141–4, 151–2, 155–7
Dickson, William Brigadier-General 113–14
Dieulafoy, Marcel-Auguste 95
dynasty(ies) 1–3, 5, 6, 8, 10, 14, 16, 19, 21, 27, 36, 38, 51, 63, 87, 91, 147–8, 150–1

East 12, 80, 88
East India Company 4, 19–20, 23, 25
East Persia Cordon 113
Eastern Committee 40, 59, 68, 74, 103, 113, 133, 153, 158
Egypt/Egyptianisation xvi, 12, 23, 36–7, 84, 106, 111, 113, 124, 133–4, 160
Ehtesham al-Saltaneh 72–3
Eight-point programme 55, 59, 67, 70, 75, 77, 87, 93, 149, 155
elections 130, 147
elite (Iranian) 1, 5, 7, 9–10, 15, 20, 33, 35, 38, 48–54, 62, 70, 73, 107, 153, 155, 157
empire(s) xii, xv–xvii, 2–4, 7–12, 14, 20–1, 23, 25–6, 28, 31–3, 36–8, 40, 45, 48–9, 52, 70, 79, 82–3, 87–91, 100–1, 103–4, 119, 131, 139–41, 144–5, 148, 150, 152, 159
enlightenment (Iranian) 3, 5, 35, 37–9, 41, 43, 45, 47, 49, 50
Enqelab-e Mashruteh See Constitutional Revolution
Entezam al-Molk 59, 63, 115, 124
Enver Pasha 47
epidemics xi, 1

Erivan 23, 139
Erzerum 90
ethnic/ethnicity(ies) xii–xiv, xvii, 7–9, 20, 45, 48, 60, 82–3, 87, 100, 141, 156–7
ethnie 8
Ettehadieh, Mansoureh 16, 98
Eulenburg Affair 70
Euphrates 87

Falkenhagen Concession 30
famine(s) xi, 1, 96, 131
Faqarat-e hashtganeh See Eight-point programme
Fath Ali Shah 5, 21
Feisal, Sheikh 86
Ferdowsi 38
finance(s) 2, 37, 40–1, 54, 56, 64, 71, 103, 105–6, 111, 112
financial(ly) 2, 6, 28–9, 36, 41–3, 57, 85, 92–4, 101–5, 107–8, 111–2, 128, 133, 157–8
Finland 144
Firouzeh 7, 148
First World War xi–xiii, xv, 2, 7, 9, 26, 28, 33, 43, 47, 48–9, 53, 70, 98, 102, 113, 120, 156, effect xi, xii, xv, 75, 96, 133, Iran xii, 1, 10, 14, 16, 31, 45, 48, 51–2, 56–7, 64–8, 71–3, 80–2, 97–8, 105, 107, 109–10, 119, 138, 146, 151, 153–7, 159, neutrality xi, 80–1, 142
Fisher, Lord 40
Firuz, Prince *See* Nosrat al-Dowleh
Foroughi, Mohammad Ali 14, 17, 59, 65, 73, 115, 129, 154, Anglo-Persian Agreement 116, 118, 120, 124, 126, 132, background/outlook 39, 63–4, 66, 73, 151, 153, 159–60, Britain 66, Churchill 129–30, delegates 73, 75, 78, 85, 129, League of Nations 85–6, 124, 160, Paris (fun) 95–6, Paris (work) 57, 63, 66, 75–6, 78, 82, 84, 92, 94–7, 100, 124, 135, 140, Perni, 73, 81, 155
Fourteen points *See* Wilson, Woodrow
France/French xv, 10, 16, 21, 55–6, 60, 62, 63, 66–7, 70, 72–6, 78–82, 84–6, 92–6, 98, 101, 106–7, 109, 111, 113–14, 121, 124, 127–8, 130, 133, 139, 154, 156, 159, Anglo-Persian Agreement 116–19, 126, 156–7, India 4, 23–4, 104, Middle East xv, 12, 56, 79, 82, 96, 100, 116, 120, 156

Freemason(s)(ry) 35, 66, 95
frontiers xiv, 7, 86–7, 103, 108–11, 129

Ganjeh 21, 23, 60, 72
Gendarmerie (Iranian) 42, 73, 114, 132
Georgia xii, xvi, 20–1, 72, 88, 145, claims 60, 83, 90–1, 108, delegation xvi, 152, independence xiii, xvi–xvii, 52, 83, Iran 73, 148, Transcaucasian Federation 83
German(s)/Germany xi, 43, 52–4, 57, 63, 73, 81, 83, 85, 91, 99, 101, 104–5, 134, 155
Ghaffar Khan 129
Gilan, Soviet Republic *See also* Kuchik Khan 146
Glanville, Lord *See also* Reuter Concession 30
Gokcha (Gokchai) 21, 83
Goldsmid, General Frederic 61
Golestan 29
Grahame, Sir George 117
Grant, Sir Hamilton 69, 102
Great Game 4, 26, 28, 30, 104
Greece xvi, 32
Grey, Sir Edward 43–4, 104, 119–20, 130

Hague 51, 94, 120
Halebja 109
Hamadan 47
Hardinge, Arthur 105
Hardinge, Lord 94, 105, 116, 144
Hartington, Lord 106
Herat 61
Herbette, Jean 96
Hodgson, Marshall 8, 89
holy Shia sites 90
Homayoun, Ehtesham 124
House, Edward 80

Imperial Bank of Persia 30, 61, 112–13
imperial nationalism 2–3, 4, 6–7, 9, 38, 60, 98, 100, 107, 123, 140, 148, 150–2, 157, 159
imperialism (Western) xii, xiv–xv, 1, 3, 9, 20, 31, 49, 51, 53, 56, 75, 79, 97, 104, 120–1, 153, 156
India xv 4, 9, 19–20, 23, 25, 40, 44, 49, 53, 69, 102, 105, 120, 133, 152, Anglo-Persian Agreement 102–4, 111, 113, 133, 157–8, army 13, 41, Iran 13–14,

20, 36, 128, security xv, 4, 12, 20, 23–6, 29, 31, 43–4, 53, 61, 68–9, 97, 103, 152
industry/industrialization 6, 28–30, 39, 118
Ingram, Edward 25–6
international law/society xii–xiv, 48–50, Rule of Law xiv, 41, 49
Iran(s) xi–xii, xv–xvii, 1–17, 19–33, 35–45, 47–88, 90–120, 123–4, 126–60
Iranian(s) xii, 1–17, 19–21, 23–8, 30–2, 35–45, 48–63, 65–87, 89–109, 111–21, 123–4, 126–55, 157–60
Iran (newspaper) 52, 71, 131
Iraq *See also* Mesopotamia xv, 108, 114, 147, 152
Ironside, General Edmund 114
irredentism/irredentist 9, 108, 139, 144, 148, 150
Isfahan 29
Islam/Islamic 8, 32, 37
Istanbul 72–3, 83, 115, 147
Italy/Italian 10, 12, 81, 156

Jahanbaksh Mirza 124
Jamalzadeh, Mohammad Ali 53
Jangalis 146
Japan 8–9, 45
Jones, Sir Harford 25
Judson, Dr. Harry Pratt 71
Julfa 31
justice xii, 43, 49, 64, 70, 80, 86, 159

Kabir, Amir (Mirza Taqi Khan) 5, 30, 37
Kahn, Albert 93
Kargozar (Kargozari) 61–2
Katouzian, Homa 16, 117, 132, 149
Kaveh (newspaper) 17, 53
Kazemzadeh, Firuz 91
Kazemzadeh, Hasan (Iranshahr) 53
Kermani, Mirza Aqa Khan 37
Kermanshah 108
Ketab-e sabz (Green Book) 57
Keynes, John Maynard 103
Khanaqin 29
Khiabani, Mohammad 146
Khoi (Khuy) 21, 48
Khorasan 29
Komisiyun-e markazi-ye ta'yin-e khesarat 56, 71, 81

Komisiyun-e ta'yin-e maqased va amal-e Iran 59, 67
Komiteh-ye Melliyun 53
Kuchik Khan *See also* Gilan, Soviet Republic academics 146
Kurds/Kurdistan *See also* Sharif Pasha xvii, 8, 45, 75–6, 82–3, 85, 87, 90, 95, 108–9, 137–8, 139, 141, 152

Lalehzar 29
Lansdowne, Lord 105
Lansing, Robert 11, 80, 82, 84, 91, 94, 115, 117
Le Temps (newspaper) 96–7, 117, 130
League of Nations xii–xiv, xvi, 49, 52, 59, 76, 85–6, 92, 99, 118–19, 121, 124–8, 130, 142–3, 149, 157, 160
Lecomte, Raymond 70, 81, 101
Lenin, Vladimir Ilyich xiii, 52
Lloyd George, David 10–2, 94, 98–101, 120, 145, 159
loans (Iran) 103, 105, 111–2, 133, 148
Loraine, Percy (Sir) 159
Luxemburg 68, 81
Luxemburg, Rosa xiii

Maclean, H 112
Majles xi 9, 42, 45, 53, 63, 70, 72, 119, 126, 130–2, 146–59
Malcolm, Sir John 20, 23, 25, 27, 32
Malkam Khan 36–8, 65, 106
mandate xiv, xvi, 68–9, 90, 93, 100–2, 111, 119, 128, 133, 138, 141, 152, 157
Marling, Charles (Sir) 58–9, 69, 134, 145, 154
Masonic Lodges *See* Freemasonry
masterly activity/inactivity 26
Mehdi Khan Qarazuglu 55
Mellat 5
Mendeli-Zohab 108–9, 139, Map 6
merchants 6, 27–8, 38–9, 41
Merv 138–9
Mesopotamia *See also* Iraq xv, 12–13, 21, 29, 69, 79, 90, 118, 134, 138, 141, 152
Mezes, Sidney Edward 80
Middle East xii–xiii, xv, 7, 9, 12, 24, 40, 70, 79, 90, 96–7, 100, 120, 144–5, 152–3, 156, 158–9

military xi–xii, xvi, 2, 4, 14, 19–21, 23–5, 30, 36, 42, 44–5, 47, 48, 51, 54, 58, 60–1, 69, 83, 90, 96–7, 102–4, 106, 110–1, 113–14, 130, 133, 137, 139–43, 145–50, 152, 157
Milyukov, Pavel Nikolayevich 52
Mirza Ali Qoli Khan 53, 55, 63, 65, 78
Mirza Reza Khan (Prince Arfa) 60
missionaries 71, 156
Mo´azzam al-Molk 59
modern xiv 2–10, 16, 21, 27, 29, 30, 32, 41, 51, 63–4, 74, 88, 98, 112–13, 138, 140, 145, 151, 157
modernisation 6, 147
modernism 5, 36–7, 74, 151
modernity 3, 4, 6, 29, 37, 66, 106
modernize/modernization 2, 4–6, 8–9, 16, 28–31, 36–7, 51, 66, 69, 101, 132, 147, 154, 157
Moghan Steppe 21, 60, 139
Mohajeran 72
Mohammad Ali Shah 9, 14, 41
Mohammad Reza Shah 148
Mohammerah xv, 31
Mojahed 146
Montagu, Edwin (Lord) 69, 102, 133, 146
Moore, Arthur 90
Moshaver al-Mamalek 39, 57–8, 62–3, 96, 123, 148–50, Anglo-Persian Agreement 115, 117–18, 142, Britain, 63, 66, 69, 73, Foroughi 73, 75, 78, 85, 96, November memorandum 55–6, Paris 75–86, 90–4, 99–101, 115–16, 123, 136–7, preparation 55, 59, 67, 70, 74, 140, 151, Treaty of Friendship 147, 154, Vosuq al-Dowleh, 62–3, 78–9, 83, 92, 98
Moshir al-Dowleh 37, 147, 149
Mostowfi al-Mamalek 62
Mosul xv
mountains 87–8, 91, 108–9, 113, 139
Mozaffar al-Din Shah 39, 41
Muslim(s) 9, 21, 36, 49–50, 60, 83, 87, 141
myth(s) 2, 8, 89, 148

Nakhchevan 4, 23, 60, 100, 108, 139, 141, 144
Napoleon 4, 23–5, 29, 95
Naser al-Din Shah 6, 28–31, 36, 38–9, 60–1, 106

nation xi–xiv, xvi–xvii, 3, 5, 7–8, 10, 16, 50, 54, 63, 72, 84, 108, 116, 126, 133, 135, 160
nationalism *See also imperial nationalism* xii, 2–9, 16, 33, 36–8, 47–8, 51, 53–4, 60, 83, 87, 98, 100, 107, 123, 135, 138, 140, 148, 150–2, 154, 157, 159, 160
nationalist(s) xii–xiii, xvi–xvii, 1–2, 7, 9–10, 14–15, 37, 45, 48, 53, 62, 64–6, 73–4, 83, 87, 91, 107, 113, 132, 134, 138, 141, 147, 150–1, 154–5, 158–9
nationalistic xi, xvi, 7, 36, 83, 98
nation-building 10, 16
Naus, Joseph 36, 41
neutral 31, 36, 52, 59, 68, 80–1, 86, 96
neutrality 16, 37, 51–2, 57, 59, 64, 80–3, 142, 155
newspaper(s) 5, 9, 14, 17, 30, 35, 38, 52–3, 71, 73, 79, 81–2, 96–8, 101, 116–18, 120, 124, 125–6, 130–2, 156
Nicolson, Harold 43, 130
Norman, Herman 147–9, 159
Nosrat al-Dowleh (Prince Firuz) 70, 115, 123–4, 146–7, 152, 154, 158, Anglo-Persian Agreement, 102, 115–16, 118, 123–31, 136–45, 149–50, 153
November memorandum 55–6
Nubar Pasha, Boghos xvi

oil xv 30, 39–41, 61, 69, 90, 105, 109, 112, 118, 127, 136, 139, 157
Oliphant, Sir Lancelot 69, 127–9, 144
Olson, William 16, 134
orientalism 35, 37, 49
Orlando, Vittorio 10, 81
Ottomans/Ottoman Empire xi–xiii, xv–xvii, 1, 7, 9, 11–2, 21, 25, 29, 31–2, 36, 45, 47–8, 53, 70, 72, 79–81, 83, 90, 99, 108, 120, 138–9, 146, 152, 156
Ouseley, Sir Gore 24–5

Pahlavi (dynasty) 2, 8, 10, 14, 16, 51, 63, 148, 151, 154, 159
Palestine 59
pan-Islamism 38, 45, 53, 146
pan-Turanian 47–8, 58
pan-Turkism 9, 47–8, 146
pandemic 95
Parliament (Iranian) *See Majles*

parti colonial 79, 96, 98, 156
paternalism/paternalistic xvi, 3, 69, 104
patrimonial(ism) 5, 12, 27, 37, 41
patriot(s) 5, 66, 131
Patton, Pier 84
Peace Conference xi–xiii, xvi–xvii, 1–4, 6, 8, 10–2, 14, 16, 20, 24, 26, 28, 30, 32, 35–6, 38, 40, 42, 44, 48, 50, 52–64, 66–76, 78–82, 84–8, 90, 92, 94, 96, 97–8, 100–2, 104, 106–8, 110, 112, 114, 116, 118, 120, 124, 126–30, 132, 134, 136, 138, 140, 142–8, 150–2, 154–6, 158–60
Peace Note xii, 52, 54
Perni, Adolphe 63, 73, 81, 128, 155
Persia Committee 40
Persian Gulf 4, 13, 19, 23, 31, 61, 68–9, 87–8
Persianate 8, 23, 38, 60, 71, 89, 139, 141
Peter the Great 4, 20
Pichon, Stephen 70, 78–9
Poincaré, Raymond 79, 156
Polak, Jakob Eduard 5
Poland xiii, 71, 96, 144
post-war xv, 1–2, 13–14, 16, 40, 49, 52–4, 68, 82, 93, 98, 135, 158, 160
pre-industrial/pre-modern 4, 7, 20–1, 27, 32–3, 39
Pretyman, Ernest 40
privileges *See* concessions
protectorate(s) xvi, 1, 12, 25, 83, 102–3, 106, 114, 124, 126–8, 132–3
Pusht-e Kuh (Pusht-i Kuh) 108

Qanun See also Mirza Malkam Khan 38
Qarazuglu, Abol-Qasim Khan 55, 62
Qazvini, Mohammad 53
Qobba 21, 60
Qolam, Hossein Khan 124
Qotur (Kotor) 108
Quai d'Orsay 70, 76, 79

race (racial) 8, 50, 89–90, 100, 108–9
Ra'd (newspaper) 97, 126, 132
railway(s) xv, 30–1, 36–7, 45, 61, 73, 92, 107, 111, 118, 138–9
Rasht 72
ratification/ratified 30, 67, 108, 121, 130–1, 136, 146–7, 149–50, 152, 157–8

realpolitik(er) 25, 54, 92, 147
Red Army *See also* Bolsheviks 140–1, 145, 147, 149
reform(s) 2–5, 9–10, 12–13, 15–16, 28–9, 31, 36–7, 39, 48, 51, 55, 61, 66, 80, 102–4, 106–7, 111–2, 114, 130–1, 136, 148–9, 153, 159
reforming 98, 112
religion/religious xiii–xiv, 8, 15, 21, 32, 37, 45, 60, 89–90, 100, 157
reparations xvi, 23, 53–4, 57, 60, 67–8, 70, 87, 90, 97, 108, 129, 155–6
republic(s) xvi, 8, 48, 100, 117, 140–1, 145–6
Reuter Concession/Baron Julius 30
revolution xv, 5, 7–10, 28–9, 35, 41–2, 44–5, 47, 49, 50, 52–3, 55, 63–6, 80, 90, 104–5, 107, 145–7, 153–4
revolutionaries xiii, xvi, 15, 53
revolutionary 9, 146, 148
Reza Khan (Pahlavi) 14, 16–17, 60, 63, 147–8, 150, 154, 159
rivers: Aras 60, 87, 138, Attrek 87, 106, 139, Jayhoun (Amou Darya) 60, 84, Murghab 60, 138–9, Tejen (Tejend) 60, 91, Tigris 61, 87
road(s) 36, 47, 139
Roshanfekran 35
Russia xi–xiii, xv–xvii, 1, 4, 5–6, 8–10, 19–21, 23–5, 27–8, 30–3, 35–7, 39, 41–2, 44–5, 47–8, 50–5, 57–61, 64, 70–3, 80–1, 83, 87, 90–1, 95–7, 100, 104–6, 113, 117, 127, 129, 134, 136, 138–40, 142, 144–6, 148, 153–5, 157, Anglo-Russian Convention 31, 39, 43–4, 49, 54–5, 69, 102, 104, 107, 118–20, 128, 134–5, 157, expansion xii, xvii, 4, 20–1, 23–4, 26–7, 32–3, 47, 108, 140, 148, Great Game xii, 25, 28, 30–1, 45, 104, 112, 115, 120

Sabahi, Houshang 16
sabotage 40, 135, 157
Safavid 21, 27, 32
Sarakhs 91, 108, 137–9, 141, 148
Sarem al-Dowleh 102, 136, 158
Schleswig (Holstein) 100
security 4, 12, 16, 23, 25–6, 29, 31, 40, 43, 58, 61, 68–9, 92, 103, 114, 128, 139, 141, 150, 152

self-determination xii–xvii, 1, 52–3, 60, 74, 97, 100, 108, 120, 141, 144, 153, 157
Shahnameh 38, 89
Shakki 21, 23, 60
Sharif Pasha xvii, 82, 85, 141
Shatt al-Arab xv
Sherley, Sir Antony 19
Shi'ism 32, 90, 100
Shiraz 29
Shirvan 21, 23, 60
Shuster, Morgan 37, 41–2, 66, 71, 104, 112, 115
Sistan 140
Social-Darwinism xiv
socialist(s) xiii, xvi, 53, 81, 95, 146, 148
Soleiman Khan, Mirza 73
South Persia Rifles 59, 105, 107, 113
sovereignty xii, xvi–xvii, 1–4, 9–10, 19, 31, 40–2, 49, 51–3, 57, 61, 67, 70, 74, 83, 86–7, 98, 100, 108, 119, 127, 129, 136, 140–1, 153, 159, 160
Soviet(s) *See also* Bolsheviks/Bolshevism 52, 58, 145–6, 148–9, 154
Spring-Rice, Sir Cecil 43
Starosselski, Colonel 113
St. Petersburg 21, 24, 41, 43, 52–3
state(s) xi–xii, xiv, 1–4, 7–11, 14, 16, 25, 27, 30–1, 35, 41, 45, 47–52, 54, 57–8, 60–1, 63–4, 68–9, 75, 80–1, 86, 94, 98, 101–2, 112, 127, 129, 131–3, 138, 141, 143, 145, 149, 152–3, 158–9
state-building 10, 148
Stockholm 53, 81
Suleimanieh 90
Sultan Abdulhamid II 45
Sunni 32, 45, 90
Swiss/Switzerland 14, 81, 113, 125
Sykes, Sir Percy 119, 130, 155
Sykes-Picot Agreement xv, 56
Syria 79, 116, 156

Tabataba'i, Seyyed Zia al-din 132, 147
Tabriz 23, 31, 41, 42, 47
Talbot, Major 38
Talesh 21, 60, 138
Taqizadeh, Hasan 53–4, 81, 84, 94, 119
tax(es) 2, 10, 28, 42, 87, 109, 112, 157

Tbilisi (Tiflis) 23, 72
teachers 35, 66, 76, 86, 95, 107, 114, 116, 124, 126, 127–8, 154, 158
Tehran 29, 31, 48, 55, 63, 66, 70, 73–4, 76–8, 80–6, 90, 93–5, 99, 101, 105, 106, 108, 110–2, 114–18, 124, 127–9, 132, 136–9, 143, 146–7, 156
telegram(s) 76–8, 80–2, 86, 91, 93, 100–1, 115, 143–4
telegraph 6, 29, 36, 59
territorialization 7–8, 47, 83
The British League of Nations Society xiii
The League to Enforce Peace xiii
Thomson, Ronald 106
Tilley, Sir John 126, 128
Tobacco Rebellion 5, 38, 41–2, 50
Topchibashev, Ali Marden Bek xvi
trade(ers)/trading xv, 4, 6, 19–20, 23, 27–8, 32, 69, 111, 119, 139, 157
traitor/traitorous 16, 62, 134
Transcaspian 8, 20–1, 44, 57, 60, 87, 89, 90, 141, 144, Maps 1/4
Transcaucasia/Transcaucasus 4, 8, 20, 48, 60, 72, 82–3, 87, 90, 97, 140–1, 143, Maps 1/5
Transcaucasian Federation *See also* Azerbaijan, Armenia and Georgia xii, 48, 83, Maps 1/3
transport 57, 104, 107, 111, 118, 128, 138–9, 148, 157
Treasurer-General 102, 111
treaty(ies) 4, 6, 21, 23–5, 27–8, 57–8, 60–1, 80, 90, 99, 100, 108–9, 118, 129, 133, 138, 141, 144–5, 148, 154, 158
Treaty of Brest-Litovsk 57–8, 61, 63
Treaty of Golestan 4, 21, 24, 53, 60, 87
Treaty of Turkmanchai 4, 6, 23, 27, 57–8, 60, 80, 90, 100, 108, 138, 144, 148
tribes/tribal xii, xvii, 7, 19, 21, 26–7, 41, 60, 86, 90, 105, 114, 138–9, 141, 148
Triumvirate *See also* Nosrat al-Dowleh, Vosuq al-Dowleh 102, 104, 107–11, 123, 135–6, 149–50, 154, 157–9
Trotsky, Leon 57
Tsereteli, Irakli xvi
Tsitsianov, General 20, 21
Turan/Turanism 48, 60, 86
Turkestan 108, 137–8, 144

Turkey(ish) *See also* Ottomans xii, xv–xvi, 7, 9, 45, 47–8, 51, 58–61, 66, 72, 87, 90, 99, 100, 108–9, 129, 138, 154–5, 157
Turkmen 19, 90–1, 139, 148
Turkmenistan 138

Ukraine 71
Ulema 21, 33, 39, 41–2, 132
ultimatum 42–3, 54, 87
understanding 44–5, 49
United States (US) xiii, xv–xvi, 10–2, 16, 37, 54–6, 59, 65–6, 68, 70–2, 74, 78–80, 82, 84–6, 91–4, 96, 98, 100, 114–21, 125–6, 131, 133, 139, 141, 154, 156–8, 159
United States Congress xiii, 121, 157, 160
Urumieh 47

Vatanparast 5
Viceroy 13, 43, 102–3, 111, 113, 120
Victorian 20
von Kühlmann, Baron Richard 57
Vosuq al-Dowleh 58, 62, 69, 78, 83–4, 124, 147, 149, 154, Anglo-Persian Agreement 3, 101–2, 107, 115, 120, 127, 131–2, 135–6, 145, 153, 156, delegation 55, 59, 62–3, 66–7, 74, 76–7, 80, 82, 85–6, 92–3, 98–9, 101, 114–15, 140, 144, 152, 158, fraud/traitor 16–17, 132, 134, 136, 158, Moshaver al-Mamalek 62–3, 76–9, 98

Washington 53, 55, 59, 63, 65, 67, 117
Watkins, Mr 112
Wellesley, Richard 25
West/Western 4–8, 20, 31–2, 39–40, 50, 74, 86, 141, 151
Westphalia, Peace of 49
White Russians 95, 145
Willock, Sir Henry 24–5
Wilson, Sir Arnold 19
Wilson, Woodrow President xii–xiv, xv, 10–2, 55, 59, 67, 71, 80, 84, 94, 99–100, 117, 120–1, 145, 156–8, Fourteen points xii–xiii, Peace Note xii, 52, 54, principles xvi, self-determination xii, xiii, xiv, xv, 60, 74
Wilsonian moment 73, 15
Wolff, Sir Henry Drummond 29, 44

Zagros mountains 139
Zohab 108, 139, Map 6
Zoroastrianism 37

www.ingramcontent.com/pod-product-compliance
Lightning Source LLC
Chambersburg PA
CBHW071833300426
44116CB00009B/1526